CQ GUIDE TO

CURRENT AMERICAN GOVERNMENT

CQ GUIDE TO

CURRENT AMERICAN GOVERNMENT

Fall 2000

CQ PRESS

A Division of Congressional Quarterly Inc.

Washington, D.C.

Congressional Quarterly Inc.

Congressional Quarterly Inc., an editorial research service and publishing company, serves clients in the fields of news, education, business, and government. It combines the specific coverage of Congress, government, and politics contained in the *CQ Weekly* with the more general subject range of an affiliated service, the *CQ Researcher*.

Under the CQ Press imprint, Congressional Quarterly also publishes college political science textbooks and public affairs paperbacks on developing issues and events, information directories, and reference books on the federal government, national elections, and politics. Titles include the *Guide to the Presidency*, the *Guide to Congress*, the *Guide to the U.S. Supreme Court*, the *Guide to U.S. Elections*, and *Politics in America*. CQ's A-Z Collection is a four-volume reference series that provides essential information about American government and the electoral process. The *CQ Almanac*, a compendium of legislation for one session of Congress, is published each year. *Congress and the Nation*, a record of government for a presidential term, is published every four years.

CQ publishes the *Daily Monitor*, a report on the current and future activities of congressional committees. An online information system, cq.com, provides immediate access to CQ's databases of legislative action, votes, schedules, profiles, and analyses.

CQ Press
A Division of Congressional Quarterly Inc.
1414 22nd St. N.W.
Washington, DC 20037
(202) 822-1475; (800) 638-1710

www.cqpress.com

Printed in the United States of America
04 03 02 01 00   5 4 3 2 1

Cover photos: *left*, Texas governor George W. Bush speaking at a campaign event in South Carolina, February 14, 2000, by Mike Segar, reprinted by permission of Reuters; *right*, Vice President Al Gore campaigning in Los Angeles, February 10, 2000, by Luke Frazza, reprinted by permission of AFP.

ISSN 0196-612-X
ISBN 1-56802-559-9

Contents

Introduction

Congressional Quarterly's *Guide to Current American Government* reprints articles selected from the *CQ Weekly* and related CQ publications. The editors chose articles that would complement existing texts with up-to-date examinations of current issues and controversies. The *Guide* is divided into four sections—foundations of American government, political participation, government institutions, and politics and public policy—that correspond with the standard framework of introductory American government textbooks.

Foundations of American Government. This section treats current issues involving the interpretation of the U.S. Constitution or affecting the broad workings the federal government. Many recent Supreme Court decisions have acted to change the way power is apportioned among the different branches and levels of government. This section analyzes two recent decisions that have contributed to a trend to return power to the states, or "federalism," and one in which the Court threw out an attempt by Congress to overrule its 1966 *Miranda* decision. The final article takes stock of the movement to amend the Constitution to require term limits for members of Congress.

Political Participation. This section, on current issues in electoral politics, features a lengthy overview of the debate about campaign finance reform, with a separate article on a bill, which was subsequently passed, aimed at closing the "527" loophole that allowed some political groups to avoid disclosure laws. Other articles from the *CQ Weekly* include a case study of the re-election bid of Rep. James E. Rogan, R-Calif., against Democratic challenger Adam Schiff, a piece about redistricting, and a study of the Republican Party's attempts to attract the votes of women. To provide background for the 2000 elections, the editors have also included historical essays about the electorate and about political parties from the new edition of CQ's *Guide to Congress* (Washington, D.C.: CQ Press, 2000).

Government Institutions. The articles in this section look at the inner workings of the major institutions of American government. The first examines the consequences of a rule change instituted by House Republicans in 1995 requiring term limits for committee chairs. The second revisits the issue of judicial vacancies. It shows how longstanding vacancies have affected the operations of two circuit courts in practice and uses the cases of two recently confirmed judges to show how complex the nomination process has become. The third argues that President Clinton's lasting legacy will be the role he has established for the federal government in overseeing the economy.

Politics and Public Policy. This section provides in-depth coverage of major social policy issues, including articles on the death penalty, trade with China, Internet privacy, and prescription drug benefits for Medicare recipients.

By reprinting the *CQ Weekly* articles as they originally appeared, the editors provide a handy source of information about contemporary political issues. The original date of publication is noted with each article to give readers a time frame for the events that are described. Although new developments inevitably occur, the editors provide updates only when they are essential to an understanding of the basic operations of American government. Page number references to related articles in the *CQ Weekly* and the *CQ Almanac* facilitate additional research on topical events. Both publications are available at many school and public libraries.

Foundations of American Government

This section focuses on the Supreme Court's role in apportioning power among the different branches of government and among the federal government and the states. Several recent Court decisions have favored a distribution of power known as *federalism*, restricting the power of Congress and returning authority to the states. This section looks at two such decisions, which have implications reaching beyond the specific issues at hand. In *Kimel v. Florida Board of Regents* the Court held that states are immune from federal age discrimination lawsuits filed by state employees. The ruling challenged Congress's ability to carry out the 14th Amendment's guarantees of due process and equal protection, which have often been used to fight discrimination. In *The United States v. Morrison* the Court struck down aspects of the Violence Against Women Act allowing women who have been the victims of violence to sue their attackers in federal court. The act had relied on Congress's constitutional authority to regulate interstate commerce, but the Court held that Congress cannot use the commerce clause to regulate behavior that has a tenuous tie to economic activity, such as violent crime.

In *Dickerson v. United States* the Court upheld its 1966 *Miranda* decision, affirming that criminal suspects must be informed of their right to remain silent and their right to counsel for their confessions to be admissible in court. In this ruling, which threw out a 1968 law that attempted to overrule *Miranda,* the Court reasserted its willingness to limit Congress's power.

The final article in this section surveys the attempts in recent years to pass a constitutional amendment requiring term limits for members of Congress. The article analyzes the political reasons why supporters of term limits have been unable to muster enough support to amend the Constitution. It then examines attempts to regain momentum for the movement by other means, such as by encouraging members to voluntarily limit their terms and by limiting the terms of state officeholders.

Justices continue a pattern of narrowing Congress' legislative prerogatives

Supreme Court Favors States In Age Bias, Gender Cases

In two cases addressing Congress' penchant for federalizing crimes and remedies, the Supreme Court continued its decade-long efforts to narrow the scope of congressional power and return authority to the states. (*Ruling, p. 4*)

The court ruled, 5-4, on Jan. 11 that states are immune from federal age discrimination lawsuits filed by state employees. And a narrow majority was openly skeptical during oral arguments Jan. 11 that Congress had the right to allow victims of gender-motivated crimes to sue their attackers in federal court — as allowed under the 1994 Violence Against Women Act (PL 103-22).

Each case is relatively narrow in scope but part of a trend by the court in the 1990s to curb congressional power.

"We've had almost a decade now in which the court in case after case is pressing the 10th and 11th Amendments," said A.E. Dick Howard, a law professor at the University of Virginia. The 10th Amendment reserves all powers not enumerated in the Constitution for the states. The 11th Amendment gives states immunity from lawsuits by citizens of another state or another country. "Taken together, this is a sea change, one of the most important constitutional shifts in decades," he said.

In the age discrimination case, *Kimel v. Florida Board of Regents*, the court found that Congress exceeded its 14th Amendment authority to enforce civil rights laws in applying to the states a 1967 law barring discrimination against older workers.

In the arguments in the Violence Against Women case, *United States v. Morrison*, justices questioned whether Congress' constitutional authority to regulate interstate commerce was an adequate justification for the Violence Against Women Act, a part of the 1994 omnibus crime law that allows victims to sue their attackers for monetary damages in federal court. (*1994 CQ Almanac, p. 273*)

But on Jan. 12, the justices unanimously upheld, under the commerce clause, Congress' ability to protect the privacy of motorists by restricting states' ability to sell information gleaned from driver's licenses. The court, in *Reno v. Condon*, said the clearly commercial aspect of the sales was sufficient to allow Congress jurisdiction.

Lawmakers expect to move early this year to reauthorize at least one of the statutes in question, the Violence Against Women Act. "These guys are on a mission," said the law's author, Sen. Joseph R. Biden Jr., D-Del., of the justices. He said in an interview Jan. 12 that the court has been "continually constraining" the breadth of congressional authority, adding, "The direction that they're moving is one that I think is quite frankly dangerous."

Howard said that since the battle between the court and the White House over President Franklin D. Roosevelt's New Deal in the late 1930s, the Supreme Court has largely deferred to Congress in defining the scope of legislative authority, especially under the commerce clause. That allowed members to believe that "they had a virtually limitless commerce power," he said.

In the past several years, however, high court decisions have nipped away at Congress' ability to legislate, both under the commerce clause and the enforcement provision of the 14th Amendment, which guarantees due process of law. (*Cases, facing page*)

Age Discrimination

The court's decision in *Kimel* continues to narrow congressional use of the 14th Amendment to carry out, through legislation, the amendment's guarantee of due process and equal protection. Justice Sandra Day O'Connor wrote the opinion for the majority, which included Chief Justice William H. Rehnquist and Associate Justices Anthony M. Kennedy, Antonin Scalia and Clarence Thomas.

Congress has used the 14th Amendment largely to fight discrimination. But to survive constitutional muster, the court said, any remedy proposed by Congress under the 14th Amendment must be "appropriate" to the situation, not too far-reaching. In *Kimel*, the court said the requirements that the Age Discrimination in Employment Act (PL 90-202) "imposes on state and local governments are disproportionate to any unconstitutional conduct that conceivably could be targeted by the Act." Age, the court held, is not a "suspect classification," a term used by the court to refer to a class of individuals, such as African-Americans, who have suffered discrimination and who deserve special protections. The court said there may be valid reasons for a state to discriminate based on age if it is "rationally related to a legitimate state interest."

The court also held that because Congress did not show a "reason to believe that state and local governments were unconstitutionally discriminating against their employees on the basis of age . . . Congress had no reason to believe that broad prophylactic legislation was necessary in this field."

At issue in the case was a set of lawsuits brought by state college faculty members and librarians against their employers, arguing that they had been denied pay increases and promotions based on their age. The plaintiffs sought monetary damages. The court noted that while its decision meant the plaintiffs could not bring a federal action, they could sue for age discrimination under state laws.

The dissenting justices, led by John Paul Stevens, said the majority was overstepping its bounds in narrowing Congress' ability to respond to discrimination. "The importance of respecting the Framers' decision to assign the business of lawmaking to the Congress dictates firm resistance to the present majority's repeated substitution of its own views of federalism for those expressed in statutes enacted by the Congress and signed by the President," Stevens wrote.

Privacy Protection

At issue in *Reno* was a 1994 law requiring states to get permission from a motorist before selling private information garnered from a driver's license application.

Congress found that many states sold such information, which can include names and vehicle type as well as more sensitive data such as addresses and Social Security numbers. Provisions of the 1994 crime law required states to allow people to opt out of such disclosures.

South Carolina challenged the law, saying Congress was violating the 10th and 11th Amendments. The 4th Circuit Court of Appeals agreed, ruling that the law was incompatible with the principles of federalism.

The Supreme Court overturned that decision, ruling that Congress has the authority under the commerce clause to regulate such sales. Rehnquist, writing for the unanimous court, said that because the personal information being regulated is an element "in interstate commerce" it was fair game for Congress. Rehnquist also said the law passed muster because it did not require South Carolina to pass a law or enforce a federal law.

Violence Against Women

Many justices seemed skeptical during the oral argument that Congress has the power under the commerce clause to grant a right to sue the victim of gender-motivated violence.

The Violence Against Women Act authorized the lawsuits as well as state and local block grants to help prevent violence against women. The law also created an anti-stalking statute and a shield law generally prohibiting a victim's sexual history from being introduced in federal court cases on sexual misconduct. (1994 Almanac, p. 273)

The 4th U.S. Circuit Court of Appeals found that Congress had exceeded its authority under the commerce clause because of a tenuous connection to commercial activity. Scalia seemed to agree that allowing Congress to claim that this kind of crime had an impact on commerce would open the door to broader regulation. "That would allow general federal criminal laws, because all crime affects interstate commerce," he said.

But Kennedy, Stevens and David H. Souter seemed more sympathetic to the argument that Congress has the right to regulate the crimes under the 14th Amendment.

In the underlying case, Christy Brzonkala, while a student at Virginia Polytechnic Institute, alleged that she had been raped by two Virginia Tech

Overruling Congress

The Supreme Court has reined in the power of Congress in more than a half-dozen decisions since 1992. The court ruled in the following cases that Congress exceeded its power under the Constitution:

1992 *New York v. United States.*
The justices struck down, 6-3, portions of a federal law (PL 99-240) making states liable for nuclear waste created by commercial reactors. The court cited the 10th Amendment, which limits Congress to powers enumerated in the Constitution and leaves other powers to the states, in ruling that Congress had exceeded its authority. (*1992 Almanac, p. 329*)

1995 *United States v. Lopez.*
The justices struck down, 5-4, portions of an anti-crime law (PL 101-647) that aimed to ban guns within 1,000 feet of schools. The court said Congress had exceeded its authority under the "commerce clause," which allows Congress to regulate interstate commerce. (*1995 Almanac, p. 6-40*)

1996 *Seminole Tribe of Florida v. Florida.*
The justices struck down, 5-4, a law (PL 100-497) that allowed tribes to file federal suits when states failed to negotiate gambling compacts. The court cited the 11th Amendment, which prohibits federal courts from adjudicating cases brought against a state by citizens of another state or country. (*1996 Almanac, p. 5-51*)

1997 *City of Boerne v. Flores.*
The justices ruled, 6-3, that Congress exceeded its powers under the 14th Amendment with a law (PL 103-141) barring states from enacting laws interfering with citizens' First Amendment rights of religious expression, unless states had a "compelling interest." The 14th Amendment allows Congress to implement equal protection laws. (*1997 Almanac, p. 5-23*)

1997 *Printz v. United States; Mack v. United States.*
The justices struck down, 5-4, a major portion of the Brady Act (PL 103-159) ordering local sheriffs to check the backgrounds of would-be gun buyers. The court cited the 10th Amendment in saying Congress had exceeded its authority. (*1997 Almanac, p. 5-21*)

1999 *Alden v. Maine.*
The justices cited the 11th Amendment in ruling, 5-4, that Congress exceeded its authority in allowing individuals to sue a state over overtime wages for violations of the 1938 Fair Labor Standards Act. (*1999 CQ Weekly, p. 1527*)

1999 *Florida v. College Savings Bank; College Savings Bank v. Florida.*
The justices cited the 11th Amendment in ruling, 5-4, that Congress exceeded its authority in enacting two laws (PL 102-560, PL 102-542) permitting lawsuits against state agencies alleging violations of federal patent and trademark laws. (*1999 CQ Weekly, p. 1527*)

students. The case was never tried in criminal court. The civil trial court found that the law exceeded Congress' constitutional authority, and the 4th U.S. Circuit Court agreed. The high court is expected to rule by the end of June.

Even as the court listened to arguments, the Senate and House prepared to reauthorize the Violence Against Women Act, which expires this year. In the Senate, Judiciary Chairman Orrin G. Hatch, R-Utah, has introduced a bill (S 245) and is working on a compromise with Biden, who introduced his own bill (S 51). In the House, the Judiciary Committee plans to take up a bill (HR 1248) by Constance A. Morella, R-Md., that would reauthorize the act and other programs dealing with domestic violence. Biden said that while the measures would "tweak" the original law, there was no intention to change the provisions now under court scrutiny. ◆

High Court Further Circumscribes Congress' Power in Ruling On Violence Against Women Act

The Supreme Court's May 15 decision striking down part of the 1994 Violence Against Women Act continues a pattern by the court's conservative majority of drawing sharp, new limits on congressional power.

The court, ruling 5-4 in *United States v. Morrison*, held that Congress exceeded its authority in a section of the law that allowed women who were victims of gender-motivated violence, such as rape, to sue their attackers in federal court. The court said the law intruded on states' power to regulate crime.

Congress included the provision in a broader initiative to curb violence against women. Other provisions of the law (PL 103-322), including an anti-stalking statute, were not affected by the court's ruling. (*1994 Almanac, p. 273*)

The decision was a victory for the court's federalist majority — although dozens of states had sent briefs to the court in support of the law.

Lawmakers blasted the ruling, but most said they recognized that the broadly written decision precluded them from redrafting the provision to pass muster. Legislation (HR 1248) to reauthorize Violence Against Women grant programs is moving through Congress and could have provided a vehicle. (*2000 CQ Weekly, p. 1110*)

Sen. Joseph R. Biden Jr., D-Del., a prime sponsor of the 1994 act, said the decision shows that "the Supreme Court has become bolder and bolder in stripping the federal government of the ability to make decisions on behalf of the American people."

Biden said he could not figure out a way to rewrite the law to allow rape victims to circumvent the ruling. Asked by The Associated Press if there were any changes that could be made to make federal rape lawsuits legal, he replied: "Yes, two new justices."

The decision could provide ammunition for Democrats who are trying to use the court's makeup as an issue in the fall's presidential election. Three justices have been mentioned as potential near-term retirees: conservative Antonin Scalia, liberal John Paul Stevens and Sandra Day O'Connor, a moderate who tends to side with conservatives on federalism issues. Any new justice appointed by a new president could shift the balance on defining the boundaries of congressional power.

Defining Commerce

In writing the law, Congress relied on its constitutional authority to regulate interstate commerce and its 14th Amendment power to provide equal protection under the law. Writing for the majority, Chief Justice William H. Rehnquist held that Congress does not have the power under the commerce clause to regulate non-economic activity. "Gender-motivated crimes of violence are not, in any sense of the phrase, economic activity," he wrote.

The case involved Christy Brzonkala, who as a freshman at Virginia Polytechnic Institute in 1994 alleged that she was raped by two students, Antonio Morrison and James Crawford. Although the school determined that there was sufficient evidence to punish Morrison, it did not do so.

Brzonkala sued under the 1994 law. The 4th U.S. Circuit Court of Appeals, based in Richmond, threw out the lawsuit, arguing that the law exceeded congressional powers.

While Rehnquist was sensitive to the situation that had brought the case before the court, he said the victim needed to look closer to home for a solution. "If the allegations here are true, no civilized system of justice could fail to provide her a remedy. . . . But under our federal system that remedy must be provided by the Commonwealth of Virginia," he wrote.

Though Congress had assembled what dissenting Justice David H. Souter called a "mountain of data" about the interstate economic effects of violence against women, Rehnquist said the congressional finding was not persuasive. Quoting a previous decision, he wrote that "simply because Congress may conclude that a particular activity substantially affects interstate commerce does not necessarily make it so."

The quote was from a 1995 case, *United States v. Lopez*, in which the court, again by a 5-4 majority, struck down a federal law prohibiting possession of a gun within 1,000 feet of a school. (*1995 Almanac, p. 6-40*)

Rehnquist relied heavily on the court's reasoning in *Lopez* in the *Morrison* ruling. "The Constitution requires a distinction between what is truly national and what is truly local," he wrote. "The concern we expressed in *Lopez* that Congress might use the Commerce Clause to completely obliterate the Constitution's distinction between national and local authority seems well founded."

Rehnquist also found that Congress could not rely on its authority under the 14th Amendment because that protection applies only to states or "state actors," not to private individuals.

Joining Rehnquist in the majority were Justices O'Connor, Scalia, Anthony M. Kennedy and Clarence Thomas. Souter wrote the dissent, joined by Justices Stevens, Ruth Bader Ginsburg and Stephen G. Breyer.

Souter found that Congress had provided more than enough testimony and evidence, over four years of hearings, to justify finding an economic interstate interest in combating violence against women. "The fact of such a substantial effect is not an issue for the courts in the first instance, but for the Congress, whose institutional capacity for gathering evidence and taking testimony far exceeds ours," he wrote. "The sufficiency of the evidence before Congress to provide a rational basis for the finding cannot seriously be questioned."

He closed with a shot at the majority opinion: "All of this convinces me that today's ebb of the commerce power rests on error, and at the same time leads me to doubt that the majority's view will prove to be enduring law." ◆

By Reaffirming Miranda Ruling, Supreme Court Underscores Its Willingness to Police Congress

In perhaps the most surprising decision of its current session, the Supreme Court on June 26 strongly reaffirmed the constitutional requirement that police warn suspects of their rights before questioning them.

In a 7-2 ruling, the court upheld its controversial 1966 decision in *Miranda v. Arizona*, which found that suspects must be informed of their rights — specifically to remain silent and to obtain counsel — in order for statements they make during interrogation to be admissible in court. The court based the decision on the Fifth Amendment's right against self-incrimination and the 14th Amendment's guarantee of due process.

Several justices who joined the majority in the current case, *Dickerson v. United States* — especially Chief Justice William H. Rehnquist, who wrote the decision — had been publicly skeptical of the *Miranda* ruling in follow-up decisions over the years, and many observers thought the law-and-order court would overturn *Miranda*.

Instead, the court struck down part of a 1968 law (PL 90-351) passed by Congress with the intention of overruling *Miranda*. The law had never been enforced. The court held that *Miranda* had provided a "constitutional rule" and as such, could be overridden only by the court, not by Congress.

It was the latest in a series of court rulings that seek to curb the reach of Congress. Earlier this year, the court ruled that Congress could not use its constitutional power to regulate interstate commerce in order to regulate behavior — such as violent crime — that had a tenuous tie to economic activity. (*CQ Weekly*, p. 1188)

A.E. Dick Howard, a law professor at the University of Virginia, said the *Dickerson* decision was "perhaps the most arresting example of the current court's willingness to draw limits on congressional power.

"Conservativism does not mean a court that's deferential," Howard said.

"We could not have a clearer example of the court's willingness to protect its own power and police Congress."

The Right to Remain Silent

The *Miranda* decision held that police must inform suspects of their rights in a formula that is now familiar to most Americans: "You have the right to remain silent. Anything you say can be used against you in a court of law. You have the right to an attorney. If you cannot afford an attorney, one will be provided for you."

The 5-4 decision was one of the most important rulings made by the activist, liberal court under Chief Justice Earl Warren. Congress quickly moved to overturn it. Lawmakers included in the massive 1968 anti-crime bill a provision that permitted "voluntary" confessions obtained without warnings. The presiding judge was given the authority to decide which confessions were voluntary. (*1968 Almanac, p. 225*)

No administration since then, from Richard M. Nixon's to Bill Clinton's, ever tried to implement the law. *Miranda* warnings remained the rule.

Indeed, Rehnquist said one reason for the court's decision not to overrule *Miranda* was the depth of public acceptance of it. "*Miranda* has become embedded in routine police practice to the point where the warnings have become part of our national culture," he wrote.

The challenge to the *Miranda* decision came from the court system. Charles Dickerson, a man accused of bank robbery and other crimes in 1997 in Alexandria, Va., tried to withdraw a confession he had given to the FBI, arguing that he had not received a *Miranda* warning before being interrogated. The U.S. District Court granted his motion, and the government appealed to the Fourth U.S. Circuit Court of Appeals, headquartered in Richmond, Va. Last year, the Fourth Circuit held that *Miranda* was not a constitutional rule, and that the 1968 law was the final say.

The Clinton administration declined to argue before the high court in favor of the 1968 law, so the court appointed Paul G. Cassell, a law professor and former clerk to Justice Antonin Scalia, to argue that side of the case.

Rehnquist, in a 15-page decision, reversed the Fourth Circuit. "Congress may not legislatively supersede our decisions interpreting and applying the Constitution," he wrote. Because *Miranda* "announced a constitutional rule," only the court can overturn it, he wrote, and the court declined to do so.

"Whether or not we agree with *Miranda's* reasoning and its resulting rule, were we addressing the issue in the first instance, the principles of *stare decisis* weigh heavily against overruling it now," he wrote. *Stare decisis* means the court should adhere to precedent.

Joining Rehnquist in the majority were Justices John Paul Stevens, Sandra Day O'Connor, Anthony M. Kennedy, David H. Souter, Ruth Bader Ginsburg and Stephen G. Breyer.

Scalia wrote a scathing 23-page dissent, in which Justice Clarence Thomas joined. Scalia said the decision to uphold the *Miranda* warning means "that this court has the power not merely to apply the Constitution but to expand it, imposing what it regards as useful 'prophylactic' restrictions upon Congress and the states. That is an immense and frightening antidemocractic power, and it does not exist."

Scalia wrote that *Miranda* was not a constitutional decision because the Constitution does not require the specific warning to ensure that a confession is not coerced. He said the 1968 law could have done this also.

"By disregarding congressional action that concededly does not violate the Constitution, the Court flagrantly offends fundamental principles of separation of powers and arrogates to itself prerogatives reserved to the representatives of the people," Scalia wrote. "Today's judgment converts *Miranda* from a milestone of judicial overreaching into the very Cheops' Pyramid (or perhaps the Sphinx would be a better analogue) of judicial arrogance." ◆

Supporters try to recruit candidates for Congress in lieu of constitutional amendment

Term Limits Movement Strikes Out in New Direction

Quick Contents

Republicans made term limits an integral part of their 1994 "Contract With America," but today the issue has all but disappeared. Many of the same GOP leaders who once supported term limits are now trying to persuade retiring Republicans to stay in Congress and help them hold on to a slim majority.

Term limits may be terminal. The issue that dominated public discourse through much of the past decade and helped sweep Republicans to power in Congress is now having to face its own mortality.

Today, just as term-limited tenures are kicking in for House GOP chairmen and for many members of the Class of 1994, the question has all but disappeared from the electoral landscape. Few candidates for Congress are running on the pledge to limit their time in office. And many of the same Republican leaders who once supported term limits are now trying to persuade retiring colleagues to stay on Capitol Hill and help them hold on to a fragile six-seat majority.

Term limits faded in part because legislative failures put them on the back burner. But they also faded because voters showed they could impose term limits without institutionalizing them.

"Term limits had legs when there was Democratic entrenchment," said John Zogby, an independent pollster. "I don't think Republicans can be considered entrenched." Yale political science professor David Mayhew agreed. "It's a solution waiting for a problem," he said.

In 1994, Republicans made term limits an integral part of their "Contract With America," 10 promises that helped them wrest control of the House from 40 years of Democratic hegemony. About two-thirds of the challengers who defeated incumbents that year signed a pledge to support a constitutional amendment on term limits, according to the advocacy group U.S. Term Limits.

But today, term limit supporters concede that Congress, after twice defeating a constitutional amendment to restrict members' service, probably will not vote on the issue again any time soon. "A constitutional amendment is not essential. What is critical is we get a Congress comprised of citizen legislators," said Paul Jacob, national director of U.S. Term Limits. Jacob and his supporters in recent years have changed their focus from pushing Congress to pass a constitutional amendment to electing more people committed to term limits. Supporters say their own polls show voters are still receptive to the issue. And they are looking to the states to reinvigorate their movement.

Voter Complacency

Zogby said term limits have not emerged as a political issue in any of his polls nor in focus groups he has convened to gauge voter sentiment heading into this fall's elections. Many political observers believe term limits may be a victim of their own success.

After Republicans rallied behind the issue in 1994, voters threw the Democrats out of power while defeating 34 incumbents in November, leading many to argue that voters could express their dissatisfaction at the ballot box and Congress did not need institutionalized term limits. "It's in remission because of the Republican takeover," Mayhew said.

This session, Republicans are facing several retirements by members who promised to limit their terms. Jacob proclaims 2000 as a record-breaking year for term-limited members stepping down from office. A total of seven House members — all Republicans — are keeping their pledge to retire this year, he said.

Several other senior Republicans are being forced to give up their committee chairmanships because back in 1995 the GOP overhauled House rules to prohibit members from chairing committees for more than six years. Chairmen who are retiring include Reps. Bill Archer, R-Texas, Bill Goodling,

House Republicans, shown on the march in 1995, swept into Washington with a 10-point agenda that included action on term limits. Now seven are stepping down.

R-Pa., and John Edward Porter, R-Ill.

But the record-breaking number of retirements by term-limited members is again being used by term limits opponents as evidence that a constitutional amendment is not needed.

A series of legislative failures also hurt the term limits movement.

Back in 1995, House Republicans held the first vote ever on a constitutional amendment to limit the time that legislators could hold office. Advocates argued that members of Congress had become too entrenched and too beholden to special interest groups. Opponents, mostly Democrats, said voters could impose term limits at election time. They said short terms would reduce legislative effectiveness and institutional memory.

The amendment fell 61 votes short of the two-thirds needed to pass and, after Senate passage, be sent on to the states for ratification. The resolution would have limited lawmakers to three two-year terms in the House and two six-year terms in the Senate. The Senate never voted on it. *(1995 CQ Almanac, p. 1-37)*

Later that year the Supreme Court, in *U.S. Term Limits Inc. v. Thornton*, struck down state-initiated term limits for members of Congress as unconstitutional. The ruling said the Constitution stipulated only three qualifications for candidacy — pertaining to age, residency and citizenship — and that the list was meant to be exclusive. *(Ruling, 1995 Almanac, p. 6-37)*

The House again voted on term limits in 1997, this time falling 69 votes short. And in 1999, Mississippi voters rejected a ballot initiative to impose limits on state legislators. *(1997 Almanac, p. 1-28)*

"Voters see there's not a need any more," said Jim Dornan, chief of staff to Rep. George Nethercutt, R-Wash. Nethercutt became the poster child of the term limits movement in 1994 when he defeated former Speaker Thomas S. Foley, D-Wash. (1965-95), while pledging to serve no more than six years.

Nethercutt, however, is now running for a fourth term. He says his pledge was a mistake and that six years is not enough time to effectively represent constituents. "Fewer and fewer candidates are taking the pledge this year," Dornan said. "If it's an issue at all, it's with a very small percentage of the electorate."

Advocates on both sides of the issue also blame — or credit — the soaring

Pledging Term Limits

In 1997, the last time the House voted on a constitutional amendment to limit congressional service to no more than 12 years, 217 members voted for the plan. That was not necessarily a promise to limit their own terms, however. Only seven members are leaving office this year in keeping with term limits pledges they made when first elected to Congress, according to the advocacy group U.S. Term Limits. Some were elected in 1992 and pledged to serve only eight years. Others were elected in 1994 and pledged to serve only six years. U.S. Term Limits says three members have opted this year to break their term limits pledge.

Keeping the pledge:

Chenoweth-Hage   Salmon

Charles T. Canady, R-Fla., elected in 1992
Helen Chenoweth-Hage, R-Idaho, elected in 1994
Tom Coburn, R-Okla., elected in 1994
Tillie Fowler, R-Fla., elected in 1992.
Jack Metcalf, R-Wash., elected in 1994
Matt Salmon, R-Ariz., elected in 1994
Mark Sanford, R-S.C., elected in 1994

Breaking the pledge:

Meehan   McInnis

Scott McInnis, R-Colo., elected in 1992
Martin T. Meehan, D-Mass., elected in 1992
George Nethercutt, R-Wash., elected in 1994

In 1994, Republicans also revised House rules to limit committee chairmen to six years. Several prominent committee and subcommittee chairmen who will lose their gavels this year have decided — for various reasons — not to seek re-election.

Among those not seeking re-election:

Ways and Means	Bill Archer, R-Texas
Education and the Workforce	Bill Goodling, R-Pa.
Budget	John R. Kasich, R-Ohio
Labor-HHS	
Appropriations Subcommittee	John Edward Porter, R-Ill.

economy with squelching the term limits movement.

"It's the same reason nobody got too excited about the president's problems. The economy is so great," said retiring Rep. Matt Salmon, R-Ariz., who is keeping the pledge he made when elected in 1994 to step down after six years. "When the economy is in good shape, voters don't mind their elected officials so much," he said.

A recent poll by Republican pollster Ed Goeas and Democrat Celinda Lake showed voters are generally happy with their elected officials.

In the poll, conducted Jan. 3-5, 65 percent of those questioned said they approved — either strongly or somewhat — of the way their lawmakers were dealing with important issues fac-

ing the nation. Only 19 percent said they strongly or somewhat disapproved of their member in Congress.

"In 1994, there was a lot of anger by voters directed in many different directions. Term limits was the beneficiary of that," Dornan said. "Term limits wasn't the answer, it was a symptom of the voters' anger."

Holding On to Hope

But supporters of a constitutional amendment to limit congressional terms say their own polls show that voters are not ready to give up on the movement.

The Republican polling and consulting group John McLaughlin & Associates conducted a survey Jan. 13 that found that a majority of voters favor limiting congressional service. Of 1,000 voters questioned, 68.8 percent said they favor placing term limits on members of Congress. When asked if they would be more or less likely to vote for a candidate who supported term limits and pledged to serve no more than three terms, 59.1 percent said they would be more likely to vote for such a candidate.

U.S. Term Limits hopes those numbers hold up as they prepare for the November elections. The group is planning a $20 million term limits campaign for this cycle, and will likely spend more than $1 million running ads against Nethercutt alone. The group, which raises its money through private donations and from its 175,000 members, launched three radio ads in Washington state this month, attacking Nethercutt for breaking his term limits pledge.

Nethercutt is considered relatively safe in his district, and no strong challengers have emerged who are running on a term limits platform, but the race could be pivotal for the movement. "If and when Nethercutt wins, that will take a lot of wind out of the sail," Dornan said. "It will be the final nail in the coffin." Term limits supporters counter that a Nethercutt defeat could help revive their movement.

U.S. Term Limits is also looking to other races across the country where term limits have emerged as an issue. In Arizona, retiring Rep. Salmon held off endorsing any candidate until he found one willing to take the pledge. He is now supporting Jeff Flake, who has pledged to serve only three terms.

Rep. Tom Coburn, R-Okla., who is keeping his 1994 pledge to step down after three terms, also declined to endorse any candidates who did not take the pledge. Coburn is backing businessman Andy Ewing, who has promised to step down after three terms.

But Ewing is facing a tough primary challenge from Steve Money, who is specifically criticizing term limits as bad policy for Oklahoma. "I think Oklahoma deserves better than an irrelevant, part-time, short-term congressman who has no agenda, no vision, no goals and who promises to not stay long enough to effectively represent the 2nd District," Money says on his campaign Web site.

Money also criticizes term limits as a

Nethercutt, shown campaigning in 1994, promised to step down after three terms but changed his mind.

SANDRA BANCROFT-BILLINGS

threat to the Republican majority. "If conservatives lose the majority in the 2000 elections it won't be because the liberals beat us, it will be because we gave up, went home and gave it to them."

Internal Changes

While U.S. Term Limits focuses on electing more pledge-takers to Congress, a new House caucus is trying to make life easier for members who have pledged to limit their terms.

Last year freshman Rep. Jim DeMint, R-S.C., launched the Citizen Legislators' Caucus, a group aimed at "enhancing the effectiveness" of short-time legislators. DeMint, who succeeded former GOP Rep. Bob Inglis (1993-99) last year — the first time someone who pledged a limited term succeeded another — says Congress' internal workings must change before term limits can be successful.

"The caucus goes right at the primary

criticism of term limits — that you can't be effective in a short period of time," DeMint said. "We want to make sure new term-limited members can hit the ground running."

Caucus members plan to act as mentors to new members serving under term limits, helping them to quickly learn about legislation and party leadership. "Those first few weeks can make a difference of whether you're on track in the first year in office," he said.

DeMint said he is also talking with leaders to encourage them not to discriminate against term-limited members when handing out committee assignments or leadership posts.

Salmon said leaders told him directly that he was denied a seat on the Commerce Committee because he pledged to limit his term. "It's all based on seniority. It doesn't make sense," Salmon said. "If the NBA operated like Congress, they would have a bunch of fat old men shooting free throws."

Looking to the States

Along with internal changes, term limit supporters are looking to the states to reinvigorate their movement.

Currently, 18 state legislatures and 38 governors serve under mandatory term limits, according to U.S. Term Limits. A petition drive is being waged in Nebraska to place an initiative on the ballot this fall to impose term limits on state legislators. And this spring, Californians will vote on an initiative that would allow candidates to voluntarily note on the election ballot whether they support term limits.

In 2000, 417 state legislators across the country are being forced out of office because of term limits, according to Jacob's group. Many of those legislators are expected to make bids for higher office, creating a huge pool of potential congressional challengers. It is those challengers who Jacob hopes will eventually lead to a re-emergence of term limits as a powerful political tool.

"Not only will we have more competitive congressional elections, but it creates that tradition," Jacob said. "In years to come, we will have a situation of a lot of states with term limits. Congressmen who don't pledge to term limits will stick out like a sore thumb." ◆

Political Participation: Elections 2000

This section of *Guide to Current American Government* focuses on the 2000 elections. To supplement the *CQ Weekly* coverage of election issues, we have included two essays reprinted from the new edition of CQ's *Guide to Congress* (Washington: CQ Press, 2000). An essay on the struggle to broaden the franchise and liberalize electoral laws provides context for recent debates about low voter turnout and under-representation of minorities. The second essay, on political parties, shows how the two-party system became established, examines the parties' influence on the legislative process, and describes the various third-party challenges to the system. We have also included an article by former CQ senior political reporter Rhodes Cook analyzing the 1996 presidential results and using the 1996 results to forecast the prospects of the 2000 candidates.

The next article in this section is a case study from the *CQ Weekly* on the re-election bid of Rep. James E. Rogan, R-Calif., who is facing a stiff challenge from moderate Democrat Adam Schiff. Rogan's campaign, which so far has emphasized his prominent role in pursuing President Clinton's impeachment, illustrates how the impeachment issue is playing out on the campaign trail. Rogan's multi-ethnic, suburban district shares demographic characteristics with many swing districts throughout the country, and political analysts are paying close attention to this race as an indicator of the Democrats' chances of recapturing either house of Congress.

The issue of campaign finance reform has received increasing attention since Sen. John McCain made it the centerpiece of his presidential bid, and there are currently several proposals before Congress for banning various forms of unregulated spending and for tightening disclosure requirements. A *CQ Weekly* article discusses the proposals against the backdrop of the political campaign season and outlines the political pressures making it unlikely that any significant reform will be passed. A subsequent article discusses the unexpected success of one of the proposals, a bill closing the "527" loophole allowing political groups to avoid disclosure laws, which was cleared by both chambers and signed into law by President Clinton in July.

This political season both parties are spending significant resources on the battle for control of state legislatures and governships—and for the right to redraw congressional districts to their own advantage after the 2000 Census results are known. A *CQ Weekly* article profiles the races in crucial states and shows how the winners will be able to influence the political landscape in the decade to come.

Another article discusses Republican efforts to close the gender gap, which reached an all-time high of 11 percentage points in the 1996 presidential elections, and to attract the support of women voters with a platform stressing education, health care reform, and tax cuts.

The last article in this section discusses the ineffectiveness of most of the "issue advocacy" television ads run by large corporations during past election cycles. Corporate spending on television ads has been ineffective in comparison with the efforts of organized labor, which have been aimed at the grass-roots level. Corporations are now trying to emulate labor's success by concentrating on voter registration drives, mailings tailored to local issues, and other grass-roots tactics.

Who Elects Congress

Few elements of the American political system have changed so markedly over the years as has the electorate. Since the early days of the nation, when the voting privilege was limited to the upper economic classes, one voting barrier after another has fallen to pressures for wider suffrage. First, men who did not own property, then women, then African Americans, and finally young people obtained the franchise. By the early 1970s virtually every adult citizen eighteen and older had won the right to vote.

But by the end of the 1990s only about half of those eligible to vote were exercising that right in high-profile presidential elections and barely one-third of those eligible were bothering to vote in midterm congressional elections. The comparatively low turnout led some observers to speculate that people stayed away from the polls because they were disillusioned with the political process. Others said concern about low turnout was overblown.

Broadening the Franchise

During the nation's first decades, all thirteen of the original states restricted voting to adult male property holders and taxpayers. The framers of the Constitution apparently were content to continue this time-honored practice. The Constitutional Convention adopted without dissent the recommendation of its Committee of Detail that qualifications for the electors of the House of Representatives "shall be the same . . . as those of the electors in the several states of the most numerous branch of their own legislatures."[1]

Under this provision fewer than half of the adult white men in the United States were eligible to vote in federal elections. With women and indentured servants disqualified, fewer than one of every four white adults could cast a ballot. Slaves also were ineligible to vote, although freed slaves could vote in some states if they met whatever other qualifications the state placed on its voters.

Those practices actually represented a liberalization of restrictions on voting that had prevailed at one time in the colonial period. Roman Catholics had been disenfranchised in almost every colony; Jews in most colonies; Quakers and Baptists in some. Not until 1842 did Rhode Island permit Jews to vote.

For half a century before the Civil War, the electorate was steadily broadened. The new western settlements supplied a stimulus for allowing all men to vote, and Jacksonian democracy encouraged its acceptance. Gradually, seven states that had limited voting strictly to men who owned property substituted a taxpaying qualification, and by the middle of the century most states had removed even that requirement.

The Fourteenth Amendment, ratified in 1868, made everyone born or naturalized in the United States a citizen and di-

Reprinted from Congressional Quarterly's Guide to Congress, 2 vols. (Washington, D.C.: CQ Press, 2000), vol. 2, 807–22.

rected Congress to reduce the number of representatives from any state that disenfranchised adult male citizens for any reason other than commission of a crime. Although no such reduction was ever made, that amendment — together with the Fifteenth Amendment, which said that the right to vote could not be denied on the basis of "race, color, or previous condition of servitude" — legally opened the polling booths to black men.

Former slaves did vote in the years immediately following the Civil War, but by the turn of the century, most southern states had in place laws and election practices that effectively barred blacks from voting. Not until passage of the Voting Rights Act of 1965 would the promise held out by the Fifteenth Amendment begin to be fulfilled.

Women fought for nearly ninety years to win their right to vote; success came with ratification of the Nineteenth Amendment in 1920. Residents of the District of Columbia were given the right to vote in presidential elections with ratification of the Twenty-third Amendment in 1961. And in 1970 Congress authorized residents of the nation's capital to elect a nonvoting delegate to the House of Representatives.

In 1971 the Twenty-sixth Amendment lowered the voting age to eighteen for federal, state, and local elections. A Supreme Court ruling in 1972 effectively required states to reduce the time citizens had to live there to be eligible to vote; no state now requires more than a thirty-day residency. By the beginning of the 1990s, only insanity, a felony conviction, or failure to meet a residency requirement barred voting-age citizens from going to the polls.

Turnout Trends

Most significant liberalizations of election law have resulted in a sharp increase in voting. From 1824 to 1856, a period of gradual relaxation in the states' property and taxpaying qualifications for voting, voter participation in presidential elections increased from 3.8 percent to 16.7 percent of the population. In 1920, when the Nineteenth Amendment gave women the franchise, it rose to 25.1 percent.

Between 1932 and 1976 both the voting-age population and the number of voters in presidential elections roughly doubled. Except for the 1948 presidential election, when barely half the people of voting age went to the polls, the turnout in the postwar years through 1968 was approximately 60 percent, according to Census Bureau surveys. This relatively high figure was attributed to a high sense of civic duty that permeated American society in the immediate postwar years, a population more rooted than it was to be later in the century, and to new civil rights laws encouraging blacks to vote.

Despite larger numbers of people voting, the rate of voter participation slumped after 1968. In that year's presidential election, 61 percent of the voting-age population went to the polls. Through successive stages, that mark fell below 50 percent in the 1996 election, the lowest level of voter turnout since 1924. Voting in the midterm elections, always lower than in presidential years, also declined.

The number of registered voters nationwide at any given time is impossible to calculate. States have different registration deadlines; people who move may be registered in more than one state at the same time, or temporarily may not be recorded in any state; and some states do not require preregistration before voting, while others do not require towns and municipalities to keep registration records.

The famous postwar baby boom, together with a lower voting age, had produced by the early 1970s a disproportionate number of young voters — voters who are the least likely to vote. In the 1972 presidential election, the first in which eighteen-year-olds could vote nationwide, some 11 million young voters entered the electorate. But the actual number of voting participants was only 4.4 million greater than in 1968, resulting in a five-point drop in the ratio of eligible to actual voters. (*See Political Parties and Elections, p. 24.*)

Voting participation continued on a general downward course throughout the rest of the century even as the baby boomers grew older. There were a few upticks in turnout in both the 1980s and 1990s, most notably in the election of 1992 — when the excitement of the nation's first baby-boom ticket (Democrats Bill Clinton and Al Gore), a well-financed independent candidate (H. Ross Perot), and the widespread perception of recession pushed the turnout above 100 million for the first and only time in the nation's history. By the late 1990s, however, turnout was again on the wane, with the presidential election of 1996 and the midterm congressional contests of 1998 posting the lowest turnout rates for elections of their type since the end of World War II.

Many reasons for the declining turnouts have been offered. Mark Mellman, a Democratic campaign consultant, has been among those who said they have detected public cynicism about the political process. "There's a sense that the political system is out of their control on one hand and not responsive on the other," Mellman has said. Campaigns that once thrived at the grassroots level — with storefront political headquarters manned by volunteers and stocked with buttons and stickers — were being waged through the more impersonal medium of television.

But another school of thought has contended that low turnout might be overrated as an indicator of voter apathy and cynicism. As expressed by Richard Scammon, former director of the U.S. Bureau of the Census: "Peace and prosperity can generally operate to keep the vote down. . . . In a sense, a low voter turnout is consent. A pool of disinterest may be valuable for a democracy."[2]

One question frequently asked is whether the results would be different if everyone voted. In a paper that they wrote in 1998, two University of California political scientists, Benjamin Highton and Raymond E. Wolfinger, answered: probably not. "The two most common demographic features of nonvoters are their residential mobility and youth, two characteristics that do not suggest political distinctiveness," they wrote. "To be sure, the poor, less educated, and minorities are overrepresented among nonvoters. But the young and the transient are even more numerous. . . . What our findings have demonstrated is that the 'party of nonvoters' is truly heterogeneous. Taken as a whole, nonvoters appear well represented by those who vote."[3]

Nonetheless, voter turnout studies by the Census Bureau have shown marked differences in participation among various

Figure 1-1   Voter Turnout, 1789–1998

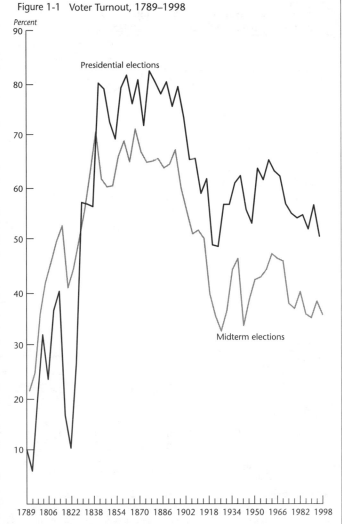

Source: Harold W. Stanley and Richard G. Niemi, *Vital Statistics on American Politics,* 7th ed. (Washington, D.C.: Congressional Quarterly, 1999).

classes of voters. Older voters tend to vote at a higher rate than younger voters. Well-educated voters tend to vote at a higher rate than those less educated. Whites tend to vote at a higher rate than blacks and Hispanics. (*See Table 1-1, p. 12.*)

Growth of Independents

Although more people identify themselves as Democrats than Republicans, there has been a steady rise over the last half century in voters who do not identify with either party. A Gallup poll released in April 1999 found that 34 percent of the American voters considered themselves Democrats, 28 percent Republicans, and 38 percent independents, with polls showing the independent strain strongest among white, young, northern, and rural voters.

Yet when it comes to the act of voter registration, most voters still sign up with one of the two major parties; at least that is the case in the twenty-seven states (and the District of Columbia) where there is such a choice to be made. According to a compilation by the political newsletter *Ballot Access News* in late 1998, Democrats had the registration advantage in thirteen states plus the District of Columbia (a total that included the four most populous states where voters can register by party —

Table 1–1   The Nation's Voters, 1980–1996
(*Percentages of voting-age Americans who said they had voted*)

	Presidential election years					Congressional election years			
	1980	1984	1988	1992	1996	1982	1986	1990	1994
Race/ethnicity									
White	61	61	59	64	56	50	47	47	47
Black	51	56	52	54	51	43	43	39	37
Hispanic	30	33	29	29	27	25	24	21	20
Gender									
Male	59	59	56	60	53	49	46	45	45
Female	59	61	58	58	56	48	46	45	45
Region									
Northeast	59	60	57	61	55	50	44	45	46
Midwest	66	66	63	67	59	55	50	49	49
South	56	57	55	59	52	42	43	42	41
West	57	59	56	59	52	51	48	45	47
Age									
18–20	36	37	33	39	31	20	19	18	17
21–24	43	44	38	46	33	28	24	22	22
25–44	59	58	54	58	49	45	41	41	39
45–64	69	70	68	70	64	62	59	56	57
65 and older	65	68	69	70	67	60	61	60	61
Employment									
Employed	62	62	58	64	55	50	46	45	46
Unemployed	41	44	39	46	37	34	31	28	29
Not in labor force	57	59	57	59	54	49	48	47	46
Education									
8 years or less	43	43	37	35	30	36	33	28	24
1–3 years high school	46	44	41	41	34	38	34	31	27
4 years high school	59	59	55	58	49	47	44	42	41
1–3 years college	67	68	65	69	61	53	50	50	50
4 or more years college	80	79	78	81	73	67	63	63	64
Total	59	60	57	61	54	49	46	45	45

Source: U.S. Bureau of the Census, current population reports on voting and registration in general elections, 1980–1996.

California, Florida, New York, and Pennsylvania). Republicans led in eight states (with the exception of New Hampshire, all in the Plains or Rocky Mountain region), and independents had the edge in six states, four of them in the Northeast (Connecticut, Maine, Massachusetts, and New Jersey).

The Black Vote: A Long, Painful Struggle

In no period of American history were all black people excluded from the polls. At the time of the Constitutional Convention, free blacks had the right of suffrage in all the original states except Georgia, South Carolina, and Virginia. Their right to vote stemmed from the fact that the first black people were brought to America not as slaves but as indentured servants, who could expect freedom after a fixed number of years' service to a master. By 1800, however, the majority of black people were held in slavery. As it grew, so did disenfranchisement. At the outbreak of the Civil War, black Americans were disfranchised, solely on the basis of their race, in all except six of the thirty-three states.

President Abraham Lincoln's Emancipation Proclamation of 1863 freed the slaves but did not accord them voting rights. To ease the impact of change on the South, Lincoln preferred to move cautiously in expanding the black electorate. After the Civil War several southern states promptly enacted "Black Codes" barring the newly liberated slaves from voting or hold-

ing office. Radical Republicans in Congress responded by passing the Reconstruction Act of 1867, which established provisional military governments in the Southern states. The return of civilian control was conditioned on their ratification of the Fourteenth Amendment, which buttressed individual liberty with "due process" and "equal protection" under the law. The amendment's second section threatened to reduce any state's representation in Congress for denying the vote to any male citizen twenty-one years of age or older.

The Reconstruction Act further stated that a secessionist state could not be readmitted to the Union unless it extended the franchise to all adult males, white and black. Congress followed in February 1869 by submitting the Fifteenth Amendment, prohibiting racial discrimination in voting, to the states. It was ratified twelve months later.

The Radical Republican majority in Congress feared that unless blacks were allowed to vote, Democrats and ex-rebels would quickly regain control of the national government. In the presidential election of 1868, in fact, Gen. Ulysses S. Grant defeated his Democratic opponent, Horatio Seymour, by fewer than 305,000 votes; the new black vote probably decided the election.

Former slaves obtained important positions in the governments formed under the Reconstruction Act of 1867. P. B. S. Pinchback served briefly as acting governor of Louisiana;

Mississippi, South Carolina, and Louisiana had black lieutenant governors. Between 1870 and 1900, southern states sent twenty-two black men to Congress — two of them, Hiram R. Revels and Blanche Kelso Bruce, represented Mississippi as senators. Bruce served a full six-year term (1875–1881) and was a presiding officer of the Republican National Convention of 1880.

The white South did not yield gracefully to this turn of events. Gunnar Myrdal noted in his landmark study of black people in America, *An American Dilemma,* that: "The Fourteenth and Fifteenth Amendments were . . . looked upon as the supreme foolishness of the North and, worse still, as an expression of ill-will of the Yankees toward the defeated South. The Negro franchise became the symbol of the humiliation of the South."[4]

After Reconstruction

Congress in 1870 passed an enforcement act to protect black voting rights in the South, but the Supreme Court in 1876 ruled that Congress had exceeded its authority. In the case of *United States v. Reese* (92 U.S. 214), the Court held that the Fifteenth Amendment did not give anyone the right to vote; it simply guaranteed the right to be free from racial discrimination in exercising that right. The extension of the right to vote itself, the Court said, was up to the states, not the federal government. Therefore, the Court said, Congress had overreached its power to enforce the Fifteenth Amendment when it enacted the 1870 law that penalized state officials who denied blacks the right to vote, or refused to count their votes, or obstructed them from voting.

At the same time, the North clearly was growing weary of the crusade for betterment of the condition of blacks. When the first federal troops were withdrawn in April 1877, the remaining Radical Reconstruction governments in the South quickly disintegrated. Some of the newly enfranchised citizens continued to vote, but by 1900, according to historian Paul Lewinson in his book *Race, Class and Party,* "all factions united in a white man's party once more, to put the Negro finally beyond the pale of political activity."[5]

Mississippi led the way in prohibiting black political activity. A new state constitution drawn up in 1890 required prospective voters to pay a poll tax of two dollars and to demonstrate their ability to read any section of the state constitution or to interpret it when read to them.

Literacy Tests for Voters

In Mississippi and other southern states that adopted voter literacy tests, care was taken not to disfranchise illiterate whites. Five states exempted white voters from literacy and some other requirements by "grandfather clauses" — regulations allowing prospective voters, if not otherwise qualified, to register if they were descended from persons who had voted, or served in the state's military forces, before 1867. Other provisions allowed illiterates to register if they owned a certain amount of property or could show themselves to be of good moral character — requirements easily twisted to exclude only blacks.

At one time or another, twenty-one states imposed literacy requirements as a condition for voting. The first to do so, Connecticut in 1855 and Massachusetts in 1857, sought to disqualify a flood of European immigrants. Between 1890 and 1910, Mississippi, South Carolina, Louisiana, North Carolina, Alabama, Virginia, Georgia, and Oklahoma adopted literacy tests — primarily to restrict the black vote.

Nineteen of the twenty-one states demanded that voters be able to read English, and all but four of them (New York, Washington, Alaska, and Hawaii) required the reading of some legal

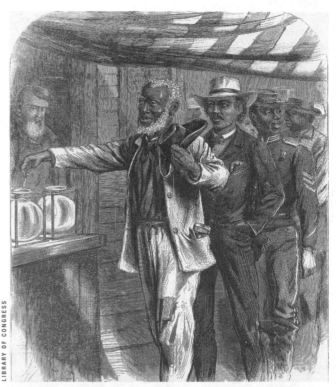

LIBRARY OF CONGRESS

Blacks, including a Union soldier, are depicted casting their first ballots in an image published November 16, 1867. In fact, it would take another hundred years to secure voting rights for African Americans.

document or passage from the state or federal Constitution. Either in lieu of or in addition to the reading requirements, fourteen states required an ability to write.

As applied in the South, literacy tests and other voting restrictions virtually disenfranchised black citizens. Outside the South the New York test was by far the most stringent, although there were seldom any complaints that it was applied in a discriminatory way. Despite pressures by civil libertarians, Congress declined for years to void literacy tests on grounds that to do so would violate a state's right to impose its own voting requirements.

Reports of extreme voter discrimination in the South gradually moved Congress to search for remedial legislation. In 1965 it passed a sweeping Voting Rights Act that suspended literacy tests in seven southern states and parts of another. Five years later Congress expanded the law to bar all voter-literacy tests.

Poll-Tax Barrier to Voting

The first poll taxes in America were substitutes for property ownership and were intended to enlarge the voting franchise. But only a few states retained them at the time of the Civil War. They were afterward revived for a far different purpose — to restrict the franchise — in all eleven states of the old Confederacy: Florida (1889), Mississippi and Tennessee (1890), Arkansas (1892), South Carolina (1895), Louisiana (1898), North Carolina (1900), Alabama (1901), Virginia and Texas (1902), and Georgia (1908).

The ostensible purpose was to "cleanse" elections of mass abuses, but the records of constitutional conventions held in five southern states during the period revealed statements praising the poll tax as a measure to bar blacks and poor whites from the polls. Some historians have asserted that the main intent of these measures was to limit the popular base of a so-called agrarian revolt inspired by the Populist Party against the existing political structure.[6]

After the Populist era many states voluntarily dropped use of the poll tax, including six southern states — North Carolina (1920), Louisiana (1934), Florida (1937), Georgia (1945), South Carolina (1951), and Tennessee (1953). Proposals to abolish the poll tax were introduced in every Congress from 1939 to 1962. By 1960 only four states still required its payment by voters. In August 1962, the House approved a constitutional amendment — already accepted by the Senate — that outlawed poll taxes in federal elections, and that amendment, the Twenty-fourth, was ratified in January 1964. In 1966 the Supreme Court held that the poll tax was an unconstitutional requirement for voting in state and local elections as well. "Voter qualifications have no relation to wealth nor to paying or not paying this or any other tax. Wealth, like race, creed, or color, is not germane to one's ability to participate intelligently in the electoral process," Justice William O. Douglas wrote for the majority in *Harper v. Virginia Board of Elections* (383 U.S. 663).

White Primaries

Even more than literacy tests or poll taxes, perhaps the most effective disfranchisement of southern blacks was their exclusion from the Democratic Party's primary elections. In the solidly Democratic South of the post-Reconstruction era, winning the party's nomination virtually assured election. Being excluded from voting in the primary was equivalent to being excluded from voting altogether.

Not until 1941 did the Supreme Court make clear that Congress had the power to regulate primary, as well as general, elections. Indeed, in a 1921 decision involving campaign spending, *Newberry v. United States* (256 U.S. 232), the Court seemed to say that Congress lacked power to regulate primary elections. This doubt about the reach of federal power encouraged the eleven states that had composed the Confederacy to begin systematic exclusion of black voters from the primary. The Democratic Party was often organized on a statewide or county basis as a private club or association that could freely exclude blacks.

The effort of Texas to use the white primary to shut blacks out of the political process came before the Supreme Court in five cases, brought over a span of twenty-five years. In 1923 the Texas Legislature passed a law forbidding blacks to vote in the state Democratic primary. Dr. L. A. Nixon, a black resident of El Paso, challenged the law, arguing that it clearly violated the Fourteenth and Fifteenth Amendments. In the case of *Nixon v. Herndon* (273 U.S. 536), decided in 1927, the Supreme Court agreed with Nixon's Fourteenth Amendment claim.

After the 1927 *Herndon* decision, the Texas Legislature authorized the executive committees of state political parties to establish their own qualifications for voting in the primary. Dr. Nixon again sued, challenging the law as racially discriminatory. Attorneys for the state argued that the Fourteenth Amendment's equal protection clause did not apply because the party, not state officials, set up the allegedly discriminatory standards.

With Justice Benjamin N. Cardozo writing for a five-man majority, the Court held in 1932 that the executive committee of the Democratic Party acted as a delegate of the state in setting voter qualifications and that its action was equivalent to state action and was thus within the scope of the equal protection guarantee, which it violated (*Nixon v. Condon*, 286 U.S. 73).

The Texas Democratic Party responded by acting without state authorization to put itself off-limits to black voters. Confronted with this situation, the Court in 1935 retreated to its *Newberry* reasoning and ruled, in *Grovey v. Townsend* (295 U.S. 45), that in this instance the party had acted not as a creature of the state but as a voluntary association of individuals. As such, its actions — even in controlling access to the vote — were not restricted by the Constitution.

In 1941 the Court switched signals again, discarding the *Newberry* doctrine in the case of *United States v. Classic* (313 U.S. 299). *Classic* was not a racial discrimination case but instead concerned a man convicted of falsifying election returns. His conviction was based on a federal law that made it a crime "to injure, oppress, threaten, or intimidate any citizen in the free exercise or enjoyment of any right or privilege secured to him by the Constitution." He challenged his conviction, arguing that the right to vote in a primary election was not a right secured by the Constitution.

But the Court upheld the conviction, ruling that the primary was an integral part of the election process. The authority of Congress under Article I, Section 4, to regulate elections included the authority to regulate primary elections, wrote Justice Stone, "when, as in this case, they are a step in the exercise by the people of their choice of representatives in Congress."

Three years later, in 1944, the Court overturned *Grovey* and held the all-white primary unconstitutional. This case, *Smith v. Allwright* (321 U.S. 649), arose out of the refusal of S. S. Allwright, a county election official, to permit Lonnie E. Smith, a black man, to vote in the 1940 Texas Democratic primary. Smith sued, saying Allwright had deprived him of his civil rights. Smith was represented by two attorneys for the National Association for the Advancement of Colored People (NAACP), William H. Hastie and Thurgood Marshall. Both were later made judges, with Marshall becoming the first black member of the Supreme Court.

The relentless effort of Texas Democrats to maintain the white primary at last came to an end in 1953 with another Supreme Court decision. In one Texas county an all-white Democratic organization conducted all-white primary elections under the name of Jaybird Club, a self-declared private club. In *Terry v. Adams* (345 U.S. 461) the Court declared this a ploy in violation of the Fifteenth Amendment.

Physical and Psychic Coercion

Throughout this period legal devices to curtail black political activity were buttressed by physical and economic intimidation. As Myrdal wrote: "Physical coercion is not so often practiced against the Negro, but the mere fact that it can be used with impunity . . . creates a psychic coercion that exists nearly everywhere in the South. . . . [I]t is no wonder that the great majority of Negroes in the South make no attempt to vote and—if they make attempts which are rebuffed—seldom demand their full rights under the federal Constitution."[7]

Any who summoned up the courage to try to register encountered various delays and harassment. The scornful question "What do you want here, nigger?" often sufficed to send a black person away. If the applicants persisted, the registrar was likely to ignore them, tell them that there were no more registration forms, or direct them to another place of registration, which, if it existed, was usually closed. Southern registrars also displayed a tendency to lose registration forms filled out by black applicants.

Voting rights was one of many reforms sought by the civil rights supporters, including Martin Luther King Jr. (front row, second from left), who marched in Washington in August 1963. Prodded by the civil rights movement, Congress began to reassert federal power to ensure the right of black citizens to vote.

NATIONAL ARCHIVES

More subtle practices limited black political participation in the North as well. With the exception of Chicago, white-controlled city machines excluded black people from any significant role in politics for the first half of the twentieth century. During that time, Congress did virtually nothing to encourage black voting.

Civil Rights Legislation

Not until the 1950s, when the civil rights movement began to gather force, did Congress, at the urging of the executive branch, begin to reassert federal power to ensure the right of black citizens to vote. Its first action was passage of the Civil Rights Act of 1957, which was intended to enforce the voting guarantee set out in the Fifteenth Amendment.

The 1957 act authorized the attorney general to bring lawsuits to halt public and private interference with the right of black people to vote, and expanded federal jurisdiction over such suits. The law also created the Civil Rights Commission to investigate and publicly disclose problems of racial discrimination, including voting problems. The investigatory procedures of the commission and the authorization of the federal lawsuits were upheld by the Supreme Court in 1960, in *United States v. Raines* (362 U.S. 17).

Responding to reports that progress in securing voting rights for blacks still was slow even under the provisions of the 1957 act, Congress in 1960 passed a measure that permitted the U.S. attorney general to sue a state for deprivation of voting rights

even if the individuals named initially as defendants — usually voting registrars — had left office. This provision remedied a situation that had arisen in a suit brought by the United States against Alabama voting officials. In addition, Title VI of the 1960 law authorized the appointment of special federal "voting referees" to oversee voter registration in counties where a federal court detected a pattern of voter discrimination.

The Civil Rights Act of 1964 mandated state adoption of standard procedures and requirements for all persons seeking to register to vote. The law also required local officials to justify rejecting an applicant who had completed the sixth grade or had equivalent evidence of intellectual competence. Other provisions of the 1964 law expedited the movement of voting rights cases to the Supreme Court.

In two cases brought under the 1964 act, *United States v. Louisiana* (380 U.S. 145) and *United States v. Mississippi* (380 U.S. 128), the Supreme Court in 1965 sanctioned the government's efforts to break the pattern of case-by-case litigation of voting rights violations. The Court upheld federal power to challenge a state's entire constitutional legal framework for voter registration and conduct of elections.

The Voting Rights Act

But progress still was slow. In Dallas County, Alabama, three new federal laws and four years of litigation had produced the registration of only 383 black voters out of a potential pool of fifteen thousand. On March 8, 1965, the Rev. Martin Luther

Constitutional Provisions for House and Senate Elections

Article I, Section 2

The House of Representatives shall be composed of Members chosen every second Year by the People of the several States, and the Electors in each State shall have the Qualifications requisite for Electors of the most numerous Branch of the State Legislature.

No Person shall be a Representative who shall not have attained to the age of twenty five Years, and been seven Years a Citizen of the United States, and who shall not, when elected, be an Inhabitant of that State in which he shall be chosen.

Representatives and direct Taxes shall be apportioned among the several States which may be included within this Union, according to their respective Numbers, which shall be determined By adding to the whole Number of free Persons, including those bound to Service for a Term of Years, and excluding Indians not taxed, three fifths of all other Persons. The actual Enumeration shall be made within three Years after the first Meeting of the Congress of the United States, and within every subsequent Term of ten Years, in such Manner as they shall by Law direct. The Number of Representatives shall not exceed one for every thirty Thousand, but each State shall have at Least one Representative; and until such enumeration shall be made, the State of New Hampshire shall be entitled to chuse three, Massachusetts eight, Rhode-Island and Providence Plantations one, Connecticut five, New York six, New Jersey four, Pennsylvania eight, Delaware one, Maryland six, Virginia ten, North Carolina five, South Carolina five, and Georgia three.

When vacancies happen in the Representation from any State, the Executive Authority thereof shall issue Writs of Election to fill such Vacancies.

Article I, Section 3

The Senate of the United States shall be composed of two Senators from each State, chosen by the Legislature thereof, for six years; and each Senator shall have one Vote.

Immediately after they shall be assembled in Consequence of the first Election, they shall be divided as equally as may be into three Classes. The Seats of the Senators of the first Class shall be vacated at the Expiration of the second Year, of the second class at the Expiration of the fourth Year, and of the third class at the Expiration of the sixth Year, so that one third may be chosen every second Year; and if Vacancies happen by Resignation, or otherwise, during the Recess of the Legislature of any State, the Executive thereof may make temporary Appointments until the next Meeting of the Legislature, which shall then fill such Vacancies.

No Person shall be a Senator who shall not have attained the Age of thirty Years, and been nine Years a Citizen of the United States, and who shall not, when elected, be an Inhabitant of that State for which he shall be chosen.

Article I, Section 4

The Times, Places and Manner of holding Elections for Senators and Representatives, shall be prescribed in each State by the Legislature thereof; but the Congress may at any time by Law make or alter such Regulations, except as to the Places of chusing Senators.

The Congress shall assemble at least once in every Year, and such Meeting shall be on the first Monday in December, unless they shall by Law appoint a different day.

Article I, Section 5

Each House shall be the Judge of the Elections, Returns and Qualifications of its own Members, and a Majority of each shall constitute a Quorum to do Business; but a smaller Number may adjourn from day to day, and may be authorized to compel the Attendance of absent Members in such Manner, and under such Penalties as each House may provide.

Amendment XIV
(Ratified July 28, 1868)

Section 2. Representatives shall be apportioned among the several States according to their respective numbers, counting the whole number of persons in each State, excluding Indians not taxed. But when the right to vote at any election for the choice of electors for President and Vice President of the United States, Representatives in Congress, the Executive and Judicial officers of a State, or the members of the Legislature thereof, is denied to any of the male inhabitants of such State, being twenty-one years of age, and citizens of the United States, or in any way abridged, except for participation in rebellion, or other crime, the basis of representation therein shall be reduced in the proportion which the number of such male citizens shall bear to the whole number of male citizens twenty-one years of age in such State.

Amendment XVII
(Ratified May 31, 1913)

The Senate of the United States shall be composed of two Senators from each State, elected by the people thereof, for six years; and each Senator shall have one vote. The electors in each State shall have the qualifications requisite for electors of the most numerous branch of the State legislatures.

When vacancies happen in the representation of any State in the Senate, the executive authority of such State shall issue writs of election to fill such vacancies: *Provided,* That the legislature of any State may empower the executive thereof to make temporary appointments until the people fill the vacancies by election as the legislature may direct.

This amendment shall not be so construed as to affect the election or term of any Senator chosen before it becomes valid as part of the Constitution.

Amendment XX
(Ratified January 23, 1933)

Section 1. The terms of the President and Vice President shall end at noon on the 20th day of January, and the terms of Senators and Representatives at noon on the 3d day of January, of the years in which such terms would have ended if this article had not been ratified; and the terms of their successors shall then begin.

Section 2. The Congress shall assemble at least once in every year, and such meeting shall begin at noon on the 3rd day of January, unless they shall by law appoint a different day.

King Jr. led a "Walk for Freedom" to dramatize the need for additional efforts in behalf of registering black voters in Selma, the county seat, and elsewhere in the South. The violence of the reaction of local white law enforcement officers and white bystanders to the peaceful demonstration drew nationwide attention to the dimensions of the problem.

A week later, President Lyndon B. Johnson addressed a joint session of Congress to ask for passage of a new voting rights measure to close legal loopholes that enabled local officials to stall black voter registration. Johnson explained that "no law that we now have on the books . . . can ensure the right to vote when local officials are determined to deny it." Later that month, NAACP official Roy Wilkins appeared before a Senate committee on behalf of the Leadership Conference on Civil Rights to urge Congress to "transform this retail litigation method of registration into a wholesale administration procedure registering all who seek to exercise their democratic birthright." Within five months Congress had approved the sweeping Voting Rights Act of 1965.

The law suspended literacy tests and provided for the appointment of federal supervisors of voter registration in all states and counties where literacy tests or similar qualifying devices were in effect on November 1, 1964, and where fewer than 50 percent of the voting-age residents had registered to vote or voted in the 1964 presidential election.

The law established criminal penalties for persons found guilty of interfering with the voting rights of others. State or county governments in areas of low voter registration were required to obtain federal approval of any new voting laws, standards, practices, or procedures before implementing them. A state or county covered by the act could escape from the law's provisions if it could persuade a three-judge federal court in the District of Columbia that no racial discrimination in registration or voting had occurred in the previous five years.

The act placed federal registration machinery in six southern states (Alabama, Georgia, Mississippi, South Carolina, Louisiana, and Virginia), Alaska, twenty-eight counties in North Carolina, three counties in Arizona, and one in Idaho.

Passage of the voting rights act heralded a significant increase in the number of blacks registered to vote. Within four years, almost a million blacks had registered to vote under its provisions. The Civil Rights Commission reported in 1968 that registration of blacks had climbed to more than 50 percent of the black voting-age population in every southern state. Before the act, black registration had exceeded 50 percent in only three: Florida, Tennessee, and Texas. The most dramatic increase occurred in Mississippi, where black registration rose from 6.7 percent to 59.8 percent of the voting-age population.[8]

Voting Law Extended

In renewing the act in 1970 for an additional five years, its supporters turned back the efforts of southern senators to dilute key provisions. State and local governments were forbidden to use literacy tests or other voter-qualifying devices, and the triggering formula was altered to apply to any state or county that used a literacy test for voting and where less than 50 percent of the voting-age residents were registered on November 1, 1968, or had voted in the 1968 general election.

Under the 1970 law, the preclearance requirement applied to those areas affected by the 1965 law and ten more: three Alaska districts; Apache County, Arizona; Imperial County, California; Elmore County, Idaho; the Bronx, Kings (Brook-lyn), and New York (Manhattan) counties, New York; and Wheeler County, Oregon.

By the time the act was due for its second extension in 1975, an estimated 2 million black people had been added to the voting rolls in the South, more than doubling the previous total. The number of blacks holding elective office also increased. The Joint Center for Political Studies reported that the number of black elected officials in the seven southern states covered by the Voting Rights act had gone up from fewer than one hundred in 1964 to 963 in just ten years. The total included one member of the House of Representatives, thirty-six state legislators, and 927 county and municipal officials.

The Voting Rights Act was renewed for seven years and substantially expanded in 1975. The triggering formula was amended to bring under coverage of the law any state or county that was using a literacy test in 1972 and where less than 50 percent of the residents eligible to vote had registered as of November 1, 1972. Two additional provisions gave greater protection to certain language minorities, defined as persons of Spanish heritage, Native Americans, Asian Americans, and Alaskan natives.

The federal preclearance provisions were expanded to apply to any jurisdiction where:

• The Census Bureau determined that more than 5 percent of the voting-age citizens were of a single language minority.

• Election materials had been printed only in English for the 1972 presidential election.

• Fewer than 50 percent of the voting-age citizens had registered for or voted in the 1972 presidential election.

These amendments significantly expanded coverage of the act, bringing in all of Alaska, Texas, and Arizona, and selected counties in several other states, including California and Florida. In addition, provisions were added requiring certain parts of the country to provide bilingual voting materials.

Congress approved a third extension of the act on June 23, 1982, two months before the law was due to expire. The 1982 legislation represented a major victory for a coalition of civil rights groups that included black, Hispanic, labor, religious, and civic organizations. Many of them had criticized President Ronald Reagan's administration for its hesitation and reservations about earlier versions and certain features of the measure.

However, the bill received widespread bipartisan support and strong backing from members of both chambers, including southerners. More than twice as many southern Democrats in both the Senate and House voted for passage in 1982 than in 1965 when the law was first approved. The steady upward trend in southern support for the act reflected changing social and political mores, and a great increase in black voting in the South.

The 1982 law had four main elements. First, it extended for twenty-five years provisions that required nine states and portions of thirteen others to obtain Justice Department approval for any changes in their election laws and procedures. Second, starting in 1984, a jurisdiction could be released from the restrictions by showing a clean voting rights record for the previous ten years. Third, it overturned a 1980 Supreme Court ruling that "intent to discriminate" must be shown to prove a violation. Fourth, it extended the bilingual election provisions through 1992.

The requirement for Justice Department approval of election-law changes figured prominently in redistricting being carried out in the affected states on the basis of the 1990 census. While that proved to be a matter of considerable controversy, there is little doubt that the Voting Rights Act has had a positive effect on the numbers of blacks winning elective office. Nationwide in January 1997, according to a compilation by the

Joint Center for Political Studies, the number of black elected officials included forty members of Congress; 579 state legislators; 387 mayors and more than 3,700 other municipal officials; more than 800 judges or magistrates; and nearly fifty police chiefs, sheriffs, and local marshals. (These totals were from the fifty states, the District of Columbia, and the Virgin Islands.)

Judicial Support

Not surprisingly, the unprecedented assertion of federal power over electoral and voting matters embodied in the Voting Rights Act was immediately challenged as exceeding the constitutional authority of Congress and encroaching on states' rights. But in 1966, in direct contrast to its post–Civil War rulings, the Supreme Court firmly backed the power of Congress to pass such a law. In that case, *South Carolina v. Katzenbach* (383 U.S. 301), the state argued that Congress had exceeded its authority in suspending South Carolina voting standards, permitting the use of federal election examiners, and adopting a "triggering" formula that affected some states but not others. At the Court's invitation, Alabama, Georgia, Louisiana, Mississippi, and Virginia filed briefs in support of South Carolina's challenge. Twenty other states filed briefs in support of the law.

Strong Court Backing

The Supreme Court rejected all constitutional challenges to the act. "Congress," wrote Chief Justice Earl Warren for the decision's 8–1 majority, "has full remedial powers [under the Fifteenth Amendment] to effectuate the constitutional prohibition against racial discrimination in voting." The federal approval requirement for new voting rules in the states covered by the act, Warren observed, "may have been an uncommon exercise of congressional power, as South Carolina contends, but the Court has recognized that exceptional conditions can justify legislative measures not otherwise appropriate."

Also in 1966, in *Katzenbach v. Morgan* (384 U.S. 641), the Court upheld the portion of the Voting Rights Act that permitted persons educated in accredited "American-flag" schools to vote even if they were unable to read and write English. The provision was aimed at enfranchising Puerto Ricans educated in such schools, living in the United States, but unable to demonstrate literacy in English.

Although the basic constitutionality of the Voting Rights Act was now settled, a steady stream of voting rights cases came to the Court in the late 1960s and the 1970s, testing the scope and application of the law. But the Court continued to back and broadly interpret the act. In the 1969 case of *Gaston County v. United States* (395 U.S. 285), for example, the Court refused to let a North Carolina county reinstate a literacy test.

Some Exceptions Allowed

In 1975, however, the Court held in *Richmond v. United States* (422 U.S. 358) that a federally approved annexation plan did not violate the Voting Rights Act — even if it reduced the percentage of black voters in the city's population — so long as there were legitimate reasons for the annexation. Despite its willingness to affirm the sweeping provisions of the 1965 law, the Court refused to interpret it as forbidding all use of racial criteria in legislative redistricting or as requiring that blacks be given proportional representation on elected bodies.

In a 1976 decision, *Beer v. United States* (425 U.S. 130), the Court upheld a city's reapportionment of the districts from which city council members were chosen. The change resulted in an increase in the number of black council members, but not in a proportional representation of black voters among the council members. The Court held that the Voting Rights Act was satisfied so long as such changes did not reduce the voting strength of racial minorities.

The next year, in *United Jewish Organizations of Williamsburgh v. Carey* (430 U.S. 144), the Court upheld New York's 1974 redistricting law, which purposely redrew certain districts to give them nonwhite majorities. The county (Kings) affected in the case was one of three in New York that had been brought under the coverage of the Voting Rights Act by the 1970 amendments to that law. The Hasidic Jewish community of the Williamsburgh section of Brooklyn objected that the new boundaries divided their voting strength between two districts. The objectors argued that such use of racial criteria in the redistricting deprived them of equal protection guaranteed by the Fourteenth Amendment and diluted their voting strength in violation of the Fifteenth Amendment.

The Constitution did not prevent all use of racial criteria in districting and apportionment, wrote Justice Byron R. White for the seven-member Supreme Court majority in that case. Nor, he continued, did it "prevent a State subject to the Voting Rights Act from deliberately creating or preserving black majorities in particular districts in order to ensure that its reapportionment plan complies with [the act]. . . ."

"There is no doubt," White continued, that the state, in drawing new district lines, "deliberately used race in a purposeful manner. But its plan represented no racial slur or stigma with respect to whites or any other race, and we discern no discrimination violative of the Fourteenth Amendment nor any abridgment of the right to vote on account of race within the meaning of the Fifteenth Amendment."

In the 1980 case of *Mobile v. Bolden* (446 U.S. 55), the Court for the first time narrowed the reach of the Voting Rights Act. Justice Potter Stewart wrote on behalf of a 6–3 majority that the fact that no black person had ever been elected city commissioner in Mobile, Alabama, under the city's challenged system of at-large elections was not enough to prove the system was in violation of the Voting Rights Act and the Constitution. "The Fifteenth Amendment does not entail the right to have Negro candidates elected," Stewart wrote, but only guaranteed that blacks would be able to "register and vote without hindrance."

Mobile Decision Overturned

The decision set off a reaction in Congress that resulted in specific language being written into the 1982 extension of the Voting Rights Act declaring that a voting practice or law that had the effect of discriminating was in violation of the federal law, whatever the local intent might have been. In 1986 the Court applied the new test to *Thornburg v. Gingles* (47 U.S. 30), ruling that six of North Carolina's multimember legislative districts impermissibly diluted the strength of black votes in the state. The fact that very few black candidates had been elected from those districts was enough to prove that the system was in violation of the law, the Court held.

In 1991 the Supreme Court relied on the 1982 revisions of the Voting Rights Act to rule that the act applied to the election of judges.

Court Decisions in the 1990s

Entering the 1990s, blacks and Hispanics were still underrepresented in Congress. To remedy this situation, the Justice Department sought to use the "preclearance" provision of the Voting Rights Act to encourage states with histories of minority voting rights violations to create so-called majority-minority districts — districts where black or Hispanic populations were in the majority.

With newly drawn majority-minority districts, the 1992 election produced a large increase in the total of black and Hispanic House members. The number of blacks jumped from twenty-six to thirty-nine, the number of Hispanics from eleven to seventeen. But some of the districts were sharply criticized as a form of racial gerrymandering because of their irregular shapes, and the Supreme Court in 1993 demonstrated that these districts would come under tough legal scrutiny.

At issue in 1993 was a district that wound its way in a snake-like fashion through central North Carolina, picking up black neighborhoods in four metropolitan areas. The district, drawn at the urging of the Justice Department, was challenged by a group of white voters who alleged that North Carolina had set up "a racially discriminatory voting process" and deprived them of the right to vote in "a color-blind" election. Their suit was dismissed by a federal district court but reinstated by the Supreme Court in a 5–4 decision, *Shaw v. Reno* (1993).

In her opinion for the Court, Justice Sandra Day O'Connor acknowledged that racial considerations could not be excluded from the redistricting process. But she said that in "some exceptional cases" a plan could be "so highly irregular that, on its face, it rationally cannot be understood as anything other than an effort to segregate voters on the basis of race." To justify such a plan, O'Connor said, the government must show that it is narrowly tailored to serve a compelling government interest.[9]

The decision in *Shaw v. Reno* returned the case to a lower court for further hearings. Meanwhile, challenges to racially drawn redistricting plans were proceeding in other states, which the Supreme Court used to refine its position on racial redistricting. In 1995 the Court struck down a Georgia plan that had created three black-majority districts, including one that stretched from the Atlanta suburbs across half the state to the coastal city of Savannah. The 5–4 vote in *Miller v. Johnson* was the same as in the North Carolina case, but the Court made clear that challenges were not limited to plans with irregularly shaped districts.

Writing for the majority, Justice Anthony M. Kennedy argued that government should not treat citizens as members of a racial class, and he said that the Georgia map could not be justified on the grounds that it was necessary to comply with the Voting Rights Act because the Justice Department had incorrectly interpreted the law to require the maximum number of majority-black districts be created. Redistricting plans were subject to challenge, Kennedy said, if race was "the predominant factor motivating the legislature's decision to place a significant number of voters within or without a particular district."

The decision was widely criticized. President Bill Clinton called the ruling "a setback in the struggle to ensure that all Americans participate fully in the electoral process." But the criticism did not sway the Court's majority. In 1996 the same five-justice majority in *Shaw v. Hunt* rejected the serpentine North Carolina district that it had scrutinized in 1993, arguing that the state had neglected traditional districting criteria, such as compactness, while overemphasizing the importance of race. The Court in *Bush v. Vera* also found that Texas had improperly used racial considerations in the drawing of three congressional districts. District maps in parts of Florida, Louisiana, New York, and Virginia were also successfully challenged on the basis of race.

Civil rights groups complained that the rulings would make it more difficult for minorities to be elected to Congress. But their warnings were tempered by the election results. In 1999 there were thirty-seven blacks in the House (down two from 1993) and eighteen Hispanics (up one from 1993).

Women's Vote: A Victory in Stages

The drive for women's suffrage, which began in the late 1830s, was closely related in the beginning to the movement for abolition of slavery. Women, because of their extensive legal disadvantages under the common law, often compared their lot to that of slaves and thus directed the bulk of their political activity against proposals for extending slavery. Women were disfranchised at every level of government. Only in New Jersey did they have a theoretical right to vote. That right had been included inadvertently in the state constitutions of 1776 and 1797, but the state legislature repealed the provision at the outset of the nineteenth century when some women actually attempted to vote.

Early victories for the women's suffrage movement came mostly in connection with school elections. Kentucky in 1838 gave the right to vote in such elections to widows and unmarried women with property that was subject to taxation for school purposes. Kansas in 1861 gave women the vote on all school questions, and by 1880 Michigan, Utah, Minnesota, Colorado, New Hampshire, and Massachusetts had followed suit.

The Woman's Rights Convention at Seneca Falls, New York, in July 1848 is generally cited as the beginning of the women's suffrage movement in the United States. But the Declaration of Principles, which Elizabeth Cady Stanton read at that meeting and which thereafter became a sacred text for the movement, was a much broader and more revolutionary document than a simple claim for the franchise.

Steps toward the Vote

Direct-action tactics first were applied by suffragists shortly after the Civil War, when Susan B. Anthony urged women to go to the polls and claim the right to vote under terms of the newly adopted Fourteenth Amendment. In the national elections of 1872, Anthony voted in her home city of Rochester, New York; she subsequently was tried and convicted of the crime of "voting without having a lawful right to vote." For almost a quarter of a century, Anthony and her followers pressed Congress for a constitutional amendment granting women's suffrage. On January 25, 1887, the Senate finally considered the proposal but rejected it by a 16–34 vote.

The suffrage forces had more success in some western states. As a territory, Wyoming extended full suffrage to women in 1869 and retained it upon becoming a state in 1890. Colorado, Utah, and Idaho granted women voting rights before the turn of the century. But after that the advocates of suffrage for women encountered stronger opposition, and it was not until the height of the Progressive movement that other states, mostly in the West, gave women full voting rights. Washington granted equal suffrage in 1910, California in 1911, Arizona, Kansas, and Oregon in 1912, Montana and Nevada in 1914, and New York in 1917.

Opponents argued that women were the "weaker sex," that their temperament was unsuited to make the kinds of decisions necessary in casting a ballot, and that suffrage might alter the relationship between the sexes. In the two decades preceding women's enfranchisement, extravagant claims were made by

Supporters of the Nineteenth Amendment— giving women the right to vote—picket the White House in 1916. The Nineteenth Amendment was ratified in 1920.

extremists on both sides. Radical feminists often insisted that women voters would be able to cleanse American politics of its corruption and usher in some ill-defined, utopian golden age. Antifranchise forces were as far-reaching in their claims. During World War I, Henry A. Wise Wood, president of the Aero Club of America, told the House Committee on Woman Suffrage that giving women the vote would mean "the dilution with the qualities of the cow of the qualities of the bull upon which all the herd's safety must depend." And the January 1917 issue of *Remonstrance*, an antisuffrage journal, cautioned that women's suffrage would lead to the nationalization of women, free love, and communism.[10]

Constitutional Amendment

On the eve of World War I, the advocates of militant tactics took the lead in a national campaign for women's rights. In the congressional elections of 1914, they set out to defeat all Democratic candidates in the nine states (which had increased to eleven by election day) where women had the right to vote. They held the majority Democrats in Congress responsible for not submitting a constitutional amendment to the states for their approval of women's voting rights. Only twenty of the forty-three challenged candidates were elected. However, this showing of electoral strength did not move President Woodrow Wilson to take up their cause.

President Wilson's opposition to a constitutional amendment prompted a series of stormy demonstrations by the suffragettes around the White House and other sites in Washington after the United States had entered World War I. The demonstrators insisted that it was unconscionable for this country to be denying its own female citizens a right to participate in government while at the same time it was fighting a war on the premise of "making the world safe for democracy."

At the direction of the administration, thousands of the women demonstrators were arrested and brought to trial. Some were beaten by hostile crowds — often made up of soldiers and sailors who viewed the demonstrations as unpatriotic. At their trials, many of the women stood mute or made speeches advocating suffrage and attacking President Wilson for his refusal to endorse the constitutional amendment.

The jailing of many of these women caused a severe housing problem for District of Columbia penal authorities and created a wave of sympathy for the suffragettes. Public support for their position was heightened by the prisoners' claims that they had been treated inhumanely and had been subjected to unsanitary conditions in prison. To protest these conditions, some of the prisoners went on a hunger strike, and the authorities resorted to forced feeding, an action that aroused even greater public sympathy.

President Wilson capitulated, announcing on January 9, 1918, his support for the proposed suffrage amendment. The House of Representatives approved it the next day by a 274–136 vote, one vote more than the necessary two-thirds majority. But the Senate fell short of the two-thirds majority in October 1918 and again in February 1919. However, when the Congress elected in November 1918 met for the first time on May 19, 1919, it took little more than two weeks to gain the required majorities in both chambers.

On August 18, 1920, Tennessee became the thirty-sixth state to approve the amendment, enough for ratification. On August 26, Secretary of State Bainbridge Colby signed a proclamation formally adding the Nineteenth Amendment to the Constitution. It stated simply that "The right of citizens of the United States to vote shall not be denied or abridged by the United States or any state on account of sex."

In the 1920 presidential election, the first in which women could vote, it was estimated that only about 30 percent of those who were eligible actually voted. Analyses of the 1924 election indicated that scarcely one-third of all eligible women voted while more than two-thirds of the eligible men had done so. The women's electoral performance came as a bitter blow to the suffragists. In more recent national elections, however, surveys by the Census Bureau have found that voting participation by women is about the same as that of men.

By the end of the twentieth century, women's representation in Congress, though, was well below half. The 106th Congress began in 1999 with sixty-five women members — nine in the Senate and fifty-six in the House — representing 12 percent of the seats in Congress. The United States ranked thirty-ninth among 160 legislatures in female representation, according to the Inter-Parliamentary Union. Sweden ranked first.

The Eighteen-Year-Old Vote

Twenty-one was the minimum voting age in every state until 1943, when Georgia lowered it to eighteen — the age at which young men were being drafted to fight in World War II. The slogan "Old enough to fight, old enough to vote" had a certain logic and public appeal. But no other state followed Georgia's lead until after the war. In 1946 South Carolina Democrats authorized eighteen-year-olds to vote in party primaries, but later withdrew that privilege. In 1955 Kentucky voters lowered the voting age to eighteen. Alaska and Hawaii, upon entering the Union in 1959, adopted minimum voting ages of nineteen and twenty, respectively.

Meanwhile, in 1954, President Dwight D. Eisenhower had proposed a constitutional amendment granting eighteen-year-olds the right to vote nationwide, but the proposal was rejected by the Senate. Eventually Congress was persuaded — perhaps by the demographics of America's fast-expanding youth population, which during the 1960s had begun to capture the nation's attention; perhaps by the separate hopes of Republicans and Democrats to win new voters; perhaps by the Vietnam War in which the young were called on to fight again. In the Voting Rights Act of 1970, Congress added a provision to lower the voting age to eighteen in all federal, state, and local elections, effective January 1, 1971.

On signing the bill into law, President Richard Nixon restated his belief that the provision was unconstitutional because Congress had no power to extend suffrage by statute, and directed Attorney General John N. Mitchell to ask for a swift court test of the law's validity. The Supreme Court, ruling in *Oregon v. Mitchell* (400 U.S. 112) only weeks before the law was due to take effect, sustained its application to federal elections but held it unconstitutional in regard to state and local elections.

After the Court ruled, Congress wasted little time in approving and sending to the states a proposed Twenty-sixth Amendment to the Constitution, stating: "The right of citizens of the United States, who are eighteen years of age or older, to vote shall not be denied or abridged by the United States or any State on account of age. The Congress shall have power to enforce this article by appropriate legislation." The proposal received final congressional approval March 23, 1971, and was ratified by the necessary three-fourths of the states by July 1, record time for a constitutional amendment.

More than 25 million Americans became eligible to vote for the first time in the 1972 presidential election. It was the biggest influx of potential voters since women won the right to vote in 1920. But the younger age group has never fulfilled its potential power at the polls; in election after election, younger voters have had the lowest turnout rate of any age category.

Removing Obstacles to Voting

In the late twentieth century the federal government and the states took steps to increase citizen participation in the electoral process. The Voting Rights Act of 1970 helped pave the way in removing residency restrictions on new voters. Another major federal initiative, the "motor-voter" law of 1993, was designed to increase the ease of voter registration. Other measures to increase voter turnout came at the state level, with a number of states experimenting with new voting methods, such as mail-in ballots.

Reducing Residency Requirements

Every state at some time has imposed a minimum period of residence in the state (and some of them a shorter period of residence in a county or voting district) as a qualification for voting. The rationale for this practice has been that individuals cannot vote intelligently, at least on state and local affairs, until they have lived in an area for a given period of time. Until the 1970s most of the states required one year's residence for voting. At one time or another, Alabama, Louisiana, Mississippi, Rhode Island, and South Carolina required residency of as much as two years.

In 1970 thirty-three states imposed residency requirements of one year, fifteen required six months, and two (New York and Pennsylvania) three months. As another condition for voting in 1970, every state except New Hampshire required voters to have lived in the same county or voting district for a stipulated period of time. The most stringent of these requirements were in Maryland and Texas, where six months was required in the county and voting district.

Federal voting rights legislation in 1970 permitted voting in presidential elections after thirty days of residence. This provision, upheld by the Supreme Court, extended the franchise to about 5 million people who might otherwise have been disqualified from voting in the 1972 presidential election. Soon thereafter the Court decided (*Dunn v. Blumstein*, 405 U.S. 330) that a state cannot constitutionally restrict the franchise to persons who lived in the state at least one year and in the county at least three months. The 6–1 opinion, rendered March 21, 1972, caused all the states to change their residency requirements. By 1980, nineteen states and the District of Columbia had no minimum residency requirement, and no other state imposed more than a thirty-day residence requirement except Arizona, which required fifty days. Ten years later, Arizona lowered its requirement to twenty-nine days.[11]

Voters Living Abroad

In 1976 President Gerald R. Ford signed legislation establishing uniform voting procedures for American citizens who lived overseas. The law gave Americans abroad the right to vote by absentee ballot in federal elections in the state in which they had their last voting address. The Senate Rules Committee had reported in May 1975 that studies showed that "nearly all of these private citizens outside of the United States in one way or another are strongly discouraged, or are even barred by the rules of the states of their last domicile, from participation in presidential and congressional elections."[12]

In 1978 Congress approved legislation that prevented states from using evidence that an American living overseas voted in a state or federal election as proof of residency for tax purposes. Sponsors said many Americans living abroad did not vote because they feared they might have to pay additional taxes.

Motor-Voter: Easing Registration Further

In most Western nations government agencies sign up voters, but the United States places the burden for qualifying for electoral participation on the citizen. Although the procedure is still somewhat cumbersome, a variety of state and federal legislation, capped by the National Voter Registration Act or so-called motor-voter act, has made voter registration more convenient.

Signed into law by President Bill Clinton in May 20, 1993, motor-voter required states to provide all eligible citizens the opportunity to register when they applied for or renewed a driver's license. It also required states to allow mail-in registration and to provide voter registration forms at agencies that supplied public assistance, such as welfare checks or help for people with

Figure 1-2   Partisan Identification, 1952–1998

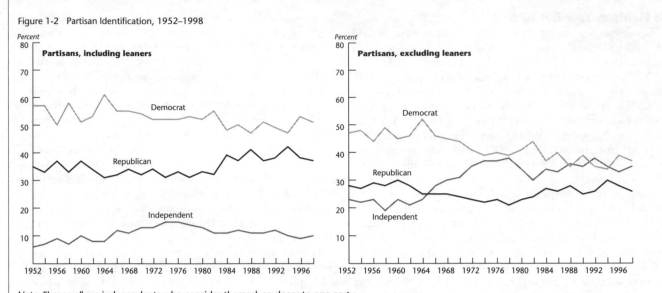

Note: "Leaners" are independents who consider themselves closer to one party.
Source: Harold W. Stanley and Richard G. Niemi, *Vital Statistics on American Politics,* 7th ed. (Washington, D.C.: Congressional Quarterly, 1999). Calculated by the authors from National Election Studies codebooks and data sets.

disabilities. Compliance with the federally mandated program was required by 1995. Costs were to be borne by the states.

Partly as a result of the legislation, a record number of new voters, some 10 million, signed up in the first three years following implementation of the act. The Federal Election Commission reported to Congress in 1996 that the United States had 143 million registered voters, or 72.8 percent of the voting-age population. The percentage was the highest since 1960, when national registration figures first became available.

Congressional Republicans had opposed the legislation on political grounds, namely that it would allow citizens of traditional Democratic constituencies — the urban poor and minorities, among others — easier access to the voting booth. Opponents also argued that easier registration could lead to election fraud.

But motor-voter had neither the negative results that critics feared nor the positive impact that supporters hoped. One year after the law was enacted, Republicans won control of both houses of Congress, which they retained in 1996 and 1998. Meanwhile, in spite of the increased number of registered voters, election turnout continued to decline in the late 1990s.

Other State Measures

By the end of the twentieth century states were also experimenting with various other measures designed to increase voter turnout, including election-day voter registration, easier absentee balloting, and elections by mail.

In the late 1970s President Jimmy Carter proposed federal legislation to allow voters to register at the polls on election day, but it was not enacted. Several states, though, have adopted election-day registration on their own, including Minnesota. In 1998, when Reform Party candidate Jesse Ventura closed fast to win the Minnesota governorship, more than 330,000 citizens registered to vote on election day (which represented 16 percent of the ballots cast).

Still, in today's busy world, when many potential voters may not have the time or capability to travel to the polls on a given day, the idea of absentee voting for all has been gaining wider acceptance. About half the states have an "early voting" option, including "no-fault" absentee voting open to all voters with no

need to plead sickness, disability, or any other reason for wanting to vote before election day. A few states, such as Colorado, Texas, and Tennessee, have tried opening voting-style booths before election day in stores or other public places.

A couple of states have tested another alternative: dispensing with voting booths altogether and conducting elections by mail to encourage higher participation. Proponents argue that the benefits of voting by mail — including convenience, speed, and lower costs — outweigh the disadvantages, including the possible abuse of the system, and the loss of the sociability that comes with gathering at the polls.

In Nevada the 1996 Republican presidential primary was held by mail-in vote. But the largest test took place in Oregon, which used mail-in votes to fill a vacant Senate seat. The winner was Democrat Ron Wyden, the first senator elected by mail.

The new procedure received good reviews. More than three-quarters of those Oregonians polled said they preferred voting by mail over going to the polling places. Women and older voters were strongest in favor of mail voting.

Oregon subsequently became the first state to decide to hold all elections by mail, approving a ballot measure in 1998 requiring vote by mail in biennial primary and general elections. The measure eliminated polling places, but it did not affect existing law allowing absentee ballots or voting at local election offices.

Notes

1. Max Farrand, ed., *The Records of the Federal Convention of 1787* (New Haven, Conn.: Yale University Press, 1966), vol. 2, 178.
2. Mellman and Scammon are quoted in *President Bush, The Challenge Ahead* (Washington, D.C.: Congressional Quarterly, 1989), 3.
3. Benjamin Highton and Raymond E. Wolfinger, "The Political Implications of Higher Turnout" (paper presented at the 1998 annual meeting of the American Political Science Association), Boston, September 1998, 10.
4. Gunnar Myrdal, *An American Dilemma: The Negro Problem and Modern Democracy* (New York: Harper and Row, 1944), 445.
5. Paul Lewinson, *Race, Class and Party: A History of Negro Suffrage and White Politics in the South* (New York: Oxford University Press, 1932), 194.

6. Frederic D. Ogden, *The Poll Tax in the South* (University: University of Alabama Press, 1958), 2–4.

7. Myrdal, *An American Dilemma*, 485.

8. U.S. Commission on Civil Rights, *Voter Participation* (May 1968), 223. See also U.S. Commission on Civil Rights, *The Voting Rights Act: Ten Years Later* (January 1975), 60.

9. Joan Biskupic and Elder Witt, *Guide to the U.S. Supreme Court* (Washington, D.C.: Congressional Quarterly, 1997), 529.

10. Mary Costello, "Women Voters," *Editorial Research Reports* (Washington, D.C.: Congressional Quarterly, 1972), 776.

11. Information from annual editions of *The Book of the States* (Washington, D.C.: The Council of State Governments), and from the Arizona Secretary of State's Office.

12. Senate Committee on Rules and Administration, "Overseas Citizens Voting Rights Act of 1975," 94th Cong., 1st sess., 1975, S Rept 94-121, 2.

Political Parties and Elections

Political parties are vital elements in the life and work of Congress and its members. Although they are not specifically mentioned in the Constitution, political parties have been important in Congress almost since its creation. The chief functions of the parties in Congress are to help select and then elect candidates for Congress, through the electoral process, and to organize and distribute power within the institution. The party that holds a majority of seats in each chamber controls all key positions of authority.

In the broadest sense, a political party is a coalition of people who join together to try to win governmental power by winning elections. Members of a party supposedly share a loosely defined set of common beliefs, although members of the same party often hold extremely different opinions and outlooks. Citizens rely on political parties to define issues, to support or oppose candidates on the basis of those issues, and then to carry out the agreed-upon policies when the party is in power.

Functions of Parties

Political parties in America serve many functions. Most important, parties help elect the president, by nominating candidates for the office and then working to get them elected. Political parties also put forward candidates for most state and local offices and help elected leaders mobilize support for their programs.

Before the Civil War a number of different parties played significant roles in Congress. Since the mid-nineteenth century, almost all members of Congress have belonged either to the Democratic or the Republican Party. Occasionally, however, some members of other parties — the Progressive Party in the early 1900s, for example — have been elected. Sometimes, a member is elected as an independent, with no affiliation to any political party.

The Democrats and Republicans each have been dominant in Congress at different times. For much of the period between the Civil War and the Great Depression of the 1930s, Republicans held majorities in both the House and the Senate. Democrats dominated through much of the rest of the century, controlling both chambers for fifty-two of the sixty-two years from the election of 1932 until the election of 1994. From 1995 to the end of the twentieth century, the Republicans held the upper hand in both the House and the Senate.

Choosing Congressional Candidates

One essential function of the parties is to provide a mechanism for choosing and supporting congressional candidates. In pre-Jacksonian times, the legislative caucus was the usual

Reprinted from Congressional Quarterly's Guide to Congress, 2 vols. (Washington, D.C.: CQ Press, 2000), vol. 2, 823–38.

method of nominating candidates for both state and federal office. From 1800 to 1824 congressional Democratic-Republicans even used the caucus to select the party's nominee for the presidency. In 1824 Andrew Jackson's followers, realizing their candidate had no chance of winning endorsement in the party caucus, set out to discredit "King Caucus" and substitute party conventions as a more democratic means of selecting the party's candidate. By 1828 most states had abandoned the caucus for the convention, and in 1832 Jacksonian Democrats sent delegates to Baltimore, where they nominated Jackson for president and Martin Van Buren for vice president.

In the early 1900s the Progressives worked to abolish the convention and replace it with the direct primary. Proponents of the primary contended that powerful organizations had seized control of the nominating conventions and frequently had ignored the preferences of the party rank and file. Under the leadership of its governor, Robert M. La Follette Sr., a leading Progressive who later served in Congress, Wisconsin in 1903 enacted the first mandatory primary law. By 1917 the direct primary had been adopted in almost every state; the convention persisted only for the selection of presidential candidates and candidates for a few state offices, and for Republican Party nominations in the Democratic South.

During this same period, the Progressives also succeeded in pushing through Congress a constitutional amendment calling for direct election of senators; they had been chosen by their state legislatures. Beginning in 1914 senators were not only elected by popular vote, but also nominated in most states through party primaries.

The direct primary considerably broadened the range of positions that a political party might take. Political scientist V. O. Key Jr. noted in his book *Politics, Parties, and Pressure Groups* that "rival factions and leaders could now fight out their differences in a campaign directed to the electorate — or a substantial segment of it — rather than be bound by the decision of an assembly of delegates."[1]

Organizing Congress

Parties also play an essential role in the internal organization of Congress. All formal authority in Congress is arranged according to party. The party that holds the majority in each chamber has the votes to select leaders such as Speaker of the House and the majority leader in the Senate. All committee and subcommittee chairmen are members of the majority party and majority party leaders control the legislative agenda. Within each political party a whip system enables party leaders to pressure party members to support the party position on important issues.

Without structures for bringing together like-minded members for common action, Congress might find itself in constant chaos as each member fought to advance his or her individual

Figure 2–1   American Political Parties 1789–1996

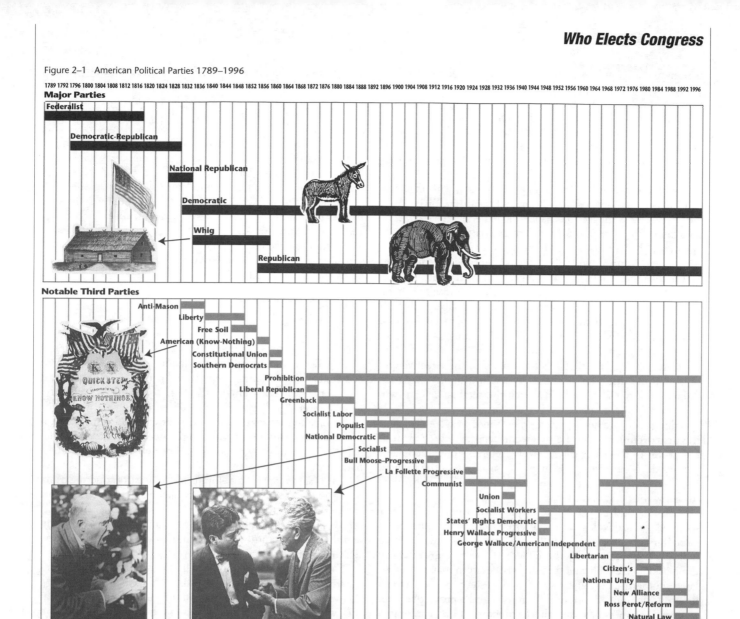

Note: Throughout U.S. history there have been several thousand political parties. For this chart Congressional Quarterly editors have selected those parties that achieved national significance during presidential election years. The spaces between the rules on this chart indicate the election year only. For example, the Constitutional Union Party and the Southern Democrats were in existence for the 1860 election only and were gone by 1864. Similarly, the Green Party first fielded a presidential candidate in 1996.

agenda. Instead, the parties help to create a system in which leaders and followers can work together in pursuit of a common program. Members, however, are under no obligation to support party positions or obey party leaders. And in recent decades, individual legislators have built their constituencies with little reference to party labels. But with the Republican takeover of Congress in 1995, partisanship — reflected in the amount of party-line voting — reached some of its highest levels in the last half of the twentieth century on both sides of Capitol Hill.

Party System: Unforeseen Development

The Founders never envisioned the importance that political parties would develop in Congress and the nation. The authors of the Constitution had little understanding of the functions of political parties; they were ambivalent, if not hostile, to the new party system as it developed in the early years of the Republic. "If I could not go to heaven but with a party, I would

not go there at all," Thomas Jefferson said in 1789.[2]

The Constitution did not mention parties, either to authorize them or prohibit them. It made possible a permanent role for parties, however, by giving citizens civil liberties and the right to organize. At the same time it erected safeguards against partisan excesses by creating a system of checks and balances within the government. The "great object" of the new government, wrote James Madison in *Federalist* No. 10, was "to secure the public good and private rights against the danger of such a faction [party], and at the same time to preserve the spirit and the form of popular government."[3]

Emergence of Parties

Parties emerged soon after the adoption of the Constitution. Those who favored the strong central government embodied in the Constitution came to be called Federalists. Led by Treasury Secretary Alexander Hamilton, they were drawn mostly from merchants and bankers in the Northeast, who favored strong government action to protect the currency from losing its value through inflation. They were opposed by a group that later became known as the Democratic-Republicans. Led by Jefferson and Madison, the Democratic-Republicans were largely southern and western farmers, who opposed a strong central government and sought government policies to make it easier to borrow money.

Party lines were fluid in the first Congresses, with members drifting between one loose coalition and the other. By the mid-1790s, however, the factions had hardened enough for one senator to observe that "the existence of two parties in Congress is apparent." Federalists generally held the upper hand in these early years, controlling the Senate and contending equally for power with the Democratic-Republicans in the House.

Although George Washington identified himself with no political party, John Adams, his successor, was unabashedly Federalist. But by 1800 Jefferson's supporters had gained a majority, and from 1801, when Jefferson replaced Adams, Democratic-Republicans occupied the White House and controlled Congress until 1829. The 1816 elections signaled the effective end of the Federalist Party, whose representation in Congress dropped off to a small minority; even the semblance of a two-party system disappeared.

Along with the dominance of the Democratic-Republicans, the first twenty years of the nineteenth century saw growth in the power of the party caucus over Congress's operations. Important decisions were made in private meetings of the Democratic-Republicans, and party members in Congress were pressed to follow the party's position.

The size and power of the Democratic-Republican Party soon led to the development of internal factions, as different regional groups struggled for influence within the only national political organization. By the mid-1820s two groups emerged: the National Republicans, a coalition of eastern manufacturers, large southern plantation owners, and westerners who favored internal economic development projects and a protective tariff against foreign goods; and the Democrats, who represented agrarian interests from the South and West and held that the common people, not the rich, should have the dominant voice in government.

The Democrats captured control of Congress in 1826 and the White House in 1828 and were to remain the dominant party in Congress for the next three decades. Showing their disgust with what they considered to be the "mob rule" of the Jacksonians, the National Republicans in 1834 changed their name to Whigs, an English political term signifying antagonism to excessive use of executive power. The Whigs twice won the presidency, in 1840 and 1848, and always held a substantial number of seats in Congress. But the Whigs were able to capture a majority of either body on only a few occasions — the 1840 and 1846 elections in the House and the 1840 and 1842 elections in the Senate.

Republican Party Founded

The Whigs faded rapidly during the 1850s and went out of existence in 1856. In their place rose the Republican Party of today. Initially, the party was composed of "Free Soil" Democrats and Whigs who opposed the extension of slavery into new territories. The party won control of the House in 1854 but lost it in 1856, even as its first presidential candidate, John Charles Fremont, was winning a third of the popular vote. During the next four years the party broadened its appeal to small

farmers and owners of small businesses by promising a homestead law for western settlement and a protective tariff. In 1858 the party recaptured control of the House and in 1860 it won the Senate and, with the election of Abraham Lincoln, the presidency.

The Republican Party controlled Congress and the presidency for most of the next seventy years. Democrats sometimes were able to win a majority of House seats and, on occasion, a Senate majority. But the Republicans, who soon gained the nickname of "Grand Old Party" (GOP), dominated the era. Backed by eastern business interests, they favored high tariffs and tight controls on the amount of money in the economy. The Democrats were the party of the South and of disaffected agricultural interests from the West. They generally sought low tariffs and liberal credit.

Two-Party Dominance

It was during this period of Republican rule that the role of the parties themselves became much more important in Congress. Although the Congress of the pre–Civil War period tended to be dominated by brilliant individuals, the postwar Senate and House were the arenas of powerful party leaders. This trend was particularly apparent in the Senate, where many of the members were "party bosses" who had gained power through political organizations in their own states. These men placed a high value on party loyalty and on the need for party discipline. They were often ready to compromise their ideals to maintain harmony within the party.

The first attempt at developing a strong party structure came in the 1870s, when New York Republican Roscoe Conkling organized a faction that controlled the Senate on procedural matters. Conkling's group had little effect on legislation, however, and the Senate returned to individualistic ways after Conkling left the Senate.

The birth of modern party discipline came in the 1890s. Republican Senators William B. Allison of Iowa and Nelson W. Aldrich of Rhode Island organized an informal group of senators, who first met only for poker and relaxation. After Allison was elected chairman of the Senate Republican Caucus, the organization of party members, in 1897, the group assumed control of the Senate. Allison used his office to solidify his control of his party and his party's control of the Senate.

Allison controlled the Steering Committee, which directed floor proceedings, and the Committee on Committees, which made committee assignments. Although chairmanship of committees was determined primarily by seniority, Allison had great leeway to appoint members to committees who would follow his wishes. Access to positions of influence soon depended on the favor and support of the party leaders.

Republicans used the caucus to work out party positions in private and then to speak in a unified voice on the Senate floor. Although they were not bound to obey the party position, members who ignored it risked losing most of their power in the Senate. The Democrats soon followed the Republicans by organizing their own internal power structure.

On the House side, Republican Speakers Thomas Bracket Reed of Maine in the 1890s and Joseph G. Cannon of Illinois in the first decade of the 1900s elicited a similar degree of party control over their rank and file. Reed's rule firmly established the authority of the majority to prevail over the minority, ending a period in which the minority used obstructionist tactics that frequently brought legislative activity in the House to a standstill.

The Republican convention of 1860 in Chicago nominated Abraham Lincoln for the presidency. Republicans controlled Congress and the presidency for most of the next seventy years. They became known as the "Grand Old Party" (GOP).

Attacks on the System

The system of strict party control was not popular among many people outside of Congress, who saw it as violating the principles of representative democracy. There were also critics of the system within Congress, including the Liberal Republicans of the 1870s and the "mugwump" antileadership Republicans of the 1880s. In addition, representatives of third parties attacked the system.

The most important of these were the Populists, who represented an agrarian reform movement based in the Midwest and West. The Populists won three Senate seats and eleven House seats in 1892. They reached their peak in the crucial election of 1896 when they and their allies won seven Senate seats and thirty House seats. Much of their program, which stressed loosening of controls on the amount of money circulated in the economy, was adopted by the Democrats, and the Populists soon faded from the scene.

The cause of reform was soon taken up by the progressives. This movement sought both economic changes, such as antitrust legislation and introduction of the income tax, and political measures aimed at opening up the system, such as direct election of senators and laws against corrupt election practices. The progressives were composed of reformist Republicans and members of the separate Progressive Party. The Bull Moose–Progressives, as they were called in honor of their leader, former president Theodore Roosevelt, elected seventeen House members in 1912. The progressives played key roles in the congressional reform movement of the early 1900s, working to reduce the autocratic power of House Speaker Cannon, and pushing for curbs on the filibuster.

Despite these attacks, the system of party control of Congress developed into a formal institution. During the 1910s, Senate Democrats and then Senate Republicans elected a single member to serve both as chairman of the party caucus and as floor leader. Soon the majority and minority leaders were the acknowledged spokespeople for their parties in the Senate. In the House the revolt against the power of the Speaker led to a great increase in the power of the party caucuses. The Democrats, who controlled the House from 1911 to 1919, worked out most legislative decisions within party meetings, and party rules obliged members to vote for the party position if it was endorsed by a two-thirds majority.

Republicans regained control of both houses of Congress in 1918, and they maintained their power until the early years of the Great Depression. However, the party was torn by deep divisions between regular forces and the progressives, who often cooperated with the Democrats in pushing legislation favorable to the economic interests of western farmers. Progressive Republicans who tried to challenge their party leadership were quickly punished by the loss of seats on important committees.

Democrats as Majority Party

The Republicans lost their exclusive control of Congress in 1930, when Democrats gained a narrow majority in the House. That election proved to be a warning sign of what was to come two years later. The 1932 elections were a watershed in the history of partisan divisions in Congress. Led by presidential candidate Franklin D. Roosevelt, who promised relief from the economic disaster that had befallen the nation, the Democrats swept to commanding majorities in both the House and Senate. By the 1936 elections, the Republicans had been reduced to a small minority. The Democrats held 331 House seats as a result of that election; the Republicans 89. The Democratic majority in the Senate was an overwhelming 76–16.

With few exceptions, the Democrats remained in complete control of Congress from then until the mid-1990s. Between 1930 and 1994, they lost their House majority only twice, in the 1946 and 1952 elections. Those elections also gave Republicans brief control of the Senate; Democrats regained control again in 1948 and 1954. The GOP also controlled the Senate during the first six years of Ronald Reagan's presidency, 1981–1987. However, Democrats regained a substantial majority in the 1986 elections, which they maintained into the early 1990s.

In 1992 Democrats won the White House for only the second time in a quarter century. But their control of both ends of Pennsylvania Avenue was short-lived. Redistricting at the beginning of the 1990s had created plenty of opportunities for the GOP, especially in the South, where the formation of a number of new majority-minority districts lowered the minority share in myriad other districts, thus enhancing Republican chances in the latter.

Democrats, as well, had suffered nationally from the perception of an arrogance of power, epitomized by a House banking scandal that was a major factor in the defeat of nineteen House incumbents (mainly Democrats) in the 1992 primary season; the number was a postwar record. Nor were the Democrats helped in 1993 and 1994 by the struggling start of the new Clinton administration, which in 1994 lobbied Congress for a complex overhaul of the nation's health care system that died in spite of the Democratic majorities in both the House and Senate.

The confluence of these factors produced a tidal wave in the 1994 elections that propelled the Republicans into power in both houses of Congress for the first time in forty years.

Divided Government

The Republican congressional takeover in 1995 returned Washington to the divided government that it has known in most of the second half of the twentieth century. Yet the combination of a Democratic president and a Republican Congress was the reverse of the combination that had existed before. *(See Table 2-1, p. 29.)*

In 1952 and 1956, Gen. Dwight D. Eisenhower, a war hero, carried the Republicans to the White House, as the GOP in 1954 slumped into its long-running minority status on Capitol Hill. Recurrent economic recessions under President Eisenhower and the vigorous campaign of presidential candidate John F. Kennedy enabled the Democrats to recapture the White House in 1960 and retain it with Lyndon B. Johnson's election in 1964.

But Republicans regained the presidency in 1968 from a Democratic Party badly split over the Vietnam War and under attack from third party candidate George C. Wallace. Richard Nixon, reelected by a huge majority in 1972, tried to create a new party alignment by courting the once solidly Democratic

South with conservative domestic programs. But the results were mixed, and the party was badly damaged when the Watergate scandal forced Nixon to resign in 1974. The scandal paved the way for Democrat Jimmy Carter to triumph in 1976.

But in 1980 a conservative tide, economic problems, and the Iranian hostage crisis swept Republican Ronald Reagan into the presidency. Eight years later his vice president, George Bush, succeeded Reagan, and in his first two years in office scored some of the highest popularity ratings of any modern president, Democrat or Republican.

As the 1990s began, there was considerable conjecture as to why the Democratic Party was able to thrive in congressional and state elections while repeatedly losing the presidency. It had become the "oddest riddle of American politics of recent years," political analyst Alan Ehrenhalt wrote in his book *The United States of Ambition*. Ehrenhalt, executive editor of Governing magazine and former political editor of the *Congressional Quarterly Weekly Report*, recalled that some observers believed voters elected Democrats to Congress to impose a deliberate check on the Republicans they sent to the White House.

Another theory — "more plausible" to the author — was that Republicans won the presidency by offering an ideology the electorate liked to hear but did not want to practice. According to this reasoning, Democrats won the lesser offices because they delivered the services and generated the government programs that the voters did not want to give up.

But the best answer, according to Ehrenhalt, was that the Democratic Party — "the party of government" — tended to attract career politicians and to benefit from their growing presence. Ehrenhalt contended that during the previous two decades in most constituencies, "Democrats have generated the best supply of talent, energy, and sheer ambition," which over time "enabled them to win an extra 10 percent of the seats in a state legislature, or an extra two or three seats in a congressional delegation. It adds up."[4]

The era that Ehrenhalt described was interrupted dramatically by the election of 1994, when Republicans not only won both houses of Congress, but also captured a majority of the nation's governorships and made inroads in the state legislatures. But whether the era of Democratic congressional dominance was over for good was open to conjecture. In the elections of 1996 and 1998, the Democrats inched back toward parity in the House and continued to hold more seats than the Republicans in the state legislatures, still a prime source of congressional candidates. *(See Table 2-2, p. 30.)*

Party Affiliation

It is probably no coincidence that the rise in divided government in the latter half of the twentieth century has coincided with the proliferation of independent voters — voters who profess no party choice. They accounted for only 16 percent of the electorate in 1937, but 32 percent — nearly a third — in 1990, and 38 percent in early 1999, according to Gallup surveys. In early 1999, 34 percent of the American voters considered themselves Democrats, 28 percent Republicans.

Yet the two major parties were still held in relatively high regard by the end of the century. When independents were asked in the 1999 Gallup survey whether they leaned to the Republican or Democratic Parties, the number that defined themselves as staunchly independent dropped to about 10 percent. Still, there was no denying that the last half of the twentieth century saw a rise in ticket-splitting, a willingness by voters of all stripes

Table 2–1 Divided Government, 1860–1998

During the last half of the twentieth century, it was not unusual for one party to occupy the White House and for the other party to dominate Congress. But for almost a century before that, beginning with the election of the first Republican president (Abraham Lincoln) in 1860, one party or the other tended to control both ends of Pennsylvania Avenue. The chart below indicates the party that won control of the House and Senate in each national election since 1860, and notes the president that was either elected then or serving at the time (in the case of midterm elections). Changes in the presidency between elections are indicated by a slash.

Election	President	Party winning control House	Party winning control Senate	Control of presidency and Congress[a]	Election	President	Party winning control House	Party winning control Senate	Control of presidency and Congress[a]
1860	Lincoln (R)	R	R	All Republican	1930	Hoover (R)	D	R	Congress Split
1862	Lincoln (R)	R	R	All Republican	1932	F. Roosevelt (D)	D	D	All Democrat
1864	Lincoln/A. Johnson (R)	R	R	All Republican[b]	1934	F. Roosevelt (D)	D	D	All Democrat
1866	A. Johnson (R)	R	R	All Republican	1936	F. Roosevelt (D)	D	D	All Democrat
1868	Grant (R)	R	R	All Republican	1938	F. Roosevelt (D)	D	D	All Democrat
1870	Grant (R)	R	R	All Republican	1940	F. Roosevelt (D)	D	D	All Democrat
1872	Grant (R)	R	R	All Republican	1942	F. Roosevelt (D)	D	D	All Democrat
1874	Grant (R)	D	R	Congress Split	1944	F. Roosevelt/Truman (D)	D	D	All Democrat
1876	Hayes (R)	D	R	Congress Split	1946	Truman (D)	R	R	Divided
1878	Hayes (R)	D	D	Divided	1948	Truman (D)	D	D	All Democrat
1880	Garfield/Arthur (R)	R	R	All Republican	1950	Truman (D)	D	D	All Democrat
1882	Arthur (R)	D	R	Congress Split	1952	Eisenhower (R)	R	R	All Republican
1884	Cleveland (D)	D	R	Congress Split	1954	Eisenhower (R)	D	D	Divided
1886	Cleveland (D)	D	R	Congress Split	1956	Eisenhower (R)	D	D	Divided
1888	B. Harrison (R)	R	R	All Republican	1958	Eisenhower (R)	D	D	Divided
1890	B. Harrison (R)	D	R	Congress Split	1960	Kennedy (D)	D	D	All Democrat
1892	Cleveland (D)	D	D	All Democrat	1962	Kennedy/L. Johnson (D)	D	D	All Democrat
1894	Cleveland (D)	R	R	Divided	1964	L. Johnson (D)	D	D	All Democrat
1896	McKinley (R)	R	R	All Republican	1966	L. Johnson (D)	D	D	All Democrat
1898	McKinley (R)	R	R	All Republican	1968	Nixon (R)	D	D	Divided
1900	McKinley/T. Roosevelt (R)	R	R	All Republican	1970	Nixon (R)	D	D	Divided
1902	T. Roosevelt (R)	R	R	All Republican	1972	Nixon/Ford (R)	D	D	Divided
1904	T. Roosevelt (R)	R	R	All Republican	1974	Ford (R)	D	D	Divided
1906	T. Roosevelt (R)	R	R	All Republican	1976	Carter (D)	D	D	All Democrat
1908	Taft (R)	R	R	All Republican	1978	Carter (D)	D	D	All Democrat
1910	Taft (R)	D	R	Congress Split	1980	Reagan (R)	D	R	Congress Split
1912	Wilson (D)	D	D	All Democrat	1982	Reagan (R)	D	R	Congress Split
1914	Wilson (D)	D	D	All Democrat	1984	Reagan (R)	D	R	Congress Split
1916	Wilson (D)	D	D	All Democrat	1986	Reagan (R)	D	D	Divided
1918	Wilson (D)	R	R	Divided	1988	Bush (R)	D	D	Divided
1920	Harding (R)	R	R	All Republican	1990	Bush (R)	D	D	Divided
1922	Harding/Coolidge (R)	R	R	All Republican	1992	Clinton (D)	D	D	All Democrat
1924	Coolidge (R)	R	R	All Republican	1994	Clinton (D)	R	R	Divided
1926	Coolidge (R)	R	R	All Republican	1996	Clinton (D)	R	R	Divided
1928	Hoover (R)	R	R	All Republican	1998	Clinton (D)	R	R	Divided

Notes: Key to abbreviations: D—Democrat; R—Republican. a. "All" indicates that one party controlled the White House and both houses of Congress. "Divided" indicates that one party held the presidency while the other party controlled both houses of Congress. "Congress Split" indicates that control of Congress was split, with one party holding the House and the other the Senate. b. The pro-Republican majority in Congress elected in 1864 was designated Unionist.

to go back and forth across the ballot rather than vote a straight-party ticket. (*See Table 2-3, p. 31.*)

Even party regulars sometimes vote for candidates in the opposing party, according to findings reported by political scientists William H. Flanigan and Nancy H. Zingale. "The proportion of strong partisans who report having voted for different parties has increased substantially since 1952," they wrote.[5]

In a comparison of voting habits in the 1952 and 1988 elections, Flanigan and Zingale noted that southern whites "have become dramatically less Democratic, while blacks throughout the country have become slightly more Democratic and the most consistently loyal Democratic group." The authors found

that Jews "have shifted away from their extremely one-sided Democratic identification" but toward independent, rather than Republican, status. Independents also made inroads among Catholics and white Protestants in the North, at the expense of both parties. Despite change, Flanigan and Zingale wrote, "there is partisan stability among both Republicans and Democrats, and the shifting of political fortunes is accomplished without intensity or extreme political appeals."[6]

Overall, according to Gallup Polls, Democrats have experienced a gradual decline in favor since 1964, when 53 percent of the voters — a record number — identified themselves with that party. However, over the course of the 1990s, voter identi-

Table 2–2 The House in the 1990s: From Democrat to Republican

The House of Representatives went from Democratic to Republican in the 1990s, fueled by the GOP upsurge in the South. But since winning control of the House in 1994, Republicans lost ground in every region except the South.

	South			West			Midwest			East				Total House			
	R	D		R	D		R	D		R	D	I		R	D	I	
1990	44	85	D	37	48	D	45	68	D	41	66	1	D	167	267	1	D
1992	52	85	D	38	55	D	44	61	D	42	57	1	D	176	258	1	D
1994	73	64	R	53	40	R	59	46	R	45	54	1	D	230	204	1	R
1996	82	55	R	51	42	R	55	50	R	39	60	1	D	227	207	1	R
1998	82	55	R	49	44	R	54	51	R	38	61	1	D	223	211	1	R
Net GOP Change[a]	+38			+12			+9			−3				+56			

Key to abbreviations: D—Democrat; I—Independent; R—Republican. Traditionally, Congressional Quarterly has defined the four regions as follows: East—Connecticut, Delaware, Maine, Maryland, Massachusetts, New Hampshire, New Jersey, New York, Pennsylvania, Rhode Island, Vermont, West Virginia; Midwest—Illinois, Indiana, Iowa, Kansas, Michigan, Minnesota, Missouri, Nebraska, North Dakota, Ohio, South Dakota, Wisconsin; South—Alabama, Arkansas, Florida, Georgia, Kentucky, Louisiana, Mississippi, North Carolina, Oklahoma, South Carolina, Tennessee, Texas, Virginia; West—Alaska, Arizona, California, Colorado, Hawaii, Idaho, Montana, Nevada, New Mexico, Oregon, Utah, Washington, Wyoming.

a. Change in GOP seats, 1990–1998.

fication with the Democrats has stayed roughly the same, while identification with the Republicans has declined and the number of self-described independents has increased.

The Gallup survey of early 1999 found a continuation of the gender gap, which had been a visible feature of American politics for the previous quarter century. While men were almost evenly divided between the Democrats and Republicans as their party of choice, women preferred the Democrats by a margin of 10 percentage points. The survey also indicated that the Democrats were supported by a "May-September" coalition of the young and elderly. Democrats were preferred by a margin of 11 percentage points over the Republicans among voters age eighteen to twenty-nine and by 10 percentage points among those age sixty-five and older. The Democrats were preferred over the Republicans by a less pronounced margin among voters in age groups in between.[7]

Party Decline in Congress

During the years after World War II in which Democrats dominated Capitol Hill, the parties suffered a noticeable decline in their influence on Congress. Parties and party leaders had much less power than they did at the beginning of the century. Members of Congress increasingly functioned as individuals rather than loyal party members, both in their electoral campaigns and in the way they voted in committee and on the floor.

In many respects, the increasing individualism was a natural outgrowth of divided government. While many districts were voting Republican for president, they were electing a Democrat to Congress. It created a situation where many members of Congress felt they had to buck their party often in order to stay in favor with their constituents.

At the same time, the growth of party primaries as a means for selecting congressional candidates added to the decline of the importance of parties. Originally introduced to reduce the power of corrupt party bosses, by giving the choice of the party nominee to party members as a whole, primaries have had the unintended effect of undermining the parties as institutions. Congressional candidates today often bypass the established party leadership in their area and appeal directly to the voters.

Other factors have contributed to the decline of the parties within Congress. In the 1950s and 1960s the conservative coalition of Republicans and southern Democrats effectively controlled both the House and Senate, and for many years it was able to frustrate efforts by the Democratic leadership to push through civil rights and other legislation. In the 1970s the congressional reform movement stripped away much of the power of the old-line party leaders. That has made it possible for members to ignore the position of the party leadership and to vote according to their own interests, without fear of much punishment. And as the century waned, interest groups took an increasingly active role in congressional campaigns, often independent of both the parties and the candidates.

Republicans and Democrats in Congress have made strong efforts in recent years to restore some of their influence in electoral politics. Each party has a House and Senate campaign committee, and all four committees play key roles in recruiting, training, organizing, and funding campaigns. The Republicans in particular have developed their campaign committees into wealthy, high-technology centers able to wage a coordinated national campaign for GOP candidates.

But nothing has rejuvenated the parties in Congress as much as the Republican takeover in 1995. Democrats were stunned. Republicans were ebullient and quickly began to push their conservative reform agenda called the Contract with America. By the end of 1995 the proportion of votes in which a majority of one party had voted against the majority of another had reached a forty-year high in both the House and Senate. The proportion of party-unity votes declined in both 1996 and 1997, but spiked upward again in 1998, a year capped in the House by the highly partisan votes to impeach President Bill Clinton.

Election of Members: Evolving Process

The creation of the U.S. Senate was a result of the "Great Compromise" at the Constitutional Convention in 1787. The small states wanted equal representation in Congress, fearing domination by the large states under a population formula. The larger states, however, naturally wished for a legislature based on population, where their strength would prevail. In resolving this dispute, delegates simply split the basis of representation between the two chambers — population for the House of Representatives, equal representation by state for the Senate. Each state was entitled to two senators.

Senate Elections

The Founders let state legislatures, instead of the people themselves, elect U.S. senators. The argument was that legislatures were more able than the electorate to give sober and reflective thought to the selection, and by doing so would take a greater supportive interest in the fledgling national government. The legislatures, after all, had chosen the members of the Continental Congress and the delegates to the Constitutional Convention.

Some legislatures looked upon the senators as their "ambassadors" to the federal government and went so far as to instruct them on how to vote. This raised severe problems of conscience among senators on occasion and resulted in several resignations.

At first, the legislatures made their own arrangements for electing senators. Many states required the two houses of the legislature, sitting separately, to agree on the same candidate. Others required a ballot of the two houses in a joint session. In 1866 Congress decided to exercise its authority. Procedures requiring concurrent majorities in both houses resulted in numerous delays and vacancies. So Congress established procedures for the legislatures to follow in the election of senators, as was authorized by the Constitution.

Article I, Section 4, states in part: "The times, places and manner of holding elections for Senators and Representatives shall be prescribed in each state by the legislature thereof; but the Congress may at any time by law make or alter such regulations, except as to the places of chusing Senators."

The new federal law required the first ballot for senator to be taken by the two houses separately. If no candidate received a majority of the vote in both houses — that is, if a deadlock resulted — then the two houses were to meet and vote jointly until a majority choice emerged. However, the new system did not have the desired effect. The requirement for a majority vote continued to result in voting deadlocks.

A notable instance occurred in Delaware at the turn of the last century. With the legislators divided between two factions of the Republican Party, and the Democrats in the minority, they could not reach agreement by the time Congress went into session on March 4, 1899. So bitter was the Republican factional dispute that neither side would support a candidate acceptable to the other. Nor would the Democrats play kingmaker by siding with one group or the other. The dispute continued throughout the 56th Congress (1899–1901), leaving the seat unfilled.

Furthermore, the term of Delaware's other Senate seat ended in 1901, necessitating another election. The same pattern prevailed, with the legislature failing to fill either Senate seat, leaving the state unrepresented in the Senate from March 4, 1901, until March 1, 1903, when at last the deadlock was broken by the choice of one faction's Senate candidate to one seat, and the other faction's candidate to the other seat.

The system had other faults besides election deadlocks. The party caucuses in the state legislatures and individual members were subject to intense and unethical lobbying by supporters of various senatorial candidates. Because of the frequency of allegations of illegal methods used in securing election, the Senate found itself involved in election disputes. The Constitution makes Congress the judge of its own members. Article I, Section 5, states that "Each House shall be the Judge of the Elections, Returns, and Qualifications of its own Members. . . ."

Critics of the legislative election of senators had still another grievance. They contended that elections to the state legislatures often were overshadowed by senatorial contests. Thus when voters went to the polls to choose their state legislators,

Table 2–3 Ticket-Splitting Between Presidential and House Candidates, 1900–1996

Year	Districts[a]	Districts with split results	
		Number	Percentage
1900	295	10	3.4
1904	310	5	1.6
1908	314	21	6.7
1912	333	84	25.2
1916	333	35	10.5
1920	344	11	3.2
1924	356	42	11.8
1928	359	68	18.9
1932	355	50	14.1
1936	361	51	14.1
1940	362	53	14.6
1944	367	41	11.2
1948	422	90	21.3
1952	435	84	19.3
1956	435	130	29.9
1960	437	114	26.1
1964	435	145	33.3
1968	435	139	32.0
1972	435	192	44.1
1976	435	124	28.5
1980	435	143	32.8
1984	435	196	45.0
1988	435	148	34.0
1992	435	100	23.0
1996	435	111	25.5

Notes: a. Before 1952 complete data are not available on every congressional district.   b. Congressional districts carried by a presidential candidate of one party and a House candidate of another party.

Source: Norman J. Ornstein, Thomas E. Mann, and Michael J. Malbin, eds., *Vital Statistics on Congress, 1997–1998* (Washington, D.C.: Congressional Quarterly, 1998), 71.

they would sometimes be urged to disregard state and local issues and vote for a legislator who promised to support a certain candidate for the U.S. Senate. This, the critics said, led to a neglect of state government. Moreover, drawn-out Senate contests tended to hold up the consideration of state business.

The main criticism of legislative elections was that they distorted, or even blocked, the will of the people. Throughout the nineteenth century, a movement for popular elections had in several states taken away from legislatures the right to choose governors and presidential electors. Now attention focused on the Senate.

Toward the turn of the century, the House on five occasions approved proposed constitutional amendments for popular Senate elections. But each time the Senate refused to act. Frustrated in Congress, the reformers began implementing various formulas for selecting Senate candidates. In some cases, party conventions endorsed nominees for senator, enabling the voters to know which candidates the legislature was likely to support.

Oregon took the lead in instituting nonbinding popular elections. Under a 1901 law, voters expressed their choice for senator in popular ballots. While the results of the vote had no legal force, the law required that the election returns be formally announced to the state legislature. When first tried, in 1902, the Oregon legislators ignored the ballot winner. But the

In 1938 Gen. Walter Faulkner of Tennessee lost his bid for a seat in the House. Here he pursues the farm vote.

DORTHEA LANGE/LIBRARY OF CONGRESSM

reformers increased their pressure, including demands that candidates for the legislature sign a pledge to vote for the winner of the popular vote. By 1908 the plan was working as its authors had hoped, with a Republican legislature electing Democrat George Chamberlain, the winner of the popular contest. Within a few years Colorado, Kansas, Minnesota, Montana, Nevada, and Oklahoma adopted the Oregon method.

It was not until 1911 that the Senate, infused with a number of progressives, both Democrats and Republicans, approved a constitutional amendment for the popular election of senators. It did so that June 12, by a vote of 64–24. The House concurred in the Senate version on May 13, 1912, by a vote of 238–39. The Seventeenth Amendment was then put before the states for their approval. It was ratified April 8, 1913.

The amendment did not bring a wholesale changeover in the Senate's membership. In fact, all but two of the twenty-five incumbents who sought election in November 1914 were successful. Seven other senators had retired or died.

House Elections

The House of Representatives was designed by the Founders to be the branch of government closest to the people. Its members, unlike the Senate or the president, were to be chosen directly by the voters. They were given two-year terms, so the people would have a chance to monitor and pass judgment on their activities at brief intervals. In addition, members of the

House, the larger of the two legislative bodies, would have relatively small constituencies.

The lower houses of the colonial and state legislatures served as a model for the U.S. House. In each state, at least one house was elected by popular vote.

The Constitution left the qualification of voters to the states, with one exception: the qualifications could be no more restrictive than for the most numerous branch of a state's own legislature. At first, property qualifications for voting were general. But a democratic trend early in the nineteenth century swept away most property qualifications, producing practically universal white male suffrage by the 1830s.

Many delegates to the Constitutional Convention preferred annual elections for the House, believing that the body should reflect as closely as possible the wishes of the people. James Madison, however, argued for a three-year term, to let the representatives gain knowledge and experience in national and local affairs. The result was a compromise on a two-year term.

The two-year term has not been universally popular. From time to time, proposals have been made to extend it. President Lyndon B. Johnson advocated a four-year term in his 1966 State of the Union address. That proposal received more applause than any other part of his speech, but it came to nothing.

The size of the original House of Representatives was written into Article I, Section 2, of the Constitution, along with directions to apportion the House according to population, as recorded in the first census in 1790. Until then, the original thirteen states were assigned the following members: New Hampshire three, Massachusetts eight, Rhode Island one, Connecticut five, New York six, New Jersey four, Pennsylvania eight, Delaware one, Maryland six, Virginia ten, North Carolina five, South Carolina five, and Georgia three. This apportionment of seats — sixty-five in all — remained in effect during the First and Second Congresses (1789–1793).

Congress in 1792 determined that the House should have one representative for every 33,000 inhabitants, 105 members in all, and fixed the number for each state. This method of dividing the population of the various states by 33,000 was devised by Thomas Jefferson and known as "rejected fractions," for all remainders were disregarded. Congress enacted a new apportionment measure, including the mathematical formula to be used, every ten years (except 1920) until a permanent law became effective in 1929.

Changing Election Practices

Five New England states at one time or another required a majority vote (50.01 percent) to win election to the House. If no candidate gained a majority, new elections were held until one contender managed to do so. But all of the states had phased out the requirement by the end of the nineteenth century. Multiple races were necessary sometimes because none of the candidates could win a majority. In the Fourth District of Massachusetts in 1848–1849, for example, twelve successive elections were held to try to choose a representative. None was successful, and the district remained unrepresented in the House during the 31st Congress (1849–1851).

Prior to ratification of the Twentieth Amendment in 1933, regular sessions of Congress began in December of odd-numbered years. There was, therefore, a long period between elections in November of even-numbered years until the beginning of the regular congressional session. As a consequence, several states moved congressional elections to odd-numbered years — a practice that continued until late in the nineteenth century.

Practices in the South

Many of the anomalies in election of U.S. representatives occurred in the South. That region's experience with slavery, Civil War, Reconstruction, and racial antagonisms created special problems for the regular electoral process.

Article I, Section 2, of the Constitution contained a formula for counting slaves for apportionment purposes: every five slaves would be counted as three persons. Thus, the total population of a state to be used in determining its congressional representation would be the free population plus three-fifths of the slave population.

After the Civil War and the emancipation of the slaves, blacks were fully counted for the purposes of apportionment. The Fourteenth Amendment, ratified in 1868, required that apportionment be based on "the whole number of persons in each State. . . ." On this basis, several southern states tried to claim immediate additional representation on their readmission to the Union. Tennessee, for example, chose an extra U.S. representative, electing him at large in 1868. Virginia took similar action in 1869 and 1870, and South Carolina in 1868 and 1870. But the House declined to seat the additional representatives, ruling that the states would have to await reapportionment after the 1870 census for any changes in their representation.

Another provision of the Fourteenth Amendment provided for reducing the House representation of any state that denied the voting franchise to any male citizen over twenty-one. This effort to prevent the southern states from denying the vote to newly freed slaves was never applied. Congress instead frequently considered election challenges filed against members-elect from the South. Between 1881 and 1897, eighteen Democrats from the former Confederate states were unseated by the House, often on charges that black voting rights were abused in their districts.

Contested Elections

Decentralization of control over elections in the United States may have strengthened participatory democracy, but it has led frequently to controversy over election results. Losing candidates and their supporters believe in many cases that more voters were on their side than the official count showed. Floyd M. Riddick wrote in *The United States Congress: Organization and Procedure*: "Seldom if ever has a Congress organized without some losing candidate for a seat in either the Senate or House contesting the right of the member-elect to be senator or representative, as the case might be, as a result of the election in which the losing candidate participated."[8]

To avert partisanship, a 1798 law established procedures to settle contested House elections. The law expired in 1804. A new law was passed in 1851 and amended in 1873 and 1875. These laws sought to give a judicial rather than partisan character to contested election proceedings, but party loyalty usually governed the outcomes.

The Federal Contested Election Act of 1969 superseded the earlier legislation. The new law, which also applied only to House contests, prescribed procedures for instituting a challenge and presenting testimony but did not establish criteria to govern decisions. It was more restrictive than earlier laws because it allowed only candidates on the ballot or bona fide write-in candidates to contest election results. Previously, anyone having an interest in a congressional election could initiate proceedings.

Senators were chosen by state legislatures until the adoption in 1913 of the Seventeenth Amendment, providing for direct popular elections. Before then, contested senatorial elections often involved accusations of corruption in the legislatures. Congress never passed a law on contested Senate elections comparable to that for the House.

The number of contested congressional elections since 1789 probably is in the hundreds, most experts agree. But an exact number has never been determined because students of the subject disagree on what constitutes a contested election.

Notes

1. V. O. Key Jr., *Politics, Parties, and Pressure Groups*, 5th ed. (New York: Crowell, 1964), 378.
2. Letter to Francis Hopkinson, March 3, 1789. Quoted in Elizabeth Frost, ed., *The Bully Pulpit: Quotations from America's Presidents* (New York: Facts on File, 1988), 149.
3. *The Federalist Papers*, with an introduction by Clinton Rossiter (New York: New American Library, 1961), 80.
4. Alan Ehrenhalt, *The United States of Ambition: Politicians, Power, and the Pursuit of Office* (New York: Times Books, 1991), 23.
5. William H. Flanigan and Nancy H. Zingale, *Political Behavior of the American Electorate* (Washington, D.C.: CQ Press, 1991), 43–44.
6. Ibid., 68, 83.
7. Lydia Saad, "Independents Rank as Largest U.S. Political Group" (Gallup News Service, April 9, 1999), 1–3.
8. Floyd M. Riddick, *The United States Congress: Organization and Procedure* (Washington, D.C.: National Capitol Publishers, 1949), 12.

The Past as Prologue:
The 1996 Presidential Election by Region and State

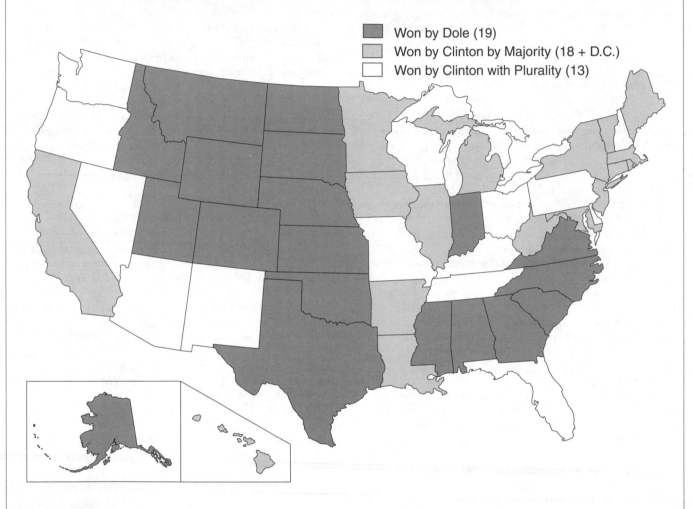

Won by Dole (19)
Won by Clinton by Majority (18 + D.C.)
Won by Clinton with Plurality (13)

The last presidential election is not always a good indicator of the one to come. But this year, a look at the 1996 election map (above) could be instructive, particularly if it is looked at beyond the normal terms of Democrat versus Republican. That one-on-one competition was pretty one-sided: 31 states (plus D.C.) and 379 electoral votes for Democrat Bill Clinton; 19 states and 159 electoral votes for Republican Bob Dole.

Rhodes Cook is an independent political analyst and author of the biennial election book America Votes (Washington, D.C.: CQ Press). His work currently appears on his political Web site, www.rhodescook.com. He can be reached at rhodescook@aol.com or through his Web site.

But Clinton was re-elected in 1996 with just 49 percent of the popular vote. Divide his states into those he won with a majority of the popular vote and those he carried with a mere plurality, and add in those that voted Republican, and one gets a reasonable idea of where the 2000 presidential race begins.

This tri-section is not a perfect overlay, to be sure. Every presidential election is different. Yet by and large, Al Gore should be strongest in most of the states that Clinton won last time with more than 50 percent of the vote. That does not mean Gore should win them all. But they would provide a starting point for Democratic strategists in exploring how to try and reach the 270 electoral votes needed to win the White House.

The 18 states (plus D.C.) that Clinton won in 1996 with a majority of the vote include virtually all the Northeast, Califor-

Table 1   1996 Electoral Votes

	Clinton		Dole
	Majority	Plurality	Dole
Northeast	100	27	0
Midwest	57	43	29
South	15	44	104
West	58	35	26
Total	230	149	159

nia, and portions of the vote-rich Frost Belt from New Jersey to Minnesota. The Clinton-majority states, plus the District of Columbia, have 230 electoral votes.

The base for George W. Bush is logically the 19 states that Dole carried, concentrated in the vast sector of the country that can be called the Republican "L." The "L" is comprised of the South, the Plains states, and the Mountain West, including Alaska, and has been the cornerstone of the Republican presidential coalition over much of the last half century.

Dole did not sweep all the states within the "L" in 1996, but the only state that he won outside it was Indiana. As mentioned, the Dole states hold 159 electoral votes.

That leaves the 13 states that Clinton won in 1996 with less than 50 percent of the vote. They represent many of the prime battlegrounds of 2000, and can be found in all parts of the country—including Pennsylvania in the Northeast, Ohio in the Midwest, and Florida in the South. Altogether, the Clinton-plurality states have 149 electoral votes.

Table 2   The 1996 Election

	Electoral Votes		Percentage of Popular Vote			
	Dems.	Reps.	Clinton (D)	Dole (R)	Perot (Reform)	Winner and Margin
National	**379**	**159**	**49%**	**41%**	**8%**	**Clinton by 8%**
Northeast	**(127)**	**(0)**				
Connecticut	8		53%	35%	10%	Clinton by 18%
Delaware	3		52%	37%	11%	Clinton by 15%
Maine	4		52%	31%	14%	Clinton by 21%
Maryland	10		54%	38%	7%	Clinton by 16%
Massachusetts	12		61%	28%	9%	Clinton by 33%
New Hampshire	4		49%	39%	10%	Clinton by 10%
New Jersey	15		54%	36%	9%	Clinton by 18%
New York	33		59%	31%	8%	Clinton by 28%
Pennsylvania	23		49%	40%	10%	Clinton by 9%
Rhode Island	4		60%	27%	11%	Clinton by 33%
Vermont	3		53%	31%	12%	Clinton by 22%
West Virginia	5		52%	37%	11%	Clinton by 15%
D.C.	3		85%	9%	2%	Clinton by 76%
Midwest	**(100)**	**(29)**				
Illinois	22		54%	37%	8%	Clinton by 17%
Indiana		12	42%	47%	11%	Dole by 5%
Iowa	7		50%	40%	9%	Clinton by 10%
Kansas		6	36%	54%	9%	Dole by 18%
Michigan	18		52%	38%	9%	Clinton by 14%
Minnesota	10		51%	35%	12%	Clinton by 16%
Missouri	11		48%	41%	10%	Clinton by 7%
Nebraska		5	35%	54%	11%	Dole by 19%
North Dakota		3	40%	47%	12%	Dole by 7%
Ohio	21		47%	41%	11%	Clinton by 6%
South Dakota		3	43%	46%	10%	Dole by 3%
Wisconsin	11		49%	38%	10%	Clinton by 11%
South	**(59)**	**(104)**				
Alabama		9	43%	50%	6%	Dole by 7%
Arkansas	6		54%	37%	8%	Clinton by 17%
Florida	25		48%	42%	9%	Clinton by 6%
Georgia		13	46%	47%	6%	Dole by 1%
Kentucky	8		46%	45%	9%	Clinton by 1%
Louisiana	9		52%	40%	7%	Clinton by 12%
Mississippi		7	44%	49%	6%	Dole by 5%
North Carolina		14	44%	49%	7%	Dole by 5%
Oklahoma		8	40%	48%	11%	Dole by 8%
South Carolina		8	44%	50%	6%	Dole by 6%
Tennessee	11		48%	46%	6%	Clinton by 2%
Texas		32	44%	49%	7%	Dole by 5%
Virginia		13	45%	47%	7%	Dole by 2%

Table 2   The 1996 Election (cont.)

	Electoral Votes		Percentage of Popular Vote			
	Dems.	Reps.	Clinton (D)	Dole (R)	Perot (Reform)	Winner and Margin
West	(93)	(26)				
Alaska		3	33%	51%	11%	Dole by 18%
Arizona	8		47%	44%	8%	Clinton by 3%
California	54		51%	38%	7%	Clinton by 13%
Colorado		8	44%	46%	7%	Dole by 2%
Hawaii	4		57%	32%	8%	Clinton by 25%
Idaho		4	34%	52%	13%	Dole by 18%
Montana		3	41%	44%	14%	Dole by 3%
Nevada	4		44%	43%	9%	Clinton by 1%
New Mexico	5		49%	42%	6%	Clinton by 7%
Oregon	7		47%	39%	9%	Clinton by 8%
Utah		5	33%	54%	10%	Dole by 21%
Washington	11		49.8%	37%	9%	Clinton by 13%
Wyoming		3	37%	50%	12%	Dole by 13%

Note: Popular vote percentages are rounded to the nearest whole percentage point, and the margins of victory are based on the differences between the Clinton and Dole percentages.

Unlikely to win on issues, a manager of Clinton's impeachment proclaims his life story

Rogan's Run: The GOP Fights For a Crucial Swing District

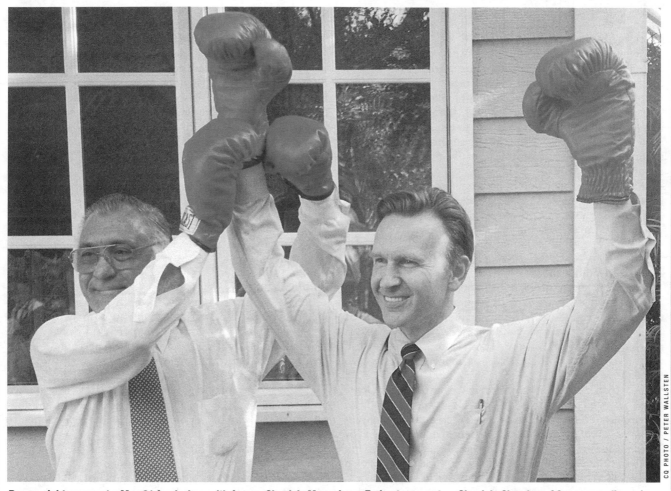

Rogan, right, poses at a May 21 fundraiser with former Glendale Mayor Larry Zarian to promote a Glendale Chamber of Commerce dinner in which Rogan and Zarian planned to be competing auctioneers. Rogan and Schiff are courting Armenian-Americans, a key swing voting bloc.

PASADENA, Calif. — It is Sunday morning in late spring at the NewLife Fellowship, a mixed-race Christian church in the northeastern suburbs of Los Angeles. As a small band plays upbeat tunes praising Jesus, children scamper about, parents settle into their seats and a man most of them know only from television waits in the front row.

This is a comfortable place for Rep. James E. Rogan, R-Calif., who likes to preach. As he takes the microphone, he asks church leaders to break tradition and let the kids remain for his testimonial. "I've got a message for them," he says, shedding his sportcoat. He tells both children and voting-age adults that he was born to a single mom on welfare, dropped out of high school and spent his teen years smoking marijuana before turning his life around, working his way through college and law school and eventually getting elected to Congress in 1996.

For many, this is not what they expected from the man who played a lead role in prosecuting a president. But in speech after speech, at churches, backyard fundraisers, graduation ceremonies and town meetings, Rogan is running for re-election in California's 27th District on his life story. And the culmination of that story — "my legacy," he says — is his starring role in the 1998 impeachment of President Clinton. "I am more proud of serving with those people on the Judiciary Committee in that exercise than anything else I have done in my professional life," he said later that day after a speech at a vocational school graduation. "I will be proud of that until the day I die." (*Impeachment, 1999 CQ Weekly, p. 2871*)

To be sure, the House's unpopular stand against Clinton is not foremost in the minds of voters, who are more interested in a proposed new freeway and the noise at the Burbank Airport. But impeachment set the stage for the race and established the character of the campaign. Rogan's visible role made him a prime target of national Democrats, who see his district as key in their fight to overcome a six-seat deficit in the House. Sensing Rogan's vulnerability, top national Democratic leaders persuaded Adam Schiff, a powerful state senator whose district encompasses Rogan's, to give up a safe seat and the Judiciary Committee chairmanship to run for Congress. Paradoxically, Schiff is downplaying the impeachment on the campaign trail because he thinks his stance on the issues can carry him to victory. But both sides cite impeachment prominently in national fundraising letters as they rake in millions of dollars from all over the country in preparation for what is expected to cost up to $10 million — and possibly be the most expensive House race in history.

Rogan's unblinking approach to the subject of impeachment illustrates the strategies unfolding in what is perhaps the most closely watched congressional race in the nation. In a district where registered Democrats were outnumbered eight years ago but now exceed Republicans by about 44 percent to 37 percent, where independents lean to the left and where an increasing number of ethnic minorities makes the terrain more treacherous for the GOP, Rogan's strategists know he cannot win on the issues. So he plans to use his best weapons — an affable personality, an inspirational life story and a Clinton-like ability to work a crowd. "It's a changed district," said National Republican Congressional Committee Chairman Thomas M. Davis III, R-Va. "This will be a race that's a close race. We conceded [that] from the beginning."

Suburban Bellwether

In some ways, California's 27th District is a bellwether for the nation: It is suburban, with suburban concerns such as traffic, noise pollution and gun control; independent voters are increasingly powerful, and its once-WASPish neighborhoods are increasingly diverse. Those factors are relevant in many of the swing districts across the country, each of which could prove vital in the fight for House control.

The struggle could be won or lost in California alone. Of the state's 52-seat delegation, 10 races are considered competitive. Three of those races have "no clear favorite," according to Congressional Quarterly's risk ratings, and all are currently held by Republicans: Rogan, Steven T. Kuykendall in the nearby 36th and Tom Campbell in Silicon Valley's 15th. But all eyes are on Rogan and Schiff. As the 27th goes, so go the swing districts, some Democratic strategists believe. "There's a recognition that if we don't win this race we probably won't win other races, that this is the best prospect we have in terms of knocking off a hard right incumbent," Schiff said. (*California, 2000 CQ Weekly, p. 1368*)

Schiff will tell voters that Rogan has spent more time in Washington worrying about the "right-wing agenda" on matters such as removing Clinton than attending to matters at home. His campaign literature attacks Rogan as anti-abortion rights, anti-gun control, unfriendly to consumers on health care issues and in favor of teaching creationism in public schools. "I'm going to make Jim Rogan the issue," Schiff says. "He has a very poor record to try to defend."

If the results of the March 7 open primary are any indication, the race will go down to the wire. In that vote, Schiff

won 48.8 percent and Rogan took 47.3 percent. Said analyst Allan Hoffenblum, publisher of the California Target Book, a report on state politics: "Rogan has to hope that it is purely a personality contest between Jim Rogan and Adam Schiff. He's got a great story. Adam Schiff better hope that it is a partisan race, Democrat vs. Republican, because if it is, he'll win."

In a sense, Schiff and Rogan can both claim the incumbent mantle. California state senators represent more constituents than U.S. congressmen. Polls show that each candidate will hold on to his base supporters — blacks, Latinos and other Democrats for Schiff; conservative independents and Republicans for Rogan — while the battle in the coming months will focus on those in the middle.

California's 27th is a collection of suburban communities northeast of Los Angeles, home to the television studios of Burbank, the old money and new diversity of Pasadena and the burgeoning minority neighborhoods of Glendale. It is traditional GOP turf, but changing demographics have altered that forever. Long gone is the "little old lady from Pasadena." Now, according to the California Target Book, 8 percent of the district's registered voters are African-American, 12 percent are Hispanic and 6 percent are Asian. It also has a large and growing group of Armenian-Americans. "This district has a lot to say about where the country is headed," Schiff said in an interview in his office in Sacramento. "Ethnically and economically it is very diverse and representative of America. [Party] registration is very close, and the issues that resonate on a national level are resonating in our district."

Unique Group

In the battle for swing voters, both sides will be courting Armenians. The district is home to as many as 17,000 registered Armenian-American voters, and they are hard to pin down as a voting bloc. (About 20 percent are independents and the rest are divided between registered Republicans and Democrats, with an edge for the GOP.) They tend to be socially conservative. "They have tended to lean Republican," said Parke Skelton, a campaign consultant to Schiff. "It's an area where we have a chance to cut into Rogan's base."

Already, Schiff's campaign has targeted the Armenian community with mail and cable television ads, Skelton said. The goal is to remind Armenians that Schiff advocated for their community as a state lawmaker, securing public funds to help produce a documentary film on the 1915 massacre of Armenians in the last days of the Ottoman Empire.

Rogan, for his part, visited Armenia last year with the

Major Issues in the Campaign

■ Impeachment	Rogan embraces his role, calling it the pinnacle of his career, while Schiff paints him as a right-wing ideologue.
■ Gun Control	Rogan supports gun rights but voted for three-day waiting period for purchases at gun shows.
■ Abortion	Schiff says Rogan, who opposes abortion rights, is out of step with the views of his constituents.
■ Health Care	Rogan accuses Schiff of shilling for trial lawyers, while Schiff faults Rogan for opposing a patient's bill of rights.

California's Vulnerable Seats Give Democrats Hope for Election Sweep

California gave the nation mall sushi and Rollerblading. Now, if Democrats get their way, the Golden State could go a long way toward delivering a power shift in Congress. Democrats are hoping for victories in the state's sprawling suburbs, where voters are moderate and the party's national agenda — gun control, health care expansion and abortion rights — might have traction.

"We have such a big state, and such a large number of seats here are vulnerable," said Art Torres, a former state senator from the Los Angeles suburbs who now heads the California Democratic Party. "We are in a pivotal position to swing control of the House."

Just six seats separate the two parties in the House, meaning that the outcomes of only a handful of elections in November could determine who gets the gavel. California, the nation's most populous state, with 52 congressional districts, boasts as many as 10 competitive races, three of which have no clear favorite to win, according to Congressional Quarterly's risk ratings.

Republican Reps. James E. Rogan and Steven T. Kuykendall are fighting for survival in L.A.-area districts dominated by Democrats, while two strong candidates are battling to replace GOP Rep. Tom Campbell, a Senate candidate, in the San Jose area. Back in Southern California, Republican

Rep. Brian P. Bilbray faces a stiff challenge from Democrat Susan Davis. Democrats say the 2000 congressional races could resemble the party's state successes in 1998, when they picked up seats in the Legislature and took the governor's office.

"California as a state is trending Democratic in the same way that many suburban districts are across the country," said John Del Cecato, spokesman for the Democratic Congressional Campaign Committee.

Republicans offer a different spin. GOP strategists say the Republicans facing tough fights reflect their districts. In many cases, they are moderates who disagree with the more conservative leadership in Congress. "With kids, my wife and I match up to the demographic of this district," said Jim Cunneen, a GOP state legislator who faces Democrat Mike Honda to succeed Campbell in the 15th. "It's a campaign about, 'I'm one of you.'"

The campaign themes in these swing races are similar. Democrats paint their opponents as right-wing extremists, tying them to former Speaker Newt Gingrich, R-Ga. (1979-99), or to the impeachment of President Clinton. Similarly, Republicans link their opponents to labor unions and trial lawyers. Both sides know that they must win the growing pool of independents — as much as 15 percent of voters in some areas.

The GOP candidates are eager for

ways to separate themselves from the leadership in Washington. In Cunneen's case, he embraces the "compassionate conservatism" of presumed GOP presidential nominee George W. Bush and, at the same time, has campaigned with Arizona Sen. John McCain of Arizona, a GOP maverick.

Rogan, probably the most conservative of the Republicans in tight races, hopes he can overcome basic disagreements with constituents on key issues by selling his compelling life story.

Kuykendall's challenger is former Rep. Jane Harman (1993-99), who gave up her seat to run unsuccessfully for governor. While the Democrats will tie Kuykendall to the national GOP, Republicans will say Harman is using Congress as a fall-back job.

Still, Democrats have an uphill battle, even in California. Democratic Reps. Lois Capps, Ellen O. Tauscher, Cal Dooley, Joe Baca and Loretta Sanchez all face competitive races, although they are each favored to win.

Marit Babin, a spokeswoman for the National Republican Congressional Committee, said even if Democrats succeed in California, they will not wrest control of the House because of GOP prospects to pick up seats in states such as Virginia and Pennsylvania. "They would have to pick up every single competitive seat out there, and that's just not going to happen," Babin said.

Armenian Assembly of America, a nonprofit educational group that lobbies in behalf of the community. He is pushing for a resolution (H Res 398) in Congress that would label the massacre of Armenians as genocide. He also hopes that his personal story will appeal to immigrants.

"Jim Rogan is talking about how 'I am a hometown guy who came from a broken family, and I made good,'" said Larry Zarian, an Armenian-American talk show host and former Republican mayor of Glendale. "The ethnic com-

munities look at him and realize he has been there for them."

Both candidates have staff members who speak Armenian, and both accuse the other of pandering. "It's really a tossup with these two guys. They both have very strong records on Armenian issues," said Peter Abajian, the Los Angeles-based western regional director for the Armenian Assembly. "Everyone's courting the middle ground, and the Armenian-American community is in position now to elect a member of Congress."

Attack Ads

The campaign has turned nasty.

In one ad airing on cable television, Rogan accuses Schiff of shilling for trial lawyers in his expressed support for plans that would give patients the ability to sue their health maintenance organizations (HMOs). The ad includes images of briefcases stuffed with cash and someone taking $100 bills. (*Managed care, 2000 CQ Weekly, p. 1274*)

A Schiff ad notes that Rogan voted against a bill (HR 2723) that would allow patients to sue their HMOs, and

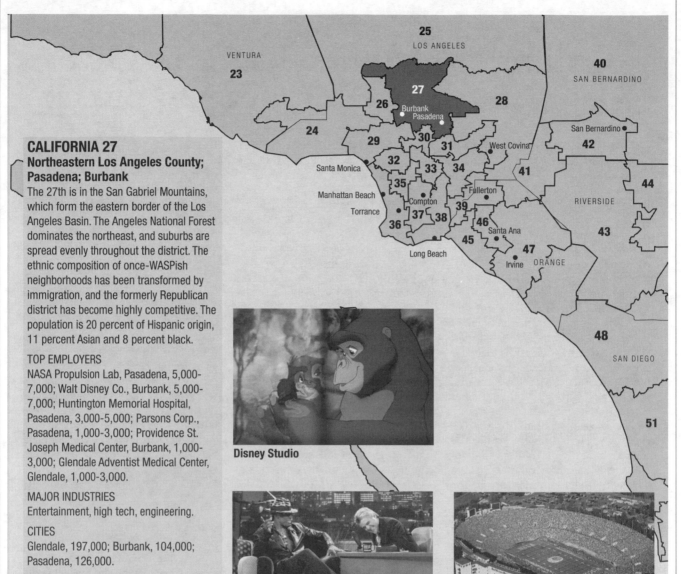

CALIFORNIA 27
Northeastern Los Angeles County; Pasadena; Burbank

The 27th is in the San Gabriel Mountains, which form the eastern border of the Los Angeles Basin. The Angeles National Forest dominates the northeast, and suburbs are spread evenly throughout the district. The ethnic composition of once-WASPish neighborhoods has been transformed by immigration, and the formerly Republican district has become highly competitive. The population is 20 percent of Hispanic origin, 11 percent Asian and 8 percent black.

TOP EMPLOYERS
NASA Propulsion Lab, Pasadena, 5,000-7,000; Walt Disney Co., Burbank, 5,000-7,000; Huntington Memorial Hospital, Pasadena, 3,000-5,000; Parsons Corp., Pasadena, 1,000-3,000; Providence St. Joseph Medical Center, Burbank, 1,000-3,000; Glendale Adventist Medical Center, Glendale, 1,000-3,000.

MAJOR INDUSTRIES
Entertainment, high tech, engineering.

CITIES
Glendale, 197,000; Burbank, 104,000; Pasadena, 126,000.

UNUSUAL FEATURES
Pasadena is home of the Rose Bowl; Burbank hosts the Disney Studio and "The Tonight Show With Jay Leno."

SOURCE: CQ's Politics in America 2000

Disney Studio

The Jay Leno show

Rose Bowl

REP. JAMES E. ROGAN (R)
Elected: 1996; 2nd term
Born: Aug. 21, 1957, San Francisco
Religion: Christian
Family: Wife, Christine; two children
Education: U. of California, Berkeley, B.A. 1979; U. of California, Los Angeles, J.D. 1983
Occupation: Lawyer
Political Highlights: California Assembly, 1994-97, majority leader, 1995-97
Committees: Commerce, Judiciary

STATE SEN. ADAM SCHIFF (D)
Elected: 1996; 1st term
Born: June 22, 1960, Framingham, Mass.
Religion: Jewish
Family: Wife, Eve; one child
Education: Stanford University, B.A. 1982; Harvard Law School, J.D. 1985
Occupation: Lawyer
Highlights: U.S. Attorney's Office, 1990-96.
Committees: Chairman, Senate Judiciary, Select on Juvenile Justice, Joint on the Arts; Insurance, Budget.

features Pasadena resident Irene McDermott, who explains that her family's HMO had refused to pay for her husband's chemotherapy treatments for cancer. McDermott says that Schiff "helped force the HMO to provide the treatment that saved Phil's life."

A Rogan ad attacks Schiff for undermining several California initiatives that passed in recent years, including Proposition 187, to limit benefits to illegal immigrants, and Proposition 227, to eliminate bilingual education. It is a risky approach in an ethnically diverse district.

This is the third time these men have faced each other — Rogan beat Schiff twice for a state assembly seat — and neither hides the animosity. "I always thought it was an interesting irony that the word arrogant has his name in it, R-O-G-A-N," Schiff said.

Rogan's aides say Schiff is a lightweight. Rogan chastises him for focusing on local issues, saying it is because Schiff cannot grasp national topics. He attacks Schiff for taking his marching orders from the "Hollywood elite" that donate to his campaign, such as Steven Spielberg, Jeffrey Katzenberg and David Geffen. Schiff accuses Rogan of neglecting the district and embellishing his stories.

Indeed, the men are a study in contrasts. Rogan is a gifted storyteller who practically worships Ronald Reagan and collects political memorabilia. He once sold off 4-by-6-inch speech note cards that Gov. Reagan gave him when he was a teenager to pay his way through school. He was a county prosecutor and judge and a Democrat who switched loyalties in 1988 because he decided the party was too liberal.

Schiff is soft-spoken and dry, and sticks closely to the national Democratic playbook as he directs an interview back to health care, gun control and Social Security. He attended Stanford University and Harvard Law School and worked as a federal prosecutor for six years.

Schiff Runs on Issues

Schiff did not have to take on Rogan for a third time. He could have enjoyed another two years as Judiciary chairman, then coasted into Congress after a state redistricting process that will be dominated by Democrats.

But he was recruited by Minority Leader Richard A. Gephardt, D-Mo., and Democratic Congressional Campaign Committee Chairman Patrick J. Kennedy, D-R.I., and decided to run

during a trip to Washington in the spring of 1999. "Talking with them helped me put the race in a national context, that I could be part of a very few races that would decide if the country would make progress on key issues," Schiff said.

Schiff argues that Rogan's stance on gun control is not in step with the district. Rogan defends the Second Amendment right to bear arms and has won support in the past from the National Rifle Association, but he opposed the NRA last year in supporting three-day waiting periods for gun purchases at gun shows.

Schiff says Rogan's opposition to abortion rights is out of step as well, as was his vote in 1999 against the so-called patient's bill of rights (HR 2723). "As much as he would like to talk about his personal history, ultimately what people are going to evaluate him on is what kind of a representative he is of the district," Schiff said. "I think he would like to deflect attention from that." Schiff said Rogan's participation in the impeachment is the most blatant example of how he "tied himself at the hip to the most hard-right, partisan elements in Congress."

Even Rogan concedes his views are probably not in line with the district's majority. "I know where the district is on abortion. I know where the district is on abolishing gun rights. I know where the district is on impeachment. I pay for polling," he said.

Of his vote on impeachment: "If all I wanted to do was get re-elected, then . . . I could have looked into the C-SPAN cameras, and said, 'As bad as this whole thing is, I'm going to do what the voters want and vote no.' I would have been hailed as an independent thinker" for bucking the GOP leadership. "I knew when I cast that vote I could have been stepping into a huge, political black abyss."

Schiff might not play the impeachment card on the campaign trail, but he hammers on it in the mail.

"Dear Friend," he wrote in a fundraising letter. "You probably remember Congressman Jim Rogan. In the partisan impeachment hearings that polarized our nation for so long, the right-wing Rogan stood out." The letter goes on to list several of Rogan's actions during the trial, after which Schiff notes: "It's an honor to run against him."

Another letter from Schiff, posted on the Web site moveon.org, says that former independent counsel Kenneth

W. Starr and House Judiciary Chairman Henry J. Hyde, R-Ill., "tried to bring down our twice-elected President disregarding the Constitution and all precedent. Standing at their side as a key leader in the impeachment was California Congressman James Rogan." Schiff continues: "I'm running for Congress because I believe that there are many more important issues that we as Americans face."

The letters recount quotes from Rogan during the trial. One reminds donors of the "shocked silence on the Senate floor" when Rogan responded to a request for information by one of the president's lawyers by saying: "Frankly, it's none of your damn business."

Wrote Sen. Barbara Boxer, D-Calif., in a national fundraising appeal for Schiff: "You may not have heard of Congressman James Rogan before the impeachment. But take it from me, the impeachment trial was not an aberration in Rogan's career. James Rogan is one of the most radical right-wing members of Congress."

Rogan has seized on the impeachment as well in national fundraising appeals to conservative donors. Through the first quarter of 2000, the most recent official reporting period, he had raised $3.9 million, according to the Committee for Responsive Politics. Typically, about a third of Rogan's donations come from outside California. In the same period, Schiff raised $1.9 million. Typically about 10 percent of his donations are from out of state. Impeachment is the "single most important factor" in attracting national attention to the race, Skelton said.

Rogan does not run from impeachment, although he knows it may not help him: "Reporters are saying the election isn't about impeachment, but it is about impeachment," he said. "Nobody had heard of Adam Schiff before impeachment. Now he's raising millions of dollars. . . . If I lose this race it will be because of impeachment. I used to draw Democrats and independents. They liked me . . . but those people supported Clinton. And they'll never support me now."

If Rogan can win, he will do it at places like the NewLife Fellowship. One congregant cornered him after the service. "I have a friend at work who says all sorts of terrible things about you," said Bob Coleman, 47, an undecided voter. "But it helps me to hear from your heart." ◆

Rhetoric aside, will parties ever change a system that serves their needs?

Campaign Overhaul Mired In Money and Loopholes

With the White House at stake and Congress in play, campaign cash is flowing this year like a bulging stream in a flash flood. Where is the record level of money coming from? Who gets it?

These are the questions on the minds of strategists and analysts, but more than ever before in modern American history, the answers are not clear. Politicians and their benefactors are forever finding holes in an already loophole-laden campaign finance system that, at one time, aimed to curb the impact of big money and assure public disclosure of those trying to influence elections.

In 2000, the leaders of both major parties and candidates across the nation are seizing upon new ways to avoid money limits and disclosure requirements. They have established nonprofit advocacy groups that raise and spend money in the shadows. They have shifted millions of dollars between state and national party organizations and used so-called soft money to avoid contribution limits. There is no evidence that anyone is breaking the law. As the Senate prepares to discuss a campaign finance overhaul at a hearing May 17, advocates of changing the system say the real scandal is that the law lets politicians avoid disclosure.

"In the world we live in today, practically speaking, there are no limits on what you can give to a campaign," said Larry Makinson, executive director of the Center for Responsive Politics, a Washington watchdog group that tracks political fundraising. "The Federal Election Commission is more useless than ever — and so are we. We're looking at a shrinking pie of reportable money, and it's frightening."

The Federal Election Commission (FEC) estimates that even without unreported money, a record-breaking $3 billion will be spent on this year's presidential and congressional races. According to the FEC, every election cycle since 1992 has set a federal spending record. Overall campaign finance activity has nearly doubled in the past 12 years.

And little of that money comes from average voters, say political watchdog groups. According to the Center for Public Integrity, a nonprofit organization that tracks political giving, less than 5 percent of Americans contribute to political campaigns, and less than one-quarter of 1 percent give $200 or more. "All the other money is coming from businesses and organizations with ulterior motives," said Peter Eisner, the center's managing director.

Eisner's group and other advocates of change say large donations from a relatively few wealthy individuals and special-interest groups have a significant influence on public policy, from sugar subsidies to tomato tariffs to Internet taxes to rules for mobile homes.

Others say the problem is time, not influence-peddling.

Former Rep. Al Swift, D-Wash. (1979-95), who led a campaign fundraising overhaul effort in the 1980s, said he believes money has become the deciding factor in winning elections — and not necessarily because it buys votes. "I don't think you can buy public policy," Swift said. "I'm more concerned about the time spent raising it."

Rep. Charles W. Stenholm, D-Texas, said the fundraising strategies that worked when he first won his seat in 1978 do not suffice any more. "Going down and having to spend hour after hour after hour on personal calls, I hate doing that," said Stenholm, who raised more than $1.5 million in the 1998 cycle in the face of a stiff challenge. "I did it last time because I had to." The fundraising can be so intense, Stenholm said, that colleagues often duck out of the Capitol during key meetings and can be found at party campaign headquarters "dialing for dollars."

Swift and the watchdog groups agree that even more disturbing than the huge amounts of money flowing through campaign committees are the millions of dollars spent by outside groups that never gets reported to the FEC.

It is all legal under the "527" tax code provision. Under this newly discovered loophole in tax and campaign law, millions of dollars are being raised by special groups that do not have to disclose their contributors. They are difficult to track, let alone outlaw, and those who want to eliminate the groups face constitutional obstacles. Group organizers say they are expressing their First Amendment right to free speech. Even foreign countries can give money to affect the outcome of American elections.

"All the fundraising problems that happened in 1996 with foreign money can now be done legally and anonymously," Makinson said. The groups "are the most dangerous loophole that's ever existed in American politics."

Limited Legislation

The political landscape in 2000 presents a dilemma for advocates of a campaign finance overhaul. While the maverick presidential campaign of Sen. John McCain, R-Ariz., placed the issue at center stage, both parties' record-breaking fundraising success gives incumbents little incentive to support change.

Several bills — including one (HR 4168) by Rep. Lloyd Doggett, D-Texas, and one (HR 3688) by Rep. Dennis Moore, D-Kan. — have been introduced in the 106th Congress to close the "527" loophole, a name that comes from the tax code provision that exempts the contributions raised by certain political organizations from taxation. However, none of those bills are expected to get so much as a hearing. Meanwhile, Sen. Joseph I. Lieberman, D-Conn., often mentioned as a possible vice presidential contender, plans to introduce two proposals May 17 to tackle "527s," with McCain as a cosponsor. One would require the groups to comply with federal election disclosure laws, and the other would require "527s" to register with the IRS and disclose donor information. *(Bills, 2000 CQ Weekly, p. 1091; fundraising, 2000 CQ Weekly, p. 881; McCain, 2000 CQ Weekly, p. 651)*

The only campaign finance bill poised to get a hearing this year is a measure (S 1816) by Sen. Chuck Hagel, R-Neb., that is scheduled to be discussed by the Rules and Administration Committee on May 17 and marked up June 14. But while Hagel's bill would limit soft money contributions to parties and committees from corporations and labor

" *[Hagel's bill] seems to be a step or an approach toward campaign finance that might receive bipartisan approval.* "

— Sen. Mitch McConnell, R-Ky., right, who has long fought campaign finance changes.

unions, it would not address the phenomenon of unreported political money. It also is silent on the parties' common practice of shifting money between national and state organizations, a strategy that would easily circumvent Hagel's soft money limits.

Even bill supporters say the measure would do little to stem the flood of campaign money. "If I started loading on to

this bill every perceived problem to cure every perceived ill, I think the reality is it would go nowhere," Hagel said in an interview May 2. McCain, whose presidential bid won only four Senate endorsements, including Hagel's, offered a blunt commentary on Hagel's bill in a May 2 interview: "It's a joke."

The House passed legislation (HR 417) in 1999 that would ban soft money in federal elections and crack down on "issue advocacy," unregulated political spending that does not directly urge the election or defeat of a candidate. McCain and Russell D. Feingold, D-Wis., offered a similar measure (S 1593) in the Senate, but a filibuster engineered by Rules and Administration Committee Chairman Mitch McConnell, R-Ky., and Majority Leader Trent Lott, R-Miss., prevented passage. *(1999 CQ Weekly, p. 2862)*

Most agree the chances of passing significant legislation this year are slim. "The political reality is that this is a presidential election year," Hagel said. "Need we say more?"

Political Impact

Even if Congress does not act on campaign finance, McCain's ability to turn the issue into the centerpiece of his presidential campaign put it center stage for the political season. McCain may have lost the GOP nomination to Texas Gov. George W. Bush, but he forced other candidates to take a stand. Now they are finding that the issue can be a useful tool.

Vice President Al Gore, the presumptive Democratic presidential nominee, has promised to make McCain's bill his first domestic policy initiative. It could prove politically astute for a candidate dogged by criticism for his 1996 fundraising tactics, including a gathering at a Buddhist temple in California.

Bush unveiled an overhaul plan earlier this year as he scurried to halt McCain's threat in the GOP primaries. The Bush plan would ban corporate and union soft money, but would allow unlimited contributions by individuals, a change that McCain said in the campaign would do little to curb big money. Bush has not made campaign finance a centerpiece of his campaign, though the issue could enhance his outsider status. Despite their differences, McCain endorsed Bush on May 9 after a brief meeting in Pittsburgh during which they discussed several issues, including campaign finance — but McCain conceded that they came to no agreement on the issue.

McConnell is a longtime opponent of campaign finance changes. But he said in an interview that Hagel's bill "seems to be a step or an approach toward campaign finance that might receive bipartisan approval." McConnell is chairman of the National Republican Senatorial Committee (NRSC),

Types of Contributions

The Federal Election Commission regulates campaign contributions and expenditures for congressional and presidential campaigns. Congress has established limits on contributions (hard money) for federal races, but few limits on spending. Spending limits have consistently been rejected by federal courts as unconstitutional. Some lawmakers have introduced legislation to regulate contributions to party committees (soft money) used for issue ads and non-federal races. The following chart outlines types of contributions with their limits and reporting requirements.

CATEGORY	DEFINITION	CONTRIBUTION LIMITS	REPORTING
Hard Money ■ Contributions to federal committees and candidates	These are political contributions from individuals or political action committees (PACs) that can be spent directly to advocate the election or defeat of a federal candidate. Direct contributions are not permitted from corporations or labor unions.	Individuals and business partnerships can contribute $1,000 per election to congressional and presidential candidates. The primary, runoff and general election are considered separate elections. Individuals and partnerships can contribute $5,000 per year to political action committees (including state and local party committees) and $20,000 per year to a national party committee. An individual or partnership cannot make total hard money contributions of more than $25,000 per year. Most PACs may contribute $5,000 per election to federal candidates and $15,000 per year to national party committees. National party committees may contribute $17,500 per cycle directly to a Senate candidate and $5,000 per election directly to a House candidate.	Hard money contributions and expenditures must be reported to the Federal Election Commission (FEC).
■ Coordinated expenditures	Political party committees such as the Republican National Committee and the Democratic Congressional Campaign Committee are permitted to spend a fixed amount of hard money in conjunction with a candidate's general election campaign. They may coordinate with the campaign on the best use of that money, but they may not give money directly to the campaign.	Limits for Senate races are set by a formula based on the voting age population of the state in which a candidate is running. Limits range from $67,560 in Delaware to $1,636,438 in California. The limit for House races for 2000 is $33,780, except in states with only one congressional district, where the limit is $67,560. State party committees may spend equal amounts or transfer their limits to national party committees, effectively doubling the national committees' expenditure limits in those states or districts.	Coordinated expenditures must be reported to the FEC by the party committee.
■ Independent expenditures	Individuals, party committees and any PAC may spend hard money independently of a candidate, advocating that candidate's election or defeat. The candidate's campaign may not coordinate with the source of the independent expenditure.	None.	Expenditures must be reported to the FEC.

which raised $40.4 million between Jan. 1, 1999 and March 31, 2000. He opposes contribution limits because he says they violate First Amendment free speech rights. McConnell said he has not decided whether to support Hagel's plan.

Democrats have jumped on the issue in the battle for control of the House, filing a civil racketeering lawsuit against Majority Whip Tom DeLay, R-Texas, for his fundraising tactics. The Democratic Congressional Campaign Committee (DCCC) filed the suit May 3, accusing DeLay of extorting campaign funds from lobbyists by exchanging policy for money and intimidating donors who tend to favor Democrats. (*2000 CQ Weekly, p. 1017*)

DeLay denied that he had broken the law, but did not disagree with the notion that he was using the nonprofit groups for campaign purposes. Rep. Patrick J. Kennedy, D-R.I., chairman of the DCCC, said that if the courts do not stop DeLay and the Republicans, they will stockpile money in secret places, and Democrats will be at a huge disadvantage in November. "We could be up against something that we don't know the full extent of, nor do the American people know the full extent of this," Kennedy told reporters May 3.

But the contradiction inherent in calling for an overhaul of a system that allows everyone to raise unprecedented sums, according to scholars, raises questions about everybody's sincerity.

"Frankly, McConnell is pursuing [Hagel's bill] as a way of deflecting political pressure," said Thomas E. Mann, who studies campaign finance issues at

CATEGORY	DEFINITION	CONTRIBUTION LIMITS	REPORTING
Soft Money ■ Direct contributions	These are contributions given mostly to national party committees to be used in state and local elections and for administrative expenses. They also pay for so-called issue ads that do not expressly advocate the election or defeat of a federal candidate.	Individuals, corporations and unions may donate unlimited amounts to national party committees and to leadership PACs, which are federal PACs associated with presidential candidates and members of Congress.	National parties must disclose soft money contributions to the FEC. Leadership PACs are not required to disclose contributions or expenditures, even though some of that money is used for leadership PAC administrative expenses.
■ Contributions to state committees and candidates	These are contributions given to political committees and candidate committees organized under state laws. The committees can use soft money for issue ads or to advocate the election or defeat of a non-federal candidate.	Limits vary by state law. In Virginia, for example, there are no limits on contributions to a state PAC. But that PAC cannot contribute directly to a federal candidate or advocate the election or defeat of a federal candidate.	Committees generally file reports with a state agency. They do not file reports with the FEC.
Contributions to Joint Fundraising Committees	These are contributions given to a fundraising committee that can collect both hard and soft money to jointly benefit a federal candidate and a national party committee. Senate campaigns often use joint fundraising committees. House candidates have used such committees to distribute hard money among several candidates.	Limits are the same as for hard and soft money. A joint fundraising committee sets a formula for allocating money collected to recipients. In some situations, the first $2,000 of a contribution is counted as hard money and goes to the candidate's campaign, while any remaining amount is treated as soft money and transferred to the national party committee.	Contributions must be disclosed to the FEC by the joint fundraising committee. Transfers of the money to the candidate's campaign committee or a party committee must be disclosed by the joint fundraiser and the recipient party committee or candidate committee.
Unregulated Money	This is money raised and spent on political activity that falls outside the scope of federal regulation. The activity can include almost any political message that does not expressly advocate the election or defeat of a federal candidate. Organizations that conduct these activities typically are created under Sections 501 and 527 of the tax code.	Individuals, corporations and unions can donate unlimited amounts to these types of organizations. A 501(c)(3) organization is generally a nonprofit charity; not all such groups are involved in politics. A 501(c)(4) organization is a social welfare group; those involved in politics are generally lobbying groups. A 527 is a political group formed to influence elections. An example of a 527 organization is Republicans for Clean Air, which aired advertisements critical of presidential candidate Sen. John McCain, R-Ariz., during this year's Republican primaries.	For 501(c)(3) and 501(c)(4) groups, the only filing requirement is an annual IRS Form 990 summarizing financial activity without listing donors or expenditures. Groups formed under Section 527 file an annual confidential tax return if they earned more than $100 in interest income.

the Brookings Institution, a Washington think tank. "And the Democrats, they're doing so well in the soft money raising business now, especially through their campaign committees, that they're not so anxious to eliminate it."

McConnell, as his party's top Senate campaign strategist, also must walk a tightrope on the campaign finance issue, with several GOP incumbents facing tough challenges in November.

"You've got a lot of nervous Republicans, particularly a lot of nervous Republicans up" for re-election, said Nor-man J. Ornstein, resident scholar at the American Enterprise Institute, a Washington think tank. Opposing campaign finance changes "makes you look foolish if you have a Republican Party that uses as its core strategy against Al Gore his campaign finance violations. If you're saying what Al Gore did is outrageous and wrong but the system is dandy, that's not a tenable position."

Sen. Spencer Abraham, R-Mich., for example, is facing an intense challenge from Democratic Rep. Debbie Stabenow in a state whose GOP prima-ry voters backed McCain over Bush. Abraham, who did not support the Mc-Cain-Feingold bill, has signed on as a cosponsor of the Hagel bill. "He does talk about it" on the campaign trail, said spokesman Joe Davis. "He thinks campaign finance reform is on the voters' minds." Abraham had raised $6.5 million for his campaign as of March 31. Stabenow had raised $3.4 million.

Sen. John Ashcroft, R-Mo., also is in a tenuous re-election position. Asked whether he had decided to ask McConnell or Lott to pass a campaign

Hoeffel-Fox II: Accounting for the Money

After Democrat Joseph M. Hoeffel, D-Pa., failed by 84 votes in a 1996 bid to unseat then-Rep. Jon D. Fox, R-Pa., he tried again in 1998 and won Pennsylvania's 13th District House seat — at a price: the two men spent about $3.2 million between them, and other organizations spent more than $1 million. Hoeffel, who raised and spent about $1.3 million, was aided by ads and mailings from labor unions and groups supporting abortion rights. Fox spent more than $1.9 million and received support from the American Medical Association and other groups. The following is a look at the sources of the men's money, how they spent it, and other groups involved.

Rep. Joseph M. Hoeffel, D-Pa.

FUNDRAISING

TOTAL RAISED: $1,269,843

SOURCE[1]	TOTAL	PACs	INDIVIDUALS
Business interests	$474,218	$37,075	$437,143
Interest groups	$160,918	$126,968	$33,950
Labor unions	$200,450	$200,450	$0
Other sources	$125,510	$2,500	$123,010

Hoeffel received 28.7 percent of his contributions from PACs, mostly labor unions. Individual contributors made up 70 percent of his total. As a group, lawyers and lobbyists were the largest individual contributors to his campaign.

SPENDING

TOTAL SPENT: $1,259,326

Broadcast advertisements and media consulting	$748,045
Payroll & office expenses	$427,588
Other consultants	$46,703
Polling	$34,372
Telephone calls	$2,618

Hoeffel's campaign spent nearly half his total, more than $626,000, between Oct. 15 and Nov. 23, 1998.

PARTY SPENDING

Democratic Congressional Campaign Committee	$8,318	Coordinated expenditures
Democratic Congressional Campaign Committee	$3,057	Direct in-kind expenditures
Pennsylvania Democratic Party	$41,780	Coordinated expenditures

OTHER GROUPS' SPENDING-Pro-Hoeffel/Anti-Fox

A Brigham Young University-led study of select 1998 races identified about 20 organizations that were involved in the Hoeffel-Fox race. The BYU study and Federal Election Commission records provide some information on how much they spent. Here is a listing of the identified groups that spent at least $1,000 independent of the two campaigns, along with some groups for which spending figures were unknown.

AFL-CIO	$117,708	Radio ads, GOTV[3]
Planned Parenthood, NARAL	$70,000[2]	Survey, GOTV
Pennsylvania AFL-CIO	$8,236	GOTV
Montgomery County AFL-CIO	Unknown	GOTV
AARP	Unknown	Mailing, GOTV
Peace Action-Delaware Valley	Unknown	Radio ads

finance bill, Ashcroft said, "Not yet." But Ashcroft's opponents at home hope the issue will haunt him on the campaign trail in November.

That is when advocates for public campaign financing hope to put an initiative on the Missouri ballot, similar to one that has passed in Maine and is being debated in Oregon, which would allow taxpayer-financed campaigns for state offices.

Ashcroft "will be forced to take a position on it," said Harriett Woods, a former Democratic lieutenant governor of Missouri and unsuccessful Senate candidate. She is on the steering committee for the state ballot initiative and a member of the national advisory board of Public Campaign, a nonprofit organization that promotes limiting the power of special interests in elections through state-level initiatives.

Woods said that as more states approve campaign changes such as public financing, Congress might take notice. "Every time a state passes it, the congressional delegation is on the hot seat," she said.

Changing Loopholes

The DCCC lawsuit may be the first effort of the new century to politicize campaign fundraising, but lawmakers have made political hay of the issue since the turn of the last century.

During his annual message to Congress in 1905, President Theodore Roosevelt called for a ban on corporate donations to political committees. Roosevelt's call for reform came after congressional hearings revealed that several corporations had secretly financed Roosevelt's 1904 campaign. (*History, p. 48*)

Efforts to overhaul the campaign system have generally surfaced in the wake of political scandal — and when one party has benefited from a campaign finance loophole more than the other.

During the 1970s and '80s, contributions from political action committees (PACs) exploded, with Democrats as the main beneficiaries. In the 1978 elections, PACs contributed $35 million to federal candidates. That rose to $60 million in 1980 and to $159 million by 1990.

During the 1988 congressional elections, House Democrats took in 66 percent of all PAC contributions. Republicans received 34 percent. The lopsided giving to Democrats continued until 1996, when PAC donations split evenly between both parties in the House.

Political watchdog groups charged

Former Rep. Jon D. Fox, R-Pa. (1995-99)

FUNDRAISING

TOTAL RAISED: $1,935,548

SOURCE[1]	TOTAL	PACs	INDIVIDUALS
Business interests	$1,164,666	$551,013	$613,653
Interest groups	$186,726	$162,701	$24,025
Labor unions	$33,148	$33,148	$0
Other sources	$72,625	$500	$72,125

Fox received 37 percent of his contributions from PACs, mostly from business-related groups and Republican and conservative leadership PACs. As a group, lawyers and lobbyists were the largest individual contributors to his campaign.

SPENDING

TOTAL SPENT: $1,921,005

Payroll & office expenses	$871,139
Broadcast advertisements and media consulting	$514,215
Direct mail	$263,612
Other consultants	$119,923
Telephone calls	$109,725
Polling	$42,392

PARTY SPENDING

National Republican Congressional Committee	$62,855	Coordinated expenditures
National Republican Congressional Committee	$152	Direct in-kind expenditures
Republican National Committee	$325,000[2]	Issue ads

OTHER GROUPS' SPENDING–Pro-Fox/Anti-Hoeffel

American Medical Association	$631,571	Television & radio ads
National Association of Realtors	$15,094	GOTV
National Right to Life	$9,000[2]	Radio ads
United Seniors PAC Inc.	$1,334	Printed materials
National Federation of Independent Business	$1,223	Unknown
The 60 Plus Coalition	Unknown	Mailing

[1] Only itemized contributions are listed

[2] Estimate

[3] Get-out-the-vote efforts

SOURCES: FEC; Center for Responsive Politics; "Outside Money: Soft Money & Issue Advocacy in the 1998 Congressional Elections," a study sponsored by Brigham Young University

that the hefty PAC donations gave big corporations special access to elected officials, who were beholden to their financial backers.

Congress attempted to curb PACs in 1989 after former Speaker Jim Wright, D-Texas (1955-89), came under attack for ethical violations and questionable financial dealings. The controversy put pressure on House Democrats to act on campaign finance legislation. Wright appointed a bipartisan task force, co-chaired by former Reps. Swift and Guy Vander Jagt, R-Mich. (1966-93), to develop an overhaul plan.

But they found little common ground. Democrats were leery of Republican efforts to enhance the role of political parties, a GOP strength. Republicans sought to curb PACs and regulate political activity by labor unions, two sources of Democratic strength. (*1990 Almanac, p. 59*)

The House and Senate also took differing positions on PACs. The Senate, whose members generally received less PAC money than House members, voted to disband PACs. The House passed language that only limited the amount candidates could take from PACs. In the end, conferees failed to reconcile their differences.

The House and Senate tried again in 1992 but again partisan differences could not be bridged. The Democratic-controlled Congress cleared legislation that set up separate systems for House and Senate races. The bill placed voluntary caps on overall spending and replaced limits on PAC and other contributions with public financing.

Republicans objected, instead favoring an overall ban on PACs. President George Bush vetoed the measure, saying it unfairly favored Democrats. (*1992 Almanac, p. 63; 1991 Almanac, p. 13*)

The PAC controversy began to subside in the 1990s, as both parties mastered PAC fundraising and a new form of campaign cash emerged: soft money. In contrast to "hard money," which is limited and goes to individual candidates, soft money is unlimited and can be used only for generic party-building activities — although in practice it often does help specific candidates through issue ads.

As the use of soft money grew in the 1990s, so did criticism.

In the 1992 federal election cycle, the Democratic and Republican cam-

From Teddy Roosevelt On: A Century of Changes

Sen. John McCain, R-Ariz., was far from first in putting campaign finance on the national agenda. It has been there for at least a century. Here are highlights:

■ **1905:** President Theodore Roosevelt says in his annual message to Congress that "all contributions by corporations to any political committee or for any political purpose should be forbidden by law." Several corporations had secretly financed Roosevelt's 1904 campaign.

■ **1907:** Congress passes the first federal campaign finance law, the Tillman Act, banning corporations and national banks from making "a money contribution in connection with any election" of candidates for federal office.

■ **1910:** Congress passes the Publicity Act, requiring House campaign committees operating in two or more states to disclose contributors of $100 or more within 30 days after an election.

■ **1911:** Congress extends filing requirements from the 1910 law to Senate elections. The law limits the amount candidates can spend to $10,000 for Senate campaigns and $5,000 for House campaigns.

■ **1925:** In reaction to the Teapot Dome scandal, Congress passes the Federal Corrupt Practices Act, which serves as the basic campaign finance law until the early 1970s. The act closes a loophole in previous laws allowing non-election year contributions to go unreported. It revises the amounts candidates can spend and prohibits offering money to anyone in exchange for a vote. The act is limited to general elections and does not apply to campaign committees operating in a single state. It contains no enforcement provisions.

■ **1939:** The Hatch Act becomes law, barring federal employees from active participation in national politics.

■ **1940:** Hatch Act revisions include a $3 million a year ceiling on fundraising and expenditures by party committees operating in two or more states and individual contribution limits of $5,000 a year. The amendments also assert Congress' right to regulate primary elections.

■ **1947:** The Taft-Hartley Act (PL 80-101) bans political contributions by labor unions.

■ **1971-72:** In response to the growing use of radio and television advertising by campaigns, the Senate passes the Federal Election Campaign Act in 1971. The House passes it in 1972, and President Richard M. Nixon signs it into law (PL 92-225). The law sets a ceiling on the amount federal candidates can spend on media advertising. It establishes strict reporting requirements for campaign committees, including those operating in only one state. It requires that reports be made public. Predicting that disclosure will eliminate corruption, Congress repeals all spending and contribution limits.

Also in 1971, Nixon signs the Revenue Act (PL 92-178), establishing the income tax checkoff to allow taxpayers to contribute to a general public campaign fund for eligible presidential candidates. *(1972 Almanac, p. 161; 1971 Almanac, pp. 875, 430)*

■ **1974:** Congress clears the Federal Election Campaign Act (PL 93-443), a comprehensive revision of the 1971 law. It creates the Federal Election Commission (FEC) and requires candidates to establish central campaign committees. It repeals the 1972 media spending limits but institutes contribution and spending limits for federal candidates and national parties. It places a $1,000 limit per election on independent expenditures in behalf of candidates. It bans cash contributions of more than $100 and all foreign contributions. It introduces some public financing of presidential elections. *(1974 Almanac, p. 611)*

■ **1975:** Several groups and individuals — including Sen. James L. Buckley, Cons-R-N.Y. (1971-77), and former Sen. Eugene J. McCarthy, D-Minn. (1959-71) — file suit, charging that the 1974 limits on contributions and expenditures impede free political speech.

■ **1976:** The Supreme Court, ruling in *Buckley v. Valeo*, upholds limits on contributions by individuals and committees and disclosure requirements for contributions of more than $100. It upholds public financing of presidential elections. But it overturns campaign spending limits, saying they violate First Amendment free speech rights. The court rules that Congress cannot unilaterally appoint FEC commissioners. *(1976 Almanac, p. 461)*

Also in 1976, Congress clears a bill (PL 94-283) that reconstitutes the FEC as a six-member panel appointed by the president and confirmed by the Senate. The law strengthens the FEC's enforcement power and sets new contribution limits. *(1976 Almanac, p. 459)*

■ **1978:** In response to complaints that the 1974 law stifles volunteer and grass-roots party activity, the FEC issues a controversial ruling that allows state parties to use money that was not permitted under federal campaign finance law — corporate and labor contributions — to pay for a portion of grass-roots and generic party activities, even if the money indirectly aids federal candidates.

■ **1979:** Amendments to the 1974 law allow state and local parties to spend as much as they want on campaign materials for volunteer activities to promote any federal candidate. The amendments allow those committees to conduct, without financial limit, certain kinds of voter registration and get-out-the-vote drives in behalf of presidential tickets. The 1978 ruling and 1979 amendments give rise to the "soft money" phenomenon. *(1979 Almanac, p. 558)*

■ **1980s-90s:** Congress fails to pass significant changes to the campaign finance system. In 1987-88, the Senate debates an overhaul bill that calls for public financing of Senate races and places aggregate limits on PAC contributions. It is shelved after a record-setting eight cloture votes. *(1988 Almanac, p. 41; 1987 Almanac, p. 33)*

■ **In 1989-90**, the House and Senate pass bills aimed at reducing campaign spending and limiting the influence of political action committees (PACs), but conferees never meet. Debate over PACs subsides in the 1990s. The 1996 presidential fundraising controversies turn the spotlight on soft money. *(1990 Almanac, p. 59)*

'527' Organizations Identified

"527" organizations are political groups that do not have to report their contributors or spending to the Federal Election Commission as long as they do not expressly call for the defeat or election of specific candidates. These issue advocacy groups are difficult to track. The political watchdog groups Common Cause and the Center for Public Integrity have identified the following:

■ **Americans for Economic Growth**
News reports have linked an associate of House Majority Whip Tom DeLay, R-Texas, with the group, which has run issue ads attacking vulnerable Democrats. DeLay denies involvement with the group, which was named in a Democratic lawsuit against DeLay.

■ **Business Leaders for Sensible Priorities**
Founded by Ben Cohen, co-founder of Ben & Jerry's Homemade Ice Cream, the group wants to cut spending for the Pentagon and increase spending for schools and health care.

■ **The Christian Coalition**
The coalition's 527 arm was created in 1999 after the IRS charged the group with crossing the line into express political advocacy. It produces voter guides and political scorecards.

■ **Citizens for Better Medicare**
Largely funded by the pharmaceutical industry, the group is spending about $25 million to $30 million on political ads promoting GOP plans to include prescription drug coverage in Medicare.

■ **Citizens for Reform**
The group is affiliated with Triad Management Services, a conservative consulting firm. It ran ads in 1997 attacking Wisconsin Democratic Sens. Russell D. Feingold and Herb Kohl, specifically for their stances against banning a controversial abortion procedure known by opponents as "partial birth" abortion.

■ **Citizens for the Republic Education Fund**
Affiliated with Triad, the group in 1998 spent about $200,000 on ads that were critical of Senate Minority Leader Tom Daschle, D-S.D.

■ **Citizens for the Republican Congress**
Formed by former Rep. Pat Saiki, R-Hawaii (1987-91), the group plans to promote GOP issues in 30 districts this year.

■ **The Club for Growth**
The membership organization was founded by National Review President Thomas L. "Dusty" Rhodes, Wall Street broker Richard Gilder and Stephen Moore, who is on leave from the Cato Institute. It is dedicated to "helping elect candidates who are advocates of the Reagan vision of limited government and lower taxes," according to its Web site.

■ **Committee for New American Leadership**
Founded by former House Speaker Newt Gingrich, R-Ga. (1979-99), the group is working to elect candidates who believe the combined "tax burden on any taxpayer should be no more than 25 percent, that the Social Security system should be personalized, and that in the 21st Century the United States has a crucial leadership role in the world," according to its Web site.

■ **League of Conservation Voters**
The league uses its "527" arm to promote candidates it sees as environmental "champions."

■ **Peace Voter Fund**
The group plans to use phone banks and voter guides to promote disarmament and human rights.

■ **The Republican Leadership Coalition**
Founded by Scott Reed, campaign manager of former Sen. Bob Dole's 1996 White House bid, the group is conducting research and running issue ads aimed at winning Hispanic support for the GOP.

■ **Republicans for Clean Air**
Formed by Texas entrepreneurs Sam and Charles Wyly, strong backers of Texas Gov. George W. Bush, the group ran ads before key March primaries attacking Bush's challenger, Sen. John McCain, R-Ariz., for his environmental record.

■ **Republican Majority Issues Committee**
DeLay has raised money for the group, which aims to spend $25 million on voter registration and issue ads to counter labor union efforts in behalf of Democrats.

■ **Saving America's Families Everyday**
House GOP Conference Chairman J.C. Watts Jr., R-Okla., is a major fundraiser for the group, which conducts polls for Republicans.

■ **Shape the Debate**
Staffed by aides to former California Gov. Pete Wilson, a Republican, the group ran ads attacking Vice President Al Gore, the presumptive Democratic presidential nominee, on campaign fundraising, Medicare and tobacco.

■ **The Sierra Club**
The organization uses its "527" arm to run issue ads on the environment. It is expected to target Bush's environmental record and to run ads in more than 20 congressional districts this year.

■ **The US Families Network**
Staffed by former DeLay aides, the group gathered $1.3 million in donations from five donors in 1998 and used the funds to further such causes as an overturn of the 1973 Supreme Court ruling legalizing abortion and limits on estate taxes.

Proposals to Overhaul Campaign Finance

The Senate Rules and Administration Committee plans to mark up a bill (S 1816) by Chuck Hagel, R-Neb., that would limit "soft money" contributions to party committees while raising limits on "hard money" contributions from individuals and political action committees (PACs). Last year the Senate failed to end a filibuster on a bill (S 1593), sponsored by John McCain, R-Ariz., and Russell D. Feingold, D-Wis., that would ban soft money. The House passed a similar bill (HR 417) on Sept. 14. Here is a synopsis of both Senate bills plus the campaign finance proposals of the presumptive presidential candidates, Republican George W. Bush and Democrat Al Gore. (*House bill, 1999 CQ Weekly, p. 2157*)

Proposal	Description
Hagel bill (S 1816)	The bill would increase limits on individual hard money donations to a candidate from $1,000 per election to $3,000. Individuals could contribute $60,000 a year to national party committees and $15,000 to other PACs, up from the current limits of $20,000 and $5,000. The total annual contribution from an individual would increase from $25,000 to $75,000. Limits on PAC contributions to candidates and other PACs would increase from $5,000 per year to $7,500. Allowable PAC contributions to national party committees would double to $30,000 per year.
	Individuals would be limited to $60,000 per year in soft money contributions to national party committees. There are currently no limits.
	The bill would require additional monthly or quarterly reports to the Federal Election Commission (FEC), including itemized entries for individuals or groups that contribute more than $200 in a year. Reports would be posted on the Internet within 24 hours. The bill would require broadcasting stations to maintain records on requests from candidates or election-related groups to purchase advertising time.
McCain-Feingold bill (S 1593)	The bill would raise the annual total contribution limit for individuals from $25,000 to $30,000. It would limit individual contributions to state political party committees, currently not regulated by federal law, to $10,000 per year.
	The bill would ban the solicitation and receipt of soft money by national political party committees. It also would ban soft money donations from a political party to a tax-exempt charitable or lobbying organization created under section 501(c) of the tax code.
	National political party committees would be required to report "all receipts and disbursements" and to itemize any transaction of more than $200 per year. The bill also would restrict the use of non-members' union dues for political purposes.
George W. Bush plan	The plan would raise hard money contribution limits by adjusting them for inflation. It would ban soft money contributions from unions and corporations, but not from individuals. The plan calls for "instant" disclosure of contributions.
	Bush's plan would restrict the use of members' and non-members' union dues for political purposes. It would prohibit lobbyists from making contributions to lawmakers while Congress was in session. It would prevent incumbent candidates from transferring money from one federal race to another (for example, from a Senate campaign to a presidential campaign).
Al Gore plan	Gore would not change current law on hard money contributions. His plan would ban soft money. It would require lobbyists to disclose contributions to members and Congress to post the information each month on the Internet. Groups running issue ads within 60 days of an election would have to disclose all funding sources. The bill would require "527" committees — political groups formed to influence elections — to file statements of organization with the FEC to maintain their tax-exempt status.
	Gore favors a $7.1 billion "Democracy Endowment" to finance general election campaigns for candidates who agree not to take private money. He also favors free broadcast time for candidates targeted by issue ads and more voluntary coverage by broadcasters in the month before an election.

paign committees raised $36.3 million and $49.8 million in soft money, respectively. Those numbers grew to $123.9 million for Democrats and $138.2 million for Republicans in 1996. Today, political parties are on their way to a new soft money record.

In the first 15 months of this election cycle, Democratic and Republican party committees raised a combined $160.5 million, according to a study by the government watchdog group Common Cause. That is nearly double the $84.6 million raised during the first 15 months of the 1995-96 cycle.

The two parties received 140 soft money donations in single amounts of $100,000 or more during the first three months of 2000, according to Common Cause.

Among those contributing massive amounts of soft money this year was tobacco giant Philip Morris Companies, which gave gifts of $100,000 each in soft money to the Republican National Committee, the National Republican Congressional Committee and the National Republican Senatorial Committee. On the Democratic side, telecommunications company SBC Communications Inc. gave the largest single soft money contribution of the year: $350,000 to the Democratic National Committee (DNC).

"We have come a long way from the days when the national parties represented their voters and acted as true grass-roots organizations," said Scott Harshbarger, president of Common Cause. "In today's soft money dominated system, the parties have become glorified mail-drops for special-interest money."

Companies that give large donations say they are merely participating in the democratic process. "No," said SBC spokesman Matthew Miller when asked if its donations are aimed at influencing public policy. "We are a major Fortune 500 firm, and as a major participant in the political process, our role is to give money not just to candidates but to political parties as well."

Miller said the large donation to the DNC was prompted by the Democratic convention being held this summer in Los Angeles, a major market for SBC.

"We want to be a good host to the Democratic Party when they have their convention in our city," Miller said. He added that SBC also gives to the GOP, and company contributions to both parties will likely even out by the end of the cycle.

Unreported Money

Although soft money has been the focus of recent campaign overhaul efforts, a new fundraising technique is emerging that some say could eclipse all other fundraising controversies.

A growing number of political groups are forming the "527s." Such groups were originally expected to report their fundraising and spending to the FEC. But as long as the groups do not expressly advocate the election or defeat of a specific candidate, they are not required to report anything. They can run ads attacking or praising a candidate; they can distribute voter guides condemning the political philosophy of candidates; and they can engage in other political activities that fall under the broad title of "issue advocacy" — all without having to abide by disclosure laws.

The use of issue ads has grown dramatically in recent years. A study by the Annenberg Public Policy Center of the University of Pennsylvania found that more than $114 million has been spent on or committed to issue ads so far this cycle. That is nearly equal to the amount spent on issue ads during the entire 1996 cycle. With six months to go until the elections, issue ad spending is expected to hit an all-time high, the study said.

The "527" groups that run issue ads can accept unlimited amounts of money from any source, including foreign governments. Because there are no public registration laws for such groups, their numbers and influence are incalculable.

The Center for Responsive Politics and Common Cause have so far compiled a list of more than a dozen "527" groups. They range ideologically from the far left to the far right. Several are affiliated with prominent special-interest groups, such as the Christian Coalition, the League of Conservation Voters and the Sierra Club. Others are independent groups, such as the Committee for New American Leadership, which was founded by former House Speaker Newt Gingrich, R-Ga. (1979-99), and seeks to cap taxes at 25 percent of income and enhance the United States' global role. The group uses the Internet and "other mechanisms for mobilizing voters so that candidates who support such issues will be elected to office," according to its Web site. Several "527s" are closely affiliated with current congressional leaders. ("527s," p. 49)

Makinson of the Center for Responsive Politics calls "527s" dangerous, but

officials who work with the groups defend their activities.

DeLay has worked closely with the Republican Majority Issues Committee, a "527" group that wants to spend $25 million on voter registration, voter turnout and issue ads this year to counter labor union activities in behalf of Democrats.

"527" groups "are legal," DeLay said. "They have been used by the left for many years." He mentioned a "527" group organized by the Sierra Club, an environmental group. "I am for full disclosure, but not for unilateral disarmament. We will continue to use legal organizations to express our point of view."

Another group, Saving America's Families Everyday (SAFE), is working to raise more than $1 million this year to conduct polls for the GOP. House Republican Conference Chairman J.C. Watts Jr. of Oklahoma is a leading fundraiser for the group.

"We're playing by the rules as they are," said Tim Crawford, executive director of SAFE. "If they change the rules and say you need to disclose your donors, we wouldn't have a problem with that." Crawford added, however, that not having to disclose donors helps fundraising. "Some donors don't want their names used so they're not pestered," he said.

Calls for Change

As Congress continues its attempts to change campaign fundraising, even those who support an overhaul concede that there is no quick fix. "No matter what system you set up, someone is going to figure it out, and you will have to pass a new law," Swift said.

Ornstein said campaign finance overhaul advocates might eventually have to agree to raise certain limits to keep up with inflation. In today's dollars, the limit on individual contributions should be about triple the $1,000 set a quarter-century ago.

Given the brain power of lawyers and experts searching for loopholes, McCain said, no law will stand forever. "There will always be corruption in American politics," he said. "That's why there are cycles of reform throughout our history. If it's cleaned up, it will stay cleaned up for another 10 or 15 years or so, and then there will be another McCain and Feingold."

As Swift put it, Congress can always pass regulations, but "you can't enforce virtue." ◆

McConnell endorses disclosure plan, provided it covers unions and businesses

Support Grows for Curbing Secrecy of '527' Political Groups

A fledgling election-year drive to correct what advocates of a campaign finance overhaul call the system's worst abuses picked up qualified support from Senate leaders and behind-the-scenes momentum in the House. But no one says it is a sure bet.

A surprise drive to require some of the most secretive organizations involved in U.S. politics to disclose their spending and contributors gained momentum the week of June 12. [*Ed. note:* The measure passed both chambers and was signed into law on July 1, 2000.]

Just days after GOP leaders failed to defeat a plan to require such confidential political groups to reveal their activities, Mitch McConnell, R-Ky., the leading Senate opponent of that effort, turned around and embraced a bill that included it — provided labor unions and business groups also would be forced to disclose more about their political activities.

The fledgling election-year move to correct what campaign finance overhaul advocates such as Sen. John McCain, R-Ariz., consider the system's worst abuses also picked up behind-the-scenes momentum in the House. There, advocates of changing campaign finance laws worked toward a promised vote by July Fourth on bipartisan legislation to require greater openness from politically active tax-exempt groups, including those that run issue ads financed by unregulated "soft money" donations.

"We believe the public — at a bare minimum — has the right to know who is spending money on advertising that seeks to influence elections, be it corporations, labor unions, wealthy individuals or foreign nationals," Reps. Christopher Shays, R-Conn., Martin T. Meehan, D-Mass., and several others said in a June 15 "Dear Colleague" letter.

The burgeoning effort on both sides of Capitol Hill comes on the heels of a Senate vote June 8 to require groups governed by Section 527 of the tax code, which currently do not have to disclose information on their political operations, to do so.

The controversial "527s" are the latest cause célèbre among advocates of tightening campaign finance laws. Such 527s include groups organized by House GOP Whip Tom DeLay of Texas to sway close House races, and an organization called Republicans for Clean Air, which ran television ads financed by wealthy Texas businessmen supporting presumptive GOP presidential nominee George W. Bush in his tough primary campaign against McCain.

Nobody says that the renewed drive on campaign finance is a sure bet to become law this year. The bitterness engulfing campaign finance issues is difficult to overstate, and efforts to expand disclosure requirements beyond 527 organizations are sure to draw powerful opposition from interest groups, including unions and business associations such as the U.S. Chamber of Commerce.

"They've decided that they're not fighting the 527 disclosure movement," Sen. Joseph I. Lieberman, D-Conn., said of Senate GOP leaders. "We want to make sure that they don't love it to death."

Driving the effort to overhaul laws on campaign finance is the potential for abuse by 527s, which can secretly accept unlimited amounts of money from unidentified contributors and spend it on political activities such as running attack ads, registering voters or distributing voter guides. Organizations across the political spectrum, from the Sierra Club to the Christian Coalition, have organized 527s. Increasingly, however, such political arms are being established by congressional leaders such as DeLay to collect large contributions. DeLay's Republican Majority Issues Committee aims to spend $25 million to elect Republicans this year.

CQ PHOTO / SCOTT J. FERRELL

McConnell, right, and Smith introduced legislation June 15 that would require greater disclosure of campaign activities by 527 groups, unions and trade associations.

Many Proposals

It is unclear just how the latest campaign overhaul effort will proceed and whether GOP leaders in either chamber can control it. House leaders — who last year unsuccessfully resisted a bill (HR 417) by Shays and Meehan to rein in soft money and make other campaign finance changes — have promised a vote by July Fourth on the issue. GOP leaders tried to quash the 527 effort, led by partisan Democrat Lloyd Doggett of Texas, but bowed to pressure from their own ranks to schedule a vote after Republican overhaul advocates threatened to vote with Democrats to bring Doggett's proposal to the floor over GOP leaders' objections. (*1999 CQ Weekly, p. 2862*)

The task of developing the House measure was assigned to moderate Amo Houghton, R-N.Y., chairman of the Ways and Means Subcommittee on Oversight, which will hold a hearing June 20. Houghton pledged to develop a bipartisan consensus, but he has to weigh the desires of overhaul advocates against the demands of GOP leaders such as DeLay, whose political activities would be affected by the drive.

"We want something we can argue is real reform and then try to get DeLay to be neutral on it," said an aide to a House GOP moderate. "We don't expect him to endorse anything."

Houghton supports disclosure requirements for 527 organizations, but wants to extend such disclosure to unions, nonprofit groups and trade associations that spend more than $10,000 on political activities such as television and radio ads, phone banks and mass mailings. His proposal would also require such groups to disclose any money they funnel to 527s, and to file quarterly reports with the IRS on their lobbying and political activities.

Shays and Meehan's approach is somewhat different. They are pushing for disclosure mandates on 527 groups, coupled with a plan modeled on an amendment by Sens. Olympia J. Snowe, R-Maine, and James M. Jeffords, R-Vt., to require disclosure of fundraising and spending by all groups that spend $10,000 per year or more on electioneering ads that mention any federal candidate. It would not apply to other political activities, such as get-out-the-vote drives. The Snowe-Jeffords plan garnered a narrow majority in the Senate in 1998 but died in a McConnell-led filibuster. (*1998 Almanac, p. 18-3*)

The measure would give nonprofits an incentive to segregate their political spending from general revenues.

GOP leaders and the campaign finance overhaul wing of the party have a longstanding antagonistic history. But given the June 8 Senate vote and the upcoming House vote, it may be impossible to put the genie back in the bottle. "If a balanced bill comes out, it may be tough for anyone to stop it," said Paul Leonard, chief of staff for Rep. Michael N. Castle, R-Del.

Constitutional Muster

The latest Senate bill (S 2742), sponsored by Gordon H. Smith, R-Ore., with the blessing of GOP leaders such as Majority Leader Trent Lott of Mississippi, appears to be an effort to wrest control of the debate from McCain and allies Lieberman and Russell D. Feingold, D-Wis. McCain dealt Lott an embarrassing loss June 8 when he succeeded in attaching a 527 disclosure measure to the fiscal 2001 defense authorization bill (S 2549).

McCain cautiously embraced the Senate GOP leadership effort even though it contained elements that he regards as "poison pills," such as a broad requirement that unions and business trade associations disclose spending not just on advertising but also on grassroots political and lobbying efforts. McConnell's foes accuse him of a vendetta against labor unions, a key Democratic ally in campaigns.

"It's clear when you read the language that what [McConnell] is trying to do is go after a lot of internal union communications and in-kind contributions," said a Senate aide to a McConnell critic.

McCain also criticized a provision in the Smith-McConnell bill that would invalidate the entire measure if any piece of it was declared unconstitutional. The effect of such a "non-severability" clause would be to invalidate disclosure requirements on 527 groups, which would be constitutional, if greater disclosure requirements on other groups were found to be unconstitutional.

Among the main legal issues is whether requiring groups to list donors of political money would violate a 1958 Supreme Court decision in *NAACP v. Alabama*. The justices held that private organizations cannot be forced to divulge their membership. Another is whether it would violate the 1976 deci-

sion in *Buckley v. Valeo* that said the government cannot require disclosure of issue advocacy activities, including election-related activities that do not expressly call for the defeat or election of a particular candidate.

McConnell said he expects anything that might pass to be challenged in the courts. He acknowledged that he thinks the bill he supports may be unconstitutional.

"I think requiring disclosure of issue advocacy is of dubious constitutionality," McConnell said at a June 15 news conference. "However, the Senate last week decided it wanted to go down this road. And so my view is, if the majority of the Senate wants to go down this path, let's make sure it's broad and effective."

The Smith-McConnell bill came in the wake of a major battle over McCain and Lieberman's more narrowly targeted effort on 527 disclosure. During debate on that measure, several Republicans embraced requiring 527s to disclose their activities, but said other groups should do so as well.

S 2742 covers trade and business associations and unions, including Democratic-tilting groups such as the Association of Trial Lawyers of America. But it would not apply to nonprofit civic and social welfare groups, such as the National Right to Life Committee, the AARP or the National Rifle Association. McConnell said such groups would unite to topple the effort if they were included.

Hagel's Bill

The developments on disclosure came as McConnell canceled a June 14 Rules and Administration Committee markup of a bill (S 1816) by Chuck Hagel, R-Neb., to increase limits on "hard money" contributions to candidates from $1,000 per election to $3,000 and to limit "soft money" giving to national party committees. The bill had a smattering of support among Democrats but is opposed by McCain and his allies.

McConnell said he called off the markup because he did not want to force panel Republicans, whose roster is dominated by senior senators such as Lott and GOP Whip Don Nickles of Oklahoma, to sit through a lengthy markup. The chance of Hagel's bill making it to the floor was remote at best, and it worsened as prospects for a disclosure-related measure brightened. ◆

Power of redistricting brings national urgency to control of state chambers

Redistricting: Campaign 2000's Wild Card

David Fisher should not be much more than a blip on the national radar screen in this election year. He is a country lawyer running for an open state Senate seat from the town of Silsbee, population 6,400, in rural east Texas, just one of thousands running for state legislatures this year.

But Fisher gets outsized attention from Washington heavyweights and fundraisers, for one reason: Of the 5,900 state legislative elections on the ballot this November, Fisher's is one of as few as 60 races that could determine control of Congress in the next decade.

Redistricting, the decennial political exercise of redrawing the House's 435 districts, is this year's election wild card. Because state legislatures generally draw the boundaries of their states' congressional districts, the winners of this year's races will be calling the shots in next year's redistricting battles. So control of state legislatures is vital to winning congressional seats through 2010.

This time around, the shift of just a few dozen state legislative seats could dramatically alter congressional line-drawing power. Analysts say the party that seizes the upper hand in state races could redraw 20 congressional districts to its partisan advantage. Considering that Republicans are defending a slender, six-seat advantage in the House, and that neither party is likely to control the House in the next Congress by more than 10 seats, the urgency becomes apparent.

Democrats are bullish on taking back the House this year. But they concede that they are in jeopardy of being locked out of the House majority in the five succeeding elections from 2002 through 2010. "If we're not careful," said Rep. Martin Frost, D-Texas, chairman of the Democratic Caucus, "we could lose it in 2002 if we don't get a good result in the control of the legislatures."

The specter of a redistricting catastrophe is not lost on Republicans either. Wes Marsh, an Arizona state House member and president of the National Republican Legislators Association (NRLA), said in a September fundraising letter that if Republicans do not maintain control of certain state legislatures, "we will face a potentially disastrous redis-

tricting situation in 2001."

In the Texas Senate, Republicans have a one-seat advantage. Democrats hope Fisher can wrest a competitive district from which a GOP incumbent is retiring. Fisher said he has already talked to Frost and other national Democratic officials. Texas Republicans, recognizing the significance of Fisher's race, are running three candidates in the March 14 primary and calling the Senate seat, as GOP Chairwoman Susan Weddington put it, "the prize" in this November's state elections.

"It's like the [college basketball] tournament," said Kevin Mack, executive director of the Democratic Legislative Campaign Committee (DLCC), which works to elect Democrats to state legislatures. "It's nameless, faceless legislators that people in Washington have never met, but they control the destiny of this town in future Congresses."

Advantage Republican

By any measure, Republicans are in a far better position than they were 10 years ago. The 2000 census is likely to show a continuing population shift from the East and Midwest to the South and West — into states that lean Republican. Those states will gain House seats under reapportionment.

Also, Republicans have made gains in state legislatures. If redistricting took place today, they would control the process in 113 House districts in 10 states. Democrats would redraw 144 districts in 13 states, and the parties would share line-drawing in 145 districts in 16 states. The other 33 districts — for a total of 435 — are either at-large districts or are controlled by special state redistricting commissions.

That is a leap for Republicans above their showing after the 1990 redistricting round, in which they controlled redistricting in just two states, Utah and New Hampshire, representing five seats. Democrats controlled 172 districts, and the parties split control in 240. That means Republicans managed to erode the Democratic advantage even under maps drawn by Democrats.

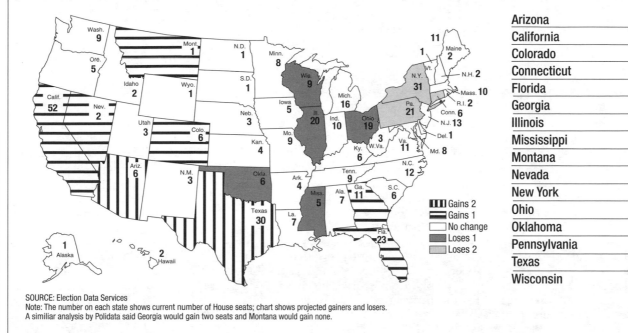

2000 Reapportionment: Projected Gainers and Losers

Arizona	+2
California	+1
Colorado	+1
Connecticut	-1
Florida	+1
Georgia	+1
Illinois	-1
Mississippi	-1
Montana	+1
Nevada	+1
New York	-2
Ohio	-1
Oklahoma	-1
Pennsylvania	-2
Texas	+2
Wisconsin	-1

Gains 2
Gains 1
No change
Loses 1
Loses 2

SOURCE: Election Data Services
Note: The number on each state shows current number of House seats; chart shows projected gainers and losers.
A similiar analysis by Polidata said Georgia would gain two seats and Montana would gain none.

"Across the whole battlefield, their [Democrats'] position is fundamentally worse than it was," said Republican National Committee (RNC) Chief of Staff Tom Cole. Republicans, after trailing for decades, have pulled to parity with Democrats in control of state legislative chambers. They control 48 to the Democrats' 49, with two chambers tied. (It adds up to 99 because Nebraska has a unicameral legislature.) After the 1990 elections, Democrats held 72 chambers.

Democrats say Republicans may be better off now, but they maintain that Democrats have a stronger state political infrastructure. After losing majorities in several states early in the decade, they fought back in 1996 and 1998. "Democrats have a three-cycle advantage in terms of state legislative politics," Mack said. The Democratic National Committee and the DLCC "have spent millions of dollars . . . building legislative majorities around the country. Republicans are latecomers to this process." Republican Marsh said as much in his September letter: "We realize that the Democrats . . . are five years ahead of us in pursuing a strong elective strategy."

Regardless of strategy, the shift of just a few state seats could alter the balance of power. If Democrats gained the right 35 state legislative seats and one governorship (Utah), they would control the drawing process for 169 seats in 17 states, compared with 60 in five states for Republicans, with 173 in 17 states split between them. If Republicans gained the right 17 legislative seats and two governorships, they would control remapping

in 182 districts in 14 states, compared with just 116 in 10 states for the Democrats, with 104 in 15 states split between them. Strategists in both parties constantly reassess which states and seats to target, but they agree that the number of battleground legislative seats is small.

Currying Favor

Congressional lawmakers play a key role in redistricting, not least because their political survival could be at stake. Redistricting is a rare instance in which members must curry favor with lesser-known state legislators. Among other things, members are expected to contribute to state campaigns. "You will see congressional delegations aggressively raising money and doing things for state legislative candidates they normally don't [care] about," said Cole, who was an Oklahoma state senator in the last redistricting round.

Said Tom Hofeller, redistricting director for the RNC: "One of my messages across to the Hill here is, Mr. Republican Congressman, you need to get personally involved in helping your legislative campaign committee. No. 1, it might be your firewall. But No. 2, even when your own people are drawing the seats, there might be some person there who thinks they can represent the state better than you can."

House Speaker J. Dennis Hastert, R-Ill., recently formed a political action committee, KOMPAC [Keep Our Majority PAC] State Victory Fund, which can divide large contributions among candidates in key races. Hastert's home state is one of the top prizes in the redis-

A Redistricting Free-for-All
In the Digital Age

Lawmakers and staff aides huddled around a computer terminal. Their goal: to redraw the legislative lines of a diverse county with a delegation increasing from nine representatives to 10.

The task was replete with land mines that invariably bedevil the redistricting process: where to shoehorn the new district, what to do about the freshman Republican wary of change, how to handle the black Democratic incumbent worried about a primary challenge. No problem. After aggressive negotiating and some clicks of the computer mouse: Voila! A new redistricting plan is produced.

Just 10 years ago this exercise would have been held in a proverbial smoke-filled room at the state Capitol at 4 a.m. But this was a simulation held in a hotel room in Burlington, Vt., where the National Conference of State Legislatures, based in Denver, conducted a three-day redistricting seminar in November.

The simulation demonstrated the need for compromise in the redistricting process. Participants had to role-play members of one of five groups with a stake in redistricting: Republicans, Democrats, African-Americans, Hispanics or citizen advocates. No two plans came out the same, even within a group.

The exercise also showed how technology is influencing the process. What was once solely the bailiwick of political insiders and statisticians now has more participants, thanks to the growth of user-friendly computer applications. Participants needed only perfunctory computer support to engage in one of politics' most complex exercises. "That simulation really showed that, with just a little bit of training, you can sit down and be drawing maps," said Tim Storey, a conference redistricting expert.

It was not long ago that mapmakers used tools now regarded as anachronistic. "Paper maps and adding machine rolls and keypunch cards to run through a mainframe computer," said Kimball W. Brace, president of the political consulting firm Election Data Services and a veteran of redistricting wars. "That's what it was like in 1980."

Tom Hofeller, redistricting director for the Republican National Committee, said the "big leap forward" in technology came in the 1990 round, when the Census Bureau produced a digital database that maps the country block by block.

The biggest change that technology will spawn in the upcoming redistricting cycle is the dramatic increase in the number of maps that will be drawn. Brace said that in 1980, about 10 plans were created per state. In 1990, it was up to 1,000. "This time around, we're talking about thousands," Brace said.

And no longer will legislators and staff members be the only ones crunching statistics. "The majority leadership in the legislative bodies will not have a monopoly of knowledge, and in redistricting, knowledge is a big factor," Hofeller said.

The growth of the Internet — once confined to scientists and the

tricting war: Democrats control the Illinois House by a 62-56 margin; Republicans have the governorship and a 32-27 lead in the Senate. "So if you've given money to that campaign committee, you may be sitting at a corner of the table when the lines are being drawn," Hofeller said.

Members of Congress ignore state legislators at their peril, because state lawmakers can use redistricting to effectively end the career of a congressional colleague. After the 1990 reapportionment, that happened to Democrats Harley O. Staggers Jr. in West Virginia and Chester G. Atkins in Massachusetts. After Massachusetts lost a seat, for example, Atkins was the "odd man out," largely because of poor relations with state leaders. Mappers chopped out territory favorable to Atkins and kept territory hospitable to Martin T. Meehan, who trounced Atkins in the 1992 primary and still holds the seat.

Using redistricting to outmaneuver an adversary is not foolproof, however. When Massachusetts lost a seat in the 1980 reapportionment, Democratic Rep. Barney Frank, a former state legislator, was said to be the "odd man out" in 1982. Hostile former colleagues paired him in a district with GOP Rep. Margaret M. Heckler, drawing most of the district from Heckler's old territory. "If you asked legislators to draw a map in which Barney Frank would never be a congressman again, this would be it," Frank said at the time. But Frank, aided by a recession that hurt GOP candidates, defeated Heckler with 60 percent of the vote.

Republicans saw their 1999 takeover of the Virginia legislature not only as a historic change in a Southern legislature long dominated by Democrats but also as an opportunity to wield some influence in redistricting. The RNC spent $400,000 on state legislative contests in

Virginia in 1999. Some dividends have already paid off. Rep. Thomas M. Davis III, R-Va., chairman of the National Republican Congressional Committee, said Feb. 2 he believes it was the prospect of redistricting that prompted Democratic Rep. Owen B. Pickett to announce Dec. 31 that he was retiring and Democratic Rep. Virgil H. Goode Jr. to announce Jan. 24 that he was becoming an independent. Goode and Pickett denied that redistricting influenced their decisions. (*Departures, 2000 CQ Weekly, p. 56*)

Reapportionment

Before state legislators can redraw congressional lines, they must wait for the official reapportionment, which is presented to the president by Dec. 31, 2000. The House is reapportioned using a formula called the "method of equal proportions," which assigns every state one congressional seat and then divides up the remaining 385 by population.

Political consultant Kimball Brace, shown Feb. 14, uses sophisticated technology to redraw House district maps.

principal researcher at the Kansas state House, expect state legislatures to put redistricting plans and detailed maps on the Internet. Plans are typically proposed in the form of legislation, and most state legislatures allow Internet users to read and track bills online. Staff members in Florida are considering a plan to post proposed redistricting maps online.

Gerrymander.com

Dean Stoecker, president of SRC, an Internet technology company based in Orange, Calif., wants to use the Internet to allow average voters to participate in redistricting. One Web site his company is designing, *www.gerrymander.com*, would allow citizens to create maps on the Internet. A second site, *www.edistricting.com*, would be geared toward legislators and would feature information about constituents. A legislator could use the

site, for example, to pinpoint all middle-class families who have children and support a waiting period for handgun purchases.

Galligan and Brace warned that the convenience of better technology could lull legislators into thinking they can postpone preparations for redistricting until after the November election. "If people are thinking that, they're going to see a light at the end of the tunnel, but the train is coming at them," Brace said.

He noted, for example, that this year's census is the first to allow respondents to identify themselves as members of two or more races. That will result in reams of new data that mapmakers must consider. "All of that data is going to make it difficult to do, and some of the cheaper and easy-to-use software is not going to be able to survive when it's trying to break through all of this information," Brace said.

Galligan said technology will not change legislators' need to push redistricting plans by means of arm-twisting and compromise. In the 125-member Kansas House, she said, any legislator who devises a plan must convince 62 colleagues to vote for it. "The technology can't make that process any easier," she said.

military — also will influence redistricting. Storey said the Internet will open up the process and allow more public access. Still, while newcomers will be able to draft maps, many may not know the legal principles on which maps must be based.

"Many of them will be flat-out unconstitutional from the start," Storey said. But he said more established groups, such as the NAACP and the Mexican American Legal Defense and Educational Fund, will have legal counsel well-schooled in redistricting case law.

Both Storey and Mary Galligan,

Fast-growing states typically gain seats and slower-growing states lose seats.

According to projections by Election Data Services, a Washington consulting firm, eight states are likely to gain seats and eight to lose. Under the projections, Arizona and Texas will each gain two seats; California, Colorado, Florida, Georgia, Montana and Nevada will gain one. New York and Pennsylvania will lose two each, and Connecticut, Illinois, Mississippi, Ohio, Oklahoma and Wisconsin will lose one.

A review by Polidata, a political analysis company based in Lake Ridge, Va., drew similar conclusions. It projects, however, that Georgia will gain two seats and Montana will gain none.

Daniel A. Smith, a political scientist at the University of Denver, said the reapportionment projections are good news for Republicans. "The states that are gaining — Florida, Texas, Arizona — have been voting more Republican,"

he said. In Arizona and Florida, Republicans currently control all three legs of what is known as the "redistricting stool" — the state House, state Senate and governor's mansion. "Just on the surface," said Smith, "it seems the traditional Democratic strongholds in the Northeast and Midwest are going to be losing seats. On the whole, where the new seats are going, [they] are probably going to be captured by Republicans."

Meanwhile, there is a continuing fight over how the census should count the population. The 1990 census undercounted millions of Americans, many of them minorities. Many statisticians and Democrats have advocated the use of statistically modified data to offset the undercount — a process called "sampling." Most Republicans oppose sampling, arguing that the Constitution stipulates an actual head count for the census.

In 1999, the Supreme Court ruled

that the Census Act, as amended in 1976 (PL 94-521), prohibits the use of statistical sampling for reapportioning congressional seats. It did not rule on the constitutionality of using sampling for redistricting. (*1999 CQ Weekly, p. 259*)

The Census Bureau plans to produce two sets of numbers, one counting heads only and one using sampling as well. The states will decide which numbers to use. Many GOP-controlled legislatures have already passed laws to prohibit the use of sampling data in redistricting. Analysts said they expect legal experts to argue that some states must use sampling to prevent infringement on minorities' voting rights.

Key States

The redistricting war is a series of 50 state-by-state chess matches, with the most crucial battles in closely matched states likely to gain or lose seats:

● **California.** With an estimated 53

Davis and Bentsen: Party Point Men In the Quest to Redraw Boundaries

The nation is focused on the race for the White House and the battle to control Congress, but party pols on Capitol Hill are quietly pulling strings in an obscure national campaign that could determine who holds congressional power for the next decade.

From their offices in the U.S. Capitol, two representatives have already spent months gauging their parties' chances of winning control of state Capitols and directing money and other resources into key legislative races. The hope: to swing control of Congress for years to come by handpicking the state legislators who will redraw congressional districts after the 2000 census.

Redistricting is always one of the most bitterly fought, politicized battles in any state legislature. But now, perhaps more than ever, the shots will be called from Capitol Hill, where the stakes are enormous.

"This is terribly important," said Rep. Ken Bentsen, D-Texas. "This will decide who controls Congress, or the House at least, for the remainder of this decade."

Bentsen is the chairman of IMPAC 2000, the Democratic group founded in 1988 to guide the party's redistricting strategy. Bentsen is pushing what he calls a "methodical" approach, using early census estimates and techies at IMPAC's Capitol Hill office to draw proposed district maps and educate his caucus on the political and legal technicalities of redrawing boundaries.

On the other side, Rep. Thomas M. Davis III, R-Va., has been devising strategies for a year to give Republicans a leg up. As chairman of the National Republican Congressional Committee, Davis says he is well-positioned to aim the GOP's big financial guns at state races. He already has one victory — the GOP's historic takeover of his home state's capital in 1999 — that he attributes in part to the work of national Republicans.

"I think we beat them to the punch because we invested in Virginia and took the Virginia legislature," Davis said in an interview. "That's my state. I understand the dynamics out there and saw the opportunity for involvement. We were out early recruiting candidates and raising money."

How important are the state races to members of Congress? Consider how closely Bentsen and Davis are following them, how easily they rattle off names of state legislators and challengers in local districts from Pennsylvania to Missouri to Texas.

Both men know that, out of thousands of legislative seats across the nation, the power shift in Congress could hinge on just a few races. "You could take eight legislative seats out of 5,000 that could make the difference of up to 20 congressional seats," said David Israelite, director of politics and governmental affairs for the Republican National Committee, which is working closely with Davis and the newly formed Republican Legislative Campaign Fund to funnel money to key campaigns. (*Chart, p. 59*)

In states where the other side leads the redistricting, each party is looking for alternatives. In California, the state Supreme Court struck a GOP-backed initiative from the March 7 ballot that would have moved redistricting powers to the courts and away from the Democrats who run state government. "We dumped $2 million into the California initiative that got struck," Davis said. "That's how much we care about California."

In Florida, where Republicans solidly control state government, Democrats are pinning their hopes on a long-shot initiative that would put an independent commission in charge of redrawing the lines.

Both parties are educating their House members on legal challenges should they lose a redistricting war. Bentsen has held meetings with almost every delegation in his caucus (he will meet with Louisiana Democrats next month) over the past year to instruct members on the law and encourage them to forge political and legal partnerships with local candidates.

"Political power alone does not ensure victory in redistricting," Bentsen said. "It's important that our members understand that. If you're in the majority you want to make sure you draw plans that stand up in court, and if you're in the minority you have to make sure you introduce a plan and prepare the legal footing to enact what you think is the most fair plan. If you can't do it through the legislature, you do it through the courts."

House members after reapportionment, California is the biggest prize in the redistricting sweepstakes. Republicans have not performed well there recently. They were trounced in the 1998 governor's race, and they trail 47-32 in the state Assembly and 25-15 in the state Senate. Democrats have a 28-24 advantage in the U.S. House delegation.

The outlook for Republicans in California is bleak. They backed a ballot initiative to require the state Supreme Court to handle redistricting, but the court in December struck it from the March primary ballot. Advocates are now gathering signatures for a similar initiative for the November ballot.

● **Texas**. If Democrats are eager to redraw the lines in California, Republicans are equally enthusiastic about Texas, which leans Republican. Nevertheless, Democrats have a 17-13 advantage in the U.S. House delegation because of what Cole called the "best Democratic redistricting job in America" in the post-1990 round.

Republican Gov. George W. Bush was re-elected in 1998 and, if elected president, would be succeeded by GOP Lt. Gov. Rick Perry. The parties will brawl for control of the legislature. Republicans hold a slender 16-15 advantage in the Senate and trail in the

State Party Breakdown

STATE	U.S. HOUSE SEATS/ PROJECTED CHANGE	GOVERNOR	STATE SENATE [1,2] (majority)	STATE SENATE SEATS UP IN 2000 [2]	STATE HOUSE [1,3] (majority)
Alabama	7 / 0	Donald Siegelman, D	23-12 (D)	none	69-36 (D)
Alaska	1 / 0	Tony Knowles, D	15-5 (R)	half	24-16 (R)
Arizona	6 / 2	Jane Dee Hull, R	16-14 (R)	all	40-20 (R)
Arkansas	4 / 0	Mike Huckabee, R	28-6 (D) [4]	half	76-23 (D) [4]
California	52 / 1	Gray Davis, D	25-15 (D)	half	47-32-1 (D)
Colorado	6 / 1	Bill Owens, R	20-15 (R)	half	40-25 (R)
Connecticut	6 /-1	John G. Rowland, R	19-17 (D)	all	96-55 (D)
Delaware	1 / 0	Thomas R. Carper, D	13-8 (D)	half	26-15 (R)
Florida	23 / 1	Jeb Bush, R	25-15 (R)	half	72-48 (R)
Georgia	11 / 1	Roy Barnes, D	33-23 (D)	all	102-78 (D)
Hawaii	2 / 0	Benjamin J. Cayetano, D	23-2 (D)	half	39-12 (D)
Idaho	2 / 0	Dirk Kempthorne, R	31-4 (R)	all	58-12 (R)
Illinois	20 /-1	George Ryan, R	32-27 (R)	one-third	62-56 (D)
Indiana	10 / 0	Frank L. O'Bannon, D	31-19 (R)	half	53-47 (D)
Iowa	5 / 0	Tom Vilsack, D	30-20 (R)	half	56-44 (R)
Kansas	4 / 0	Bill Graves, R	27-13 (R)	all	77-48 (D)
Kentucky	6 / 0	Paul E. Patton, D	20-18 (R)	half	66-34 (D)
Louisiana	7 / 0	Mike Foster, R	28-11 (D)	none	76-29 (D)
Maine	2 / 0	Angus King, I	20-14-1 (D)	all	79-71-1 (D)
Maryland	8 / 0	Parris N. Glendening, D	32-15 (D)	none	106-35 (D)
Massachusetts	10 / 0	Paul Cellucci, R	33-7 (D)	all	131-28-1 (D)
Michigan	16 / 0	John Engler, R	23-15 (R)	none	58-52 (R)
Minnesota	8 / 0	Jesse Ventura, I	40-26-1 (D)	all	71-63 (R)
Mississippi	5 /-1	Ronnie Musgrove, D	34-18 (D)	none	86-33-3 (D)
Missouri	9 / 0	Mel Carnahan, D	18-16 (D) [4]	half	86-76-1 (D)
Montana	1 / 1	Marc Racicot, R	32-18 (R)	half	59-41 (R)
Nebraska	3 / 0	Mike Johanns, R	*	half	*
Nevada	2 / 1	Kenny Guinn, R	12-9 (R)	half	28-14 (D)
New Hampshire	2 / 0	Jeanne Shaheen, D	13-11 (D)	all	246-153-1 (R)
New Jersey	13 / 0	Christine Todd Whitman, R	24-16 (R)	none	45-35 (R)
New Mexico	3 / 0	Gary E. Johnson, R	25-17 (D)	all	40-30 (D)
New York	31 /-2	George E. Pataki, R	35-26 (R)	all	98-52 (D)
North Carolina	12 / 0	James B. Hunt Jr., D	35-15 (D)	all	66-54 (D)
North Dakota	1 / 0	Edward T. Schafer, R	31-18 (R)	half	64-34 (R)
Ohio	19 /-1	Bob Taft, R	21-12 (R)	half	59-40 (R)
Oklahoma	6 /-1	Frank Keating, R	33-15 (D)	half	61-40 (D)
Oregon	5 / 0	John Kitzhaber, D	17-13-1 (R)	half	34-25-1 (R)
Pennsylvania	21 /-2	Tom Ridge, R	30-20 (R)	half	103-100 (R)
Rhode Island	2 / 0	Lincoln C. Almond, R	42-8 (D)	all	86-13-1 (D)
South Carolina	6 / 0	Jim Hodges, D	24-22 (D)	all	68-56 (R)
South Dakota	1 / 0	William J. Janklow, R	22-13 (R)	all	51-19-1 (R)
Tennessee	9 / 0	Don Sundquist, R	18-15 (D)	half	59-40 (D)
Texas	30 / 2	George W. Bush, R	16-15 (R)	half	78-72 (D)
Utah	3 / 0	Michael O. Leavitt, R	18-11 (R)	half	54-21 (R)
Vermont	1 / 0	Howard Dean, D	17-13 (D)	all	77-67-6 (D)
Virginia	11 / 0	James S. Gilmore III, R	21-19 (R)	none	52-47-1 (R)
Washington	9 / 0	Gary Locke, D	27-22 (D)	half	49-49
West Virginia	3 / 0	Cecil H. Underwood, R	29-5 (D)	half	75-25 (D)
Wisconsin	9 /-1	Tommy G. Thompson, R	17-16 (D)	half	55-44 (R)
Wyoming	1 / 0	Jim Geringer, R	20-10 (R)	half	43-17 (R)

*Nebraska has a 49-seat nonpartisan unicameral Legislature.

[1] All third-party members and independents are grouped together.

[2] These states have an odd number of Senate seats; therefore, one more or one less than half the seats are up: Arkansas, Colorado, Delaware, Hawaii, Nebraska, Nevada, North Dakota, Ohio, Tennessee, Texas, Utah, Washington and Wisconsin.

[3] All state House members are up in 2000 in every state except Alabama, Louisiana, Maryland, Mississippi, New Jersey and Virginia. House members in Alabama and Maryland have four-year terms, with the next election in 2002. The other states have odd-year state legislative elections.

[4] One vacancy.

SOURCE: National Conference of State Legislatures

House by 78-72.

● **Pennsylvania.** The GOP has Republican Gov. Tom Ridge, who was re-elected in 1998, and they lead 30-20 in the state Senate. The battleground will be the state House, which Republicans control, 103-100.

● **Illinois.** Democrats are up in the state House, 62-56, and trail in the Senate, 32-27. Republican George H. Ryan was elected governor in 1998.

● **Michigan.** Republicans control the governorship — John Engler was re-elected in 1998 — and the GOP-controlled state Senate is not up for election until 2002. Democrats hope to win the state House, which Republicans control, 58-52.

● **Wisconsin.** Republicans have a 55-44 lead in the state House, and Democrats cling to a one-seat lead in the Senate, 17-16. Republican Gov. Tommy G. Thompson was re-elected in 1998.

● **Other battlegrounds.** The legislature and governorship are up for grabs in two other battleground states. In Indiana, Republicans comfortably control the Senate and Democrats narrowly control the House; GOP Rep. David M. McIntosh is challenging Democratic Gov. Frank L. O'Bannon. In Missouri, Democrats narrowly control both chambers (86-76-1 in the House, 18-16 in the Senate). Democratic state Treasurer Bob Holden and Republican Rep. James M. Talent are locked in a competitive contest to succeed Democratic Gov. Mel Carnahan.

Republicans hold a 30-18 advantage in governorships, with two independents, and most of this year's 11 gubernatorial races will have little impact on redistricting — partially because several of the 11 states have only one U.S. House representative.

Support Groups

The redistricting battles will be fought in individual states, but both parties are relying on national party groups for assistance.

The pre-eminent Democratic redistricting organization is IMPAC 2000, founded by former Rep. Vic Fazio, D-Calif. (1979-99), in 1988. It aims to provide technical and financial assistance to key state campaigns and legal assistance for Democrats who want to challenge GOP maps. "The main focus is to prepare members of the House Democratic Caucus for the 2001 redistricting," said Rep. Ken Bentsen, D-Texas, chairman of IMPAC 2000 since

January 1999. Bentsen and IMPAC apprise Democrats about what their territory might look like after redistricting.

The DLCC wants to elect Democratic state legislatures. Mack said the 11-member staff uses a list of 17 components of a modern campaign committee to assess the effectiveness of state legislative campaigns.

Republicans hope to parlay their traditional fundraising advantages into campaign success. On Feb. 2, Republican National Committee Chairman Jim Nicholson announced the creation of the Republican Legislative Campaign Fund (RLCF) to help fund key state legislative contests. "We will help them raise the resources to deliver the Republican message to their states' voters," Nicholson said. He said it would be a "multimillion-dollar effort." The NRLA, the Republican Governors' Association and the National Republican Congressional Committee (NRCC) also have stakes in redistricting. The NRCC in December gave $750,000 to McIntosh's gubernatorial campaign.

There are many stakeholders in redistricting — congressional incumbents, state legislators looking to run for Congress, governors, citizen groups and political parties — and current technology allows virtually anyone to draw a congressional map.

Some incumbents are notorious for resistance to even marginal change to their district lines, even if they are likely to win re-election by a landslide. That attitude often runs counter to the team goal of crafting districts favorable to electing as many party members as possible. "Incumbents really don't want new voters because they have to find out about those people; they have to do work," said Minnesota state Sen. Lawrence J. Pogemiller, a Democrat.

The alliances that sometimes form in redistricting make for some strange bedfellows. In the early 1990s, the Bush administration's Justice Department signed off on plans to boost congressional representation by racial minorities by concentrating them in a few districts, a process known as "packing."

Nowhere is that phenomenon more evident than in Georgia, which in 1991 had nine House Democrats — including one black, John Lewis — and one Republican, then-Minority Whip Newt Gingrich. With the GOP's tacit blessing, mapmakers sculpted two contorted black-majority districts that

practically ensured the election of black Democrats Sanford D. Bishop Jr. and Cynthia A. McKinney. But it also enhanced Republican prospects in heavily white and conservative outlying districts. Georgia's delegation now has eight white Republicans and three black Democrats.

One lesson of redistricting, analysts say, is that there is no such thing as a universally popular congressional district map. "There is no perfect map," Pogemiller said. "Whatever map you do, someone's not going to feel good."

Litigation

Analysts say the next redistricting round will spawn an avalanche of litigation. In the 1990s, 41 of the 44 states with multimember House delegations wound up in court over their congressional redistricting plans.

As in the 1990 round, the political parties will try to use the courts to get more palatable plans. One strategy both sides will employ is shopping for sympathetic judges. Kimball W. Brace, president of Election Data Services, said that in the 1990s some Republicans thwarted Democrats who controlled redistricting by getting courts to overturn Democratic plans. "Some Democrats in 1990 thought, 'Hey, we control all three legs of the redistricting stool, we should be able to draw the plan,' " Brace said. "They forgot a redistricting stool really has four legs, and the courts are that fourth leg."

Mark Rush, a political scientist at Washington & Lee University in Lexington, Va., said the next president will reshape the Supreme Court, which has decided several recent redistricting cases in close votes. In a 5-4 decision in January, the high court limited the Justice Department's authority to block proposed changes that might dilute the voting strength of minority groups. Under the 1965 Voting Rights Act (PL 89-110), all or part of 16 states must have their redistricting plans "precleared" by the Justice Department or by the U.S. District Court for the District of Columbia.

Peter Roff, a Republican analyst who edits a newsletter on redistricting issues, noted that this year's presidential election will also influence how Justice considers state redistricting plans next year. "You can assume that a Republican Justice Department would view things differently from a Democratic Justice Department," Roff said. ◆

Few States' Redistricting Procedures Depart From the Legislative Path

In most states, redistricting adheres to the model of how a bill becomes a law: New district lines are proposed as legislation and referred to committees in both chambers. After floor debate and amendments, the legislature can pass the bill and send it to the governor, who can sign it or veto it. In most states, the legislature can override a veto with a two-thirds majority vote.

A three-fifths vote is required to override a veto in five of these "textbook" states — Illinois, Maryland, Nebraska, Ohio and Rhode Island. A simple majority overrides a veto in Alabama, Arkansas, Kentucky, Tennessee and West Virginia. In North Carolina, the governor has no veto on redistricting.

At least six states will have only one representative following reapportionment and no need to carve out districts: Alaska, Delaware, North Dakota, South Dakota, Vermont and Wyoming. Montana's status is uncertain.

The following are exceptions to the textbook:

Commission States

Five states provide for commissions to redraw district lines, bypassing the legislative process:

Hawaii. A nine-member commission is to be appointed by March 1, 2001, made up of two appointees by the Senate president, two by the House Speaker and two each by the minority party in each chamber. The eight members select the ninth member. The commission has 150 days to redraw the district map.

Idaho. Voters in 1994 approved a constitutional amendment creating a six-member Commission for Reapportionment to draw new district boundaries. The Democratic and Republican leaders in the state House and Senate each select one member, as do the two state party chairmen. Commissioners have 90 days to finish a plan.

Montana. A five-member commission draws the plan. Democratic and Republican leaders in both chambers select one member each. Those four members select the fifth. No panelist may be a public official. The commission must produce a redistricting plan 90 days after census figures are available. The plan is submitted to the secretary of State and becomes law. This procedure will be moot if Montana fails to gain a second congressional seat.

New Jersey. New Jersey voters in 1995 passed a constitutional amendment creating a 13-member redistricting commission. Two commissioners each are appointed by the Democratic and Republican leaders in the Senate and House, and two each are selected by state party chairmen. The 13th person, selected by at least seven others, is an "independent member" who heads the commission. The commission must draw new district lines by Jan. 15, 2002. If no plan receives at least seven votes, the two plans with the most votes are submitted to the state Supreme Court, which selects the final proposal.

Washington. A five-member Redistricting Commission is empaneled to redraw district lines. The Democratic and Republican leaders in the House and Senate each appoint one member; those four panelists choose a non-voting fifth member as chairman. Three members must approve a plan and present it to the state legislature by Jan. 1, 2002; the legislature can amend the plan by a two-thirds vote. If the commission fails to meet its deadline, the state Supreme Court must complete redistricting by April 30, 2002.

Quirks of the Process

Other states that give their legislatures primary responsibility for redrawing congressional districts have idiosyncrasies that set them apart:

Connecticut. The state legislature appoints an eight-member reapportionment committee consisting of four senators and four House members. The committee has until Aug. 1, 2001, to send a plan to the legislature. If it fails to do so, a nine-member reapportionment commission will be created. Again, eight members of the commission would be selected, in equal numbers, by party leaders. The ninth member would be selected by the other eight. The commission must submit a plan by Oct. 30, 2001.

Indiana. If the legislature fails to meet an April 29, 2001, deadline to pass a congressional remap, the task will be performed by a redistricting commission consisting of the state House Speaker, the Senate president, the chairmen of the House and Senate redistricting committees and a fifth member appointed by the governor. The commission proposal would be an interim plan; the legislature may subsequently pass its own plan.

Iowa. Responsibility for redrawing the lines lies with the legislature's nonpartisan Legislative Service Bureau, which devises a plan based on population counts and without regard to party registration statistics, election results or incumbents' addresses. The bureau must submit a plan to the legislature by April 1, 2001, or within two months of receiving census data, whichever is later. The legislature can reject the first two plans proposed by the bureau, then may amend a possible third.

Maine. Redistricting begins with a 15-member advisory commission, made up mostly of appointees by Democratic and Republican party officials. The commission must submit its redistricting plan no later than 90 days after the 2003 legislative session begins. The legislature must adopt the commission's plan, or a proposal of its own, within 30 days. If it fails, the state Supreme Court draws the plan.

No longer preaching smaller is better, party tries for a more appealing domestic agenda

GOP Hopes for Receptive Ears Across the Gender Gap

Bush, who is reaching out to women as a "compassionate conservative," shakes hands as he works the crowd at the Aiken County, S.C., Republican Women's presidential rally Feb. 16.

If Republicans want to win the White House and preserve their power in Congress, they will have to reach out to voters like Robin Wanner. Wanner, 35, a single mother who lives in the New York suburbs, is so busy looking for affordable child care and scrimping to cover the rent that she cannot follow the daily bickering in Washington. But she has a gut feeling about the lay of the political land.

"The Democrats support more of my ideals," says Wanner, a student activities coordinator at Marymount College in Tarrytown. The Republicans? "They're not pro-choice. . . . They're for the rich people."

Wanner, a registered Democrat who is undecided on who to support for president, is not unique. Her sentiments represent perhaps the GOP's biggest obstacle this November: the sense among women that Republicans are not on their side. In election after election, the so-called gender gap has plagued GOP candidates, from presidential contenders to congressional hopefuls. This year, most polls show the gender gap is alive and well. Consider also that female voters have outnumbered their male

counterparts in recent elections, and the situation looks even more grim for the GOP. Republicans hope to hold on to the House, where they have a slim, 222-211, advantage. "Women will determine the next president this November," says Sen. Dianne Feinstein, D-Calif., "and women will decide who controls the Congress."

Republicans are not ceding any ground. The party's presumptive presidential nominee, Texas Gov. George W. Bush, preaches a philosophy of "compassionate conservatism" that supporters say is tailor-made for women. He was one of the few Republicans to eliminate the gender gap in his state campaigns, tallying 65 percent of the women's vote on his way to a 68 percent re-election romp in 1998. Recently, he has tried to capitalize on education, a key issue for women, by campaigning at schools and calling for more federal dollars to fight illiteracy.

Congressional leaders would like to rely on Bush's coattails, but they know that will not suffice, especially in the wake of a bruising primary season that pushed Bush toward the political right and prompted him to take a hardline stance against abortion rights. GOP leaders have been busy crafting a congressional agenda they say should please most women, emphasizing issues such as education, health care, Social Security and tax cuts — and de-emphasizing their 1994 calls for smaller government.

Republicans also believe they have neutralized the Democrats' advantage on abortion by pushing an appealing bill (HR 3660) to ban the procedure they call "partial-birth abortion." President Clinton vetoed the ban in 1997, and the Democrat who hopes to succeed him, Vice President Al Gore, supported the veto. (1998 *Almanac*, p. 3-7)

Abortion, says GOP pollster Kelly-anne Fitzpatrick, is "conspicuous by its absence" from the debate, ranking far below education, health care and Social Security in polls measuring what matters most to women. That trend gives Republicans hope that this year could be their chance to close the gender gap.

With eight months to go before Election Day 2000, both parties are fighting to lure the approximately 45 percent of female voters who consider themselves politically independent. Despite the gender gap's persistence, certain swing voting blocs could give Republicans a chance to woo women: single white women, seniors, suburban mothers and Baby Boomers.

"I don't think you pander by working on issues that you interpret to be important to women [exclusively], because I don't think those exist anymore," said Rep. Jennifer Dunn, R-Wash., who has made it a priority to hone the GOP message to make it more universally appealing. "Women are working now more than ever, and starting businesses. They have a broad array of issues that they have interest in."

Two events this spring will underscore the battle for the women's vote: the annual Republican Women Leaders Forum on April 25-27, hosted by Dunn and Sen. Kay Bailey Hutchison, R-Texas, and the "Million Mom March" on Washington on May 14, hosted by advocates of gun control.

Image Problem

Why all the attention to women? Not only do they outnumber men in the United States, but women also are voting in greater numbers than ever before and deciding the outcomes of more elections. According to statistics compiled by Rutgers University's Center for the American Woman and Politics, about 56 percent of voting-age women turned out in 1996, compared with 53 percent

Budget and Taxes Breakdown

The National Republican Congressional Committee (NRCC) says 57 percent of all voters in 41 swing districts favor the Republican position on the budget and taxes, while 33 percent favor the Democratic position, and 11 percent are undecided. Here is how pollsters for the NRCC phrased the question, followed by the responses, broken down by gender with several subcategories:

Which one comes closer to your own view?

■ *Generally Republicans say that the American people are overtaxed and the tax system is unfair especially to middle-class families which is why we need to eliminate the marriage tax penalty which on average would give middle-class families $1,400 per year.*

■ *Generally Democrats say passing any tax cut right now is a risky scheme could very well hurt our economy and would take away the government's ability to invest in the problems facing Americans like protecting Social Security, improving education, and health care.*

Response by Gender Groups

Men	Republicans	Democrats	Women	Republicans	Democrats
All	59	32	All	55	33
Ticket-splitters	60	29	Working women	58	29
Married with children	63	29	Homemaker	52	36
			Women under 40	59	32
			Women over 40	54	33
			Ticket-splitters	55	27
			Married with children	65	25

The poll was conducted in January for the NRCC by Fabrizio, McLaughlin & Associates. The overall margin of error is 3 percentage points.

of their male counterparts. In raw numbers, female voters outnumbered men by more than 7 million. Indeed, female voters have outnumbered men, if only slightly, since the 1960s. The same is true in off-year congressional elections.

The gender gap reached an all-time high in 1996, when exit polls showed 54 percent of women supporting Clinton, compared with 43 percent of men. The gap was 4 points in 1992.

In congressional races since the 1980s, according to exit poll data compiled by Rutgers, the gender gap has been a consistent factor.

Political scientists attribute the gender gap to the Democratic Party's focus on governmental activism, which women generally support — in part because many women either accept government aid or provide aid in such support roles as nurses, teachers or social workers.

The GOP, experts say, has not helped matters with its emphasis on making government smaller and limiting social welfare programs. The largest gender gap in congressional elections cited by Rutgers occurred in 1994, the year former Rep. Newt Gingrich, R-Ga. (1979-99), marshaled the GOP takeover of

Congress and then became Speaker. Fifty-four percent of women voted for a Democratic House member that year, while 43 percent of men did so.

A recent poll conducted for EMILY's List, an advocacy group that works to elect Democratic women who support abortion rights, found that 45 percent of women had a positive feeling about Democrats in Congress, compared with 35 percent who felt positively about the GOP. The poll found a 6-point gender gap over whether Congress is doing a good job: 48 percent of women approved of Congress' work, compared with 54 percent of men.

"The Republicans have a bit of an image problem with women voters across the country," said Susan J. Carroll, senior research associate at Rutgers' Center for the American Woman and Politics. "The main image of Congress is the image from the Newt Gingrich years, of a Congress controlled by Republicans that seemed a bit more on the extreme and was more interested in cutting back social programs."

The EMILY's List report, compiled by Washington Democratic pollsters Celinda Lake and Geoff Garin, says

Women's Priorities

A Gallup Poll conducted Feb. 23-27 found that the top concerns of women were health care, education and lower taxes. The women, asked an open-ended question, were allowed to mention three topics. The question was: "Regardless of who wins the election, what single issue or challenge are you most interested in having the next president address when he takes office next January?" The margin of error was 3 percent.

Issue	Total %	White	Non-White
Health care	20%	22%	15%
Education	17	17	19
Lowering taxes	13	13	12
Maintaining Social Security	11	11	9
Economic issues	10	11	4
Stance on abortion	6	7	2
Medicare policy	6	6	7
Less crime	4	4	5

Other topics, mentioned by 3 percent of respondents or less, included child care, welfare issues, honesty and integrity, caring for seniors, defense issues and unemployment. Non-whites were more likely than whites to mention such topics as child care, welfare and unemployment.

SOURCE: The Gallup Organization

that a 5-point margin that women gave Democratic candidates for Congress in 1998 "propelled Democrats to a net gain of five seats." Citing their data showing that women favor Democratic candidates for Congress over Republicans 41 percent to 34 percent, Lake and Garin say support among women for Democrats "undoubtedly will have significant implications for the battle to control Congress in the 2000 election."

That may be true, but a poll conducted for the National Republican Congressional Committee (NRCC) suggests the Democrats will not have the advantage with women in 41 swing congressional districts. According to the NRCC poll, women in those districts favor a GOP candidate over a Democrat 48 percent to 30 percent. (NRCC poll, p. 63)

New Image?

Republicans such as Dunn do not deny that their party has an image problem. To the contrary, they have acknowledged it and worked to find solutions. "We know that that's been a problem," Dunn said. "We understand the problem much better now."

The party, Dunn says, is pushing legislation that it believes women will like. Candidates are encouraged to talk about the House's vote Feb. 10 to eliminate the so-called marriage penalty tax

— a bill (HR 6) Dunn says would help women because their salaries often cause a couple to get hit harder by income taxes. (2000 CQ Weekly, p. 290)

They are talking about GOP-backed legislation (HR 7) to create education savings accounts to help families pay for college, and vouchers and charter schools to give parents more flexibility in finding quality education for their children. (2000 CQ Weekly, p. 667)

Candidates, Dunn says, can talk about tax cuts that she says help women as much as men, because more women are taking responsibility for household finances. Dunn says women will like GOP plans to shore up Social Security while giving people the opportunity to invest their savings, because more women are investing, and women live longer than men. For that reason, Dunn says, women will like the GOP's support for a bill (HR 5) to lift the Social Security earnings limit for certain seniors. (2000 CQ Weekly, p. 658)

Indeed, the rhetoric of 2000 is far different from 1994's "Contract With America," the House GOP's legislative agenda. Rather than repeatedly calling for smaller government, GOP leaders from Bush to House Speaker J. Dennis Hastert of Illinois to Senate Majority Leader Trent Lott of Mississippi are talking about the role that government can play in improving schools and helping

families plan their retirements.

Opinion polls show the GOP could be onto something. A February Gallup Poll of 1,205 adult women conducted for the Internet site www.women.com found that health care ranked first on the list of challenges women want the new president to address. Twenty percent cited health care as their greatest priority, 17 percent cited education, 13 percent pointed to lower taxes and 11 percent cited maintaining Social Security.

Rep. James E. Rogan, R-Calif., knows that he must push a "compassionate" agenda if he hopes to stave off a challenge from Democratic state Sen. Adam Schiff. That is why Rogan, whose seat is a prime target of Capitol Hill Democrats, sent a mailing to 35,000 women this year stressing education, health care and Social Security. Rogan went a step beyond the national GOP agenda, citing his support for certain gun control initiatives. "I don't view women as a swing group. They are the basis of my constituency," Rogan said in an interview.

Democrats are confident that women will not be swayed. They plan to stick to core issues — such as abortion rights, gun control, a managed-care overhaul and a prescription drug benefit for Medicare recipients — that separate them from the GOP and draw heavy support from women. "As the election approaches, there will be an intense focus on choice and gun safety," Feinstein said. "In the [presidential] debates, there will be a real focus on those two issues." Schiff, for example, notes prominently on his Web site that Rogan believes "a woman does not have a right to choose and that gun control is unnecessary."

Although abortion ranks low now, political scientists say Gore and other Democrats can turn it into a defining issue by pointing out that the next president could make Supreme Court appointments that determine the fate of Roe v. Wade, the landmark 1973 ruling that guaranteed abortion rights. Democrats can produce ads that depict Bush as appeasing Christian conservatives in South Carolina with his stance against abortion.

"It could be the Willie Horton issue of the next election," said Karen O'Connor, chairman of the government department at American University, referring to the 1988 ad campaign that helped doom the presidential hopes of Democrat Michael S. Dukakis by portraying him as too liberal on crime.

Women in Congress

There are 56 women in the House, 17 Republicans and 39 Democrats. Forty-four of the 56 are in districts considered "safe" for the incumbent party, according to CQ ratings. The outlook for the districts is as follows:

REPUBLICAN

	State/District (Elected)	Outlook
Judy Biggert	Illinois 13 (1998)	Safe
Mary Bono	California 44 (1998)	Safe
Helen Chenoweth-Hage[1]	Idaho 1 (1994)	Safe
Barbara Cubin	Wyoming (1994)	Safe
Jennifer Dunn	Washington 8 (1992)	Safe
Jo Ann Emerson	Missouri 8 (1996)	Safe
Tillie Fowler[1]	Florida 4 (1992)	Safe
Kay Granger	Texas 12 (1996)	Safe
Nancy L. Johnson	Connecticut 6 (1982)	Safe
Sue W. Kelly	New York 19 (1994)	Safe
Constance A. Morella	Maryland 8 (1986)	Safe
Sue Myrick	North Carolina 9 (1994)	Safe
Anne M. Northup	Kentucky 3 (1996)	Republican favored
Deborah Pryce	Ohio 15 (1992)	Safe
Ileana Ros-Lehtinen	Florida 18 (1989)	Safe
Marge Roukema[2]	New Jersey 5 (1980)	Safe
Heather A. Wilson	New Mexico 1 (1998)	Leans Republican

DEMOCRATIC

	State/District (Elected)	Outlook
Tammy Baldwin	Wisconsin 2 (1998)	Democrat favored
Shelley Berkley	Nevada 1 (1998)	Leans Democratic
Corrine Brown	Florida 3 (1992)	Democrat favored
Lois Capps	California 22 (1998)	Leans Democratic
Julia Carson	Indiana 10 (1996)	Democrat favored
Eva Clayton	North Carolina 1 (1992)	Safe
Pat Danner	Missouri 6 (1992)	Safe
Diana DeGette	Colorado 1 (1996)	Safe
Rosa DeLauro	Connecticut 3 (1990)	Safe
Anna G. Eshoo	California 14 (1992)	Safe
Darlene Hooley	Oregon 5 (1996)	Democrat favored

DEMOCRATIC cont.

	State/District (Elected)	Outlook
Sheila Jackson-Lee	Texas 18 (1994)	Safe
Eddie Bernice Johnson	Texas 30 (1992)	Safe
Stephanie Tubbs Jones	Ohio 11 (1998)	Safe
Marcy Kaptur	Ohio 9 (1982)	Safe
Carolyn Cheeks Kilpatrick	Michigan 15 (1996)	Safe
Barbara Lee	California 9 (1998)	Safe
Zoe Lofgren	California 16 (1994)	Safe
Nita M. Lowey	New York 18 (1988)	Safe
Carolyn B. Maloney	New York 14 (1992)	Safe
Carolyn McCarthy	New York 4 (1996)	Leans Democratic
Karen McCarthy	Missouri 5 (1994)	Safe
Cynthia A. McKinney	Georgia 4 (1992)	Safe
Carrie P. Meek	Florida 17 (1992)	Safe
Juanita Millender-McDonald	California 37 (1996)	Safe
Patsy T. Mink[3]	Hawaii 2 (1990)	Safe
Grace F. Napolitano	California 34 (1998)	Safe
Nancy Pelosi	California 8 (1987)	Safe
Lynn Rivers	Michigan 13 (1994)	Safe
Lucille Roybal-Allard	California 33 (1992)	Safe
Loretta Sanchez	California 46 (1996)	Democrat favored
Jan Schakowsky	Illinois 9 (1998)	Safe
Louise M. Slaughter	New York 28 (1986)	Safe
Debbie Stabenow[4]	Michigan 8 (1996)	No clear favorite
Ellen O. Tauscher	California 10 (1996)	Democrat favored
Karen L. Thurman	Florida 5 (1992)	Safe
Nydia M. Velázquez	New York 12 (1992)	Safe
Maxine Waters	California 35 (1990)	Safe
Lynn Woolsey	California 6 (1992)	Safe

[1] *These two women are retiring; Republicans are expected to hold the seats.*
[2] *Roukema faces a tough primary; the GOP is expected to hold the seat.*
[3] *Mink also served 1965-77.*
[4] *Stabenow's seat will be open; she is running for the Senate.*

Of abortion, O'Connor said: "It doesn't show up in the polls because we haven't been talking about it a lot. When you get to situations like back in the late 1980s, when it looked like the Supreme Court might overturn *Roe v. Wade*, there was a lot of attention paid to it."

The challenge for Republicans, Dunn says, is to turn the legislative agenda into an effective campaign message. "If we don't explain all these things in ways that are personally relevant to women, they are so busy these days, they might not be aware of what we're working on," Dunn says. Another part of the strategy is to showcase female GOP candidates and incumbents, who can help spread the message. (*Candidates, p. 66; incumbents, this page*)

Recent polling of 41 targeted, swing districts for the NRCC suggests the GOP could find attentive ears. When presented with Republican and Democratic rhetoric on issues such as taxes, Social Security and education, the poll indicated that women support the Republican message.

The EMILY's List poll suggests a GOP advantage on certain issues im-

Competitive Female Candidates

Six female House challengers have been rated by CQ as having at least an even chance of winning the election in November.

REPUBLICAN
Melissa A. Hart / Pennsylvania 4th. Incumbent Democrat Ron Klink is running for the Senate. The race has no clear favorite. Eight Democrats are running in the April 4 primary to challenge Hart, a state senator.

DEMOCRATS

Byrum

Diane Byrum / Michigan 8th. Incumbent Democrat Debbie Stabenow is running for the Senate. State Sen. Byrum faces GOP state Sen. Mike Rogers; there is no clear favorite.

Lauren Beth Gash / Illinois 10th. GOP Rep. John Edward Porter is retiring. State Rep. Gash faces Porter aide Mark Kirk in a race with no clear favorite.

Jane Harman / California 36th. Former Rep. Harman (1993-99) is challenging GOP Rep. Steven T. Kuykendall in a race with no clear favorite.

Nancy Keenan/ Montana at-large. GOP Rep. Rick Hill is retiring. Keenan, a top state education official, faces GOP former Lt. Gov. Dennis Rehberg in a race with no clear favorite.

Hilda Solis / California 31st. State Sen. Solis defeated Rep. Matthew G. Martinez in the primary and has no GOP opponent.

Other candidates with a chance include Republican Shelley Moore Capito in West Virginia's 2nd District, which leans Democratic, and Democrats Linda Chapin in Florida's 8th, Susan Davis in California's 49th and Maryellen O'Shaughnessy in Ohio's 12th . The three districts lean Republican.

portant to some voters, including moral values and keeping America strong. Women also give Republicans an edge on "strengthening families," ethics and personal responsibility.

Democratic partisans, however, believe the GOP message on key issues is not in line with what most women believe. The EMILY's List survey, conducted in January, gives Democrats a big advantage on the issues that Republicans hope to seize. By a 17 percentage-point margin, for example, women favor the Democrats' approach to education. On health care, Democrats lead by 22 points; they lead by 23 points on retirement and Social Security, by 27 points on the environment and by 19 points on "looking out for the middle class."

As the campaign heats up, both parties will focus on the women in the middle, those who identify themselves as independents and who rank education, moral values, crime and health care as priorities.

Swing Voters

Who are the swing voters? Perhaps the most important women up for grabs this year are Baby Boomers, not only because of their numbers but also because of the range of issues motivating them to vote. "For the first time in our country's history we have a bloc of voters who are bookended by children on one end and elderly parents on the other, both of whom depend on [women] for something," said GOP pollster Fitzpatrick. According to the Democratic poll for EMILY's List, white Baby Boomers ages 40 to 54 favor a GOP congressional candidate by a narrow, 4-point margin.

The same poll identifies another up-for-grabs group, called "cross-pressured women," typically in their 30s and 40s, who are married with children and live in the suburbs. They favor Democrats on social issues and health care but trust Republicans more on morality. This is a broader socioeconomic group than the "soccer moms" sought in past elections, making up about 18 percent of the likely female electorate, according to EMILY's List. They favor a Republican congressional candidate by a narrow margin and give broad support to Bush.

A group identified by Democratic pollsters Lake and Garin as "prime-time seniors," or women ages 60 to 74, identify themselves as Democrats by a slight margin, but favor GOP congressional candidates and Bush for president. They make up about 10 percent

of likely female voters and cite Social Security, morals, health care, crime and education as priorities.

The Bush Factor

Democrats hate to admit it, but Bush presents a perplexing puzzle. Despite the data giving Democrats key advantages in wooing women voters, Bush erased the problem in Texas and may be able to do the same on the national stage. A recent USA Today/ CNN/Gallup Poll showed Gore ahead among women, 50 percent to 44 percent — fairly close to the 5-point margin of error.

"Maybe it's because he's not so well known," said National Organization for Women President Patricia Ireland, asked why Bush has been doing well among women. "He is affable; at least he appears to be less pompous and puffed up than some of the candidates." Ireland predicted: "I don't think he will wear well with time." Pollsters Lake and Garin called Bush's support among women "shallow," arguing that when voters are informed of Bush's record on key issues such as the environment, they grow less impressed.

Republicans see Bush's allure differently. "Bush is very, very good in connecting with women," Dunn said. "You start paying attention to the language he uses: 'No child is a second-rate child. We want to leave no child behind. We want the American dream to touch every willing heart.' That makes a woman stop and think."

Some Republicans suggest that Bush can enhance his appeal to women by naming a female running mate. Topping that list is former presidential contender Elizabeth Dole, whose short-lived campaign drew heavy support from women. Other possibilities include Maine Sen. Olympia J. Snowe, New Jersey Gov. Christine Todd Whitman, Arizona Gov. Jane Dee Hull (who endorsed Bush over Arizona Sen. John McCain) and former U.N. Ambassador Jeanne Kirkpatrick.

If Bush chooses a woman as his running mate, Gore might feel pressure to do the same. His list could include Feinstein or Maryland Lt. Gov. Kathleen Kennedy Townsend.

It is not clear what impact, if any, a female running mate would have on swing female voters. In 1984, when Democrat Walter F. Mondale chose Rep. Geraldine A. Ferraro of New York as his running mate, the ticket never had a chance; President Ronald Reagan won the majority of the women's vote. ◆

Corporations and trade groups urged to take a page from labor's playbook

Rx for Business: Grass Roots

Corporations are finding that air superiority does not always win the electoral war. Their challenge now is to recruit an army of pro-business voters.

Trying to mimic the success of labor unions' grass-roots political organization, business groups are urging their members to take the millions of dollars they have been spending on expensive television ads and use it instead for mailings, phone calls and brochures to persuade employees to support select candidates and turn out in November.

The Washington-based effort, led by the Business-Industry Political Action Committee (BIPAC), involves extensive use of the Internet. It aims to replicate the strength unions displayed during the 1998 elections, when nearly one-quarter of all voters were members of union households.

"We're saying to the business community: 'We spend a lot of money, and we're trying to suggest that we're not spending it very smart compared to the other groups,'" said R. Bruce Josten, executive vice president for government affairs at the Chamber. "We're trying to build an organization, beginning in these elections, that can show it has the capacity to make a difference."

A May 24 House vote to grant China permanent normal trade status — business' top priority — showed the importance, but also the vulnerability, of labor's grass-roots power. A united business community poured on millions of dollars in campaign contributions, advocacy ads and lobbying to beat back a challenge from unions, which bitterly opposed the bill.

The measure passed by a wider-than-expected margin, due to support from Republicans. Democrats were clearly worried about losing union support in November if they voted for the bill. In the end, however, many made the calculation they would hold on to labor backing even if they voted for the bill, because of their party's historical ties with the union movement.

Top 10 Spenders

Following are the top 10 spenders on corporate communications in the 1997-98 election cycle and the amount they spent, compiled from Federal Election Commission records.

Labor unions have made the most effective use of the strategy, although business groups hope to catch up.

1. AFL-CIO	$2,510,966
2. National Assn of Realtors	$614,754
3. National Federation of Independent Business	$271,417
4. National Rifle Association	$164,648
5. Washington State Labor Council, AFL-CIO	$108,321
6. Wisconsin Education Association Council	$87,933
7. Sierra Club	$80,045
8. New York State AFL-CIO	$78,844
9. American Federation of Teachers	$73,346
10. Chamber of Commerce for the USA	$61,101

BIPAC and its sponsors, which include such groups as the U.S. Chamber of Commerce and the National Association of Manufacturers, have named their organizing effort Project 2000.

The move is a clear nod to the supremacy of organized labor in the "ground war" aspect of politics: identifying and turning out potential voters through face-to-face contact, flyers and phone banks.

While labor has long been a political force because of its ability to activate its members, its current prowess at voter turnout developed after the 1996 elections.

That year, the labor movement spent millions on television "issue ads" — political messages that do not specifically call for the election or defeat of a federal candidate — to try to help Democrats win back the House. The strategy did not work. In a November when President Clinton was handily re-elected, Democrats did not take back the House.

Labor leaders switched tactics in 1998, concentrating on turnout while party-funded ads dominated the airwaves. A recent study by the Brennan Center for Justice at the New York University School of Law found that 65 percent of all television "issue ads" in the top 75 media markets during the last election were sponsored by political parties, not by interest groups.

Labor credits the switch in tactics as one reason House Democrats posted a five-seat gain in 1998. That lesson is not lost on Project 2000's supporters.

"In the past, we have tried to raise some money to do some issue advertisements," said Alan M. Kranowitz, senior vice president for government relations at the National Association of Wholesaler-Distributors, a federation of trade associations. "We reached the conclusion that the airwaves are tied up and the ads just bounce off people's heads."

This year, the group will be spending money on getting members and their employees registered to vote.

Strategists for labor agree that political parties have a diminished role in organizing voters for elections.

"Parties, by and large, don't exist anymore," Steve Rosenthal, political director for the AFL-CIO, said in February at a forum on the 1998 congressional elections. "Parties have become a vehicle to move money into elections."

Internet-Fueled Democracy

Project 2000's Web site (www.politikit.com), the centerpiece of BIPAC's effort, collects and publishes Federal Election Commission (FEC) guides and legal opinions on campaign contributions and independent expenditures, two ways that business can spend money on elections.

It lets users pick a congressional district and find instructions on voter registration and absentee ballots. Other features include custom voting records (how candidates voted on issues of importance to business) and candidate questionnaires.

"You could be a retailer in Idaho, go into that site, press a couple buttons and have a print-out of how Congress voted over time," Josten said. "It stands today as one of the best tools available to the business community."

One component of Project 2000 is "corporate communications," a little-used part of campaign finance law that allows companies, trade associations and labor unions to promote specific candidates in mailings and phone calls that reach only their employees and members of those groups, not the general public.

"Business has been terrible at corporate communications," said BIPAC Vice President Darrell Shull, who is heading the Project 2000 effort. "We're urging them to put their names on materials, because they are credible spokespeople in their communities."

FEC regulations permit unlimited spending on such efforts, but they have mostly been the domain of unions. A review of FEC data lists 241 corporate communication accounts, of which all but 66 are affiliated with labor unions. Some have been active for years, while others came alive for only a single race.

The National Federation of Independent Business, which represents small companies, is one group that has used its corporate communications account during the past several election cycles. In February and March it sent faxes and mailings totaling $4,440 to its members in nine states. The National Association of Realtors spent about $28,000 to help elect Rep. Johnny Isakson, R-Ga., in 1999.

Labor Still Gives More

Those figures are just a fraction of what some Democratic candidates have received, especially from unions. Vice President Al Gore's presidential campaign benefited from $174,493 in corporate communications by unions during the 2000 primary season, according to FEC records.

California groups, mostly unions, spent $88,189 in get-out-the-vote efforts in support of Rep. Joe Baca, D-Calif., during a special election last fall. The National Republican Congressional Committee tried to mount an absentee

ballot effort in that race, but its candidate, Elia Pirozzi, lost by 2,672 votes.

Several local and state Realtors' groups also have created communications accounts, along with organizations associated with environmental and anti-abortion movements. Those efforts usually involve a single House or Senate seat and do not have much connection to broader issues.

Project 2000 also emphasizes other areas of political involvement that do not include direct donations to candidates and political parties. Business leaders cite individual elections where, given a better turnout among the business community, a race won by a Democrat might have gone to the GOP.

One example is Connecticut's 5th District, where two-term Democratic Rep. Jim Maloney held off Republican Mark Nielsen by just 2,343 votes in 1998, the second-closest House race in the nation that year.

Maloney's district contains some of Connecticut's wealthiest towns, such as Waterbury and Danbury, and is considered one of the most politically competitive in the nation. Kranowitz called Nielsen's loss "appalling."

Any new grass-roots organization would mostly benefit Republicans, who are closely allied with corporations. Democrats, however, have boasted of making inroads, especially in raising unrestricted "soft money" contributions. A number of corporate donors have increased their support of Democratic Party committees during the current election cycle, FEC records show.

The telecommunications firm SBC Communications Inc. has given $641,150 in soft money to Democratic committees during the current election cycle, up from $160,361 during the previous cycle. The company has also boosted its contributions to Republican committees, although not as much.

Soft money contributions have not been effective in motivating business owners and employees at the ballot box, some business leaders say, in part because the ads are often tailored to support or oppose a candidate rather than to encourage voting.

"We cannot rely on political parties to advocate our issues or turn out our base," Shull said. "Soft money is not the cure."

Message Control

As a case in point, Shull cited the 1998 Kentucky Senate race between

then-Rep. Scotty Baesler (1993-99), a Democrat, and Republican Jim Bunning. The Kentucky GOP, aided by soft money from the national party, spent at least $500,000 on broadcast ads, some of which advocated positions that were anathema to business.

One television ad criticized Baesler's 1993 vote for the North American Free Trade Agreement (PL 103-182) and said it had led to the loss of manufacturing jobs in Kentucky. The ad asked viewers to call Baesler and voice their disapproval. Bunning won. *(1993 CQ Almanac, p. 171)*

Project 2000's backers concede that their effort might not pay off in this year's elections, but perhaps in 2002 or 2004. By that time, they say, the disparate business community should be able to organize and deliver a pro-business vote to counter labor.

Unions may be counting on their grass roots, but have not abandoned the airwaves. They have turned to television this year, running advertisements on issues such as China's trade status. Organized labor plans to continue its emphasis on face-to-face contact, however, during this election cycle.

What the business community can't match, beside labor's experienced operation, is the strong ties union members have to their affiliates, said the AFL-CIO's Rosenthal in a May 25 interview.

"Beyond the organization, what people don't understand is the intensity and depth of the relationship that union members have with their union," he said. "They expect to get political information from the union."

In the meantime, neither BIPAC nor other business groups and their political action committees will stop contributing money to congressional candidates or parties. One of Project 2000's provisions details the rules for making political donations and offers suggestions on the most competitive races. Even that practice might need some fine-tuning, said the Chamber's Josten.

His message: Giving money for access to lawmakers is "not a political strategy." A better tactic, he said, is working to elect pro-business representatives — a much easier task than trying to change the minds of elected officials once they assume office.

"The political parties used to do a very good job registering and turning people out to vote — before they went to the air," he said. "It's about votes, it's not about who has the best ad." ◆

Government Institutions

The articles in this section provide insight into the workings of the major institutions of American government, focusing in this issue on term limits for committee chairs in Congress, judicial vacancies, and the legacy of the Clinton presidency.

In 1995 House Republicans imposed a three-term, six-year limit on committee chairmanships. If Republicans maintain control of the House after the 2000 elections, most current chairs will reach this limit, setting up an intra-party contest for several coveted posts. The first article in this section examines the effect this competition is having on party unity and speculates on how the policy will influence the legislative process. Some observers believe that so much turnover in top positions, and the loss of many experienced lawmakers, will have a negative influence, while others see the change as a welcome addition of new perspectives and fresh talent.

An article on judicial vacancies describes the nomination process for Judges Richard Paez and Marsha Berzon, who were recently confirmed to the 9th U.S. Circuit Court of Appeals after years of delay. It also discusses whether longstanding vacancies have hurt the courts' ability to manage their caseloads, using the 9th and 4th Circuit Courts as examples, and discusses a plan for dividing the unwieldy 9th Circuit into two circuits.

The lasting legacy of President Clinton's presidency, the final article in this section argues, will probably be the role he has established for the government in maintaining and bolstering the nation's economic health. The article charts the evolution of Clinton's fiscal policy from his initial days in office, looks at broad economic indicators during his presidency, and examines to what extent the economic gains of the 1990s can rightfully be credited to the actions of the federal government.

Junior members vie to prove their mettle while others prepare for life in rank and file

Chairmen's Term Limits Already Shaking Up House

Quick Contents

Republicans voted in 1995 to limit committee chairmen to six years, but as the first deadline approaches, they are scrambling to figure out how term limits will affect their personal and party agendas — assuming they can keep control of the House. Some say term limits will energize the party, but others warn that they are driving experienced lawmakers out to pasture.

Arguably the best thing that could happen to Pennsylvania Republican Bud Shuster next year is for Democrats to win control of the House. That way, the man who has ruled the Transportation and Infrastructure Committee for six years could stay on as the panel's top Republican and continue his close working relationship with top Democrat and presumptive Chairman James L. Oberstar of Minnesota. "We're joined at the hip," Oberstar said of his relationship with Shuster.

If Republicans hold on to their narrow majority, House rules require that Shuster — along with seven other committee chairmen and dozens of subcommittee chairmen — relinquish control of their fiefdoms. Shuster would be pushed down to chair the Ground Transportation Subcommittee. He still would be able to earmark pet projects, but he would not have the power of the chairman or even the ranking member.

The rule limiting committee chairmen to six years, enacted in 1995 as part of the Republicans' "Contract With America," is aimed at bringing fresh blood to the party leadership and preventing a small group of old bulls from dictating House policy.

But as the first deadline for chairmen approaches at the end of 2000, Republicans are scrambling to figure out how term limits will affect their personal and party agendas. Some say it will energize the party, inspiring ambitious lawmakers to prove their worth, working extra hard on issues and raising money for the party. "It will create a competitive environment," said Michael Franc, vice president of government relations at the Heritage Foundation and former communications director for House Majority Leader Dick Armey, R-Texas. "Anyone aspiring to be a chair is going to be at the top of their game for the next few months."

Others warn that term limits will hurt the party and the House by driving experienced legislators out to pasture. "It's a dumbing down of Congress," said Sherwood Boehlert, R-N.Y. "We're losing proven performers."

Already, four senior Republicans have announced that they will retire this year as a direct result of term limits on chairmanships: Bill Archer of Texas, chairman of the Ways and Means Committee; Bill Goodling of Pennsylvania, chairman of Education and the Workforce; Thomas J. Bliley Jr. of Virginia, chairman of Commerce, and John Edward Porter, R-Ill., chairman of the Appropriations subcommittee funding the departments of Labor, Health and Human Services (HHS), and Education.

Those open seats could prove pivotal in the GOP's fight to hold on to its six-seat majority. "This is uncharted territory for us," said John A. Boehner, R-Ohio. "Everybody is moving very gingerly."

These transitions have raised concern that legislative authority could pass from elected lawmakers to unelected staff members. Others say term limits may have a particularly adverse effect on the GOP majority. "Experience matters," said Richard F. Fenno Jr., professor of political science at the University of Rochester. "When you give up experience, you give up a lot. You give up influence."

Party Politics

With term limits looming, scores of junior members began jockeying for chairmanships more than a year ago. They lobbied the leadership and raised their profiles on issues of importance to their committee of choice. They have been campaigning across the country for GOP candidates and raising millions in campaign dollars to prove their party loyalty. Committee chairmen are nominated by party leaders, led by Speaker J. Dennis Hastert, R-Ill., then ratified by the GOP Conference.

W. J. "Billy" Tauzin, R-La., and Michael G. Oxley, R-Ohio, the two top contenders for Commerce chairman, are working furiously. Tauzin is well on his way to raising $10 million for the Republican Party in the 1999-2000 election cycle. That includes not only money he has raised from his personal campaign fund and his political action committee — the Bayou Leader PAC — but also from hosting party fundraisers. On March 16, Tauzin hosted the National Republican Congressional Committee's annual fundraiser in Washington, which is estimated to have

CQ PHOTO / SCOTT J. FERRELL

Armed Services Committee Chairman Floyd D. Spence, R-S.C., shown in 1998, is among a dozen full committee chairmen who must step down after three consecutive terms as chairman. Bob Stump, R-Ariz., left, is next in line but will be challenged by Curt Weldon, R-Pa. Another possible contender is Duncan Hunter, R-Calif. Spence could become chairman of the Military Procurement Subcommittee.

raised more than $7.2 million. Hours after that event, Tauzin flew to Georgia to hold a fundraiser for Rep. Mac Collins.

Last January, Oxley chaired a $10,000-a-plate fundraiser in New York that took in more than $1 million. Overall, Oxley takes credit for bringing in $3 million this cycle. "He has raised more this year than ever before," said Oxley spokeswoman Peggy Peterson, who notes that Oxley has been fundraising since 1986. "The majority is threatened this year, and it is inspiring everybody to help their colleagues." Peterson also conceded that the fundraising does not hurt Oxley's effort to take over the Commerce Committee.

Another potential chairman-in-waiting, Curt Weldon, R-Pa., has pledged to raise $1 million for GOP candidates this cycle. He has so far campaigned for GOP candidates in 10 districts across the country and plans to visit at least 50 more by November. Weldon is seventh in seniority on the Armed Services panel and insists he is "not running for anything," but his aggressive campaigning and fundraising, as well as his increased profile on military issues this session, suggest otherwise. Current panel Chairman Floyd D. Spence, R-S.C., is stepping down, and Weldon would be challenging Bob Stump, R-Ariz., who is next in line and says he intends to go for the post. Weldon this January launched a political action committee, the Committee for a

United Republican Team (CURT PAC).

Numerous PACs have been organized by would-be chairmen in the past few years. Among them are the Common Sense Leadership Fund, organized in 1998 by Saxby Chambliss, R-Ga., who is eyeing the Budget Committee; the Fund for a Free Market America, started in 1998 by Rep. Philip M. Crane, R-Ill., who is next in line at Ways and Means; and the Wisconsin Leadership PAC, begun last year by Wisconsin Reps. F. James Sensenbrenner Jr. and Tom Petri, who are vying respectively for the Judiciary and the Education and the Workforce panels. *(PACS, p. 75)*

The PACs have received tens of thousands of dollars from corporations with business before the committees that are up for grabs. For example, Tauzin and Oxley's PACs received contributions from the employees and federal PACs of numerous telecommunications and tobacco companies, which fall under the jurisdiction of the Commerce Committee. Contributors included Bell-South Corp. ($3,000 to Oxley, $2,500 to Tauzin in 1999) and R.J. Reynolds Tobacco Holdings Inc. ($4,000 to Oxley, $1000 to Tauzin in 1999).

Among donations from Crane's PAC last year were $2,000 each to Reps. George Nethercutt, R-Wash., Tom Tancredo, R-Colo., and Joe Skeen, R-N.M. Crane gave $9,000 to GOP candidates who are challenging incum-

Musical Chairs

In 1995, Republicans imposed a three-term, six-year limit on committee chairmen. Most will reach that limit at the end of 2000, setting up some heated GOP contests for the posts — assuming Republicans maintain control of the House. If a panel's current chairman has not reached the limit and is not retiring, the panel is not listed.

COMMITTEE	CURRENT CHAIRMAN	107TH CONGRESS CONTENDERS
Appropriations Agriculture	Joe Skeen, R-N.M., has reached the three-term limit and is eyeing the Interior Subcommittee chairmanship.	Jay Dickey, R-Ark., is third in line on the subcommittee and interested in the seat, but he may be too far down in full committee seniority to become a cardinal. Henry Bonilla, R-Texas, has more full committee seniority and could be chosen for the post.
Commerce, Justice, State	Harold Rogers, R-Ky., has reached the three-term limit and may seek the chairmanship at Labor-HHS.	Jim Kolbe, R-Ariz., has not yet served three terms as chairman of the Treasury-Postal Service Subcommittee, but his strong interest in trade may entice him to try to jump to this panel.
Energy & Water	Ron Packard, R-Calif., has not yet served three terms but is retiring from Congress.	Sonny Callahan, R-Ala., who has reached the limit on Foreign Operations, may be interested. He unsuccessfully sought the gavel in the 105th Congress.
Foreign Operations	Callahan has reached the three-term limit and may be interested in Transportation or Energy & Water.	Frank R. Wolf, R-Va., who must give up Transportation, is seeking the chairmanship of Foreign Operations, although more moderate members may oppose the move.
Interior	Ralph Regula, R-Ohio, has reached the three-term limit and may seek the chairmanship at Labor-HHS.	Skeen is said to have his eyes on the Interior Subcommittee.
Labor-HHS	John Edward Porter, R-Ill., has reached the three-term limit and is retiring.	Rogers, whose district's major industry is health care, may want to move from Commerce-Justice-State to Labor-HHS. Regula, who must give up Interior, also may be interested. Ernest Istook, R-Okla., has not finished six years as District of Columbia chairman, but may want to move to Labor-HHS. Bonilla is next in line on the subcommittee.
Transportation	Wolf has reached the three-term limit and may seek the chairmanship at Foreign Operations.	Callahan tried to get this subcommittee in the 105th Congress and may be interested again.
Armed Services	Floyd D. Spence, R-S.C., has reached the three-term limit. He is next in line for the Military Procurement Subcommittee.	Curt Weldon, R-Pa., will challenge Bob Stump, R-Ariz., who is next in line. Another possible challenger is Duncan Hunter, R-Calif.
Banking and Financial Services	Jim Leach, R-Iowa, has reached the three-term limit and may seek the chairmanship of International Relations.	Next in line is Marge Roukema, R-N.J. She may be challenged by Richard H. Baker, R-La., and Rick A. Lazio, R-N.Y.
Budget	John R. Kasich, R-Ohio, has reached the three-term limit and is retiring.	Saxby Chambliss, R-Ga., and Jim Nussle, R-Iowa, are actively pursuing the seat. Also interested are Peter Hoekstra, R-Mich., Nick Smith, R-Mich., and John E. Sununu, R-N.H.

COMMITTEE	CURRENT CHAIRMAN	107TH CONGRESS CONTENDERS
Commerce	Thomas J. Bliley Jr., R-Va., has reached the three-term limit and is retiring.	Michael G. Oxley, R-Ohio, and W.J. "Billy" Tauzin, R-La., are running aggressive campaigns for the seat. Joe L. Barton, R-Texas, has expressed interest.
Education and the Workforce	Bill Goodling, R-Pa., has reached the three-term limit and is retiring.	Tom Petri, R-Wis., at left, is next in line but may be challenged by Hoekstra and John A. Boehner, R-Ohio.
House Administration	Bill Thomas, R-Calif., has reached the three-term limit and is seeking the chairmanship at Ways and Means.	Boehner is likely to get this post if he does not win Education and the Workforce. Otherwise, the next likely chairman is Vernon J. Ehlers, R-Mich.
International Relations	Benjamin A. Gilman, R-N.Y., has reached the three-term limit. He is not seeking any other full committee chairmanship but may get a subcommittee post.	Banking Chairman Leach may seek the post, but Doug Bereuter, R-Neb., who has less seniority than Leach, is interested in the spot.
Judiciary	Henry J. Hyde, R-Ill., has reached the three-term limit but some are pushing for a waiver to allow him to continue as chairman.	If Hyde does not get a waiver, his likely successor is F. James Sensenbrenner Jr., R-Wis.
Resources	Don Young, R-Alaska, has reached the three-term limit and is likely to become chairman of Transportation and Infrastructure.	James V. Hansen, R-Utah, is likely to get the post unless Tauzin, who is more senior, fails to receive the Commerce post.
Science	Sensenbrenner has been chairman since 1997. He may move to Judiciary if Hyde does not get a waiver to remain there as chairman.	If Sensenbrenner, at left, moves, the next likely chairman is Sherwood Boehlert, R-N.Y.
Small Business	James M. Talent, R-Mo., is running for governor.	Donald Manzullo, R-Ill., is fourth in line but likely to get the post. Larry Combest, R-Texas, has more seniority but is expected to stay as chairman of Agriculture, and Joel Hefley, R-Colo., appears more interested in subcommittees on Armed Services and Resources.
Transportation and Infrastructure	Bud Shuster, R-Pa., has reached the three-term limit and is seeking the chairmanship of the influential Ground Transportation Subcommittee.	Young is the likely successor.
Veterans' Affairs	Stump has reached the three-term limit and is next in line at Armed Services, but may be challenged.	The next likely chairman is Christopher H. Smith, R-N.J.
Ways and Means	Bill Archer, R-Texas, has reached the three-term limit and is retiring.	Philip M. Crane, R-Ill., at left, is next in line. He took a medical leave March 21 to be treated for alcohol dependency. Thomas is expected to offer a tough challenge. E. Clay Shaw Jr., R-Fla., is a possibility.

bent Democrats or running for open seats. Petri and Sensenbrenner's PAC gave $1,000 to two other Wisconsinites, Reps. Mark Green and Paul D. Ryan, as well as to several GOP challengers.

All this party unity has made for some odd alliances. Richard H. Baker, R-La., who is expected to challenge Marge Roukema, R-N.J., for the chairmanship at Banking and Financial Services, recently gave $1,000 to her troubled primary re-election campaign. Roukema points to the contribution as evidence that Baker supports her bid for the Banking seat, but Baker can use it as evidence that he is a loyal Republican who puts party needs above his own.

Eyes on the Prize

Although some say the competition is profitable for the party, others, including Hastert, fear the committee races could fracture the conference. Hastert has threatened retribution against lawmakers who become too aggressive in their committee campaigns. "That will weigh heavily on who will be chair," Hastert said in a recent interview.

In reaction to Hastert's warnings, most lawmakers seeking chairmanships deny it in public. They say their efforts to raise funds and campaign for colleagues is altruistic, showing party loyalty. But they are still maneuvering behind the scenes.

Seniority, the traditional standard for selecting chairmen, is likely to be abandoned next year. Many junior members are promoting their legislative acumen — and in some cases their IQ and physical stamina — in hopes of vaulting over more senior members.

One such race — for the Ways and Means Committee — is expected to turn ugly, as Bill Thomas, R-Calif., an aggressive and sharp-tongued legislator, challenges Crane, who has a decade more seniority. Thomas, like others expected to run for chairmanships, says he is not campaigning for anything.

Crane on March 21 took a 30-day medical leave of absence from the House to receive treatment for alcohol dependency. "Alcoholism is a disease, and I must deal with it directly and decisively," Crane said in a written statement. "I look forward with anticipation to returning soon in order to continue my work in the House and to returning to family, friends, colleagues, and supporters in good health."

Along with his statement, Crane included comments from Archer praising him for his decision to seek treatment and saying he looks forward to Crane's "return to his extraordinary career in Congress and on the Ways and Means Committee."

Another possibility for the post is E. Clay Shaw Jr., R-Fla., who acknowledged his interest in the seat but said it was "too early to speculate" about whether he would run for it.

Roukema also played down her race for Banking. "I haven't been waging an aggressive campaign for it," she said. However, she is quick to point out her legislative record on banking issues, and said the "leadership recognizes" her abilities as a lawmaker. If selected, she would likely be the GOP's only female chairman.

Losing Experience

When the House amended its rules in 1995 to limit committee and subcommittee chairmen to six years, Republicans heralded the change as a key part of the "devolution of authority from federal lawmakers and bureaucrats back to individual citizens." No House Republicans voted against the rules change, which passed on the first day of the Republican takeover. (*1995 Almanac, p. 1-12*)

But this year, some outgoing chairmen express fear that legislative authority will pass from elected lawmakers to unelected staff members.

"The stupid part about term limits is the only people left with institutional history are people who are not elected," Goodling said. "Whoever takes over as the new chairmen — do they have the institutional knowledge? If not, the staff will have more influence."

Porter agrees.

"If you see members with no experience on a subcommittee take over as chair, there will be a big influence from subcommittee staff," Porter said.

The influence of staff will be particularly potent on Appropriations because subcommittee chairmen, known as "cardinals," are chosen based on seniority on the full committee, not the subcommittee. Under that system, a member who ranks high in overall seniority can be named to head a subcommittee on which he has never served. The new cardinal's expertise on that panel's issues could be minimal.

Of the 13 Appropriations subcommittee chairmen, six must give up their seats because of term limits. A seventh, Ron Packard, R-Calif., whose term on the Energy and Water panel has not run out, is retiring from Congress along with one of the six, Porter.

The other term-limited cardinals are expected to jump to the head of other Appropriations subcommittees, which in turn is likely to prompt chairmen who have not reached the limit to nonetheless seek an open slot on a more desirable panel. In the end, as many as 11 of the 13 subcommittees could have new chairmen next year if the GOP keeps control. The two expected to stay put are Jerry Lewis, R-Calif., at Defense and James T. Walsh, R-N.Y., at VA-HUD.

Porter said the new cardinals will have to rely not only on staff aides for help, but also upon more junior subcommittee members.

Some lawmakers, such as Boehlert, predict committee term limits will hurt the institution by draining the House of valuable legislative knowledge. Others say term limits could affect the way Republicans govern and the likelihood of their holding the House. Said Fenno, of the University of Rochester: "Republicans in Congress over the last six years have had an awful lot of trouble learning how to run the place. There's a lot at stake. They're trying to learn how to govern and, at the same time, [they're injecting] internal party controversy into a party already crippled by internal differences."

New Energy

Others, however, say the negative impact on legislation will be minimal.

"There will always be a learning curve when you become a chair," said Franc of the Heritage Foundation. "But it's going to be a lot less difficult than [in 1994]. It was night and day when everything flipped over. Even junior members were given the gavel."

Most lawmakers now maneuvering for full committee chairmanships have headed subcommittees previously, experience that Franc said will ease the transition. He added that the unfolding races will energize lawmakers and the GOP agenda. Indeed, Weldon, in his bid for Armed Services, is aggressively promoting his work on national security issues.

"The issue of defense and national security . . . needs to be raised to a higher level," Weldon said in an interview. "There are a lot more things we need to be doing. Rather than complaining about it . . . I'm doing it myself." Weldon points out that in the

Seeking Chairmanships

These lawmakers are seeking committee chairmanships and have organized political action committees (PACs) to raise money for fellow Republicans. The money goes to candidates or campaign committees.

COMMITTEE	MEMBER	PAC	WHEN ORGANIZED	DONATIONS (cycle contributed)
Armed Services	Curt Weldon, R-Pa.	Committee for United Republican Team (CURT PAC)	January 2000	$0 *(1999-2000)*
Budget	Saxby Chambliss, R-Ga.	Common Sense Leadership Fund	May 1998	$44,500 *(1997-1998)* $3,000 *(1999-2000)*
	Jim Nussle, R-Iowa	Great Dane PAC	August 1999	$0 *(1999-2000)*
Commerce	Michael G. Oxley, R-Ohio	Leadership PAC 2000	March 1996	$139,000 *(1997-1998)* $46,000 *(1999-2000)*
	W.J. "Billy" Tauzin, R-La.	Bayou Leader PAC	October 1997	$101,654 *(1997-1998)* $44,662 *(1999-2000)*
Education and the Workforce	Tom Petri, R-Wis.	The Wisconsin Leadership PAC	June 1999	$6,000 *(1999-2000)*
	John A. Boehner, R-Ohio *	The Freedom Project	September 1995	$481,665 *(1997-1998)* $226,763 *(1999-2000)*
Judiciary	F. James Sensenbrenner Jr., R-Wis.	The Wisconsin Leadership PAC	June 1999	$6,000 *(1999-2000)*
Science	Sherwood Boehlert, R-N.Y.	TR Fund	April 1996	$96,126 *(1997-1998)* $3,000 *(1999-2000)*
Transportation and Infrastructure	Don Young, R-Alaska	Midnight Sun PAC	May 1999	$20,396 *(1999-2000)*
Ways and Means	Philip M. Crane, R-Ill.	Fund for a Free Market America	September 1998	$0 *(1997-1998)* $19,000 *(1999-2000)*
	E. Clay Shaw Jr., R-Fla.	Sunshine PAC	March 1998	$36,000 *(1997-1998)* $0 *(1999-2000)*
	Bill Thomas, R-Calif.	Congressional Majority Committee	1993	$5,440 *(1997-1998)* $2,000 *(1999-2000)*

* Boehner is also seeking the chairmanship of the House Administration Committee.

SOURCE: Federal Election Commission

105th Congress he served on a special committee that looked into Chinese espionage, and that Hastert recently named him to a Speaker's task force on U.S.-Russian relations. (*Espionage*, *1998 Almanac*, *p. 16-28*)

Tauzin also has talked about his plans for the Commerce Committee. He said he would give subcommittee chairmen more power over staff hiring, which is currently controlled by the full committee chairman. Tauzin said he would also re-establish the Telecommunications and Finance Subcommittee. In the 105th Congress, the panel was turned into the Telecommunications, Trade and Consumer Protection panel and handed to Tauzin as a reward for his switch to the Republican Party. Tauzin said he would give the Telecom-munications Subcommittee to Oxley.

The issue of Tauzin's relatively new membership in the GOP will be a factor in the race. Oxley refers to himself as the "most senior Republican on the committee," while Tauzin touts his overall seniority. "If the litmus test for being a good Republican is that you had to be born one, Ronald Reagan would have never been president," said Tauzin spokesman Ken Johnson.

Lateral Moves

While some chairmen facing term limits — such as Spence and International Relations Chairman Benjamin A. Gilman, R-N.Y., who are not seeking other full committee posts — may have to adjust next year to life as sub-committee chairman among the rank and file, others will get a chance to lead a different panel.

In a controversial edict last year, Hastert ruled that Republicans could play musical chairs, jumping from one top spot to another.

Among those expected to seek another top post is Banking Chairman Jim Leach, R-Iowa, who is in line to take over International Relations. But Leach faces a challenge from Doug Bereuter, R-Neb., who is two slots below him in seniority.

Bereuter earlier this year passed up a chance to run for the Senate seat being vacated by Democrat Bob Kerrey, who is retiring, because Bereuter hopes to move into the International Relations post. Many conservative Republicans give Bereuter the upper hand, saying

Democrats Spurn Limits

As House Democrats watch their Republican colleagues compete with each other for committee chairmanships left open by incumbents subject to term limits, they say they will get rid of limits on chairmanships if they win control of the House.

"My personal point of view is that the [term limits] rule has caused the Republicans great difficulty in being able to retain their senior members and keep experienced lawmakers in Congress," said Rep. Martin Frost, D-Texas, chairman of the Democratic Caucus. "They have lost some of their very good members who still had productive years ahead."

The retirement of several GOP chairmen who were limited to three terms, or six years, at their committee posts — including Labor-HHS Appropriations Subcommittee Chairman John Edward Porter, R-Ill., whose 10th District could go Democratic — has given Democrats increased hope of taking control of the House in 2001. The current ratio is 222-211, with two independents.

If Democrats win the majority, they will have to adopt new rules to get rid of committee term limits. Frost said they can do that without stirring up too much controversy.

The House must approve a new rules package every year. So Democrats, rather than having to vote to strip term limits from House rules, can put forward a new set of rules without the limits.

Frost also pointed out that Democrats have party rules to ensure that chairmen do not stay at the top of their committees if their colleagues feel they can no longer serve effectively.

Under Democratic Caucus policy, every full committee and Appropriations subcommittee chairman is subject to an up or down vote at the beginning of each Congress. If a majority of the caucus votes against a chairman, the floor is then open to nominations for a replacement.

The same rule currently applies to Democratic ranking members.

"We have a procedure in place that lets the caucus decide . . . when people remain too long and are no longer personally able to do the job," Frost said.

Before the 102nd Congress convened, House Democrats used the procedure to topple two chairmen — Frank Annunzio of Illinois (1965-93) from the House Administration Committee, and Glenn M. Anderson of California (1969-93) from the Public Works chairmanship. (*1991 Almanac, p. 3*)

Frost said if his party takes control next year, he does not anticipate any challenges to Democrats set to become chairmen. Democratic lawmakers from conservative and liberal wings of the party also said that current ranking members would have a smooth transition to the chairmanships.

Members of the conservative Democratic Blue Dog Coalition said they were not planning to challenge more liberal members. Instead, they said they would make sure there are no challenges to any Blue Dogs. Under a Democratic House, two Blue Dogs would be in line for chairmanships: Charles W. Stenholm of Texas at the Agriculture Committee and Ralph M. Hall of Texas at the Science Committee.

More liberal lawmakers also said they were satisfied with the lineup. "I think we're in a very strong position in terms of both full and subcommittee chairs," said Peter A. DeFazio of Oregon, chairman of the Progressive Caucus, whose membership includes five of the 20 Democrats in line for chairmanships: George Miller of California at Education and the Workforce, John Conyers Jr. of Michigan at Judiciary, Lane Evans of Illinois at Veterans' Affairs, Henry A. Waxman of California at Government Reform and Nydia M. Velázquez of New York at Small Business.

Leach, a member of the moderate Tuesday Group, has strayed from the party line too many times. Bereuter, who also serves on Banking, said Leach asked him to take the Banking chairmanship and forgo a run for International Relations, but he declined.

One chairman facing a term limit may get a chance to hang on to his committee. Some Republicans are quietly pushing the leadership to grant Henry J. Hyde, R-Ill., a waiver from the term-limit rule to allow him to stay on as Judiciary chairman.

The waiver movement could get a boost from Bliley's recent decision to retire. Had he stayed on, he likely would have demanded a waiver if Hyde got one. With Bliley's departure, it may be easier to allow Hyde — who won praise for his calm and steady handling of the impeachment hearings against President Clinton — to hold on. (*Bliley retirement, 2000 CQ Weekly, p. 529*)

Hyde says he is not seeking a waiver and is happy to join the rank and file.

But the transition could prove awkward for some outgoing chairmen, particularly Shuster. Shuster has a reputation as the "king of asphalt" for his forceful handling of the Transportation Committee and his ability to direct pet projects to his district. Some predict it could be a less-than-smooth transition if Shuster hands the gavel to would-be Chairman Don Young, R-Alaska. (*Shuster, 2000 CQ Weekly, p. 576*)

"Shuster has highways and bridges in his blood," Oberstar said. "He knows the nuances of the process."

Boehlert, the panel's fourth-ranking Republican, said he expects Shuster to influence the committee from beyond the podium. "As long as he serves, he will have influence far beyond any single member, simply because he is so conversant with the issues." Young says he expects a "good working relationship" with Shuster and will consult him regularly. "We'll do an agenda together," Young said. "It's a committee together, not just Bud Shuster's, not just Don Young's."

But one retiring chairman said he is glad he does not have to deal with a change from king to commoner. "I wouldn't want to be sitting on a committee as a former chair," Goodling said. "No matter how hard you tried not to second-guess the new chairman, people will constantly come to you. No matter how hard the old chairman tries to keep the press away, or the lobbyists away, or other members away, it's going to happen." ◆

Bill would cut big 9th circuit in half; both sides of issue rest their case on short-staffed 4th

Longstanding Judicial Vacancies Revive 'Smaller Is Better' Crusade

RICHMOND, Va. — Other judges may be complaining about their workloads, but J. Harvie Wilkinson III does not believe a federal appeals court has to be big to be effective. He has argued against filling the vacancies on the bench of the Richmond-based 4th U.S. Circuit Court of Appeals, where he has been the chief judge since February 1996.

"Courts weren't meant to be that big," Wilkinson, first named to the federal bench in 1984 by President Ronald Reagan, said in a Feb. 25 interview.

His circuit has four vacancies and 11 active judges, which he thinks is sufficient to manage its caseload.

Not everyone agrees.

The Judicial Conference of the United States has designated two of the four vacancies as emergencies, meaning the circuit — which includes Virginia, Maryland, North and South Carolina, and West Virginia — has a caseload in excess of 500 filings. The median time for disposition of a case by the 4th Circuit is 8.9 months, compared with a national median for appeals courts of 12 months.

Patrick J. Leahy of Vermont, the ranking Democrat on the Senate Judiciary Committee, said March 3 that the vacancies in the 4th Circuit and elsewhere mean that "prosecutors have to plea bargain cases they don't want to" or else run afoul of speedy-trial rules. For years, Leahy and other Democrats have accused Senate Republicans of political foot-dragging on President Clinton's judicial nominations in hopes of winning back the White House in 2001.

On the other side of the country, the 9th U.S. Circuit Court of Appeals — by far the biggest circuit — has four vacancies among its 28 authorized judges, with two just filled. The Senate voted March 9 to confirm Richard A. Paez and Marsha L. Berzon as appellate judges. All four openings have been designated emergencies.

Of those four, one has existed since the seat was created in 1990. Another has existed since 1994, and two others opened in 1999.

The 9th Circuit's median disposition time is 14.2 months per case.

Conservative critics have charged that

the 9th Circuit is a liberal behemoth, a huge court out of touch with the people it serves. Its jurisdiction includes more than 50 million people in states from Alaska to Nevada to Hawaii. That has led some, including Senate Judiciary Committee Chairman Orrin G. Hatch, R-Utah, to endorse legislation that would split the massive circuit.

Vacancies are only one of several issues that members of Congress are looking at more closely these days, given the increasing importance of the circuit courts. As the Supreme Court hears fewer and fewer cases, "the courts of appeals have become our regional Supreme Courts," said Sheldon Goldman, a political science professor at the University of Massachusetts at Amherst.

The 'Liberal' Circuit

"I think the 9th Circuit is a circuit that is very much out of touch with mainstream America," Senate Majority Leader Trent Lott, R-Miss., said March 7, explaining in part why he would vote against Paez and Berzon. "[It has] been overruled in something over 80 out of the last 100 cases that have been appealed to the Supreme Court."

Based in San Francisco, the 9th Circuit includes Alaska, Arizona, California, Hawaii, Idaho, Montana, Nevada, Oregon, Washington, Guam and the Northern Mariana Islands.

There have been efforts over the years to carve the circuit into smaller units. In 1997, an attempt by the Senate to cut the court into two sections eventually was scaled back to

Quick Contents

The need to fill vacancies on the federal bench is viewed differently from the East and West coasts. The 4th U.S. Circuit Court of Appeals manages its docket with four vacancies, while the massive 9th Circuit, which has had six vacancies, is overwhelmed.

By the Numbers

	4th Circuit	9th Circuit	U.S.
Appellate judgeships	15	28	179
Vacancies	4 (27%)	4 (14%)	22 (12%)
Nominations pending	1	4*	16*
District judgeships	51	97	636
Vacancies	1 (2%)	12 (12%)	52 (8%)
Nominations pending	1	3	19

* Senate confirmed three nominees the week of March 6, two of them for the 9th Circuit.

SOURCE: The Administrative Office of the U.S. Courts

CQ Weekly March 11, 2000

Senate Confirms Paez and Berzon
To 9th Circuit After Years of Impasse

After years of delay and controversy — including charges that Republicans opposed some judicial nominees based on their race and ethnicity — the Senate on March 9 voted to confirm Richard A. Paez and Marsha L. Berzon to lifetime seats on the 9th U.S. Circuit Court of Appeals.

The vote for Paez was 59-29; the vote for Berzon was 64-34. (*Votes 40 and 38, 2000 CQ Weekly, p. 564*)

Opposition to Paez and Berzon stemmed both from their backgrounds and from the fact that they were appointed to serve on the massive 9th Circuit, a court that conservatives say is too liberal and out of touch with its constituents. (*Circuits, p. 77*)

On March 7, the Senate confirmed, 93-0, Julio M. Fuentes to be a judge on the 3rd U.S. Circuit Court of Appeals, which hears cases from New Jersey, Pennsylvania, Delaware and the U.S. Virgin Islands. (*Vote 34, 2000 CQ Weekly, p. 564*)

Fuentes will be the first Hispanic on that court. He was confirmed just one day short of the first anniversary of his nomination.

The Senate has confirmed seven judicial nominees this year. Another two have been approved by the Judiciary Committee and await floor action, while 33 are pending before the committee.

Thirty-nine vacancies have no nominee named.

Paez's Problems

President Clinton decided in 1996 to elevate Paez, 52, a U.S. District Court judge in central California. Clinton resubmitted the nomination at the start of the 106th Congress. The Senate Judiciary Committee approved his nomination, 10-8, on July 29, 1999.

Berzon, 54, a labor lawyer, was first nominated in January 1998. Clinton renominated her in early 1999, and the Judiciary Committee reported out her nomination on July 1, 1999.

But the nominations lingered on the calendar until Senate Majority Leader Trent Lott, R-Miss., agreed last year to bring the pair up for a vote before March 15 in order to end a Democratic hold on a nominee to the Tennessee Valley Authority who was supported by Lott. (*1999 CQ Weekly, p. 2714*)

According to Democrats, Paez spent longer waiting for confirmation than any previous nominee. The seat he will fill has been vacant since January 1996.

Vice President Al Gore, who rushed to Washington from the presidential campaign trail in case he was needed to break a tie vote, urged the Senate to act more rapidly on future nominations. "When it comes to our judiciary, justice delayed is still justice denied. So today I say to the Senate majority once again, stop holding our justice system hostage," Gore said.

"It has been a tortured path to this day," said Democratic Sen. Barbara Boxer of California, a key supporter of Paez and Berzon. "Thank goodness that Richard and Marsha hung in there."

Republicans had raised objections to Paez on several fronts, including his handling of a trial dealing with abortion protesters and his ruling in a case dealing with human rights in Burma.

Most recently, Republican Sen. Jeff Sessions of Alabama — who lost a bid for a federal judgeship in 1986 when the Judiciary Committee rejected him — raised questions about Paez's sentencing of John Huang, a key figure in the campaign fundraising scandal that grew out of the Clinton-Gore 1996 re-election campaign.

Based on the recommendation made and evidence presented by the Justice Department, Paez sentenced Huang to no jail time.

"We ought not to be doing this," Sessions said March 8. "We ought not to be shoving this thing through."

A motion by Sessions to delay consideration of Paez's nomination indefinitely failed, 31-67. (*Vote 39, 2000 CQ Weekly, p. 564*)

Lott said he opposed Paez because of "highly questionable rulings and political statements while sitting on the bench. . . . You should assume the bench and keep your mouth shut."

But Paez won the support of Judiciary Committee Chairman Orrin G. Hatch, R-Utah, and 13 other Republicans crossed party lines to vote for him.

Berzon's Record

Berzon, a San Francisco lawyer, has specialized in employment discrimination cases and has prepared many briefs for the Supreme Court, including four she personally argued before the justices.

Berzon seemed to be more a victim of the GOP's antipathy toward the 9th Circuit than anything specific she had done. While many Republicans included her with Paez, the objections generally had to do with Paez's statements or rulings.

For example, Jim Bunning, R-Ky., said on March 8 that he opposed Berzon's nomination because "looking at her past and the causes which she has pushed show that, if confirmed, she is not going to help steer the 9th Circuit toward the judicial mainstream."

Lott was even more oblique: "When you look at her position on many issues that will come before the court, there's high doubt about the basis of her confirmation."

But even more Republicans defected in favor of Berzon. Nineteen Republicans crossed party lines to support her confirmation.

Gordon H. Smith, R-Ore., summed up his reason for supporting Paez's nomination this way: "I didn't find anything that disqualified him, so I voted yes."

a provision in the fiscal 1998 appropriations bill for the departments of Commerce, Justice and State (PL 105-119) creating a commission to study the structure of the circuits. *(1997 Almanac, p. 5-18)*

That commission, headed by former Supreme Court Justice Byron R. White, recommended that the 9th Circuit be divided into three sections for administrative purposes, but it did not go as far as Republicans had wanted. The commission did not call for a split of the circuit itself. Congress has not acted on the recommendation.

The debates over Paez and Berzon have resurrected the issue for the GOP. Alaska Republican Sen. Frank H. Murkowski on March 7 introduced legislation (S 2184) that would halve the court. Hatch cosponsored the bill.

The smaller 9th Circuit would include Arizona, California and Nevada. A new 12th Circuit would get the other states: Alaska, Hawaii, Idaho, Montana, Oregon, Washington, Guam and the Northern Mariana Islands.

Murkowski said the population served by the current circuit court is expected to grow to 63 million by 2010 — a 26 percent increase.

But it is not clear whether subdividing the court would really get at the heart of the complaint of many Republicans — what they perceive as the liberal nature of the court. "It is the furthest-left circuit in the American judiciary, and there is no doubt about it," said Sen. Jeff Sessions, R-Ala.

"The 9th Circuit is notorious for its anti-law enforcement record, its frequent creation of new rights for criminals and defendants, often in the face of clearly established law," said Robert C. Smith, R-N.H.

Many Republicans point to the numerous times the Supreme Court has overruled the 9th Circuit as evidence of the court's liberal activism. Most recently, on March 6 the Supreme Court unanimously overruled a 9th Circuit decision upholding a Washington state law that imposed stricter regulations on oil tankers than federal law. The court held that the federal government's power to regulate maritime law trumps state power.

The 'Conservative' Bench

Meanwhile, the 4th Circuit is gaining a reputation for its conservative rulings. A recent series of decisions by the court, appealed to the Supreme Court, have given the high court the opportunity to re-examine the scope of some federal laws.

For example, the justices are reviewing a decision by the 4th Circuit that limited the Miranda warning given to criminal suspects, and they seemed sympathetic to the 4th Circuit's reasoning when it threw out part of the 1994 Violence Against Women Act (PL 103-322). *(2000 CQ Weekly, p. 80; 1994 Almanac, p. 273)*

The 4th Circuit — which now has six GOP appointees and five named by Democratic presidents — has never had a black judge. President Clinton has nominated two African-Americans, at different times, for one of the open seats,

but neither has had a hearing. That is because the Senate confirmation process defers to home-state senators.

According to tradition, both senators from the nominee's state are supposed to turn in a form to the Judiciary Committee before its hearing, noting whether they support the nominee.

Sen. Jesse Helms, R-N.C., has never returned the slips for the nominated blacks on the 4th Circuit, and the vacancy is one that is supposed to be filled by a North Carolinian. That means Clinton's most recent nominee, James A. Wynn Jr., is unlikely to even get a chance to testify.

Helms argues that the court is doing well without any additional judges. And he has the support of the court's chief judge. "My view is that we're doing a fine job with the personnel that we have," Wilkinson said. "We're on top of our docket."

The court is certainly a busy one. The docket of oral arguments for the first week in March listed 74 cases. Each case is argued before a three-judge panel — for most of the March arguments, four panels were to meet simultaneously.

Judges are required to be familiar with a vast range of issues, from copyright infringement to National Labor Relations Board decisions to the regulations regarding railroad crossings.

The court heard a variety of criminal cases, including one in which it was asked to determine whether a juvenile who had helped rob a bank with a sawed-off shotgun should be tried in federal, not state, court.

The San Francisco-based 9th U.S. Circuit Court of Appeals handles cases from Alaska, Arizona, California, Hawaii, Idaho, Montana, Nevada, Oregon and Washington.

The courtroom is an interesting mix of the formal and the familiar. Lawyers approach the bench and introduce themselves with, "May it please the court," just as is done at the Supreme Court. Also as at the high court, each argument is carefully timed — most only get 10 minutes per side, though some cases, involving black-lung disease, for example, get 15 minutes.

But at the end of each case, the senior judge gavels down the case, and the judges come down from the dais, shake hands and chat with the lawyers.

Each panel must have three judges in order to conduct business. With only 11 active judges on the 4th Circuit, the panel led by Wilkinson included an African-American district court judge, who was "sitting by designation" to help the appellate court hear its cases. ◆

Historians may conclude that a growing economy did much of Clinton's work for him

A Legacy of Budget Surpluses And Thriving Markets

When economic historians start writing about President Clinton's role as steward of the federal budget and the U.S. economy, they will not be writing about the enactment of sweeping new entitlement programs, a revitalization of organized labor or any other themes from the Democratic agenda.

More likely, they will consider Clinton's most enduring and significant economic actions to be his firm backing of a Federal Reserve chairman beloved by Wall Street, his pursuit of a free trade agenda loathed by many in his party, and his success in leading the Democrats in Congress to adopt a sustained program of deficit reduction and debt repayment.

And despite what Clinton himself probably imagined when he took office and submitted his first bold budget proposal seven years ago — his promise to focus "like a laser beam" on economic woes was manifest in an ill-starred and quickly scuttled $16.3 billion economic stimulus plan — the president today is eager to have the textbooks of tomorrow focus on low interest rates, the democratization of participation in securities

investing and the boom in stock prices that occurred on his watch.

As his administration enters its final year and unveils its last full-blown budget proposal — to be delivered to Capitol Hill on Feb. 7 — Clinton boasts repeatedly that he has taken the lead in sustaining the nation's record period of economic growth by holding the size of the government in check, eliminating the deficit and calling for a prudent apportioning of the newly arrived surplus. He is still proud of his signature on the tax law (PL 103-66) enacted during his first year in office without a single GOP vote, which called for $240 billion in new revenue over the ensuing five years. He considers it a catalyst for deficit reduction and, by extension, for continued prosperity that validates a long-term economic role for the federal government. *(1993 Almanac, p. 107)*

"What we decided to do was to go for the deficit reduction," Clinton said at a Feb. 1 news briefing, "because we knew if we didn't

CQ Weekly Feb. 5, 2000

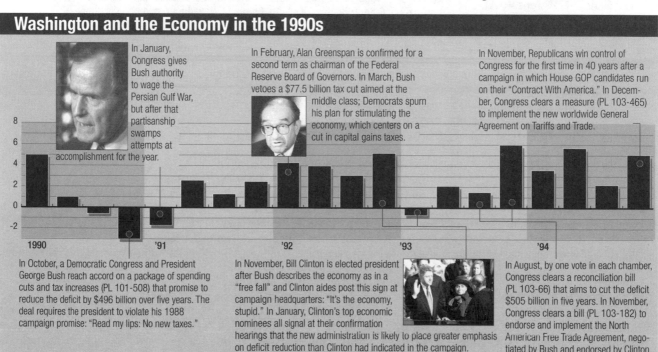

Washington and the Economy in the 1990s

In January, Congress gives Bush authority to wage the Persian Gulf War, but after that partisanship swamps attempts at accomplishment for the year.

In February, Alan Greenspan is confirmed for a second term as chairman of the Federal Reserve Board of Governors. In March, Bush vetoes a $77.5 billion tax cut aimed at the middle class; Democrats spurn his plan for stimulating the economy, which centers on a cut in capital gains taxes.

In November, Republicans win control of Congress for the first time in 40 years after a campaign in which House GOP candidates run on their "Contract With America." In December, Congress clears a measure (PL 103-465) to implement the new worldwide General Agreement on Tariffs and Trade.

8
6
4
2
0
-2

1990   '91   '92   '93   '94

In October, a Democratic Congress and President George Bush reach accord on a package of spending cuts and tax increases (PL 101-508) that promise to reduce the deficit by $496 billion over five years. The deal requires the president to violate his 1988 campaign promise: "Read my lips: No new taxes."

In November, Bill Clinton is elected president after Bush describes the economy as in a "free fall" and Clinton aides post this sign at campaign headquarters: "It's the economy, stupid." In January, Clinton's top economic nominees all signal at their confirmation hearings that the new administration is likely to place greater emphasis on deficit reduction than Clinton had indicated in the campaign.

In August, by one vote in each chamber, Congress clears a reconciliation bill (PL 103-66) that aims to cut the deficit $505 billion in five years. In November, Congress clears a bill (PL 103-182) to endorse and implement the North American Free Trade Agreement, negotiated by Bush and endorsed by Clinton.

turn the economy around, we would never get to spend the money, anyway. In other words, you're not going to be able to put the money into education or health care or anything else if you don't turn the economy around."

Truth or Spin?

That is his story, and he's sticking to it. But how much credit is rightfully his for keeping the fire lit under the economy? That debate will no doubt draw much attention from both his allies and his enemies as the Clinton administration moves toward its denouement. Most Republicans will have little of it, to be sure; they have hammered Clinton throughout his tenure for being a spendthrift. And, in fact, Clinton has proposed a dizzying array of new programs and spending initiatives, in full knowledge that many of them never would be embraced by Congress — neither by his fellow Democrats, who controlled the Capitol during the first two years of the administration, nor by the Republicans who have set the legislative agenda since.

The budget Clinton submits for fiscal 2001

will not be his last; he will transmit another one just before leaving office, either to give the next Democratic president a starting point or to provide a symbolic counterpoint to whatever fiscal policy is promised by a Republican preparing to enter the White House.

Still, this year's budget request will climax a presidential era of surprisingly conservative fiscal policy when the numbers are evaluated from a broad perspective. Budgeting during the Clinton administration has largely increased discretionary appropriations at close to the rate of inflation, with no fundamental shift in federal spending priorities other than the law (PL 104-193) that shifted responsibility for welfare to the states. (*1996 Almanac, p. 6-3*)

And when measured as a percentage of the gross domestic product (GDP) — the sum total of the value of all the goods and services generated by the U.S. economy — federal spending has dropped: Outlays accounted for 21.5 percent of the GDP in fiscal 1993 but only 18.7 percent in fiscal 1999, according to the Congressional Budget Office (CBO).

By comparison, federal spending as a

The National Bureau of Economic Research used a complex formula to decide that the economy has now been growing for a record 107 consecutive months. As measured solely by the gross domestic product (GDP), however, the economy shrank once in that period, just as Clinton took office. The timeline shows the percentage change in the GDP in each quarter of the last decade and some of the key events that Washington policy-makers say have kept the expansion going.

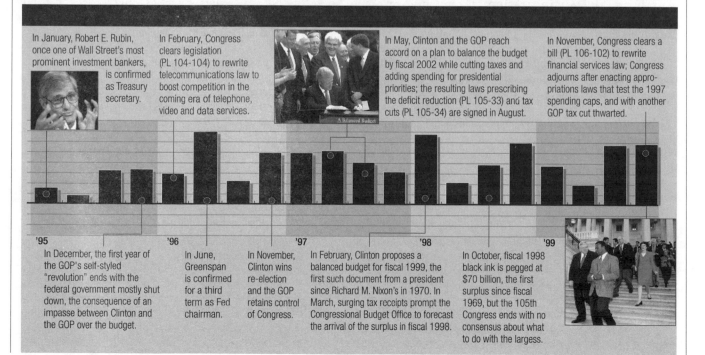

In January, Robert E. Rubin, once one of Wall Street's most prominent investment bankers, is confirmed as Treasury secretary.

In February, Congress clears legislation (PL 104-104) to rewrite telecommunications law to boost competition in the coming era of telephone, video and data services.

In May, Clinton and the GOP reach accord on a plan to balance the budget by fiscal 2002 while cutting taxes and adding spending for presidential priorities; the resulting laws prescribing the deficit reduction (PL 105-33) and tax cuts (PL 105-34) are signed in August.

In November, Congress clears a bill (PL 106-102) to rewrite financial services law; Congress adjourns after enacting appropriations laws that test the 1997 spending caps, and with another GOP tax cut thwarted.

A Balanced Budget

'95   '96   '97   '98   '99

In December, the first year of the GOP's self-styled "revolution" ends with the federal government mostly shut down, the consequence of an impasse between Clinton and the GOP over the budget.

In June, Greenspan is confirmed for a third term as Fed chairman.

In November, Clinton wins re-election and the GOP retains control of Congress.

In February, Clinton proposes a balanced budget for fiscal 1999, the first such document from a president since Richard M. Nixon's in 1970. In March, surging tax receipts prompt the Congressional Budget Office to forecast the arrival of the surplus in fiscal 1998.

In October, fiscal 1998 black ink is pegged at $70 billion, the first surplus since fiscal 1969, but the 105th Congress ends with no consensus about what to do with the largess.

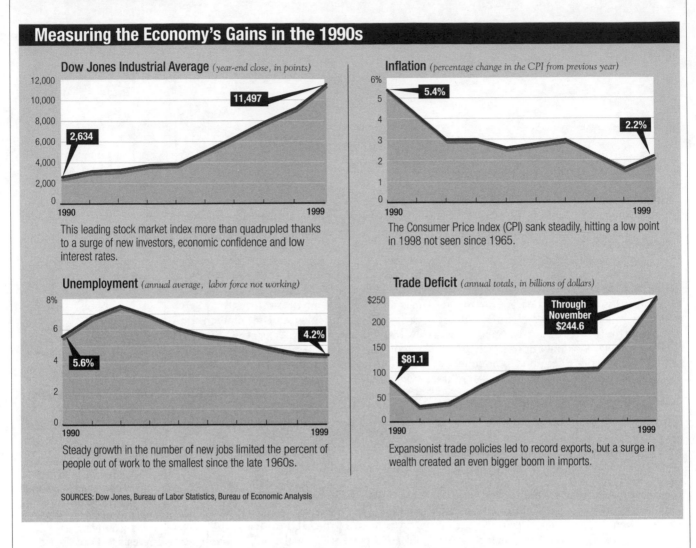

Measuring the Economy's Gains in the 1990s

Dow Jones Industrial Average *(year-end close, in points)*

2,634

11,497

This leading stock market index more than quadrupled thanks to a surge of new investors, economic confidence and low interest rates.

Inflation *(percentage change in the CPI from previous year)*

5.4%

2.2%

The Consumer Price Index (CPI) sank steadily, hitting a low point in 1998 not seen since 1965.

Unemployment *(annual average, labor force not working)*

5.6%

4.2%

Steady growth in the number of new jobs limited the percent of people out of work to the smallest since the late 1960s.

Trade Deficit *(annual totals, in billions of dollars)*

Through November $244.6

$81.1

Expansionist trade policies led to record exports, but a surge in wealth created an even bigger boom in imports.

SOURCES: Dow Jones, Bureau of Labor Statistics, Bureau of Economic Analysis

---

share of the economy ranged from 21.2 percent to as high as 23.5 percent during the administration of Ronald Reagan, the last two-term president. This was largely because his lasting economic legacy included a dramatic boost in defense spending that, his supporters say, aided the domestic economy and helped to end the Cold War.

Of course, the Clinton record is aided immensely by the fact that the economy has grown at a far faster pace than government spending. Angela Antonelli, director of economic policy studies for the Heritage Foundation, a conservative think tank, believes that Clinton will be remembered for ratcheting up domestic spending at the expense of defense spending. Starting with his Jan. 27 State of the Union address, she said, Clinton proposed a "reckless level of spending" that, if enacted, would seriously hamper the ability of his successors to pay down the debt. (*2000 CQ Weekly, p. 174*)

"Spending levels have a significant

impact on the economy," Antonelli observed in a Feb. 1 interview, and too much government spending is the greatest threat to economic growth. "When government gets out of the way, the economy does well."

The nation is fortunate that the strong economy has kept low the portion of the GDP attributable to federal outlays, she said, but if the economy slows, any new spending initiatives that Clinton manages to enact will exacerbate the downturn.

Quiet Budget Exit

This year, Clinton will unveil a budget that ignores the statutory spending caps that he and Congress agreed to as part of the 1997 budget-balancing law (PL 105-33). Whether overtly or covertly, the Republican Congress seems destined to go along. But overall, the fiscal 2001 debate will round out Clinton's impact on budgeting with a whimper. The most important new proposal will be an expansion of Medicare, the federal medical insur-

ance program for senior citizens and the disabled, to cover prescription drugs. Even if Congress accepts some version, Clinton's budget will still project long-term surpluses.

"I want to have fewer gimmicks in this budget than we had last year," Clinton said in explaining his reason for ignoring the spending caps. "What I tried to do is take the money [enacted for this year] and make it the baseline, and then assume a reasonable amount of inflation based on the spending patterns of the last five years or so."

Few are likely to point out that such a formula rolls back the budget debate to the late 1980s, when the GOP said that the only way to rein in government would be to scrap the "current services" concept favored by Democrats, in which budgeting for each program starts with the assumption of an inflationary increase. That is because a new era of potential plenty has arrived for budget writers. Under even its most pessimistic set of assumptions, the CBO projects budget surpluses during the

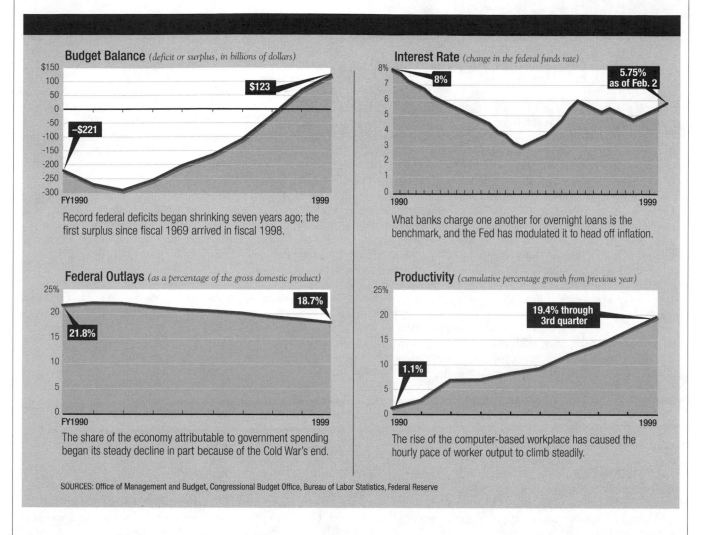

Budget Balance *(deficit or surplus, in billions of dollars)*

$123

−$221

FY1990 — 1999

Record federal deficits began shrinking seven years ago; the first surplus since fiscal 1969 arrived in fiscal 1998.

Interest Rate *(change in the federal funds rate)*

8%

5.75% as of Feb. 2

1990 — 1999

What banks charge one another for overnight loans is the benchmark, and the Fed has modulated it to head off inflation.

Federal Outlays *(as a percentage of the gross domestic product)*

21.8%

18.7%

FY1990 — 1999

The share of the economy attributable to government spending began its steady decline in part because of the Cold War's end.

Productivity *(cumulative percentage growth from previous year)*

19.4% through 3rd quarter

1.1%

1990 — 1999

The rise of the computer-based workplace has caused the hourly pace of worker output to climb steadily.

SOURCES: Office of Management and Budget, Congressional Budget Office, Bureau of Labor Statistics, Federal Reserve

coming decades of a size and duration never before seen in American history. (*2000 CQ Weekly, p. 177*)

In addition to providing an exciting new research opportunity for political scientists, this new era of surplus could fundamentally change the way members of Congress and the president do their jobs. Members of both parties are talking more seriously than ever about switching to a two-year budget cycle, a feat that becomes more workable as Congress moves away from its self-imposed, deficit-era straitjackets — the caps on discretionary spending and the "pay-as-you-go" rules designed to make tax cuts and entitlement expansions a zero-sum game. Both could be shown the door soon by Republicans eager for tax breaks and Democrats excited about new spending opportunities. (*Budgeting, 2000 CQ Weekly, p. 241*)

Partisan Battle Lines Shift

Ground rules for partisan fights over the budget already are evolving. While the most serious battles in Congress dur-

ing the past decade have been over tax increases and spending cuts, the debate now centers on whether surpluses should be used mostly for tax cuts or spending increases. Members of both parties appear to be shrugging off warnings from budget watchdogs that debt reduction should be Congress' first priority, maintaining instead that there is plenty of extra cash to pay down the debt even with tax cuts or spending increases, or both. (*2000 CQ Weekly, p. 120*)

The General Accounting Office, which audits government programs for Congress, issued a report Feb. 1 urging lawmakers to make debt reduction their highest priority. "Reducing interest payments on the debt . . . is critical to providing the fiscal flexibility to address future needs and commitments," the agency's comptroller general, David M. Walker, told the Senate Budget Committee. He said that spending the surplus elsewhere would squander a "golden opportunity" for Congress to get its fiscal house in order.

While Republicans chided Clinton

for proposing to, in effect, hamper debt-reduction efforts with his proposal-filled State of the Union message, the GOP has a big wish list of its own for using revenue that could otherwise service the debt.

"We will have tax cuts every year — every year that I'm majority leader and every year the Republicans are in the majority," Senate Majority Leader Trent Lott, R-Miss., said Feb. 1. One such bill (HR 6), to alleviate the "marriage penalty" in the tax code, is expected on the House floor the week of Feb. 7. (*Taxes, 2000 CQ Weekly, p. 238*)

Among those urging restraint on apportioning the surplus is John M. Spratt Jr., D-S.C., the ranking Democrat on the House Budget Committee. He notes that the CBO forecast based on limiting discretionary spending increases to the rate of inflation starting next year yields $861 billion in cumulative surpluses over the ensuing decade, if the surplus reserved for Social Security is untouched. But that happens only in the absence of a tax cut or a big economic downturn. And there is pressure to spend faster than the current inflation rate. Thus, Spratt calculates, a more realistic 10-year surplus would be "certainly under $500 billion."

New Pressures on the Horizon

The National Bureau of Economic Research declared Feb. 1 that the economic expansion had reached a record 107 consecutive months, besting the period from March 1961 to December 1969. While the ongoing surge helped to erase the three-decade headache of deficit politics for Congress — and has meant manifest good news to most Americans — it has created a potential problem: a dramatically widening wealth gap between the most prosperous and the most poor.

Even if those on the lowest end of the economic scales have made real inflation-adjusted gains in their economic status, huge wealth disparities inevitably provoke calls for government action, said David C. Colander, a historian of economic thought at Middlebury College. The call for federal action will be particularly strong when an economic slowdown or downturn occurs, and lower income Americans "will demand enormous amounts of redistribution," Colander said.

Many economists and political observers see government's role in macroeconomics declining, with factors such as global trade and technological advances having far more important effects. Although the current expansion officially began in April 1991, it would be inaccurate to suggest that the United States was a nation in economic peril in the years before Clinton took office. In general, the economy has been growing strongly since 1983. In fact, Clinton himself recently acknowledged that a restructuring of the American business sector — which began in the 1980s in response to global competitive pressures — was an important factor in today's good economic times.

The last recession, which ended in 1991, was relatively mild and brief; the economy had already begun rebounding even as Clinton was campaigning against President George Bush on the theme that he would take a more activist role in righting economic ills. (*Timeline, pp. 80-81*)

In recent years, whether the White House was occupied by a Democrat or Republican, whether deficits were up or down, whether taxes were cut or raised, the economy seemed to go its own way. The U.S. annual GDP has not contracted for two years in a row since 1975. The economy grew despite the deficits that mushroomed under Reagan, and while taxes were cut and then raised during his presidency. The economy stumbled as Bush signed a tax increase in 1990 but grew after Clinton's 1993 tax increase.

Most economists believe that "the fiscal policy of the president and Congress plays a relatively small role in what goes on in the economy," said James R. Horney, a chief forecaster for the CBO from 1992 to 1999 and now a senior fellow at the Center on Budget and Policy Priorities, a liberal think tank.

The best thing federal lawmakers can do for the economy usually is to avoid actions that would hurt growth, he said in a Feb. 1 interview. Horney's organization and other budget watchdog groups are warning that Congress and some of the presidential candidates are poised to do exactly what they should not do: endanger the economy by pushing for big tax cuts or spending increases that would claim the projected budget surpluses, slow debt repayment and endanger growth.

Colander agreed that the best thing a president can do for the economy is to stay out of the way. He concludes that Clinton generally has done so, but that the public does not accept the extremely limited role presidents may play in guiding the economy. That is another reason the next recession will spur calls for government intervention, he said.

An Evolving Economic Focus

Early in his presidency, Clinton saw the federal budget as a tool for economic stimulation and job creation, as well as a safety net for the unemployed or under-employed. Clinton won the presidency by suggesting he would use the government to prime the pump on a sluggish economy; he sounded less interested in partaking in other government economic roles, such as keeping the financial markets happy and restraining inflation.

While he signaled a shift toward an interest in deficit reduction with his initial nominees for top economic posts — including Senate Finance Committee Chairman Lloyd Bentsen, D-Texas (1971-93), for Treasury secretary and House Budget Committee Chairman Leon E. Panetta, D-Calif. (1977-93), for Office of Management and Budget director — Clinton remained frustrated with the early fiscal-policy positioning of his administration. "We stand for lower deficits and free trade and the bond market. Isn't that great," Clinton said sarcastically at an April 1993 staff meeting, according to Bob Woodward's account of Clinton's first year, "The Agenda."

Seven years later, Clinton declared a respect for the role of government in maintaining economic health that went far beyond the types of job training programs and low-income tax credits that filled the book detailing his initial campaign platform, "Putting People First." The record expansion "was earned by the American people through hard work, high technology, open markets and fiscal discipline," he said at a Feb. 1 news briefing. "We ought to be determined to continue, to deepen, to improve."

Speaking at the same event, Senate Minority Leader Tom Daschle, D-S.D., said of the economic expansion, "it's no accident that it's happening now. It's a result of discipline, it's a result of real, sound fiscal and monetary leadership, and we can take great pride in it."

At another event the same day, Clinton shared the credit with Alan Greenspan, who he said "sensed somewhere along the way there was something fundamentally different going on, and he realized he did not have to stop it because we had 'X' years at 3.5 or 4 percent growth, or some other indicator that always before had been a good rule of thumb." On Feb. 3, the Senate confirmed Greenspan to a fourth term as chairman of the Federal Reserve. (*Story, p. 85*)

The Budget as History

In many ways, both the Reagan and Bush eras were defined by fights over the budget. The Reagan era is remembered for tax cuts, domestic spending cuts, increased defense spending and a ballooning deficit. Although Republicans often blame the Democratically controlled Congress for deficit spending during the 1980s, Reagan never submitted a balanced budget for congressional consideration, and the budget he submitted to Congress during his final full year in office called for a $129.5 billion deficit. (*1988 Almanac, p.181*)

For Bush, the decision to break the

One Who Gets Credit

Among those given credit for the economy are Clinton; Rubin, his second Treasury secretary, left; and Greenspan. They are shown at a 1998 economic conference.

With a bipartisan chorus giving him much of the credit for an economic expansion of record duration, the Senate voted 89-4 on Feb. 3 to confirm Alan Greenspan for a fourth term as chairman of the Federal Reserve Board of Governors. (*Vote 6, 2000 CQ Weekly, p. 268*)

Confirmation came one day after the Fed raised the federal funds interest rate — what banks charge one another for overnight loans — by one quarter of a percentage point, to 5.75 percent. It was the fourth time the Fed has raised that benchmark since June in an effort to temper the pace of the economy's growth and thereby keep inflation in check.

But the action gave fresh ammunition to the small cadre of Greenspan critics in the Senate, who say his moves against inflation have an unwelcome trickle-down effect, by making it more difficult for many people to obtain financing for new home purchases or business expenses. "My farmers, who are already hurting enough," lamented Tom Harkin, D-Iowa, "are going to get hit again." Byron L. Dorgan, D-N.D., called the rate increases "a tax on every single American."

Fewer sided with that view this time than these detractors had predicted, and fewer than when Greenspan was last reconfirmed, four years ago. His new term as chairman begins in June and runs to June 2004, when he will be 78. (*Background, 2000 CQ Weekly, pp. 183, 55; 1996 Almanac p. 2-62*)

Greenspan boosters noted that Feb. 1 — the day the Senate Banking Committee endorsed the nomination by voice vote — marked a new record for uninterrupted economic growth. Chairman Phil Gramm, R-Texas, said Greenspan deserved a large share of credit for "complementing the tight fiscal policy of the administration and Congress with a monetary policy that has allowed our economy to grow." He said that "a strong case can be made that Alan Greenspan is the greatest central banker in the history of the world."

President Clinton urged Gramm to move on his nomination of Carol J. Parry, a former Chase Manhattan Bank executive, to a vacant Fed seat. Gramm said he would meet with Parry soon. He has denied any intent to keep Fed vacancies open for a new president to fill next year.

"no new taxes" pledge of his 1988 campaign and compromise two years later with the Democrats in Congress will forever figure prominently in discussions of his domestic policy legacy. (*1990 Almanac, p. 111*)

G. William Hoagland, chief of staff of the Senate Budget Committee, said that 1990 tax increase, and Bush's decision to compromise and accept it, do not get nearly enough credit for laying the groundwork for the surpluses that exist today. The savings and loan crisis chewed up the revenue generated by the Bush tax increase, Hoagland said, but that does not change the fact that the nation would have run even deeper deficits and accumulated more debt in the 1990s without the additional revenue, and the federal government would be making larger interest payments on the debt today.

Unlike Reagan and Bush, Clinton's fiscal legacy will be largely disconnected from federal budget politics, Colander said. Instead, it will be marked by presidential action — or absence thereof — that helped bolster the economy and create a surge in tax revenues that helped to balance the budget just months after Clinton's accord with the GOP Congress set out a five-year path for doing so. (*1997 Almanac, p. 2-18*)

Many of these successes must be shared with others. In addition to Greenspan's oft-praised leadership, former Treasury Secretary Robert E. Rubin is widely credited with helping to contain the Asian financial crisis of the late 1990s before it spread to the United States.

Throughout his tenure, Clinton cast about for accomplishments that would define his presidency. His first initiative with big budgetary implications was his attempt to create universal health coverage, which ended in disarray and embarrassment. If enacted, this year's proposed expansion of Medicare to cover prescription drugs could be his most significant, enduring new spending initiative. The welfare overhaul will be a significant marker, but it would not have happened without the election of a Republican Congress in 1994.

So in the end, Clinton raised taxes without sacrificing a second term, pressed to limit defense spending after the Cold War, added a handful of modest programs like AmeriCorps — and allowed a growing economy to balance the budget on his watch. ◆

Politics and Public Policy

Articles in this section discuss major policy issues that have come before Congress in recent months. Some of these were being debated in mid-summer 2000 and might be enacted into law before the current Congress adjourns and the fall elections are held. Others will remain unresolved but are sure to become campaign issues.

This section begins with an article about the debate over the death penalty, an issue that has been following Texas governor George W. Bush on the campaign trail. The article surveys the reasons why the debate has been renewed and discusses proposals now before Congress, including legislation that would give prisoners easier access to DNA testing and legislation that aims to improve the quality of counsel in capital cases.

On May 24 the House passed a bill that would grant China permanent normal trade relations. A bill liberalizing trade with China would be an important step toward fulfilling President Clinton's broad agenda of pursuing market-opening policies and advancing long-term policy goals through international commerce. An article on the House bill details the political maneuvering that took place in the days leading up to the bill's passage, provides an overview of the relations between the two countries in recent times, and speculates about the bill's prospects in the Senate. A separate article examines the likely political consequences of the vote for members on each side of the issue.

A heated debate is beginning over whether Congress should take action to protect the privacy of Internet users. The next article examines some of the measures proposed by consumer advocates for restricting the rights of companies to share information about consumers without their consent. Online businesses, concerned that consent requirements would destroy the valuable ability to deliver sales pitches to targeted groups over the Internet, have begun working with some members to establish a common ground. A related article discusses possible law enforcement responses to computer hacker attacks, some of which could possibly compromise the privacy of individual users.

The final article in this section discusses proposals for giving Medicare beneficiaries prescription drug coverage, an issue critical to attracting the votes of seniors.

The Death Penalty: Shifting Perspectives

Rep. Henry J. Hyde is no bleeding heart liberal. So his support for a fresh look at the fairness of the death penalty shows just how much the debate has shifted in recent years.

"I am not yet ready to reject capital punishment in all circumstances," Hyde, R-Ill., said in an interview May 3. "But I think we all have had second thoughts." Those who believe in the system, he said, "have had our confidence shaken" by stories of innocent people narrowly avoiding execution.

Hyde is responding to a chorus of national leaders who are calling for a re-examination of the death penalty, which is allowed in 38 states and in federal law. Since the Supreme Court reinstated the penalty in 1976, about 600 people have been executed. During the same time, 87 death row inmates have been freed after proving their innocence.

The death penalty has been controversial for decades, and those on the political left who oppose it on moral grounds have tried for years to eliminate it without success. To the contrary, the 1990s brought an increase in both the number of crimes punishable by death and in annual executions, from 23 in 1990 to 98 in 1999.

The difference now is that leading voices asking for a re-evaluation are conservatives such as Christian Coalition founder Pat Robertson and columnist George Will. Their arguments center not on the morality of the punishment — most conservatives agree it is appropriate and morally justified — but on whether the system is functioning properly or too often ensnaring the innocent.

Indeed, there is concern that Congress went too far in the 1990s by limiting death row inmates' right to appeal and eliminating funds for federal centers that helped train lawyers in capital punishment law. Others argue that states and the federal government are failing to accommodate new technologies — such as DNA testing — that could help prisoners exonerate themselves.

House and Senate lawmakers have introduced legislation that would make it easier for prisoners to get access to DNA tests, while requiring the 38 states that impose the death penalty to ensure that defendants get adequate legal representation. Congress is likely to hold hearings on these measures sometime this year. Still, some top Republicans prefer that Congress not get involved, particularly in an election year in which the presumptive GOP presidential nominee, Texas Gov. George W. Bush, leads the state that leads the nation in executions.

Energizing the Debate

Republican Gov. George Ryan of Illinois energized the death penalty debate in January when he declared a moratorium on executions in his state after 13 people were released from death row upon proving their innocence. And on May 18 the New Hampshire Legislature became the first in decades to vote to repeal the death penalty — although Democratic Gov. Jeanne Shaheen vetoed the bill the next day.

Democratic Rep. Jesse L. Jackson Jr. of Illinois and Democratic Sen. Russell D. Feingold of Wisconsin have introduced legislation (HR 4162, S 2463) that would impose a national moratorium on executions. Feingold's measure would halt executions until a blue-ribbon panel examined the death penalty system and recommended improvements. States that allow the death penalty could not resume executions until Congress repealed the moratorium. These measures have little chance of passage, however, in a Congress in which the majority has voted for tougher capital punishment laws.

More likely to be considered are a Senate bill (S 2073) by Patrick J. Leahy, D-Vt., and a House bill (HR 4167) by Bill Delahunt, D-Mass., and cosponsored by Ray LaHood, R-Ill., that would ease prisoners' access to DNA tests, which map genetic information from evidence left at the scene of a crime that can help people prove their innocence. The bills also would require states that allow the death penalty to improve the quality of counsel in capital cases in order to qualify for $400 million in federal crime-fighting grants.

House Speaker J. Dennis Hastert, R-Ill., a supporter of the

CQ Weekly June 3, 2000

Number of People Executed, By Jurisdiction

Since the Supreme Court reinstated the death penalty in 1976, 30 states have executed 598 prisoners. One person was executed in 1977 and 98 were executed in 1999 — the highest number since 1951, when 105 prisoners were executed. Of the 598 executed, 342 were white, 211 were black, 34 were Hispanic and 11 were from other racial or ethnic groups. Thirteen jurisdictions have no death penalty: Alaska, Hawaii, Iowa, Maine, Massachusetts, Michigan, Minnesota, North Dakota, Rhode Island, Vermont, West Virginia, Wisconsin and the District of Columbia.

STATE	NUMBER EXECUTED 1977-99
Texas	199
Virginia	73
Florida	44
Missouri	41
Louisiana	25
South Carolina	24
Georgia	23
Arkansas	21
Alabama	19
Arizona	19
Oklahoma	19
North Carolina	15
Illinois	12
Delaware	10
Nevada	8
California	7
Indiana	7
Utah	6
Mississippi	4
Maryland	3
Nebraska	3
Pennsylvania	3
Washington	3
Kentucky	2
Montana	2
Oregon	2
Colorado	1
Idaho	1
Ohio	1
Wyoming	1

SOURCE: Bureau of Justice Statistics

death penalty, has said he wants HR 4167 to get a thorough examination. Hyde, chairman of the House Judiciary Committee, and his Senate counterpart, Orrin G. Hatch, R-Utah, have both said they want to hold hearings this year.

Not all Republicans agree that Congress should get involved. "It's something that I don't think Congress will speak to for the time being," Senate Republican Policy Committee Chairman Larry E. Craig, R-Idaho, said May 2.

Senate Majority Leader Trent Lott, R-Miss., has indicated he feels the same way, as has Texas Gov. Bush. Texas leads the states in the number of executions from 1977 through 1999, with 199. Virginia is second, with 73. Bush has said he is "confident that every person who has been put to death in Texas under my watch has been guilty of the crime charged." Still, on June 1, Bush ordered an execution halted for 30 days to allow new DNA testing, and Virginia Gov. James S. Gilmore III ordered new DNA tests for a man imprisoned for 17 years.

Lott may want to keep the death penalty debate out of the Senate until after the November election. Further, prosecutors are concerned that the anti-death penalty campaign is just the opening salvo in attacks on tough sentences for criminals — although ironically it could help those who support the death penalty by neutralizing arguments that the system is unfair.

Steve Stewart, prosecuting attorney for Clark County, Ind., said that while "those of us in the business are concerned that our system is an accurate one . . . I think the claims have been greatly exaggerated." He added: "It would be ridiculous for any prosecutor to try to keep out any DNA evidence." The fear among prosecutors, Stewart said, is that "ultimately, any law [Congress] may pass could let a killer back out on the streets."

Lott and others may not be able to stave off hearings if momentum continues to build. The issue seems likely to get considerable attention this summer, when the federal government may use its new execution chamber in Terre Haute, Ind., for the first time. The last federal execution took place in Iowa in 1963 when Victor Feguer was hanged for kidnapping and killing a doctor. Now Juan Raul Garza, convicted of three murders, has exhausted all appeals and faces execution. (*Federal death row, p. 92*)

Changing Tide

The renewed national debate on the death penalty reflects a marked change in direction and circumstances. In the past two decades, members of Congress, responding to increasing public frustration with crime, have extended the death penalty to cover more than 60 crimes and have sped up executions by limiting a convicted person's right to appeal. A 1978 Gallup Poll found that 62 percent of Americans supported the death penalty. By 1994, that percentage had risen to 80 percent. (*History, p. 90*)

But the violent crime rate has dropped in each of the past seven years. With new stories every month about people who came within days of execution for crimes they did not commit, public support for the death penalty dropped in 2000 to 66 percent, according to a Gallup Poll, its lowest level since 1981.

Two events this year have helped focus attention on the death penalty. The first was Gov. Ryan's decision Jan. 31 to impose a moratorium in Illinois, which has executed 12 people since 1977. The moratorium will last until a 14-member panel appointed by Ryan on March 9 completes a review. "I can only draw one conclusion: Our system is broken," he said that day. The panel is headed by former U.S. District Judge Frank Mc-Garr and includes former Democratic Sen. Paul Simon of Illinois (1985-97), and novelist and lawyer Scott Turow. Former FBI and CIA Director William H. Webster is a special adviser.

Another goad was the publication

Landmark Rulings and Laws On the Death Penalty

These are the key federal laws and Supreme Court rulings affecting the death penalty system:

■ **1972:** The Supreme Court ruling in *Furman v. Georgia* nullifies all death penalty statutes in the United States. The justices rule, 5-4, that the death penalty violates the Eighth Amendment because judges and juries have so much discretion that the results are "arbitrary, irrational, and deprived defendants of due process of law." The Eighth Amendment to the Bill of Rights provides that in dealing with the accused, "Excessive bail shall not be required, nor excessive fines imposed, nor cruel and unusual punishments inflicted." Justice Potter Stewart describes the existing process as "cruel and unusual in the same way that being struck by lightning is cruel and unusual."

■ **1974:** Congress passes a law (PL 93-366) imposing the death penalty for anyone guilty of aircraft hijacking resulting in a death. Members say the statute is narrow and specific enough to pass constitutional muster. *(1974 Almanac, p. 275)*

■ **1976:** The Supreme Court rules, 7-2, in *Gregg v. Georgia* and related cases that death as a punishment for first-degree murder is not necessarily cruel and unusual punishment. The court rules that laws that provide for a two-part criminal procedure — one to determine guilt and one for sentencing — are constitutional because they allow the judge and jury to consider an offender's character and the particular circumstances of a crime. The court rules, 5-4, in *Woodson v. North Carolina* that mandatory death penalties for first-degree murder are unconstitutional.

■ **1977:** The Supreme Court rules, 7-2, in *Coker v. Georgia* that the death penalty for rape is a disproportionate penalty forbidden under the Eighth Amendment.

■ **1982:** The high court rules, 5-4, in *Enmund v. Florida* that it is cruel and unusual punishment for the driver of a getaway car to be sentenced to death after conviction for first-degree murder if he did not witness or commit the crime.

■ **1986:** In *Ford v. Wainwright,* the high court rules, 5-4, that it is unconstitutional to execute an insane prisoner.

■ **1987:** The Supreme Court rules, 5-4, in *McClesky v. Kemp* that a defendant may not use broad evidence of racial disparities in death sentencing as evidence of racial discrimination in his own sentence.

■ **1988:** President George Bush signs the anti-drug law (PL 100-690) that authorizes the death penalty for anyone who causes the death of a local law enforcement officer and for drug-related felonies resulting in death. *(1988 Almanac, p. 85)*

■ **1989:** The high court rules, 5-4, in *Penry v. Lynaugh* that it is not cruel and unusual punishment to execute a mentally retarded person. It rules, 5-4, in *Stanford v. Kentucky* that it is not cruel and unusual punishment to execute juveniles ages 16 and 17.

■ **1991:** In *Payne v. Tennessee,* the court rules, 6-3, that it is permissible to use "victim impact statements" during sentencing hearings in capital cases. Such statements refer to evidence regarding the emotional impact of a murder on the victim's family. In *McClesky v. Zant,* the court rules, 6-3, to effectively make it

in February of "Actual Innocence," a book by New York Daily News columnist Jim Dwyer and O.J. Simpson's lawyers Barry Scheck and Peter Neufeld, about people released from death row, sometimes after decades in prison. Scheck and Neufeld head the Innocence Project at the Benjamin N. Cardozo School of Law in New York, which seeks to free the wrongly convicted. The project has secured the release of 37 inmates so far.

According to the book, newly tested DNA evidence secured the release of 67 people between 1992 and 1999. The book lists reasons for so many incorrect convictions, from incompetent lawyers to questionable actions by police and prosecutors to victims convinced they have identified their attacker, only to

have later evidence prove them wrong.

Columnist Will wrote that the book "compels the conclusion that many innocent people are in prison, and some innocent people have been executed."

Hollywood has taken note of the book, too. A recent three-episode story in "The Practice," a popular ABC drama, featured a man on death row who had inadequate counsel, who could not get DNA evidence retested and who was convicted, in part, on the testimony of a drunken eyewitness — a scenario straight

out of "Actual Innocence."

On May 11, the Constitution Project, a nonprofit, bipartisan group formed to focus public attention on constitutional issues, announced the formation of the National Committee to Prevent Wrongful Executions. Former FBI Director William Sessions is a member,

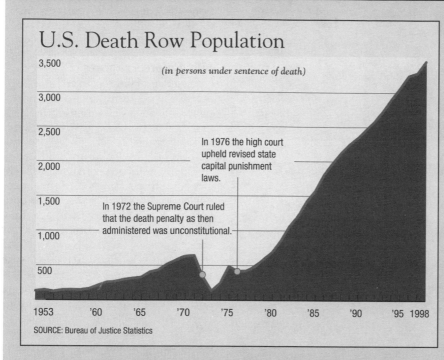

U.S. Death Row Population

(in persons under sentence of death)

3,500
3,000
2,500
2,000
1,500
1,000
500

In 1976 the high court upheld revised state capital punishment laws.

In 1972 the Supreme Court ruled that the death penalty as then administered was unconstitutional.

1953 '60 '65 '70 '75 '80 '85 '90 '95 1998

SOURCE: Bureau of Justice Statistics

extremely difficult for multiple habeas corpus petitions to be heard. Such a petition seeks review of a conviction, asserting that an inmate's constitutional rights have been violated.

■ **February 1994:** In his dissent in *Callins v. James*, in which the court denied a review in a Texas death penalty case, Justice Harry A. Blackmun declares that he will no longer vote to uphold death sentences. He says he hopes that the "court eventually will conclude that the effort

to eliminate arbitrariness while preserving fairness in the infliction of death is so plainly doomed to failure that it and the death penalty must be abandoned altogether."

■ **September 1994:** President Clinton signs comprehensive anti-crime legislation (PL 103-322). The law includes provisions authorizing the federal death penalty for dozens of crimes if they result in death, including hostage taking, carjacking, sexual exploitation of children, drive-by shootings, kidnapping, racketeering

and torture. It also authorizes the death penalty for genocide, civil rights murders and murder of federal witnesses. *(1994 Almanac, p. 273)*

■ **1996:** Clinton signs anti-terrorism legislation (PL 104-132) that includes death penalty provisions. The law restricts the ability of state and federal prisoners to challenge the constitutionality of their convictions in federal court. For prisoners on death row to obtain a second round of federal review, they must file a petition within six months of exhausting state appeals. A panel of federal appellate judges needs to see new evidence that shows "clear and convincing" proof of a defendant's innocence. The panel's decision cannot be appealed. The death penalty becomes available for cases of international terrorism resulting in death. *(1996 Almanac, p. 5-18)*

■ **1998:** Upholding the spirit of the 1996 anti-terrorism legislation, the high court rules, 5-4, in *Calderon v. Thompson*, that the 9th U.S. Circuit Court of Appeals committed a "grave abuse of discretion" by halting the execution of a convicted rapist and murderer in California. It also rules that an appeals court may change a state death sentence only if presented with "clear and convincing evidence" of a defendant's innocence.

as are former Clinton White House counsel Charles F.C. Ruff and Beth Wilkinson, the federal prosecutor who tried the Oklahoma City bombing case.

On May 18, after a decadelong campaign by activists against capital punishment, the New Hampshire Senate voted 14-10 to repeal the state's death penalty. The state House passed the legislation March 9. But Gov. Shaheen vetoed the measure May 19, saying she believed that some crimes are so heinous they should be punishable by death.

History

The death penalty was legal in most jurisdictions until 1972, when the Supreme Court ruling in *Furman v. Georgia* struck down most statutes, saying the punishment was inflicted too

arbitrarily. States then rewrote their statutes and in 1976, in *Gregg v. Georgia*, the court held that the new laws were constitutional. *(1976 Almanac, p. 951; 1972 Almanac, p. 87)*

Gary Gilmore was the first person executed after the *Gregg* decision. He was killed by firing squad in Utah on Jan. 17, 1977. Congress did not enact broad death penalty legislation until 1988, when members made some drug offenses subject to capital punishment (PL 100-690). In the 1994 omnibus anti-crime bill (PL 103-322), Congress expanded the number of crimes subject to the death penalty to about 60. *(1994 Almanac, p. 273, 1988 Almanac, p. 85)*

In 1996, Congress passed legislation (PL 104-132) dramatically limiting the appeals process for state and federal

prisoners convicted of capital crimes. The law set time limits for appeals and forbade federal judges from overturning a state court verdict if it was "reasonable." *(1996 Almanac, p. 5-18)*

In 1995, Congress eliminated funding for a federal judiciary program that paid for Death Penalty Resource Centers, where attorneys in capital cases could get legal advice from experts on complicated capital punishment law. Critics of the centers said they had become magnets for anti-death penalty advocates. But critics of the death penalty often cite inadequate counsel — such as the lawyer who appeared to sleep through a trial in Texas — as a major reason for convictions of the innocent. *(Representation, p. 93)*

LaHood said some of these changes

Federal Convicts on Death Row

There are 17 people on federal death row, including four sentenced under the 1988 anti-drug abuse law (PL 100-690) and 13 sentenced under the 1994 anti-crime bill (PL 103-322), which broadened the definition of capital crimes.

Sentenced under the 1988 law were:

■ **Richard Tipton**
Sentenced in February 1993 for participating in a series of drug-related murders in Richmond, Va.

■ **Cory Johnson**
Sentenced in February 1993 for the same crimes as Tipton.

■ **James H. Roane Jr.**
Sentenced in February 1993 for the same crimes as Tipton and Johnson.

■ **Juan Raul Garza**
Sentenced in August 1993 for the murder of three drug traffickers in Texas. He faces execution this summer.

Sentenced under the 1994 law were:

■ **Louis Jones**
Sentenced in November 1995 for the kidnap-murder of a female soldier in Texas. The U.S. Supreme Court confirmed the conviction on June 21, 1999.

■ **Orlando Hall**
Sentenced in November 1995 for the abduction, sexual assault and murder of a 16-year-old female in Fort Worth, Texas.

■ **Bruce Webster**
Sentenced in June 1996 for the same crime as Hall.

■ **Bountaem Chanthadara**
Sentenced in October 1996 for the armed robbery-murder of the female proprietor of a Chinese restaurant in Wichita, Kan.

■ **Anthony Battle**
Sentenced in March 1997 for the murder of a prison guard at the federal penitentiary in Atlanta.

■ **Timothy McVeigh**
Sentenced in June 1997 for the bombing of the Oklahoma City federal building in 1995. The U.S. Supreme Court denied a review on March 8, 1999.

■ **Jeffrey Paul**
Sentenced in June 1997 for the robbery-murder of a retired National Park Service employee on federal land in Arkansas.

■ **Darryl Alamont Johnson**
Sentenced on Nov. 17, 1997, for ordering the murder of two informants in Illinois in connection with the Gangster Disciples drug conspiracy cases.

■ **Aquilia Barnette**
Sentenced Feb. 10, 1998, for murdering his former girlfriend in Virginia and for murdering a man in North Carolina during a carjacking.

■ **Billie Jerome Allen**
Sentenced in March 1998 for the fatal shooting of a bank guard during a robbery in St. Louis.

■ **Norris Holder**
Sentenced in April 1998 for the same crime as Allen.

■ **David Paul Hammer**
Sentenced on July 24, 1998, for killing an inmate at the federal penitentiary at Allenwood, Pa. Hammer was serving three consecutive 400-year sentences after being convicted in Oklahoma of car theft, kidnapping and shooting with the intent to kill.

■ **Richard Thomas Stitt**
Sentenced in November 1998 for ordering the murder of three people in Norfolk, Va.

might have led to current dissatisfaction with the death penalty system. "I think they will get re-examined" when lawmakers consider his bill, he said.

Bills Before Congress

Hyde and Hatch plan to hold hearings on legislation that would address two major areas of contention in death penalty cases: DNA testing and defense attorneys.

The bills by Delahunt and Leahy would allow anyone convicted in a federal court to ask for DNA testing of key evidence. Current law is unclear concerning a prisoner's right to get these tests, especially after conviction. Only three states — Illinois, New York and Washington — explicitly authorize DNA testing after a conviction. Moreover, many death row prisoners were convicted prior to recent developments in DNA testing, according to "Actual Innocence." The new technology allows for accurate results on small samples taken many years ago.

"From a prosecutor's point of view . . . I'd be all for it," said Leahy, a former prosecutor. "If you've got the right person, it would probably help you" get a conviction, he said. Senate Judiciary Chairman Hatch agreed: "To the extent that DNA could alleviate doubt, we should use it."

The bills would require that in federal cases, the federal government keep all biological crime evidence to allow for requests for DNA testing, unless the prisoner was given 90 days' notice that the government intended to destroy the material. To obtain a DNA test, inmates would have to show that the evidence was related to their conviction and that they wanted a test that had not been performed already.

Under the bills, states would have to adopt similar rules to be eligible for federal DNA grant funds. Under current "new evidence" laws in some states, defendants have only a few months after conviction in which they can introduce new evidence — effectively prohibiting new tests on old evidence.

The bills also would draw on the federal government's authority under the 14th Amendment to prohibit states from denying requests for DNA testing that could provide exculpatory evidence or evidence that could help a case. States would have to inform jurors in capital cases of all sentencing options, in order to be eligible for federal truth-in-sentencing grants — money awarded to

Congress Considers Taking a Role In Improving Quality of Counsel

Carl Johnson, convicted of killing a 75-year-old security guard during a robbery, was executed in Texas in 1995. The Texas high court had declined to overturn his conviction, although Johnson claimed he had inadequate legal representation. Among Johnson's complaints: His attorney slept through part of the trial.

The U.S. Supreme Court ruled in 1963 in *Gideon v. Wainwright* that anyone — rich or poor — facing serious criminal charges is entitled to a lawyer. The plaintiff in that case, Clarence Earl Gideon, was eventually acquitted. In his retrial for burglary charges, his attorney investigated the crime scene and took apart the prosecution's case.

That lawyer was apparently well prepared. As the case of Carl Johnson suggests, and many critics of the death penalty contend, not all defense lawyers measure up. Nearly 40 years after *Gideon*, one of the biggest battles in the fight over the death penalty is whether those on trial for their lives are adequately represented. According to "Actual Innocence," a book by death penalty lawyers Barry Scheck and Peter Neufeld and reporter Jim Dwyer, about one-quarter of capital prisoners who are ultimately proved innocent had poor legal counsel at some point during their case.

Grab Bag of Laws

In federal death penalty cases, the appointment of counsel is standard procedure for defendants who cannot afford an attorney. The federal government reimburses the attorneys at $125 an hour (more than most states

pay) and allows for expenses. The average cost for a federal death penalty defense, which typically takes eight years, is $130,000.

In state death penalty cases, appointment of counsel depends on the state. Moreover, many states do not appoint lawyers during state appeals, which come after conviction but before federal appeals. When an inmate reaches the final level of federal appeal, paid counsel is appointed. Under current law, no evidence may be introduced in the final federal appeal that has not already been introduced at the state level.

Procedure for appointing counsel varies from state to state. California and New York, for example, have well-funded public defender's offices with experience in handling capital cases. Texas does not have a centralized system. Each of the state's 254 counties can decide whether to have a public defender's office.

"Most states that impose the death penalty most frequently do not have a public defender system," said Elisabeth Semel, director of the American Bar Association's Death Penalty Representation Project, which tries to find lawyers to work without compensation for indigents in capital cases.

States and counties that do not have a public defender system rely on counsel appointed by the trial judge. Payment of appointees varies widely. In Mississippi, the fee is a flat $1,000 for a capital trial, plus expenses. In Louisiana, some lawyers are paid only for expenses.

"It's a mess," said death penalty at-

torney Martin McClain, who has been involved in capital cases in Florida, Missouri, New York and Wyoming. In states that pay little, he said, "you get the bottom-of-the-barrel attorneys who are desperate for money."

Congressional Proposal

The House and Senate Judiciary committees may hold hearings this year on legislation (HR 4167, S 2073) that aims to improve the quality of counsel in capital cases. It would require the 38 states that allow the death penalty to meet certain criteria to qualify for $400 million in federal crime-fighting grants. Patrick J. Leahy of Vermont, sponsor of the Senate bill and ranking Democrat on Judiciary, said there is no reason Congress cannot tell states "to get that [money], there are some things you have to do."

Under both bills, states would be required to set up a central, independent authority to appoint lawyers for indigents in capital cases and to pay attorneys a "reasonable" hourly rate as well as administrative costs.

The bills also would authorize capital representation grants to public and private organizations to help train and recruit qualified lawyers, similar to the Death Penalty Resource Centers, which lost congressional funding in 1995. Some conservatives said the centers had become lobbying forces for anti-death penalty activists. Semel said the centers got many clients released from death row. "They were victims of their own success," she said.

states that require prisoners to serve at least 85 percent of their sentences.

The bills would remove barriers to moving a case to federal court if a state failed to provide the defendant with adequate legal services. They also would increase federal funding for public and private groups to help defense lawyers in capital cases do a better job.

For those wrongly convicted in federal cases, the bills would authorize com-

pensation of up to $50,000 a year per year in prison for non-death penalty cases and up to $100,000 in capital cases.

The bills would limit the federal government's ability to seek the death penalty in states or jurisdictions, including the District of Columbia, that do not permit the death penalty. And the bills would allow federal juries to impose a life sentence instead of the death penalty in drug kingpin cases. LaHood, who sup-

ports the death penalty, is optimistic about his bipartisan proposal. "This is really catching fire," he said.

Hastert, like LaHood, is no death penalty foe. He voted for the 1988 law that reinstated the federal death penalty and for other measures to extend it. But he supports hearings on the Delahunt-LaHood plan. "We have to make sure only guilty people end up on death row," he said May 4. ◆

Despite solid House vote, smooth going from here is not a given

Big Victory for China Trade Needs Senate's Blessing

An unexpectedly strong House vote to usher China into the new global economy is evidence that a bipartisan coalition can be formed in Congress to endorse trade expansion — but only when the benefits are overwhelmingly embraced by American business, and only if the concerns of detractors and skeptics are addressed head-on.

Such was the case as President Clinton worked with Speaker J. Dennis Hastert, R-Ill. and his tenacious majority whip, Tom DeLay, R-Texas, to secure House passage on May 24 of the legislation (HR 4444) that would make permanent China's standing as a regular trading partner of the United States, ensuring that U.S. goods and services reap the full benefits of a market-opening deal that the administration reached with Beijing last year.

The vote was 237-197, the majority formed when better than one-third of the chamber's Democrats joined nearly three-quarters of its Republicans. (*Vote 228, 2000 CQ Weekly, p. 1306*)

That 30-vote margin was the result of patient negotiations, all-out lobbying by business coalitions and not-so-subtle dealmaking by the White House. It was also a step toward a broader approach to trade policy, which the administration was criticized for pushing in the most recent round of talks by the World Trade Organization (WTO) — one that recognizes human rights, labor standards and other issues as relevant in charting economic relations between nations.

But those very provisions, crafted to win over perhaps 30 House members and guarantee victory, may well lead to delays in the Senate. Majority Leader Trent Lott, R-Miss., would prefer to pass a bill without the add-ons and says he is inclined to send the House bill to committee instead of directly to the Senate floor after the Memorial Day recess.

There is little chance such a delay would dampen Senate enthusiasm for the proposal; at least 70 senators are said to be committed to voting "yes." Forestalling the vote until the time of the Independence Day recess, however, would make supporters anxious, and they seem certain to pressure Lott to rethink his statements and to quickly clear the House bill. If the Senate passes its own, more straightforward bill (S 2277) or amends the House's legislation, the issue will have to return to the House for reconsideration.

"Another vote over here is not something everybody's looking forward to," said Thomas J. Donohue, president of the U.S. Chamber of Commerce, which made House passage of the bill the object of an intense and expensive campaign.

Clinton and House Republican leaders said they intended to press the Senate to take up the House bill. "I am confident it too will act swiftly to advance these interests," Clinton said May 24. "I will be speaking with many senators in the days ahead to ensure that we continue to move ahead to get this done as promptly as possible."

By abandoning an annual renewal of China's normal trade relations (NTR) status, both bills would pave the way for that nation to join the WTO and allow the United States to join in fostering a new economy in the most populous nation on Earth. The House bill also includes provisions designed to protect domestic industries harmed by surges in Chinese imports and to monitor Chinese human rights and labor abuses, the key concerns of those opposed to expanding trade with Beijing. (*Highlights, p. 96*)

If the Senate were to make only slight changes to that package, a conference to work out differences between the two chambers could be finished quickly, members said, and the House would probably be able to clear the bill.

Such movement would cement what history may view as Clinton's most significant achievement — bolstering the U.S. economy and advancing long-term foreign policy goals through international commerce. The pivotal decisions would have come at the bookends of his presidency. Congress cleared the North American Free Trade Agreement (NAFTA) at Clinton's urging in 1993. Along with the overhaul of the welfare system, the balancing of the federal budget and the saga of impeachment, the advancement of market-opening policies would likely rate at the top of the Clinton legacy.

A Host of Pressures

But the more circuitous the route the Senate takes, and the more skeptical senators are of the changes the House crafted to keep the proposal alive, the more trouble that could come from a legislative body that not only was designed to thoroughly vet contentious proposals, but also is in the throes of a particularly nasty period of partisan ill will. (*Story, 2000 CQ Weekly, p. 1255*)

"I don't anticipate a jurisdictional roadblock being erected to our being able to do this in a timely fashion, but anything is possible in this place," said Joseph R. Biden Jr. of Delaware, the ranking Democrat on the Foreign Relations Committee, which is likely to hold hearings on the House bill.

Though Lott and Minority Leader Tom Daschle, D-S.D., both support the China measure, they will have to work together to keep members from fatally amending it. While most of those amendments likely would be tabled — or thwarted in advance with a successful vote to invoke cloture, or limit debate — a roster of contentious amendments could drag out Senate debate for more than a week.

Ideas being floated as amendments include an overhaul of campaign finance law. Lobbying on the China bill, which has included thousands of dollars in campaign contributions from both businesses and unions, would provide opponents of the current system with ample evidence to damn it. John McCain of Arizona, who made changing the way money influences politics the centerpiece of his Republican presidential cam-

paign, said May 24 that he reserves the right to try to offer his bill (S 1593) as an amendment. If that happens, Lott said that he would hold McCain responsible for killing the China legislation. *(Background, 2000 CQ Weekly, p. 1084)*

At the same time, Robert G. Torricelli, D-N.J., and Fred Thompson, R-Tenn., held a news conference May 25 to announce that they were introducing a bill (S 2645) to set up an annual presidential review of China's record in supplying nuclear weapons and technology to nations that may not be friendly to the United States, and to require the president to take action if he determines that such transfers are taking place. They said they may attempt to attach that measure to the trade bill as an amendment, though they could be persuaded to move it as a parallel measure just before or after the Senate takes up the China bill. Still, both Torricelli and Thompson would probably vote for the China bill even if their measure were not considered.

Senators more hostile to the bill — generally the most liberal and the most conservative lawmakers — also were readying amendments.

Paul Wellstone, D-Minn., will focus his efforts on monitoring human rights, labor rights and the environment in China and will also touch on agriculture policy, according to his spokesman, Jim Farrell. He said the senator's aim is not to stall the bill but to foster a comprehensive debate.

Foreign Relations Committee Chairman Jesse Helms, R-N.C., enunciated the same goal. In a statement

Last-minute appeals and vote counting were rampant in the hours before the May 24 vote. Bennie Thompson, D-Miss., top left, is wooed outside the Capitol by lobbyist Jake Jones of the AFL-CIO, as Samuel L. Maury, president of the Business Roundtable, approaches over Jones' left shoulder. U.S. Chamber of Commerce President Thomas J. Donohue, near right, confers with Roy Blunt, R-Mo., chief deputy majority whip. Textile and apparel workers' lobbyist Ann Hoffman, below, presses a point with Joseph M. Hoeffel, D-Pa.

Highlights of the House Bill

The heart of the measure (HR 4444) that the House passed, 237-197, on May 24 was the legislative language President Clinton unveiled March 8 for making permanent the favorable trade treatment the United States now affords China one year at a time. Additional provisions were added in the week before the vote in a bid to secure the support of blocs of wavering lawmakers.

ISSUE	DESCRIPTION
Normal Trade Relations	The bill would authorize the president to exempt China from the Jackson-Vanik amendment to the 1974 Trade Act (PL 93-618), and to extend permanent, non-discriminatory treatment to Chinese goods once China is accepted into the World Trade Organization (WTO). Under Jackson-Vanik, normal, non-discriminatory trade status — currently known as normal trade relations (NTR) — can only be extended to some communist countries for one year at a time.
Presidential Certification	Before granting permanent NTR, the president would have to certify to Congress that the terms for China's entry into the WTO are as rigorous as those agreed to between the U.S. and Beijing in 1999.
Anti-Surge Safeguards	The president could increase tariffs and quotas to provide relief to specific domestic industries and workers in response to instances when the U.S. International Trade Commission found that a surge of Chinese imports threatened to disrupt the U.S. market.
Human Rights and Labor Commission	A 23-member commission, its members appointed by Congress and the president, would be created to monitor human rights and labor issues in China. The commission would submit an annual report of its findings on internationally recognized freedoms, such as freedom from torture and from being jailed for political views or advocacy of human rights; freedom from arbitrary arrest, detention or exile; the right to a fair public trial by an independent tribunal; freedom of choice in employment; and freedom of religion.
World Trade Organization Compliance	The Office of the U.S. Trade Representative would be required to issue an annual report on China's compliance with multilateral and bilateral trade agreements. The WTO would be urged to carry out an annual review of China's compliance.
Forced Labor	An interagency task force, headed by the Treasury Department, would be created to monitor imports and promote effective enforcement of U.S. laws barring goods made with forced or prison labor.
Trade Pact Enforcement	Federal agencies would receive additional resources to monitor and enforce trade agreements with China and other nations.
Technical Assistance	The Commerce, State and Labor departments would be directed to provide training and technical assistance to help China develop its labor and commercial laws.
Taiwan	The bill would express the sense of Congress that the WTO should accept Taiwan as a member at the same time China joins.
Radio Free Asia, Voice of America	The bill would authorize $99 million in fiscal 2001 for Radio Free Asia and the Voice of America to expand broadcasts to China and neighboring countries.

May 24, he predicted "robust" Senate deliberations that would delve into prison labor, religious persecution, human rights abuses, proliferation of nuclear weapons, and military threats to Taiwan. "We are going to have a debate, Mr. Clinton. And we are going to have votes, perhaps uncomfortable votes, on a range of issues relating to China," Helms said.

While Lott said in a floor speech May 25 that he did not want to move to limit amendments — a tactic that has increasingly infuriated Democrats — Daschle told reporters May 24 that he would try to quell any attempts by Democrats to offer amendments on some of their main legislative priorities, such as gun control and prescription drug coverage for Medicare beneficiaries.

In addition to the threatened amendments, Lott faces a rapidly dwindling legislative session. When Congress returns the week of June 5, only 11 legislative weeks will remain before Oct. 6, the target adjournment date for the 106th Congress. And the Senate has passed just one fiscal 2001 appropriations bill.

Appropriations Committee Chairman Ted Stevens, R-Alaska, said May 23 that he would push for the Senate to complete action on all 13 spending measures before the China bill is taken up. "Why should we take it up when we can't get other things done?" Stevens asked.

Mitch McConnell, R-Ky., also espoused such a view. The China bill "ought to be the last thing we do after the president signs the last appropriations bill" or "the first thing President Bush will do," he said, referring to Texas Gov. George W. Bush, the presumed GOP nominee.

While such comments indicated some GOP belief that holding up Clinton's capstone legislative achievement might give them some advantages — either in the perennial fight over government funding or perhaps in the campaign — some lobbyists sensed that the Senate, which has received scant attention or campaign largess on the China bill, wants to ensure that it does not pass the measure without receiving some of the political benefits House members garnered.

"There are too many strong supporters over there for this to get derailed, but they certainly want to leverage it as much as they possibly can," said former Rep. Dave McCurdy, D-Okla. (1981-

Enacting Trade Bill Would Not Bridge All That Divides U.S. and China

If the Senate does as is widely expected and joins the House in voting to grant Beijing permanent normal trade relations (NTR), Congress will have provided an opportunity for Sino-American relations to follow a more constructive path.

Still, differences between the two nations — on issues from Taiwan to human rights to nuclear proliferation — remain profound and likely will continue to flare. And many players, including Congress, could still knock relations off course, according to analysts and the senators who will take the next key vote in the trade debate.

"This moves China in the direction of reform, openness, accountability, transparency," said former House Foreign Affairs Committee Chairman Lee H. Hamilton, D-Ind., (1965-99), an expert on Sino-American relations. "But it's not going to be an immediate turnaround. This is going to remain a very difficult relationship for years to come."

Hamilton and many lawmakers nonetheless contend that passage would benefit the relationship of the United States and China both in the short run and in the long term.

John Kerry, D-Mass., a member of the Senate Foreign Relations Committee and a backer of President Clinton's trade proposal, discounts any prospects for a dramatic consequence. "Trade is trade; it's not going to have a profound impact," he said, but congressional backing of a more stable trade relationship "helps the atmosphere" leading to the possibility of accord on other issues.

Permanent NTR "keeps the door open for a huge number of conversations, exchanges which are important," said Richard G. Lugar of Indiana, a senior panel Republican. "It's a signal of whether we want to have much of a relationship or we don't."

Richard H. Solomon, assistant secretary of state for East Asian and Pacific Affairs in the Bush administration, said the vote comes at a "crucial decision point" in China, Taiwan and the United States about how to manage the strategic and economic relationships among the three entities.

House Vote Shows Deep Split

The House's 237-197 vote May 24 demonstrated the deep splits in the United States over relations with China, Solomon said. He noted that Chinese leaders too are "deeply divided" over their relations with the United States and economic reform, while the May 20 inauguration of pro-independence leader Chen Shui-bian underlined political differences on Taiwan, which China considers a renegade province. (*2000 CQ Weekly, p. 675*)

Yet, in recent weeks, all three players have taken steps that could help relations.

In his inaugural speech, Chen repeated a campaign pledge not to declare independence unless Beijing attacks. A day later, he said he was willing to consider opening direct trade, transportation and postal links with the mainland. The trade links could become particularly important if Taiwan, as expected, joins the World Trade Organization (WTO) soon after China.

Beijing, which launched a fusillade of bellicose rhetoric surrounding Chen's election, has since backed down; now Chinese officials say they are willing to wait for him to agree that both governments are part of the same nation without specifying whether Beijing or Taipei is in charge.

"This positions everyone for a new phase that is more constructive than during the last few years, when relations have been more confrontational," Solomon said.

In the longer term, analysts and lawmakers said, the economic change fostered by China's entry into the WTO could bolster political change by spreading Western values and technology while closing state-run factories, thus cutting into the communist parties' political base. "WTO becomes the lever to bring about fundamental change," Hamilton said.

"It's a big step forward, all of whose impacts we can't foresee right now," said Sen. Joseph I. Lieberman, D-Conn., but "some things in China will continue to bother us."

To that end, the House trade measure (HR 4444) includes provisions that highlight the continuing and deep differences between the two countries: establishment of a commission to monitor China's human rights behavior; requirements for an annual review of trade agreements; a potential annual vote on China's human rights practices; additional funds for democracy-building; and creation of a task force on prison and forced labor. (*Highlights, p. 96*)

If the Senate embraces that language, Congress presumably could disrupt U.S.-China relations in the years ahead, just as the annual congressional review of Beijing's trade status has for the past decade. In addition, the Senate still could consider its version (S 693) of a House-passed bill (HR 1838) to strengthen military-to-military ties between the United States and Taiwan. Beijing vigorously opposes the legislation. (*2000 CQ Weekly, p. 953*)

Some senators also fret that if China becomes more prosperous, it will use its new wealth to become a greater threat to the United States and Taiwan. They say it is now up to China to take steps to lower tensions. "The future of U.S.-China relations is going to be determined by China's behavior in the future," said Tim Hutchinson, R-Ark., a leading critic of Beijing.

Another critic, Jon Kyl, R-Ariz., wondered in a May 23 interview whether, in the long run, potential benefits from an improved U.S.-China relationship will be seen as having outweighed the surrender of congressional leverage over China's behavior. "I'm not sure what the end result will be. They ought to be grateful, and relations ought to improve. We'll see."

Analyzing the House Vote

In recent weeks, proponents from both parties of a proposal to make permanent China's status as a normal trading partner of the United States had talked of the same formula for winning House passage: At least 70 Democrats would need to join about 150 Republicans to form the majority. But the roll call May 24 exceeded those expectations: the bill (HR 4444) passed with the votes of 73 Democrats (35 percent of the caucus) and 164 Republicans (74 percent of the caucus) The two independents both voted "no"; one lawmaker, Joe Scarborough, R-Fla., did not vote. *(Vote 228, 2000 CQ Weekly, p. 1306)*

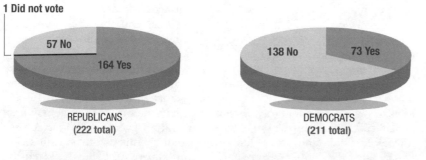

1 Did not vote

57 No
164 Yes
**REPUBLICANS
(222 total)**

138 No   73 Yes
**DEMOCRATS
(211 total)**

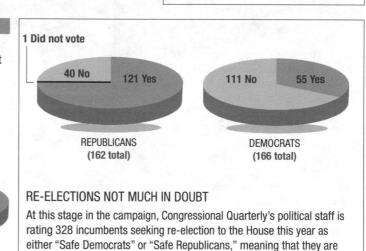

Yes   No

30   23   23   54

REPUBLICANS   DEMOCRATS

SWING VOTE VETERANS

Thirty percent of the House membership, or 130 members, have mixed voting records on the seven previous key trade votes of the past decade, and so were initially seen as pivotal to the outcome by lobbyists on both sides. But, in the end, they voted 53-77 against the China measure. *(Background, 2000 CQ Weekly, p. 449)*

Twelve percent of the members of the House won their most recent race with 55 percent of the vote or less — a traditional way to identify lawmakers with tenuous holds on their seats. Among these are 27 members (12 D, 15 R) who won re-election in 1998, 22 members (13 D, 9 R) sent to Washington in 1998, and two members (one of each party) elected in 1999 special elections.

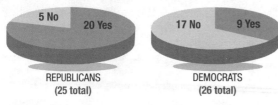

5 No
20 Yes
**REPUBLICANS
(25 total)**

17 No   9 Yes
**DEMOCRATS
(26 total)**

1 Did not vote

40 No   121 Yes
**REPUBLICANS
(162 total)**

111 No   55 Yes
**DEMOCRATS
(166 total)**

RE-ELECTIONS NOT MUCH IN DOUBT

At this stage in the campaign, Congressional Quarterly's political staff is rating 328 incumbents seeking re-election to the House this year as either "Safe Democrats" or "Safe Republicans," meaning that they are virtually certain to hold the seat in November.

95), president of the Electronics Industries Alliance, a high-tech group pushing for expanded trade with China.

Pivotal Promises

The House had been considered the main battleground for the bill since U.S. Trade Representative Charlene Barshefsky and Chinese Premier Zhu Rongji reached agreement in November on a trade pact. China promised to greatly cut its tariffs and other barriers to U.S. imports and investments, while the Clinton administration promised to press for the removal of China from the dwindling list of nations subject to only short-term standing as a regular

U.S. trade partner. Under the 1974 trade law (PL 93-618), the president is required to annually review tariff and quota treatment for some communist nations, including China, and to base renewal decisions on whether the country allows free immigration, a throwback to the days of the Soviet Union. *(2000 CQ Weekly, p. 1168)*

Because Clinton will not be able to permanently normalize China's trade treatment until the legislation is enacted and China joins the WTO — both of which are not likely to occur before China's current NTR status expires July 3 — during the first week of June the president is expected to announce that

he will renew the country's status for another year. It is not clear, however, whether the House will vote on a joint resolution disapproving of the president's decision. Such a measure has been put to a vote annually, although never successfully, for the past decade.

Many members had long expressed frustration that the annual U.S. review of Beijing's policies did not spur much democratization in China — even in years such as 1992, when the House twice voted to place conditions on China's trade standing because of its human rights record. *(1992 Almanac, p. 157)*

But when confronted this year with the proposal to permanently extend

DEMOGRAPHIC CONSIDERATIONS

Congressional Quarterly classifies districts as urban when at least 60 percent of its residents live within central cities of a metropolitan area. Suburban districts are those where 60 percent or more live in a metropolitan area but outside a central city. Rural districts are those where 60 percent live outside a metropolitan area and outside towns with populations of 25,000 or more. The remaining districts are designated as mixed. *(1997 Almanac, p. 10-3)*

URBAN (68 total)

Republican
- Yes: 9
- No: 0

Democrat
- Yes: 22
- No: 37

RURAL (57 total)[2]

Republican
- Yes: 29
- No: 6

Democrat
- Yes: 8
- No: 13

SUBURBAN (159 total)

Republican
- Yes: 61 [1]
- No: 27

Democrat
- Yes: 16
- No: 54

MIXED (151 total)[2]

Republican
- Yes: 65
- No: 24

Democrat
- Yes: 27
- No: 34

■ Yes ▨ No

[1]One Republican did not vote
[2]Independent voted "no"

ECONOMIC CONSIDERATIONS

LABOR'S INFLUENCE

- 22 Yes
- 86 No

These 108 House Democrats, or 52 percent of the caucus, received at least 20 percent of their total contributions for their most recent campaigns from labor political action committees.

SOURCE: Federal Election Commission

WHITE-COLLAR DISTRICTS

- 63 Yes
- 43 No

In these 106 districts, at least 65 percent of workers held white-collar jobs at the time of the 1990 census. (The average district had 57.4 percent white-collar employment then.)

BLUE-COLLAR DISTRICTS

- 22 Yes
- 35 No

These 57 lawmakers represent districts in which blue-collar jobs accounted for at least 35 percent of the work force in 1990. (The average district was 26.7 percent blue-collar then.)

AGRICULTURAL DISTRICTS

- 43 Yes
- 17 No

These 60 districts are where farm workers were at least 4 percent of the work force in 1995, the last time the statistic was compiled by House district. (The average district was 2.2 percent.)

WEALTHIER DISTRICTS

- 44 Yes
- 24 No

The median family income in these 68 districts topped $40,000 at the time of the 1990 census. (The average district's median family income at that time was $30,711.)

SOURCE: Census Bureau

NTR, a status that greatly reduces Chinese tariffs on imports, a number of those lawmakers said they would just as soon keep the annual review as a potential cudgel.

Businesses joined together to fight that inclination tooth and nail, and they spent millions of dollars — on both sides of the partisan aisle — in their efforts. The Business Roundtable, a group of executives from large corporations, estimates it will spend $10 million on advertisements, lobbying and other expenses by the time the bill is enacted. At the same time, labor unions, religious groups, veterans organizations, human rights advocates and environmentalists also countered with an intense, though less costly, campaign.

As a result, the pivotal bloc of undecided lawmakers described themselves as feeling under siege — not only from lobbyists on both sides, but also from the president and his Cabinet and from some impassioned constituents.

Two in the eye of the storm were Democrats Gregory W. Meeks of New York and Rubén Hinojosa of Texas. They were ultimately the only two wavering lawmakers who took the administration up on its offer of a trip to China this spring to assess its behavior, and its market potential, firsthand. The factors they said they considered in weighing their decisions were a microcosm of what House members as a whole faced.

Meeks' district includes John F. Kennedy International Airport, which stands to gain from increased commerce with China, but it is also home to a strong contingent of unionized workers concerned that jobs like theirs could be exported.

Hinojosa's Rio Grande Valley district, one of the poorest in the nation, is desperate to find jobs and new outlets for its small businesses and manufacturing efforts. Its constituents also have some concerns that the NAFTA law (PL 103-182), which lowered U.S.-Mexican trade barriers in 1993, also

"I was not confident at any point that was a 'gimme,' " Philip M. Crane, R-Ill., chairman of the Ways and Means Trade Subcommittee, said at a news conference after the May 24 vote with Rules Chairman David Dreier, R-Calif., left, and Majority Whip Tom DeLay, R-Texas.

shifted some production to lower-wage Mexico and brought environmental problems across the border. Critics cite NAFTA as an ominous precedent for what may happen in China, where workers are paid even less and environmental conditions are already some of the worst in the world.

At a May 23 news conference where they announced their intention to vote "yes," Meeks and Hinojosa said that the biggest impression left by their trip was of the Chinese people. "I came away with the feeling that they were just like the average American citizen," Meeks said.

The trip alone was not convincing enough. In the end, their decisions were eased by progress on an unrelated bill. Clinton and Hastert agreed May 22 on a package of legislation to help impoverished inner cities and rural areas through tax cuts and other development incentives. (*Story, 2000 CQ Weekly, p. 1263*)

Commerce Secretary William M. Daley acknowledged in a press briefing May 23 that the timing of that deal was no coincidence. He said there was a strong desire "by a number of members, especially minority members, that as we move forward with trade, we address some of the difficult areas of our nation."

In addition, Hinojosa was influenced by an administration promise that the EPA would quickly complete its required review before a gas pipeline across southern Texas may open. That also swayed previously undecided Sil-

vestre Reyes, D-Texas, and secured what had been tenuous support from Solomon P. Ortiz, D-Texas.

Other local matters were also addressed by the administration. Democrat Robert E. "Bud" Cramer voted "yes" after the Commerce Department vowed to reconsider a plan to close a national weather station in his tornado-prone Alabama district. Democratic Caucus Chairman Martin Frost voted "yes" after the Northrop Grumman Corp. signaled, in an internal memorandum, that it would stay put in Dallas after reaching agreements with the Navy and the city.

Meeks' decision was eased by senior New York Democrat Charles B. Rangel's announcement May 16 that he would vote for the bill. Clinton, Republican leaders and House Democrats in favor of the China bill cited Rangel's influence in securing "yes" votes. Tim Roemer, D-Ind., a Democratic whip for the bill, referred often to "Rangel coattails."

The three groups with which Rangel is most influential split on the bill: eight of 19 New York Democrats voted "yes," nine of the 36 Congressional Black Caucus members did so, and so did 11 of the 16 Democrats on the Ways and Means Committee, of which Rangel is the ranking member.

The bill split various other blocs of votes, as well. Rural representatives voted overwhelmingly for it but urban and suburban lawmakers did not, for example. Electoral considerations appeared to

have little influence on members' votes: Republicans and Democrats with narrow holds on their seats — as well as those with certain prospects for re-election — voted for and against the bill in percentages that echoed the House as a whole. (*Analysis, pp. 98-99*)

The vote, and the six hours of floor debate beforehand, were somewhat anti-climactic. Nine minutes into the 15-minute period for voting, the "yes" votes surpassed 218 — the absolute majority of the House — and applause broke out on the floor. No members entered the well at the last moment to change their votes once passage of the bill was assured.

Legislating From the Center

The prospects of passage appeared to solidify with the decision by the House GOP leadership to embrace the proposals of Sander M. Levin, D-Mich. After receiving encouragement from senior Ways and Means Committee Republican Bill Thomas of California and others, Levin worked for months to craft a proposal that would address the China-specific concerns of human rights advocates, labor leaders and those who feared that China would never follow through on its trade promises.

As the vote drew near, Levin joined forces with Doug Bereuter, R-Neb., who had been putting together a similar proposal. Working with Trade Subcommittee Chairman Philip M. Crane, R-Ill., and others, their package was credited with winning over as many as 30 members, many of them Democrats. In the end, the bill passed with 19 votes to spare.

The Ways and Means Committee attached the anti-surge portion of the Levin-Bereuter proposal to its bill at its May 17 markup. The Rules Committee agreed May 23 to a procedure under which the rest of the proposal was automatically attached to the bill when the resolution setting the rules for floor debate (H Res 510) was adopted by the House. That same procedure amended the bill with a list of specific human rights abuses that would have to be addressed by the commission the bill would create, and it added a $99 million authorization for news broadcasts into China, a priority of undecided John Edward Porter, R-Ill., who then announced support for the bill.

The vote to adopt the rule was 294-136. (*Vote 225, 2000 CQ Weekly p. 1304*)

Unions and Pro-Trade Democrats: Estrangement but No Divorce

In the weeks before the May 24 House vote on granting permanent normal trade relations to China, organized labor threatened to make the bill (HR 4444) a litmus test for its support in November's elections.

Unions may have a hard time making that threat stick for the simple reason that there is one imperative that trumps the China vote — regaining Democratic control of the House.

Lawmakers say they will have ample opportunity to make up with unions in coming weeks and are already reminding them why a Democratic House is vital to their interests. On May 25, a House committee voted on party lines to block federal rules to combat repetitive stress injuries in the work force. Health care and minimum wage battles are also brewing. (*Ergonomics, 2000 CQ Weekly, p. 1280*)

"Labor will be right back on issues of ergonomics and the minimum wage," said Rep. Richard E. Neal, D-Mass., who voted for the China bill but still proudly touts his 96 percent record of voting with organized labor.

Neal said labor's political clout is far from waning. "All you have to do is look at what labor did two years ago — all the money it raised and spent" for Democrats, he said.

The majority of unions' staunchest allies toed the labor line on China: Four out of five Democrats who received 20 percent or more of their contributions in the last election from union political action committees opposed the bill. (*Vote analysis, p. 98*)

Those House Democrats who did back the legislation said union lobbying, in the end, was only one of a host of considerations on an issue that ran far deeper than workers vs. business.

"It's a very difficult, complex issue," said Max Sandlin of Texas. Although Sandlin received 26 percent of his money from labor during his last election, he voted for the bill.

Sandlin said he weighed a variety of topics — from national security and

Sweeney

religious freedom to human rights, as well as labor concerns — before deciding, the night before the vote, how he would come down.

Several unions dispatched emissaries to Sandlin's office to make the case against the bill. He also met with President Clinton three times and was called by Secretary of State Madeleine K. Albright, Secretary of Health and Human Services Donna E. Shalala and U.S. Trade Representative Charlene Barshefsky. Three days before the vote, he also had a 40-minute phone conversation with former chairman of the Joint Chiefs of Staff Colin Powell, who argued that human rights improvements in China could be best achieved through U.S. engagement.

Passage "is not an indication that labor is losing its political power. It's just such a complex issue," Sandlin said.

Charles B. Rangel of New York, perhaps the most important pro-labor Democrat for the bill, used a matrimo-

nial metaphor to describe his party's relationship with unions: "When you've been married for a number of years and you have one major disappointment, you don't walk out."

He attacked unions, such as the United Auto Workers, that threatened to use the China vote as a litmus test for future support. "That was either poor judgment or arrogance," Rangel told reporters May 23.

Labor's Disappointment

At a news conference May 25, the morning after the bill's passage, AFL-CIO officials predicted that rank-and-file members would punish traditional Democratic allies who voted for the measure by showing a lack of enthusiasm this fall, rather than casting their lots elsewhere. "They're not going to turn to the other side," said Richard Trumka, the group's secretary-treasurer. "They're going to stay at home."

He pointedly noted, however, that pro-trade Democrats have "made a difficult job more difficult," meaning the party's bid to win control of the House.

In 1998, the union household share of the electorate was 22 percent — up from 14 percent in 1994, the previous midterm election — and that record labor turnout helped the Democrats gain a net of five House seats.

AFL-CIO President John Sweeney said that this fall, his group would reprise the type of aggressive get-out-the-vote effort that boosted union turnout last time. While he described himself as "angry" at Democrats — Clinton in particular — who worked to win passage of the China bill, he said he would leave it to the rank and file to decide how much weight to give the China vote.

"I would hope that [unions] understand that their future has a lot more to do with who is elected president than whether or not" the China bill passes, Senate Minority Leader Tom Daschle, D-S.D., a supporter of the measure, said May 24.

While applauding the House endorsement of permanent NTR, top Chinese government officials May 25 denounced as an unwarranted intrusion the provision in the bill calling for a new commission to monitor Chinese labor and human rights. Their statements signaled that, while the bill could herald a new era in Sino-American relations, deep divisions between the two nations will not soon disappear. (*Story, p. 97*)

Presidential Effort

The deep partisan divisions in Washington, however, were put on hold in the days surrounding the House debate. Majority Leader Dick Armey, R-Texas, who normally prizes his role as a Clinton nemesis, said at a May 24 news conference that he was "proud of the effort the president made."

At the start of the year, proponents of the trade initiative feared that Clinton would back away from the bill to aid Vice President Al Gore, who was caught between his loyalty to the administration and his desire for union support in his bid for the presidency. Instead, Clinton made much of his time available to win over undecided Democrats. Robert T. Matsui of California, the main Democratic vote-counter for the bill in the House, said that many to whom Clinton paid the most attention voted for the bill.

In the House, Clinton relied not only on Matsui but also on Roemer, Cal Dooley of California and James P. Moran of Virginia, leaders of the centrist New Democrat coalition. For them, winning one-third of Democrats to their side on a trade issue in a highly contested election year was something to crow about. "It showed that when we put our minds to it, we can govern from the center out," Moran said.

Roemer identified 50 of those in his party who voted "yes" as New Democrats — somewhat of a consolation prize for unions. While they lost the vote, they were still able to muster their core constituency of Democrats to vote against the bill. And of the 46

Democrats who hail from five of the states seen as pivotal to a presidential victory this year — New Jersey, Pennsylvania, Illinois, Ohio and Michigan — only Levin and Tom Sawyer of Ohio cast votes in favor of the bill.

The Down Side

Such factors did little to lift the spirits of the main opponents who had worked vociferously against the bill. Some union officials threatened to refrain from helping to re-elect Democrats who crossed them on the vote. (*Story, p. 101*)

At a news conference after the bill passed, Bonior and Nancy Pelosi, D-Calif., who had to wait through more than an hour of celebratory comments from Hastert's and Matsui's groups before they could face reporters in the House Radio-TV studio, found it difficult to conceal their frustration and exhaustion. "The burden is now on members of Congress who voted for this legislation and on the president of the United States to produce some results," Pelosi said.

Bonior was more upbeat, saying that the "no" vote from 45 percent of the House meant that concern about globalization would not go away.

"We will win this" in the long run, he said. "There's a real good feeling I have about what we did today."

Opponents attempted to make passage of the bill more difficult by offering a motion to recommit the bill to Ways and Means with the requirement that it add language saying China's permanent normal trade status would be revoked if it attacked or blockaded Taiwan. China regards Taiwan as a renegade province, and it has threatened military action against it in the recent past. The proposal was designed to make the China vote more difficult for Republicans, but it was defeated, 176-258. (*Vote 227, 2000 CQ Weekly, p. 1304*)

Consideration of the bill had proved divisive for both parties, but it was Democrats who were most split. Some likened the Democratic division over trade, in its fervor and import, to the GOP split over abortion. And

many Democrats expressed frustration that Clinton — who pushed NAFTA to enactment one year before Democrats lost control of the House — would push another trade measure just months before Democrats have a chance to win back the majority.

The 237 votes for the China bill were three more than the number who voted in the House for NAFTA. Members such as Matsui said that the president was more engaged and focused on the China debate than he had been on the first trade debate of his presidency, although in that case 102 Democrats took his side, 29 more than did so on May 24.

Shortly after the vote, Democrats began trying to rally around the party. Levin said he agreed with bill opponents that the next president would have to address labor and environmental standards before he would win fast-track trading authority. That authority, which requires Congress to vote up or down on trade agreements the president negotiates, expired in 1994, and Clinton has been unable to win it back. (*1998 Almanac, p. 23-3*)

The day after the vote, Clinton called Minority Leader Richard A. Gephardt, D-Mo., who had opposed the bill, and Bonior to the White House to discuss prescription drugs for Medicare recipients, a proposal Democrats are firmly behind.

Business leaders responded to union threats by offering to cross the country to personally thank the Democrats who sided with them. Still, Donohue noted, the Chamber of Commerce would not be endorsing or contributing to Democratic supporters, who may have a history of voting against the business group 80 percent of the time. That could leave some Democrats in a difficult position.

But Levin, whose district is home to Teamsters President James P. Hoffa and a host of union members, said he was not worried. "When voters look at issues in 2000, they're going to look at all of the issues, at the whole person," he said. ◆

In competitive districts, members' China vote could help swing control of the House

Candidates Face Consequences of China Vote

Sprawling along the western bank of the Willamette River, Oregon's "Silicon Forest" is home to thousands of people with much to gain if the United States allows free trade with China. A large Intel computer chip plant is there, and shoe-giant Nike is headquartered nearby. Scores of small, high-tech companies dot the map.

So when David Wu, the freshman Democrat who represents the area in the U.S. House, announced that he would fight any effort to reach out to Beijing, political strategists took notice. In this year's precision battle for control of the House, every district counts.

"I can't for the life of me know why Wu is voting against this. In Portland, Oregon?" said Rep. Thomas M. Davis III, chairman of the National Republican Congressional Committee (NRCC). "Along the coast, it's a very hot issue for members who are on the wrong side."

Wu, a native of Taiwan and the only Chinese-American member of Congress, calls his stance a "bottom line." He said May 11: "It's heart. It's soul. It's conscience."

His contest, and several other close races, are part of the calculation as wavering members decide which way to vote the week of May 22 on permanent normal trade relations with China. Whatever happens, the debate will continue on the campaign trail months later. (*China, 2000 CQ Weekly, p. 1164*)

Indeed, the China issue could be a factor in any competitive district heavily influenced by labor, business or both. In California's 15th District, the heart of Silicon Valley, the issue is a factor in the race to succeed Rep. Tom Campbell, a Republican who is challenging Democratic Sen. Dianne Feinstein. Democrat Mike Honda, a labor

Wu, right, talks at a Rotary Club gathering April 18 in his Portland office about his opposition to permanent free trade with China.

union ally, has broken with the unions to support the China bill (HR 4444), while Honda's opponent, Jim Cunneen, supports the bill but makes known Honda's ties to labor.

In California's agricultural 23rd District, Republican Rep. Elton Gallegly lost some traditional support for his reelection bid because of his opposition to normal trade relations with China. The president of the Ventura County Farm Bureau recently announced an endorsement of the Democrat in the race, real estate lawyer Michael Case.

And the political ripples could flow beyond the battle for Congress. Democratic Reps. Martin T. Meehan and Edward J. Markey of Massachusetts both have statewide aspirations and are wary of upsetting such a key base as labor. Both are undecided on China trade.

In the fight for Congress, campaign contributors are passionate on both sides. Farmers, computer makers, software developers, textile companies and other industries see China as a potentially booming marketplace. Labor unions see China as a bastion of cheap workers that will steal American jobs. Meanwhile, religious conservatives see China as an evil empire that persecutes Christians and other religious minorities. The political landscape is riddled with fault lines for politicians balanc-

ing between constituents and contributors. "It plays different in different districts," Davis said.

Wu, who won in 1998 with 50.1 percent of the vote, is favored to win reelection but is not considered safe — although he may have become a bit safer after the GOP primary May 16. His Republican opponent, conservative state Sen. Charles Starr, defeated a more moderate candidate that Washington strategists had hoped would be a formidable challenger to Wu in November. Starr has sent mixed signals on China trade, saying he admires Wu's stance but supports trade. "It can't help but be an issue that will define the two candidates and will play a part in people's decision-making," Starr said in an interview.

Wu estimates that his China vote will cost him $400,000 in business contributions for 2000. Still, he has substantial support in other arenas. In 1998 he raised $1.6 million, with the largest single contributions coming from labor unions that support his stance on trade.

But even if the primary strengthened Wu's incumbency, he remains a shining example for Republicans hoping to paint Democrats as unfriendly to business and the high-tech industry.

Democrats, who hope to win at least six seats in November to overcome the majority taken by the GOP six years ago, cannot afford to dismiss any competitive district. Among 435 races, the outcome could be decided in as few as a dozen.

Said Davis: "For businesses, companies, employees, for investors who believe that American goods can prosper in [the] 96 percent of the world that is not American consumers, I think the Republican Party in the House is their home. That's the message we're willing to take to the streets and we're willing to take to districts."

Indeed, Davis uses the GOP leadership's unity on China trade to the NRCC's advantage in fundraising. In presentations to business and high-tech PACs, Davis uses trade group rankings to show that Republicans are more friendly to their interests. One slide, titled "Critical Issues for America's IT Economy," compares the "yea" votes on China trade by GOP House leaders with the "nay" votes by Minority Leader Richard A. Gephardt, D-Mo., Minority Whip David E. Bonior, D-Mich., and Democratic Congressional Campaign Committee Chairman Patrick J. Kennedy, D-R.I.

House Democrats, whose leaders and rank-and-file are divided on the issue, must either stick with their traditional labor supporters or risk angering their most loyal base.

Passions on Both Sides

In an election year in which candidates are talking about dining room table topics such as health care, Social Security and education, the arcane topic of permanent normal trade relations (or PNTR, in Beltway speak) is generally not the stuff of sound bites or flashy direct mail brochures. There is no Million Manufacturer March for supporters of free trade.

So why all the hand-wringing by the undecideds? Though strategists and scholars agree that China trade is not a hot topic on most Main Streets, there are places, such as Oregon's 1st District, where executives and employees are paying attention.

"The issue splits both parties," said James A. Thurber, director of the Center for Congressional and Presidential Studies at American University. The election fallout "depends on local issues and how well-organized the grass roots are locally. This is not an air war issue. It is a ground war issue."

Rep. Bill McCollum, R-Fla., a trade supporter who is running for the Senate, says the issue occasionally pops up on the campaign trail. He told reporters at a breakfast May 11 that people have not objected to his stand. "Most of the time it comes up in terms of, 'What do you think about China?' People are concerned about China."

McCollum is campaigning in a state where trade is an emotional subject. Citrus growers and other farmers in central and northern Florida tend to support trade. But it can be a tricky question for Cuban-Americans in the Miami area — typically GOP voters that McCollum will need in his primary election — who draw the line at the Florida Straits. Mc-

Collum differentiated May 11 between Cuba and China, saying China was a dictatorship open to a free market, while Cuba's Communist system was not an appropriate trading partner.

In the poor, working-class, rural 4th District of Alabama, Rep. Robert B. Aderholt is in a quandary. He is one of the few Republicans still undecided on China, and no wonder: His district consists largely of unionized workers who labor on chicken and tree farms. The district is socially conservative, and Aderholt says he has been lobbied heavily by some conservative Christians to vote against China trade.

Aderholt is favored to win re-election over his Democratic opponent, former Alabama first lady Marsha Folsom, but he knows that even a few thousand voters motivated by a single issue can make a difference. He also has financial support from industries favoring the trade bill, and business advocates have come calling. "I want to do the right thing," he said May 11. "But usually I do what I know my district wants, and I don't want to do anything that's not in line with what the district thinks."

Divided Democrats

For Republicans, Aderholt is the exception. The party's congressional leadership is united on the issue, and the presumptive GOP presidential nominee, Texas Gov. George W. Bush, supports the bill as well.

In the months leading up to Nov. 7, Democrats are more likely to trip over one of those China land mines.

President Clinton, free of the constraints of running for re-election, is pushing hard for the bill, telephoning undecided House members and barnstorming the country. But Vice President Al Gore, wary of irritating labor unions in his bid for the White House, has not taken a leadership role on the issue, although he supports passage.

Quite conspicuously, Gephardt, the man who would be House Speaker if Democrats won the majority, has steered clear of the fray. He announced his opposition to the bill in a speech April 19 near St. Louis, thousands of miles from the Capitol, and he has made it known that he will not lobby Democrats.

That task has been left to lawmakers such as Wu and Bonior, a longtime labor union friend, on one side, and Reps. Robert T. Matsui and Cal Dooley of California on the other.

The division pleases conservatives and Republicans. Marshall Wittmann, legislative affairs director for the conservative Heritage Foundation, likens the trade dispute within the Democratic Party to the abortion issue in GOP circles, where moderates often disagree with the party establishment's opposition to abortion rights.

"It really highlights the tension between the old Democrats and the new Democrats," Wittmann said of the China trade debate. "For any party, you don't want to have an issue that divides you from your base. The PNTR issue divides the Democratic Party from its largest organized constituency, which is the labor movement."

For Democrats, unions offer more than campaign dollars. They provide election ground soldiers, volunteers who stuff envelopes and ring doorbells. "Any time you have a divide like that, it has the potential to weaken voter turnout and deflate the base," Wittmann added.

In some ways, Gephardt is a convenient stopgap. Unionists upset about Clinton and Gore can take solace that Gephardt, one of the nation's top Democrats, is on their side.

"When you look at the fact that President Clinton is a strong supporter of PNTR, when you look at [Senate Minority Leader] Tom Daschle, who is a strong supporter of PNTR, in some ways it was important to have one of our Democratic leaders who was showing some sensitivity to the concerns of a very important constituency," Dooley said. "The way that Dick has handled himself has helped him and the party to maintain very strong and positive ties to labor."

When undecided Democrats complain to him that they are risking damaged relations with labor, Dooley says he assures them that unions still prefer to help Democrats win the majority.

Back in Oregon's 1st District, David Wu can expect a pounding from lobbyists on the other side. "David Wu is going to have to look his constituents in the face and say, 'I voted against your interests,' " said William Morley, chief trade lobbyist for the U.S. Chamber of Commerce. "He's turning his back on his constituents in Portland, where trade is a huge, huge employer. He's doing the wrong thing."

Says Wu: "If the voters choose to remove me for this, then so be it. I'll go home with a clean conscience and peace in my heart." ◆

Hill moves cautiously to address concerns, either in broad-based or industry-specific bills

Internet Privacy Issue Beginning to Click

It is a rare political issue that can bring together Phyllis Schlafly, founder of the conservative Eagle Forum, Nadine Strossen, president of the liberal American Civil Liberties Union, and consumer activist Ralph Nader. Yet these three find themselves on the same side in a crucial battle heating up in the 106th Congress: the push to protect the privacy of consumers who surf and shop on the Internet.

"We have a deep and common interest on this issue," Schlafly said March 21. "Personal information should be controlled by the individual consumer. It should not be controlled by business." Schlafly and her allies contend legislation is needed to ensure that sensitive consumer data is protected.

This unusual alliance across the political spectrum mirrors the concerns about privacy that have spread among American consumers as Internet commerce has exploded. People are worried about who is privy to the data that streams through telephone lines and computer networks every time they click their mouse on a World Wide Web page or volunteer information to an online merchant or an Internet service provider.

More ominously, a majority of Americans fear they could lose their jobs or be denied loans because of inaccurate or incomplete personal information they provide to online retailers, banks and other businesses on the Internet, according to a recent survey by Harris Polls.

In response to these fears, President Clinton is promising to try to do more to protect the sensitive information of consumers cruising the Internet. He has vowed to press Congress on the proposal he made in his State of the Union address in January for new safeguards for medical and financial records.

"Our administration has encouraged Internet firms to work together to raise privacy standards. The response has been good," Clinton said March 3 to a group of business leaders at a meeting in Silicon Valley sponsored by the Aspen Institute, a private educational group. "But the American people know it's still not enough."

Growing consumer worries and the expec-

tation of a Clinton proposal are increasing the likelihood lawmakers will take some action this year to better protect privacy, possibly as part of a broad measure covering all commerce on the Internet or through smaller, industry-specific bills.

The battle over the shape and timing of such legislation is already under way. On one side are Clinton, consumer advocates and lawmakers such as Sen. Richard C. Shelby, R-Ala., and Rep. Edward J. Markey, D-Mass., who would give consumers considerable additional control over the data that online companies can collect and release. On the other side are lawmakers who are wary of acting — especially in a short, election year session — on an issue that might slow the growth of Internet commerce.

These lawmakers, including House Majority Leader Dick Armey, R-Texas, and Rep. Zoe Lofgren, D-Calif., side with high-tech companies that want Congress to let industry set a voluntary system to protect privacy.

Both sides agree that the debate has potentially massive consequences for the bur-

Quick Contents

Privacy advocates are pushing for greater protection of data in specific industries:

● Utilities — an electricity deregulation bill, HR 2944, would restrict the release of consumer billing data.

● Health care — a proposed bill, S 573, would ensure the privacy of health records.

● Financial services — S 1903 and HR 3320 would slap tougher restrictions on data-sharing by banks, brokers and insurers.

CQ PHOTO / DOUGLAS GRAHAM

Sen. Richard C. Shelby, R-Ala., speaks at a March 23 briefing of the Congressional Privacy Caucus, focused on consumer protections in the financial services industry.

geoning Internet economy. Forrester Research, a market research firm, estimates that U.S. online sales will grow to $184.5 billion in 2004 from $20.2 billion last year. Failure to ensure the privacy of information sent into cyberspace could turn off consumers. But excessive controls on the collection and sharing of information could hurt online companies that rely on advertising revenue to survive.

"We should seize on this issue," said Rep. Bob Barr, R-Ga., who calls for strong consumer safeguards. "It's going to be a hot issue. There's no doubt about it."

Hard-to-Digest Cookies

At the heart of the privacy debate are marketing practices employed by operators of commercial Internet sites. The sites are often designed to transfer small files, or cookies, onto the hard drives of potential customers. The cookies are used to track visitors' comings and goings; an analysis of those electronic footprints, or "clickstream," is then used by merchants to zap specially tailored ads to the customers' computer screens.

Worries about consumer profiling grew in January when DoubleClick Inc., an Internet marketing company, unveiled a plan to link its collection of online browsing histories to shopping records of consumers that included their names and addresses. The plan would have brushed aside the veil of anonymity that computer users have when they cruise the Internet.

In response to a storm of public complaints, the company backed down, saying it had mistakenly acted "in the absence of government and industry privacy standards." It is now awaiting the outcome of an investigation of its practices by the Federal Trade Commission (FTC) and the debate in Congress.

Consumer Advocates

Consumer advocates want broad legislation similar to a bill (S 2063) proposed by Sen. Robert G. Torricelli, D-N.J., that would bar companies from sharing information without giving notice to consumers and getting their consent.

Requiring consent, they say, would provide real control over personal information. And notice rules would ensure enforcement by providing grounds for the FTC to investigate companies that violate their own posted policies.

Industry Wants '99 Law Changed

Banks, insurers and securities brokers won a mixed victory last year when lawmakers included an industry-backed compromise on customer privacy protection in the financial services overhaul law (PL 106-102).

The act let the industry share some of the transaction history of its customers with unrelated companies, unless consumers opt out of such arrangements. It set weaker restrictions than consumer advocates had sought on the sharing of customer information among affiliated companies. (*1999 CQ Weekly, 2797*)

But industry also got something it did not bargain for: A provision stating that the federal standard was a floor, permitting states to adopt stricter privacy protection laws.

Now, more than 20 states are considering proposals to go beyond federal law. The toughest measures, pending in legislatures in at least eight states including California, Iowa and Massachusetts, would require companies to get written consent before disclosing consumers' personal information to other businesses.

"If all states do their own thing, we're going to have a patchwork system that will be impossible to navigate," said Allen R. Caskie, executive director of the privacy project of the Financial Services Coordinating Council, which represents the American Bankers Association, the American Council of Life Insurers and others.

To head off that possibility, Caskie and the industry are going back to Congress, seeking a single national standard to pre-empt pending state proposals. The industry's quest carries a big risk: To get the trump card it wants, it may have to accept tighter federal restrictions on use of customer information. For privacy advocates to agree to a single national standard, they will insist that it be far stricter than the 1999 law.

"It is a sham law," Sen. Richard C. Shelby, R-Ala, said of the 1999 act. "It does not give consumers true privacy protection."

He joined Paul S. Sarbanes of Maryland, the top Democrat on the Senate Banking, Housing and Urban Affairs Committee, in inserting the provision to allow tougher state laws in the 1999 act. (*1999 CQ Weekly, p. 2500*)

Shelby and Sarbanes say that any new federal standard pre-empting state law would have to require companies to get express consent of consumers before sharing financial records with unaffiliated companies, rather than putting the onus on consumers to opt out. Such language is contained in a Shelby bill (S 1903).

President Clinton likely will play a key role in the debate. He promised in his State of the Union address Jan. 27 to follow up on the steps taken by Congress last year to protect financial records privacy. "Soon I will send legislation to [the Congress] to finish that job," he said. (*2000 CQ Weekly, p. 180*)

The administration has yet to send a formal proposal to lawmakers.

At a minimum, Clinton is expected to ask lawmakers to extend the privacy restrictions for unaffiliated companies in the 1999 law to affiliated companies. He has so far not sought a federal pre-emption of state laws.

The biggest hurdle industry faces may be the unwillingness of key lawmakers to reopen the debate. Phil Gramm, R-Texas, chairman of the Senate Banking, Housing and Urban Affairs Committee, and Jim Leach, R-Iowa, chairman of the House Banking and Financial Services Committee, say they are sympathetic to the need for privacy protection. But they are reluctant to take sides when there is little hope for compromise.

"The new law needs time to work," Gramm said.

Similar requirements would be established by a bill (S 854) sponsored by Sen. Patrick J. Leahy, D-Vt., and another bill (HR 3321) by Markey.

All three bills would apply across-the-board to any company doing business on the Internet. But consumer advocates and their allies in Congress are considering an industry-by-industry approach as well.

In February, four lawmakers established a bipartisan Congressional Privacy Caucus to develop a range of proposals. Sens. Shelby and Richard H. Bryan, D-Nev., and Reps. Joe L. Barton, R-Texas, and Markey said they would pursue a two-track strategy of promoting broad measures and industry-specific bills to set consumer consent requirements for information sharing.

"We need a dual approach because it is doubtful we can do a broad-based bill in this Congress," Barton said in a March 16 interview.

He and other members of the coalition want to promote legislation similar to existing laws that prevent unauthorized persons from getting sensitive private information.

In 1998, lawmakers required parental consent before businesses could collect any information from children online. The provision was part of an omnibus spending law (PL 105-277). (*1998 Almanac, p. 22-10*)

In three earlier measures, Congress: in 1984 barred disclosure of cable television billing records showing program choices without prior approval (PL 98-549); in 1986 barred unauthorized access to electronic communications, including e-mail (PL 99-508); and in 1988 banned release of video rental records without consent (PL 100-618).

The video rental privacy law was a response to the disclosure in the media of a list of videos rented by former Appeals Court Judge Robert H. Bork during his 1987 confirmation hearing for a vacant seat on the Supreme Court. (*1984 Almanac, p. 287; 1986 Almanac, p. 88; 1988 Almanac, p. 120*)

A bill sponsored by Shelby (S 1903) would require financial service companies to get consent before sharing any consumer financial information with other companies. Markey has introduced a companion bill (HR 3320). (*Banking, 2000 CQ Weekly, p. 638*)

Consumer advocates would like to raise the issue of privacy protection in conference committee deliberations on bills (S 761 and HR 1714) that would

U.S. Online Retail Projections

With more and more Americans shopping online, retail sales over the Internet are expected to rise from almost $3 billion in 1997 to $185 billion in 2004. Along with the growing popularity, however, has come growing concern about the privacy of online transactions and data.

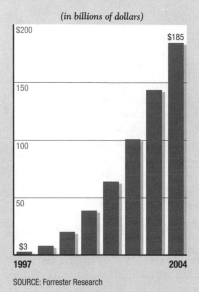

(*in billions of dollars*)

SOURCE: Forrester Research

authorize the use of electronic signatures, including identification codes and hand-written signatures on touch-sensitive computer screens, to make deals on the Internet. But Barton and other lawmakers say conferees are unlikely to support a consumer consent requirement. (*2000 CQ Weekly, p. 107*)

Barton and Markey have had more success in laying the groundwork for a debate on privacy in a bill (HR 2944) to open the nation's $220 billion electricity industry to competition. The bill includes a measure that would prevent electric utilities from disclosing a customer's billing records without permission. The measure is awaiting a markup in the full House Commerce Committee. (*2000 CQ Weekly, p. 478*)

Industry Response

Online businesses strongly oppose any legislation to set privacy protection requirements.

Privacy legislation, they fear, could be a prelude to more bills and far-reaching federal regulation of the Internet. The companies also argue that legislation is not needed because customers will shun companies that do not adopt acceptable standards for privacy

and for conducting business. (*1999 CQ Weekly, p. 2028*)

NetCoalition.com, a policy group representing 10 top online businesses, said March 20 that it would step up lobbying efforts against measures that could "thwart initiative, slow economic growth or limit consumers' choices." The group's members include DoubleClick; Amazon.com, the online book seller; and Emusic.com, an online music provider.

"NetCoalition will intensify the dialogue that is vital for understanding the dynamic nature of the Internet," said Jerry Yang, a co-founder of the Internet portal operator Yahoo! Inc., one of the group's members.

Other trade groups, such as the Information Technology Industry Council, which represents more than two dozen high-tech companies, are also trying to block legislation. In a letter to leaders of both chambers Feb. 3, the council urged support for a "private-sector led approach and not broad federal Internet privacy legislation."

The industry points to two voluntary programs that monitor privacy protection policies of companies as proof of the success of self-regulation.

The Virginia-based Council of Better Business Bureaus, a nonprofit group that monitors business practices, operates one of the programs, called BBBOnline. The program oversees privacy protection practices of more than 400 companies, including IBM Corp., Bank of America Corp., Procter & Gamble and America Online Inc.

The second program is run by TRUSTe, a nonprofit California-based privacy watchdog. The group has signed up more than 1,000 companies including eBay Inc., E*TRADE Group Inc., and Yahoo! Inc.

Both programs certify that participating companies comply with a five-part fair practices standard developed by the industry and the FTC. The guidelines require companies to give customers notice of what is collected and shared, a choice to opt out, the ability to correct bad data, information on security and a contact for complaints.

Businesses say the guidelines ensure customers can make informed decisions on whether to continue using an Internet site. They argue that consumer advocates would nullify one of the Internet's greatest strengths — its ability to deliver rifle-shot sales pitches — by making consent a prerequisite for tracking consumer habits.

Shane Ham, a technology policy analyst for the Progressive Policy Institute, a think tank sponsored by the centrist Democratic Leadership Council, said the industry's fear of lost revenue was probably justified. "A consent requirement would kill the business plans of many free Internet Web sites," Ham said. The institute recently urged lawmakers to give business more time to regulate itself and to "resist the urge to panic."

With consumer advocates and online businesses sharply divided on whether there is a need for legislation, leaders of both parties have been cautious about taking sides. Some, including Senate Majority Trent Lott, R-Miss., Speaker J. Dennis Hastert, R-Ill., Senate Minority Leader Tom Daschle, D-S.D., and House Minority Leader Richard A. Gephardt, D-Mo., have all tended to lean toward giving the industry more time to regulate itself.

"I'm going to have to think about that issue. I need more time,'" Lott said in an interview March 7.

Neither party's emergent presidential nominee — Vice President Al Gore or Texas GOP Gov. George W. Bush — has taken a stance on whether specific legislation is needed. With little direction from political leaders and little time to reach a compromise, since Congress is already in the third month of an election-shortened session, some lawmakers have been reluctant to take a strong stand on either side of the issue.

"All of us are very concerned that we don't mess up the Internet," said Sen. Larry E. Craig, R-Idaho. "I can feel the grass roots is beginning to become alarmed. But there is little agreement on what to do. I don't think this issue has matured yet."

Middle Ground

If a consensus is to emerge on this issue, it may come from the efforts of some key lawmakers including Senate Judiciary Committee Chairman Orrin G. Hatch, R-Utah, and House Commerce Telecommunications and Consumer Protection Subcommittee Chairman W.J. "Billy" Tauzin, R-La., who are trying broker a deal between industry and consumer groups.

Tauzin plans to sponsor a retreat in May where lobbyists and lawmakers can discuss the issue of privacy protection and look for common ground. "I

need to know what I'm for before I can say what I'm against," Tauzin said. "The retreat will give members a chance to focus on this."

One of the proposals being discussed is the creation of a two-tiered system to restrict the sharing of personal information by companies. Businesses would be required to get consumers' consent before they shared the most sensitive data, including financial and medical files; a lower level of protection would be imposed for other information that advertisers collect, including a consumer's name, e-mail address, preferences for products and services, and Internet browsing habits.

Like Tauzin, Hatch is trying to discuss the issue with lobbyists on both sides. He says it will be difficult to draw the line between what is sensitive information and what is not, but that he wants to try. He is betting that online businesses will eventually come to the table to discuss broad legislation.

"The big companies know that privacy protection is good for business," Hatch said. One company, America Online Inc.(AOL), the nation's biggest Internet service provider, has already expressed interest in Hatch's efforts.

During a Senate Judiciary Committee hearing last month to discuss his company's pending merger with media giant Time Warner Inc., AOL Chairman and CEO Stephen M. Case said he would not have "an allergic reaction" to legislation. "If there is something that really deals with the issue in a focused way so that every consumer has the kind of basic principles of notice and choice . . . we would be supportive," he said.

Other vehicles for possible compromise include a bill (S 809) sponsored by Sens. Conrad Burns, R-Mont., and Ron Wyden, D-Ore., and a bill (HR 1685) sponsored by Reps. Robert W. Goodlatte, R-Va., and Rick Boucher, D-Va.

Both bills would establish broad rules covering all businesses on the Internet. But, instead of requiring express consent for any information sharing, these bills would use the industry's guidelines for self-regulation as a starting point. The bills would give companies leeway if they provide notice about the information they collect and what they plan to do with it.

Consumer advocates argue the two bills would give consumers little, if any, control over information sharing if the company disclosed its intentions fully in advance.

But online businesses contend that even these bills, which echo the industry's own standards, go too far by giving the FTC too much authority to establish rules that could strangle the growth of the Internet.

With the two sides far apart, Tauzin said lawmakers would probably wait until release of a new FTC study on Internet privacy before trying to move on legislation. The agency plans to release its third annual survey of privacy policies of Internet Web sites by June.

A similar study sponsored by the agency last year examined 361 of the busiest 7,500 World Wide Web sites in the country. It found that 93 percent of those sites collected personal information, but only 44 percent posted privacy notices. Only 10 percent complied with all the fair practice guidelines developed by the industry and the FTC, which require companies to divulge plans for handling personal information and offer the consumer a chance to opt out.

Mary J. Culnan, a professor at Georgetown University's school of business who conducted the study for the FTC last year, said the new survey could provide support for legislation if it finds that most companies are not complying with the guidelines. "The real question now is whether the patience of Congress and the FTC has run thin," she said.

As it often does, Congress may simply decide to study the issue itself.

High-tech companies are rallying behind a bill (HR 4049) sponsored by Reps. Asa Hutchinson, R-Ark., and James P. Moran, D-Va., to create a bipartisan commission to conduct an 18-month study and make recommendations on privacy protection. The proposal is similar to a bill (S 1901) sponsored by Sen. Herb Kohl, D-Wis.

While Congress decides how it will handle the issue, U.S. trading partners are moving on their own restrictions.

Legislation pending in Canada would require consumer consent for the sharing of sensitive information by companies, including certain financial and medical records.

A directive by the European Union (EU) that took effect in 1998 barred the sharing of personal information by companies unless a consumer has given his consent

On February 23 the Commerce Department announced a deal with the EU to require American companies to give consumers in Europe a chance to opt out of information-sharing. ◆

Lawmakers, Industry Debate How to Tackle 'Cybercrime' Without Jeopardizing Privacy

The recent surge of computer hacker attacks on private and government Internet sites brought members of Congress face-to-face with cybercrime the week of Feb. 28, in a series of hearings that revealed sometimes sharp differences between the lawmakers and the technology industry on how to respond.

The hearings were prompted largely by the recent "denial of service" attacks on popular commercial Web sites, such as Yahoo!, Amazon.com and eBay, that pointed out the vulnerabilities of the booming e-commerce sector.

At three separate hearings, lawmakers learned that those attacks — still under investigation but believed to have been carried out by vandals using unsophisticated technology — were only a small part of a far more pervasive problem that is frustrating law enforcement and national security officials.

Witnesses told the congressional panels that the sheer variety of ways in which computer systems can be sabotaged — embodied in technical terms such as "cross-site scripting," "IP spoofing" and "SYN attacks" — threatens everything from personal financial data to electric power grids and crucial military command systems.

"Cybercrime presents the most fundamental challenge for law enforcement in the 21st century," Michael A. Vatis, director of the FBI's National Infrastructure Protection Center, told a joint hearing of the Senate Criminal Justice Oversight Subcommittee and the House Judiciary Subcommittee on Crime on Feb. 29. "A criminal sitting on the other side of the planet is now capable of stealthily infiltrating a computer network in this country to steal money, abscond with proprietary information or shut down e-commerce sites."

The hearings included an appearance by Kevin Mitnick, who has been described as one of the world's most notorious computer hackers, before the Senate Governmental Affairs Commit-

McCollum, right, and Sen. Strom Thurmond, R-S.C., left, conduct a Feb. 29 joint hearing investigating hacker attacks on private and government Web sites.

tee on March 2. Mitnick, 36, who was recently released after serving 59 months in federal prison for computer crimes, testified that he penetrated the computer systems of the IRS, the Social Security Administration, and large corporations such as Motorola Inc. and Sun Microsystems Inc. for the thrill and intellectual challenge, not to make money stealing secret information.

Mitnick, who led the FBI on a three-year manhunt that ended in 1995, said he would never have been caught had government officials not cooperated with telephone companies and Internet service providers in tracing his electronic footprints. He urged that federal agencies train employees to be aware of "social engineering" — tricking people into revealing passwords and other vital information.

Lawmakers offered their own suggestions, which ranged from modifying existing laws to address new types of electronic attacks, to increasing appropriations for federal computer crime-fighting efforts. Some urged caution, worried that increased electronic security measures could compromise personal privacy.

Underscoring the deliberations was the realization that while Congress can spend more money for increased security on government computers, it cannot dictate how the private sector responds or what technological solutions will be developed.

"At this stage, government should not force companies to take better security precautions, but we can set an example. Regretfully, thus far, we have been a woefully poor example," said Sen. Joseph I. Lieberman, D-Conn., cosponsor of a bill (S 1993) with Sen. Fred Thompson, R-Tenn., that would coordinate electronic security measures within the federal government and give the Office of Management and Budget oversight responsibilities.

As if to underscore Lieberman's contention, hackers infiltrated the Web site of House Speaker J. Dennis Hastert, R-Ill., the week of Feb. 28 and defaced the home page. Parts of the site (http://speakernews.house.gov) were briefly taken down.

Among other measures aimed at toughening existing laws to address cybercrimes is a bill (S 2092) introduced Feb. 24 by Sens. Jon Kyl, R-Ariz., and Charles E. Schumer, D-N.Y., that would provide law enforcement officials with expanded authority to trap and trace computer signals and would lower the barriers for federal prosecution of computer criminals. (*2000 CQ Weekly, p. 420*)

Schumer said Feb. 29, "The rules governing law enforcement have not kept pace with our changing technology, and this legislation is designed to make sure law enforcement has the tools it needs to keep up."

Deputy Attorney General Eric H. Holder Jr. endorsed the ideas embodied in the proposal at the Feb. 29 hearing.

But technology companies pointedly warned lawmakers not to micro-manage the world of cyberspace, saying the private sector is better equipped to respond quickly to new developments in computer crime. Instead, tech executives urged the federal government and private industry to improve the way they share information about emerging threats.

"Cooperation, not regulation or legislation, will ensure that the Internet remains secure and at the same time open to the broadest possible public access," Charles Giancarlo, senior vice president of Cisco Systems Inc., the world's largest manufacturer of computer hardware for the Internet, told lawmakers at the Feb. 29 hearing.

"National security is traditionally viewed as a government responsibility. Infrastructure security, however, does not lend itself to government management," said Howard Schmidt, chief information security officer for Microsoft Corp., the world's largest software maker. "The private sector has the knowledge and expertise to help fight against computer crimes on the infrastructures on which they operate."

Some lawmakers cautioned that increased surveillance of electronic signals could compromise individuals' privacy and vowed to block any legislation that would create a national security network. Lawmakers have already expressed concern about companies' ability to profile individuals by mining data from their online purchases, postings on Internet message boards and Web-browsing activity.

"In no circumstance will I support the creation of a nationwide computer security system that functions by monitoring and profiling online activities of millions of Americans," said Rep. Bob Barr, R-Ga., one of the most vocal privacy advocates in Congress, at the Feb. 29 hearing.

At the very least, lawmakers indicated, they may increase the Clinton administration's budget request for programs to fight computer crime through the appropriations process. The White House is requesting a $37 million increase in the Department of Justice's computer crime budget for fiscal 2001, which would bring total funding to $138 million. But House Judiciary Crime Subcommittee Chairman Bill McCollum, R-Fla., sounded incredulous when Justice Department officials told him the amount included $850,000 for additional prosecutors.

"And that's going to be enough, in light of what we're seeing here? You think you're going to have to come back and ask for more?" McCollum asked Holder.

Serious Federal Concerns

While disruption of commercial Web sites was the main focus of attention, the hearings also revealed serious security concerns surrounding government sites. Jack L. Brock Jr., director of governmentwide and defense information systems for the General Accounting Office (GAO), told the Senate Governmental Affairs Committee on March 2 that 22 of the largest federal agencies were not adequately protecting key operations from computer attacks. Of particular concern is the Department of Defense, which GAO found suffered "pervasive weaknesses" in information security.

"Government officials are increasingly worried about attacks from individuals and groups with malicious intentions, such as terrorists and nations engaging in information warfare," Brock told lawmakers.

A number of recent incidents have heightened concern about computers being used to wage information warfare and compromise national security. Last spring for example, during military operations against Yugoslavia in response to the Kosovo conflict, computer hackers in Belgrade tampered with NATO's Web site, saturated its e-mail system and sent computer viruses by e-mail.

Hackers believed to be working from Russia also broke into the Pentagon's computer network and other large government information systems last year, capturing large amounts of unclassified but sensitive information, including data on nuclear weapons and research labs. A 1998 incident that investigators labeled "Solar Sunrise" illustrated how teenagers in the United States and Israel could break into numerous military computer systems. While the pranksters did not obtain classified information, the incident raised fears about more malicious intruders. (*1998 CQ Weekly, p. 675*)

Security experts told members of the Senate Armed Services Emerging Threats and Capabilities Subcommittee on March 1 that part of the problem stems from the government's reliance on commercial "off the shelf" software that can be easily penetrated. Because of the rapid growth of the Internet and the development of increasingly complex communications systems, single solutions — such as erecting new firewalls or using encryption software to scramble messages — may not be enough to ward off intruders.

"The organizations that have applied a 'silver bullet' are lulled into a false sense of security and become less vigilant, but single solutions applied once are neither foolproof nor adequate," Stephen E. Cross, director of the software engineering institute at Carnegie Mellon University in Pittsburgh, told the subcommittee. The institute runs the CERT Coordination Center, which coordinates computer security efforts with Internet companies and the government.

Government and private officials indicated that the likely remedy is to try to improve the way agencies share information about threats in cyberspace. The Pentagon, for instance, recently designated the U.S. Space Command in Colorado Springs, Colo., as the lead military agency for coordinating network security efforts. The task involves safeguarding a network of 10,000 separate computer systems with 1.5 million individual computers located at 637 military bases and other locations.

But Mitnick, the ex-hacker, said officials must also focus on human factors, such as the ability to trick people into divulging sensitive information about computer systems. He noted that he was often able to pierce secure corporate computer systems simply by placing a phone call and posing as a worker with a computer problem.

"The methods that will most effectively minimize the ability of intruders to compromise information security are comprehensive user training and education," Mitnick said. ◆

Senate rejects Democratic measure; House GOP plans a vote before July Fourth recess

Parties Fighting Toward a Standoff Over Prescription Drug Benefits

The wrangling over a Medicare prescription drug benefit, which has crept toward center stage for weeks, took a leading role on Capitol Hill the week of June 19 with both parties pushing bills on an issue they view as critical to capturing seniors' votes in the November elections.

Senate Democrats on June 20 introduced a "bipartisan" measure to give Medicare beneficiaries drug coverage. Backers said the measure could be the basis for a compromise on prescription drugs this year, but two days later they tried to force Republicans to fold it into the fiscal 2001 Labor, Health and Human Services, and Education appropriations bill (HR 4577).

Richard J. Durbin, D-Ill., said the vote on prescription drugs would "really define the difference in values between the two parties." A few moments later, Phil Gramm, R-Texas, called the Democrats' maneuvering "politics at its worst." The Democrats' amendment eventually was rejected, 44 to 53. (*Vote 144, 2000 CQ Weekly, p. 1552; Labor-HHS, p. 1538*)

House GOP leaders, meanwhile, pushed ahead with plans to vote on their drug bill (HR 4680) before the July Fourth recess, concerned that allowing the $39.7 billion package to linger longer would weaken chances for passage, especially since President Clinton and Democrats continue to describe it as a "false promise" that would benefit insurers and drug manufacturers more than seniors.

The Ways and Means Committee approved the GOP bill June 21 along party lines, 23-14. The action came after Democrats failed, on a 14-23 vote, to substitute their own measure, which would have given drug coverage to seniors and added some $21 billion for payments to hospitals, nursing homes and other Medicare providers who say they are still hurting from spending cuts made in the 1997 budget law (PL 105-33). (*1997 Almanac, p. 2-47*)

Dubious Prospects

Despite the push by both parties the week of June 19, prospects are slim for enactment of any prescription drug legislation this year. Vast differences between the two parties' measures have kept a bipartisan consensus

from emerging, and the number of days in the legislative calendar is dwindling.

"I don't think there's enough time to do it this year," said Martin Corry, director of federal affairs for AARP, the lobbying group for seniors.

Sen. John B. Breaux, D-La., said the Senate skirmish all but guarantees that prescription drug legislation is dead for the year. "We're going to end up with nothing come the end of this year but an issue," he told reporters after the vote.

Still, even if no new drug benefit is created, the debate lays the groundwork for action when the 107th Congress and a new administration take office next year. Once the elections are over, lawmakers may find it easier to find common ground on the tough questions that must be answered before the 35-year-old entitlement program can be expanded to include prescription drugs. Among them: Should benefits be determined by the federal government or private sector, and when should so-called catastrophic coverage begin for beneficiaries with high drug bills?

Seniors Lobbyists Pleased

Despite the partisan rancor heard during the debate, advocates for the elderly are pleased with the ongoing discussion. "This debate is now over how, not whether," to add prescription drugs to Medicare, said Corry.

Quick Contents

Both parties are championing a Medicare drug benefit to win seniors' votes this fall, but vast differences remain between their proposals, and prospects are slim for legislation to be enacted this session.

Durbin, shown at a 1997 hearing, said the June 22 Senate vote on a Medicare drug benefit would define the differences between the two parties.

Looking for Closure on Managed Care, Conferees Reach Out to Norwood

Even as Congress dived into one politically charged health care battle on prescription drugs, congressional Republicans launched an all-out effort to bring another fight — the one over managed care — to a final bell.

As of June 23, however, the GOP negotiators were discovering how wide the disagreements remain among themselves.

Stung by Democratic charges that they were stalling the managed-care overhaul effort, GOP members of a House-Senate conference committee began a marathon series of meetings June 21 to reach an agreement among themselves that would resolve the vast differences between their managed-care bills (HR 2990).

By June 22, the late-night negotiations included not only House Speaker J. Dennis Hastert, R-Ill., but Rep. Charlie Norwood — the Georgia Republican who rammed the House bill through over the leadership's objections. (1999 CQ Weekly, p. 2354)

Hastert, viewing a managed-care bill as critical to preserving the GOP majority in the House, had pushed the negotiators to wrap things up June 22. But the two sides remained stuck on how much to expand patients' ability to sue managed-care plans and how many people should be covered by the new federal rules.

Norwood remained nonplussed by the talks. In an angry statement released June 23, he said the Republicans were weeks away from an agreement that could be signed into law. "What I heard discussed will never pass muster with either the Republicans or Democrats in the House that voted for the original bill," he said.

The statement did not endear him to Senate Republicans, who said the discussions were far enough along that staffers were starting to draft legislative language.

Senate Republicans are trying for a quick deal as well, but they are in less danger of losing their majority

and are putting less emphasis on deadlines. "I don't know whether it will be tomorrow or several weeks from now, but this summer we will pass a Patients' Bill of Rights," Senate Majority Leader Trent Lott, R-Miss., told reporters June 21.

To do that, the Republican conferees concluded that they needed Norwood's help after all. Hastert did not name him to the conference committee, and all but one of the House GOP conferees opposed his bill because they thought it went too far in exposing managed-care plans and employers to lawsuits.

In recent weeks, however, Norwood said Hastert has been in constant touch, and Senate Assistant Majority Leader Don Nickles, R-Okla. — the manager of the Senate bill and an outspoken critic of the House bill — held his first face-to-face meeting with Norwood on June 21. The next day, Hastert brought Norwood into the negotiations.

It is not hard to see why. Norwood's bill attracted 68 Republican votes in the House, and his support may be crucial in winning their votes for any conference report. In addition, he is now the only link the Republicans have to Democrats such as John D. Dingell of Michigan, the cosponsor of the House bill.

A Republican Deal?

The Republicans decided to talk among themselves after concluding they could not do business with the Democrats — a conclusion they reached when Sen. Edward M. Kennedy, D-Mass., embarrassed them June 8 by forcing a Senate vote on the House bill. The Senate tabled, or killed, 51-48, a Kennedy effort to attach the House managed-care bill — without its GOP-sponsored provisions to increase access to health insurance — to the fiscal 2001 defense authorization legislation (S 2549). (2000 CQ Weekly, p. 1391)

Still, GOP leaders maintain they are not under any illusions they can push a compromise bill through Congress without Democratic votes. And Norwood said he is telling them that strategy would not work in the House anyway. "Democrats kind of walked away from the table," Nickles told reporters June 21, but "we'll be bringing back the Democrats before too long."

In their June 4 offer to the Democratic conferees, Senate Republicans proposed letting patients sue managed-care plans in federal court if the plan refused to comply with the ruling of the external reviewers.

To extend the core patient protections, such as direct access to specialists and coverage of emergency services, to all 193 million privately insured Americans without pre-empting state laws, the GOP compromise would allow governors to certify that they had state patient protection laws at least as strong as the federal protections.

Norwood said he has not dismissed either idea on its face, but there are still major disagreements. He said state courts must decide the fights over quality of care — whether a managed-care plan did not provide enough of a benefit, such as a long enough hospital stay, or delayed a treatment for so long that it was no longer useful to the patient. Senate Republicans, however, want to keep any lawsuits against managed-care plans in federal courts so that employers would face one consistent set of liability rules, rather than 50 different ones.

The core patient protections are another matter. Senate Republicans do not want to pre-empt state laws, so they would leave those laws alone if the governors say they are as strong as the new federal protections. Norwood, however, said some kind of oversight body — not necessarily the Department of Health and Human Services — would have to make sure the state laws really exist and are as strong as the governors say they are.

While the prescription drug issue has been a top legislative priority for months for House Republicans, Senate GOP leaders have moved more slowly. "The prescription drug proposal can explode in costs if isn't done carefully," Senate Majority Whip Don Nickles, R-Okla., told reporters June 20.

Senate Finance Committee members have recently begun meeting privately to try to develop a legislative compromise on prescription drugs. On June 20, several members of that panel, including Democrats Bob Graham of Florida and Charles S. Robb of Virginia, came forward with their own drug plan, which tried to find the middle ground between the House Republican bill and Clinton's prescription drug proposal. *(Background, 2000 CQ Weekly, p. 1436)*

The Graham plan would offer coverage beginning in fiscal 2003, with beneficiaries paying premiums on an income-related scale. Most beneficiaries would pay 50 percent of the premium's cost; wealthier seniors would pay up to 75 percent. After meeting a $250 deductible, seniors would pay half their drug costs up to $3,500 and Medicare would pay the remainder. For costs between $3,500 and $4,000, beneficiaries would pay 25 percent and Medicare 75 percent. Medicare would pay all expenses above $4,000.

Both the House GOP bill and Clinton's plan would initially pay half of beneficiaries' expenses, up to $2,100 and $2,000, respectively, and increase over the life of both bills. In the House Republican plan, catastrophic coverage would begin in fiscal 2003 when beneficiaries' expenses reached $6,000. Clinton has proposed setting aside $35 billion of the federal budget surplus to begin catastrophic coverage in fiscal 2006.

Democrats said Graham's proposal, which Robb offered June 22 as an amendment to the Labor-HHS bill, should be approved because Republicans had nothing to offer. "We've waited for years for your prescription drug benefit. But there's nothing for us to consider from the Republican side,"

Durbin said.

Senate Republicans complained that Democrats were trying to rush to the floor a proposal that few members had read, that had not been reviewed by the committees of jurisdiction and that would increase Medicare spending by billions of dollars. "The last thing we need to do is put our Medicare program at greater risk," said Finance Committee Chairman William V. Roth Jr., R-Del.

Exchanges between Ways and Means Republicans and Democrats were just as combative as those on the Senate floor when the committee met June 21 to mark up legislation sponsored by Health Subcommittee Chairman Bill Thomas, R-Calif.

His package would look to the private insurance market to create drug benefit packages that would be available to all beneficiaries, an approach that Democrats and insurers have criticized. The Health Insurance Association of America has said its members would not write such policies because they would be too expensive.

A Different View

At least one company has embraced the Thomas plan. Per G.H. Lofberg, the chairman of Merck-Medco Managed Care, a division of the drug manufacturer Merck & Co., told Thomas in a June 21 letter that his company would be willing to develop a drug plan for seniors and participate in "what we expect will be a highly competitive market." Thomas said the letter was evidence that the private market would offer drug policies to seniors.

Charles B. Rangel of New York, the panel's ranking Democrat, said the GOP bill would privatize the Medicare program "and give the money not to the people but to the insurance companies." Pete Stark, D-Calif., called the Republican plan "a prescription for failure" because it would not give the government enough power to ensure that beneficiaries received comprehensive drug coverage at affordable rates.

Benjamin L. Cardin, D-Md., offered

an amendment that would have allowed the government to create a standard package of drug benefits available to all Medicare beneficiaries. It failed on a 14-22 party-line vote.

Ways and Means Democrats, led by Stark, later offered a substitute drug package that, like Clinton's, would pay up to half of beneficiaries' costs, up to $2,000 in 2003 and 2004, rising to half of $5,000 in 2009. Unlike Clinton's plan, it would begin catastrophic coverage in 2003 once a senior's out-of-pocket costs reached $4,000.

Stark said his proposal, which failed on a party-line vote, 14-23, would "provide a defined benefit on which [seniors] can depend for uniform benefits across this country." Thomas faulted it for relying too heavily on future budget surpluses for funding.

Thomas and House Speaker J. Dennis Hastert, R-Ill., said June 21 that House Republicans would work to give Medicare providers more money later this year, most likely after the widely anticipated Congressional Budget Office mid-session review, which could add $40 billion to the budget surplus.

Thomas said he was confident House Republicans would support his drug plan even without any additional "givebacks" for Medicare providers.

"That wouldn't affect the vote one way or the other," said Thomas. "You can't spend money you don't have."

Should Thomas' bill fail, Republicans may be able to find more Medicare money via "lockbox" legislation (HR 3859) the House passed June 20 by a vote of 420-2. That measure would require any Medicare surpluses to be used only for the Medicare program. That could include giving more money to hospitals, nursing homes, managed-care plans and other Medicare providers. *(Story, 2000 CQ Weekly, p. 1518; Vote 297, p. 1554)*

The "lockbox" legislation was dropped from the GOP drug bill to showcase it on the House floor. "This was so important it should stand on its own," said Wally Herger, R-Calif. ◆

Appendix

The Legislative Process in Brief

Note: Parliamentary terms used below are defined in the glossary.

Introduction of Bills

A House member (including the resident commissioner of Puerto Rico and non-voting delegates of the District of Columbia, Guam, the Virgin Islands and American Samoa) may introduce any one of several types of bills and resolutions by handing it to the clerk of the House or placing it in a box called the hopper. A senator first gains recognition of the presiding officer to announce the introduction of a bill. If objection is offered by any senator, the introduction of the bill is postponed until the following day.

As the next step in either the House or Senate, the bill is numbered, referred to the appropriate committee, labeled with the sponsor's name and sent to the Government Printing Office so that copies can be made for subsequent study and action. Senate bills may be jointly sponsored and carry several senators' names. Until 1978, the House limited the number of members who could cosponsor any one bill; the ceiling was eliminated at the beginning of the 96th Congress. A bill written in the executive branch and proposed as an administration measure usually is introduced by the chairman of the congressional committee that has jurisdiction.

Bills — Prefixed with HR in the House, S in the Senate, followed by a number. Used as the form for most legislation, whether general or special, public or private.

Joint Resolutions — Designated H J Res or S J Res. Subject to the same procedure as bills, with the exception of a joint resolution proposing an amendment to the Constitution. The latter must be approved by two-thirds of both houses and is thereupon sent directly to the administrator of general services for submission to the states for ratification instead of being presented to the president for his approval.

Concurrent Resolutions — Designated H Con Res or S Con Res. Used for matters affecting the operations of both houses. These resolutions do not become law.

Resolutions — Designated H Res or S Res. Used for a matter concerning the operation of either house alone and adopted only by the chamber in which it originates.

Committee Action

With few exceptions, bills are referred to the appropriate standing committees. The job of referral formally is the responsibility of the Speaker of the House and the presiding officer of the Senate, but this task usually is carried out on their behalf by the parliamentarians of the House and Senate. Precedent, statute and the jurisdictional mandates of the committees as set forth in the rules of the House and Senate determine which committees receive what kinds of bills. An exception is the referral of private bills, which are sent to whatever committee is designated by their sponsors. Bills are technically considered "read for the first time" when referred to House committees.

When a bill reaches a committee it is placed on the committee's calendar. At that time the bill comes under the sharpest congressional focus. Its chances for passage are quickly determined — and the great majority of bills falls by the legislative roadside. Failure of a committee to act on a bill is equivalent to killing it; the measure can be withdrawn from the committee's purview only by a discharge petition signed by a majority of the House membership on House bills, or by adoption of a special resolution in the Senate. Discharge attempts rarely succeed.

The first committee action taken on a bill usually is a request for comment on it by interested agencies of the government. The committee chairman may assign the bill to a subcommittee for study and hearings, or it may be considered by the full committee. Hearings may be public, closed (executive session) or both. A subcommittee, after considering a bill, reports to the full committee its recommendations for action and any proposed amendments.

The full committee then votes on its recommendation to the House or Senate. This procedure is called "ordering a bill reported." Occasionally a committee may order a bill reported unfavorably; most of the time a report, submitted by the chairman of the committee to the House or Senate, calls for favorable action on the measure since the committee can effectively "kill" a bill by simply failing to take any action.

After the bill is reported, the committee chairman instructs the staff to prepare a written report. The report describes the purposes and scope of the bill, explains the committee revisions, notes proposed changes in existing law and, usually, includes the views of the executive branch agencies consulted. Often committee members opposing a measure issue dissenting minority statements that are included in the report.

Usually, the committee "marks up" or proposes amendments to the bill. If they are substantial and the measure is complicated, the committee may order a "clean bill" introduced, which will embody the proposed amendments. The original bill then is put aside and the clean bill, with a new number, is reported to the floor.

The chamber must approve, alter or reject the committee amendments before the bill itself can be put to a vote.

Floor Action

After a bill is reported back to the house where it originated, it is placed on the calendar.

There are five legislative calendars in the House, issued in one cumulative calendar titled *Calendars of the United States House of Representatives and History of Legislation.* The House

This graphic shows the most typical way in which proposed legislation is enacted into law. There are more complicated, as well as simpler, routes, and most bills never become law. The process is illustrated with two hypothetical bills, House bill No. 1 (HR 1) and Senate bill No. 2 (S 2). Bills must be passed by both houses in identical form before they can be sent to the president. The path of HR 1 is traced by a gray line, that of S 2 by a black line. In practice, most bills begin as similar proposals in both houses.

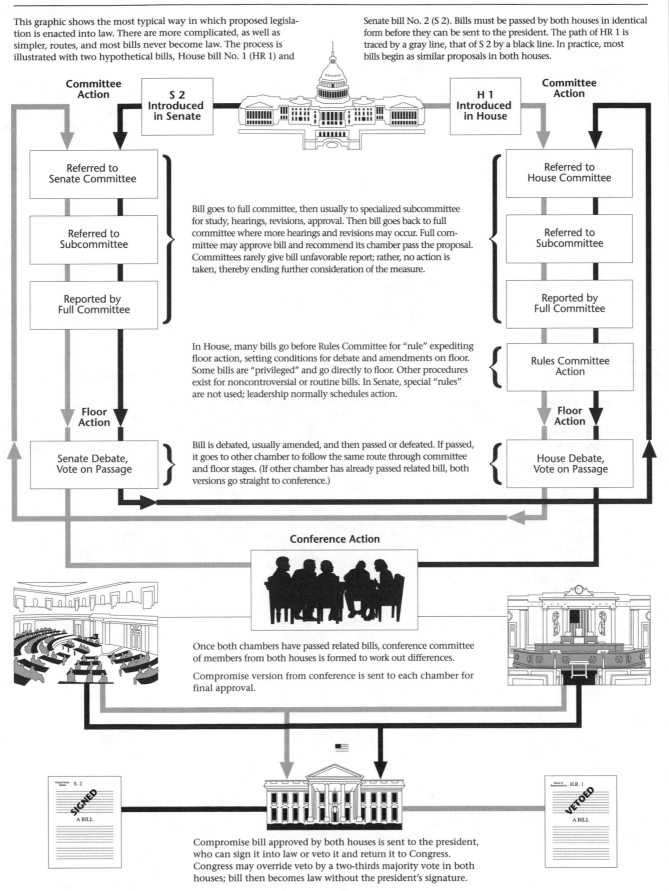

Committee Action

S 2 Introduced in Senate

H 1 Introduced in House

Committee Action

Referred to Senate Committee

Referred to Subcommittee

Reported by Full Committee

Bill goes to full committee, then usually to specialized subcommittee for study, hearings, revisions, approval. Then bill goes back to full committee where more hearings and revisions may occur. Full committee may approve bill and recommend its chamber pass the proposal. Committees rarely give bill unfavorable report; rather, no action is taken, thereby ending further consideration of the measure.

Referred to House Committee

Referred to Subcommittee

Reported by Full Committee

In House, many bills go before Rules Committee for "rule" expediting floor action, setting conditions for debate and amendments on floor. Some bills are "privileged" and go directly to floor. Other procedures exist for noncontroversial or routine bills. In Senate, special "rules" are not used; leadership normally schedules action.

Rules Committee Action

Floor Action

Senate Debate, Vote on Passage

Bill is debated, usually amended, and then passed or defeated. If passed, it goes to other chamber to follow the same route through committee and floor stages. (If other chamber has already passed related bill, both versions go straight to conference.)

Floor Action

House Debate, Vote on Passage

Conference Action

Once both chambers have passed related bills, conference committee of members from both houses is formed to work out differences.

Compromise version from conference is sent to each chamber for final approval.

S. 2 — SIGNED — A BILL

H.R. 1 — VETOED — A BILL

Compromise bill approved by both houses is sent to the president, who can sign it into law or veto it and return it to Congress. Congress may override veto by a two-thirds majority vote in both houses; bill then becomes law without the president's signature.

calendars are:

The Union Calendar to which are referred bills raising revenues, general appropriations bills and any measures directly or indirectly appropriating money or property. It is the Calendar of the Committee of the Whole House on the State of the Union.

The House Calendar to which are referred bills of public character not raising revenue or appropriating money.

The Corrections Calendar to which are referred bills to repeal rules and regulations deemed excessive or unnecessary when the Corrections Calendar is called the second and fourth Tuesday of each month. (Instituted in the 104th Congress to replace the seldom-used Consent Calendar.) A three-fifths majority is required for passage.

The Private Calendar to which are referred bills for relief in the nature of claims against the United States or private immigration bills that are passed without debate when the Private Calendar is called the first and third Tuesdays of each month.

The Discharge Calendar to which are referred motions to discharge committees when the necessary signatures are signed to a discharge petition.

There is only one legislative calendar in the Senate and one "executive calendar" for treaties and nominations submitted to the Senate. When the Senate Calendar is called, each senator is limited to five minutes' debate on each bill.

Debate. A bill is brought to debate by varying procedures. If a routine measure, it may await the call of the calendar. If it is urgent or important, it can be taken up in the Senate either by unanimous consent or by a majority vote. The majority leader, in consultation with the minority leader and others, schedules the bills that will be taken up for debate.

In the House, precedence is granted if a special rule is obtained from the Rules Committee. A request for a special rule usually is made by the chairman of the committee that favorably reported the bill, supported by the bill's sponsor and other committee members. The request, considered by the Rules Committee in the same fashion that other committees consider legislative measures, is in the form of a resolution providing for immediate consideration of the bill. The Rules Committee reports the resolution to the House where it is debated and voted on in the same fashion as regular bills. If the Rules Committee fails to report a rule requested by a committee, there are several ways to bring the bill to the House floor — under suspension of the rules, on Calendar Wednesday or by a discharge motion.

The resolutions providing special rules are important because they specify how long the bill may be debated and whether it may be amended from the floor. If floor amendments are banned, the bill is considered under a "closed rule," which permits only members of the committee that first reported the measure to the House to alter its language, subject to chamber acceptance.

When a bill is debated under an "open rule," amendments may be offered from the floor. Committee amendments always are taken up first but may be changed, as may all amendments up to the second degree; that is, an amendment to an amendment to an amendment is not in order.

Duration of debate in the House depends on whether the bill is under discussion by the House proper or before the House when it is sitting as the Committee of the Whole House on the State of the Union. In the former, the amount of time for debate either is determined by special rule or is allocated with an hour for each member if the measure is under consideration without a rule. In the Committee of the Whole the amount of time agreed on for general debate is equally divided between proponents and opponents. At the end of general discussion, the bill is read section by section for amendment. Debate on an amendment is limited to five minutes for each side; this is called the "five-minute rule." In practice, amendments regularly are debated more than ten minutes, with members gaining the floor by offering pro forma amendments or obtaining unanimous consent to speak longer than five minutes.

Senate debate usually is unlimited. It can be halted only by unanimous consent by "cloture," which requires a three-fifths majority of the entire Senate except for proposed changes in the Senate rules. The latter requires a two-thirds vote.

The House considers almost all important bills within a parliamentary framework known as the Committee of the Whole. It is not a committee as the word usually is understood; it is the full House meeting under another name for the purpose of speeding action on legislation. Technically, the House sits as the Committee of the Whole when it considers any tax measure or bill dealing with public appropriations. It also can resolve itself into the Committee of the Whole if a member moves to do so and the motion is carried. The Speaker appoints a member to serve as the chairman. The rules of the House permit the Committee of the Whole to meet when a quorum of 100 members is present on the floor and to amend and act on bills, within certain time limitations. When the Committee of the Whole has acted, it "rises," the Speaker returns as the presiding officer of the House and the member appointed chairman of the Committee of the Whole reports the action of the committee and its recommendations. The Committee of the Whole cannot pass a bill; instead it reports the measure to the full House with whatever changes it has approved. The full House then may pass or reject the bill — or, on occasion, recommit the bill to committee. Amendments adopted in the Committee of the Whole may be put to a second vote in the full House.

Votes. Voting on bills may occur repeatedly before they are finally approved or rejected. The House votes on the rule for the bill and on various amendments to the bill. Voting on amendments often is a more illuminating test of a bill's support than is the final tally. Sometimes members approve final passage of bills after vigorously supporting amendments that, if adopted, would have scuttled the legislation.

The Senate has three different methods of voting: an untabulated voice vote, a standing vote (called a division) and a recorded roll call to which members answer "yea" or "nay" when their names are called. The House also employs voice and standing votes, but since January 1973 yeas and nays have been recorded by an electronic voting device, eliminating the need for time-consuming roll calls.

Another method of voting, used in the House only, is the teller vote. Traditionally, members filed up the center aisle past counters; only vote totals were announced. Since 1971, one-fifth of a quorum can demand that the votes of individual members be recorded, thereby forcing them to take a public position on amendments to key bills. Electronic voting now is commonly used for this purpose.

After amendments to a bill have been voted upon, a vote may be taken on a motion to recommit the bill to committee. If carried, this vote removes the bill from the chamber's calendar and is usually a death blow to the bill. If the motion is unsuccessful, the bill then is "read for the third time." An actual reading usually is dispensed with. Until 1965, an opponent of a bill could delay this move by objecting and asking for a full reading of an engrossed (certified in final form) copy of the bill. After the "third reading," the vote on final passage is taken.

Examples of Legislative Documents

The final vote may be followed by a motion to reconsider, and this motion may be followed by a move to lay the motion on the table. Usually, those voting for the bill's passage vote for the tabling motion, thus safeguarding the final passage action. With that, the bill has been formally passed by the chamber. While a motion to reconsider a Senate vote is pending on a bill, the measure cannot be sent to the House.

Action in Second House

After a bill is passed it is sent to the other chamber. This body may then take one of several steps. It may pass the bill as is — accepting the other chamber's language. It may send the bill to committee for scrutiny or alteration, or reject the entire bill, advising the other house of its actions. Or it simply may ignore the bill submitted while it continues work on its own version of the proposed legislation. Frequently, one chamber may approve a version of a bill that is greatly at variance with the version already passed by the other house, and then substitute its contents for the language of the other, retaining only the latter's bill number.

A provision of the Legislative Reorganization Act of 1970 permits a separate House vote on any non-germane amendment added by the Senate to a House-passed bill and requires a majority vote to retain the amendment. Previously the House was forced to act on the bill as a whole; the only way to defeat the non-germane amendment was to reject the entire bill.

Often the second chamber makes only minor changes. If these are readily agreed to by the other house, the bill then is routed to the president. However, if the opposite chamber significantly alters the bill submitted to it, the measure usually is "sent to conference." The chamber that has possession of the "papers" (engrossed bill, engrossed amendments, messages of transmittal) requests a conference and the other chamber must agree to it. If the second house does not agree, the bill dies.

Conference, Final Action

Conference. A conference works out conflicting House and Senate versions of a legislative bill. The conferees usually are senior members appointed by the presiding officers of the two houses, from the committees that managed the bills. Under this arrangement the conferees of one house have the duty of trying to maintain their chamber's position in the face of amending actions by the conferees (also referred to as "managers") of the other house.

The number of conferees from each chamber may vary, the range usually being from three to nine members in each group, depending upon the length or complexity of the bill involved. There may be five representatives and three senators on the conference committee, or the reverse. But a majority vote controls the action of each group so that a large representation does not give one chamber a voting advantage over the other chamber's conferees.

Theoretically, conferees are not allowed to write new legislation in reconciling the two versions before them, but this curb sometimes is bypassed. Many bills have been put into acceptable compromise form only after new language was provided by the conferees. The 1970 Reorganization Act attempted to tighten restrictions on conferees by forbidding them to introduce any language on a topic that neither chamber sent to conference or to modify any topic beyond the scope of the different House and Senate versions.

Frequently the ironing out of difficulties takes days or even weeks. Conferences on involved appropriations bills sometimes are particularly drawn out.

As a conference proceeds, conferees reconcile differences between the versions, but generally they grant concessions only insofar as they remain sure that the chamber they represent will accept the compromises. Occasionally, uncertainty over how either house will react, or the positive refusal of a chamber to back down on a disputed amendment, results in an impasse, and the bills die in conference even though each was approved by its sponsoring chamber.

Conferees sometimes go back to their respective chambers for further instructions, when they report certain portions in disagreement. Then the chamber concerned can either "recede and concur" in the amendment of the other house or "insist on its amendment."

When the conferees have reached agreement, they prepare a conference report embodying their recommendations (compromises). The report, in document form, must be submitted to each house.

The conference report must be approved by each house. Consequently, approval of the report is approval of the compromise bill. In the order of voting on conference reports, the chamber which asked for a conference yields to the other chamber the opportunity to vote first.

Final Steps. After a bill has been passed by both the House and Senate in identical form, all of the original papers are sent to the enrolling clerk of the chamber in which the bill originated. He then prepares an enrolled bill, which is printed on parchment paper. When this bill has been certified as correct by the secretary of the Senate or the clerk of the House, depending on which chamber originated the bill, it is signed first (no matter whether it originated in the Senate or House) by the Speaker of the House and then by the president of the Senate. It is next sent to the White House to await action.

If the president approves the bill, he signs it, dates it and usually writes the word "approved" on the document. If he does not sign it within 10 days (Sundays excepted) and Congress is in session, the bill becomes law without his signature.

However, should Congress adjourn before the 10 days expire, and the president has failed to sign the measure, it does not become law. This procedure is called the pocket veto.

A president vetoes a bill by refusing to sign it and, before the 10-day period expires, returning it to Congress with a message stating his reasons. The message is sent to the chamber that originated the bill. If no action is taken on the message, the bill dies. Congress, however, can attempt to override the president's veto and enact the bill, "the objections of the president to the contrary notwithstanding." Overriding a veto requires a two-thirds vote of those present, who must number a quorum and vote by roll call.

Debate can precede this vote, with motions permitted to lay the message on the table, postpone action on it or refer it to committee. If the president's veto is overridden by a two-thirds vote in both houses, the bill becomes law. Otherwise it is dead.

When bills are passed finally and signed, or passed over a veto, they are given law numbers in numerical order as they become law. There are two series of numbers, one for public and one for private laws, starting at the number "1" for each two-year term of Congress. They are then identified by law number and by Congress — for example, Private Law 21, 97th Congress; Public Law 250, 97th Congress (or PL 97–250).

The Budget Process in Brief

Through the budget process, the president and Congress decide how much to spend and tax during the upcoming fiscal year. More specifically, they decide how much to spend on each activity, ensure that the government spends no more and spends it only for that activity, and report on that spending at the end of each budget cycle.

The President's Budget

The law requires that, by the first Monday in February, the president submit to Congress his proposed federal budget for the next fiscal year, which begins on October 1. In order to accomplish this, the president establishes general budget and fiscal policy guidelines. Based on these guidelines, executive branch agencies make requests for funds and submit them to the White House's Office of Management and Budget (OMB) nearly a year prior to the start of a new fiscal year. The OMB, receiving direction from the president and administration official, reviews the agencies' requests and develops a detailed budget by December. From December to January the OMB prepares the budget documents, so that the president can deliver it to Congress in February.

The president's budget is the executive branch's plan for the next year — but it is just a proposal. After receiving it, Congress has its own budget process to follow from February to October. Only after Congress passes the required spending bills — and the president signs them — has the government created its actual budget.

Action in Congress

Congress first must pass a "budget resolution" — a framework within which the members of Congress will make their decisions about spending and taxes. It includes targets for total spending, total revenues, and the deficit, and allocations within the spending target for the two types of spending — discretionary and mandatory.

Discretionary spending, which currently accounts for about 33 percent of all federal spending, is what the president and Congress must decide to spend for the next year through the thirteen annual appropriations bills. It includes money for such activities as the FBI and the Coast Guard, for housing and education, for NASA and highway and bridge construction, and for defense and foreign aid.

Mandatory spending, which currently accounts for 67 percent of all spending, is authorized by laws that have already been passed. It includes entitlement spending — such as for Social Security, Medicare, veterans' benefits, and food stamps — through which individuals receive benefits because they are eligible based on their age, income, or other criteria. It also includes interest on the national debt, which the government pays to individuals and institutions that hold Treasury bonds and other government securities. The only way the president

and Congress can change the spending on entitlement and other mandatory programs is if they change the laws that authorized the programs.

Currently, the law imposes a limit or "cap" through 1998 on total annual discretionary spending. Within the cap, however, the president and Congress can, and often do, change the spending levels from year to year for the thousands of individual federal programs.

In addition, the law requires that legislation that would raise mandatory spending or lower revenues — compared to existing law — be offset by spending cuts or revenue increases. This requirement, called "pay-as-you-go" is designed to prevent new legislation from increasing the deficit.

Once Congress passes the budget resolution, it turns its attention to passing the thirteen annual appropriations bills and, if it chooses, "authorizing" bills to change the laws governing mandatory spending and revenues.

Congress begins by examining the president's budget in detail. Scores of committees and subcommittees hold hearings on proposals under their jurisdiction. The House and Senate Armed Services Authorizing Committees, and the Defense and Military Construction Subcommittees of the Appropriations Committees, for instance, hold hearings on the president's defense budget. The White House budget director, cabinet officers, and other administration officials work with Congress as it accepts some of the president's proposals, rejects others, and changes still others. Congress can change funding levels, eliminate programs, or add programs not requested by the president. It can add or eliminate taxes and other sources of revenue, or make other changes that affect the amount of revenue collected. Congressional rules require that these committees and subcommittees take actions that reflect the congressional budget resolution.

The president's budget, the budget resolution, and the appropriations or authorizing bills measure spending in two ways — "budget authority" and "outlays." Budget authority is what the law authorizes the federal government to spend for certain programs, projects, or activities. What the government actually spends in a particular year, however, is an outlay. For example, when the government decides to build a space exploration system, the president and Congress may agree to appropriate $1 billion in budget authority. But the space system may take ten years to build. Thus, the government may spend $100 million in outlays in the first year to begin construction and the remaining $900 million during the next nine years as the construction continues.

Congress must provide budget authority before the federal agencies can obligate the government to make outlays. When Congress fails to complete action on one or more of the regular annual appropriations bills before the fiscal year begins on October 1, budget authority may be made on a temporary basis through continuing resolutions. Continuing resolutions make budget authority available for limited periods of time, generally at rates related through some formula to the rate provided in the previous year's appropriation.

Monitoring the Budget

Once Congress passes and the president signs the federal appropriations bills or authorizing laws for the fiscal year, the government monitors the budget through (1) agency program managers and budget officials, including the Inspectors General, who report only to the agency head; (2) the Office of Management and Budget; (3) congressional committees; and (4) the General Accounting Office, an auditing arm of Congress.

This oversight is designed to (1) ensure that agencies comply with legal limits on spending, and that they use budget authority only for the purposes intended; (2) see that programs are operating consistently with legal requirements and existing policy; and (3) ensure that programs are well managed and achieving the intended results.

The president may withhold appropriated amounts from obligation only under certain limited circumstances — to provide for contingencies, to achieve savings made possible through changes in requirements or greater efficiency of operations, or as otherwise provided by law. The Impoundment Control Act of 1974 specifies the procedures that must be followed if funds are withheld. Congress can also cancel previous authorized budget authority by passing a rescissions bill — but it also must be signed by the president.

Glossary of Congressional Terms

Absolute Majority—A vote requiring approval by a majority of all members of a house rather than a majority of members present and voting. Also referred to as constitutional majority.

Act—(1) A bill passed in identical form by both houses of Congress and signed into law by the president or enacted over his veto. A bill also becomes an act without the president's signature if he does not return it to Congress within 10 days (Sundays excepted) and if Congress has not adjourned within that period. (2) Also, the technical term for a bill passed by at least one house and engrossed.

Adjourn for More Than Three Days—Under Article I, Section 5, of the Constitution, neither house may adjourn for more than three days without the approval of the other. The necessary approval is given in a concurrent resolution and agreed to by both houses, which may permit one or both to take such an adjournment.

Adjournment Sine Die—Final adjournment of an annual or two-year session of Congress; literally, adjournment without a day. The two houses must agree to a privileged concurrent resolution for such an adjournment. A sine die adjournment precludes Congress from meeting again until the next constitutionally fixed date of a session (January 3 of the following year) unless Congress determines otherwise by law or the president calls it into special session. Article II, Section 3, of the Constitution authorizes the president to adjourn both houses until such time as he thinks proper when the two houses cannot agree to a time of adjournment, but no president has ever exercised this authority.

Adjournment to a Day (and Time) Certain—An adjournment that fixes the next date and time of meeting for one or both houses. It does not end an annual session of Congress.

Advice and Consent—The Senate's constitutional role in consenting to or rejecting the president's nominations to executive branch and judicial offices and the treaties he submits. Confirmation of nominees requires a simple majority vote of the senators present and voting. Treaties must be approved by a two-thirds majority of senators present and voting.

Amendment—A formal proposal to alter the text of a bill, resolution, amendment, motion, treaty, or some other text. Technically, it is a motion. An amendment may strike out (eliminate) part of a text, insert new text, or strike out and insert—that is, replace all or part of the text with new text. The texts of amendments considered on the floor are printed in full in the *Congressional Record*.

Amendment in the Nature of a Substitute—Usually, an amendment to replace the entire text of a measure. It strikes out everything after the enacting clause and inserts a version that may be somewhat, substantially, or entirely different. When a committee adopts extensive amendments to a measure, it often incorporates them into such an amendment. Occasionally, the term is applied to an amendment that replaces a major portion of a measure's text.

Annual Authorization—Legislation that authorizes appropriations for a single fiscal year and usually for a specific amount. Under the rules of the authorization-appropriation process, an annually authorized agency or program must be reauthorized each year if it is to receive appropriations for that year. Sometimes Congress fails to enact the reauthorization but nevertheless provides appropriations to continue the program, circumventing the rules by one means or another.

Appeal—A member's formal challenge of a ruling or decision by the presiding officer. On appeal, a house or a committee may overturn the ruling by majority vote. The right of appeal ensures the body against arbitrary control by the chair. Appeals are rarely made in the House and are even more rarely successful. Rulings are more frequently appealed in the Senate and occasionally overturned, in part because its presiding officer is not the majority party's leader, as in the House.

Apportionment—The action, after each decennial census, of allocating the number of members in the House of Representatives to each state. By law, the total number of House members (not counting delegates and a resident commissioner) is fixed at 435. The number allotted to each state is based approximately on its proportion of the nation's total population. Since the Constitution guarantees each state one representative no matter how small its population, exact proportional distribution is virtually impossible. The mathematical formula currently used to determine the apportionment is called the Method of Equal Proportions. (*See Method of Equal Proportions.*)

Appropriation—(1) Legislative language that permits a federal agency to incur obligations and make payments from the Treasury for specified purposes, usually during a specified period of time. (2) The specific amount of money made available by such language. The Constitution prohibits payments from the Treasury except "in Consequence of Appropriations made by Law." With some exceptions, the rules of both houses forbid consideration of appropriations for purposes that are unauthorized in law or of appropriation amounts larger than those authorized in law. The House of Representatives claims the exclusive right to originate appropriation bills—a claim the Senate denies in theory but accepts in practice.

Authorization—(1) A statutory provision that establishes or continues a federal agency, activity or program for a fixed or indefinite period of time. It may also establish policies and restrictions and deal with organizational and administrative matters. (2) A statutory provision that authorizes appropriations for an agency, activity, or program. The appropriations may be authorized for one year, several years, or an indefinite period of time, and the authorization may be for a specific amount of money or an indefinite amount ("such sums as may be necessary"). Authorizations of specific amounts are construed as ceilings on the amounts that subsequently may be appropriated in an appropriation bill, but not as minimums; either house may appropriate lesser amounts or nothing at all.

Backdoor Spending Authority—Authority to incur obligations that evades the normal congressional appropriations process because it is provided in legislation other than appropriation acts. The most common forms are borrowing authority, contract authority, and entitlement authority.

Baseline—A projection of the levels of federal spending, revenues, and the resulting budgetary surpluses or deficits for the upcoming and subsequent fiscal years, taking into account laws enacted to date and assuming no new policy decisions. It provides a benchmark for measuring the budgetary effects of proposed changes in federal revenues or spending, assuming certain economic conditions.

Bill—The term for the chief vehicle Congress uses for enacting laws. Bills that originate in the House of Representatives are designated as H.R., those in the Senate as S., followed by a number assigned in the order in which they are introduced during a two-year Congress. A bill becomes a law if passed in identical language by both houses and signed by the president, or passed over his veto, or if the president fails to sign it within 10 days after he has received it while Congress is in session.

Bills and Resolutions Introduced—Members formally present measures to their respective houses by delivering them to a clerk in the chamber when their house is in session. Both houses permit any number of members to join in introducing a bill or resolution. The first member listed on the measure is the sponsor; the other members listed are its cosponsors.

Bills and Resolutions Referred—After a bill or resolution is introduced, it is normally sent to one or more committees that have jurisdiction over its subject, as defined by House and Senate rules and precedents. A Senate measure is usually referred to the committee with jurisdiction over the predominant subject of its text, but it may be sent to two or more committees by unanimous consent or on a motion offered jointly by the majority and minority leaders. In the House, a rule requires the Speaker to refer a measure to the committee that has primary jurisdiction. The Speaker is also authorized to refer measures sequentially to additional committees.

Borrowing Authority—Statutory authority permitting a federal agency, such as the Export-Import Bank, to borrow money from the public or the Treasury to finance its operations. It is a form of backdoor spending. To bring such spending under the control of the congressional appropriation process, the Congressional Budget Act requires that new borrowing authori-

ty shall be effective only to the extent and in such amounts as are provided in appropriations acts.

Budget—A detailed statement of actual or anticipated revenues and expenditures during an accounting period. For the national government, the period is the federal fiscal year (October 1–September 30). The budget usually refers to the president's budget submission to Congress early each calendar year. The president's budget estimates federal government income and spending for the upcoming fiscal year and contains detailed recommendations for appropriation, revenue, and other legislation. Congress is not required to accept or even vote directly on the president's proposals, and it often revises the president's budget extensively. (*See Fiscal Year.*)

Budget Act—Common name for the Congressional Budget and Impoundment Control Act of 1974, which established the basic procedures of the current congressional budget process; created the House and Senate Budget committees; and enacted procedures for reconciliation, deferrals, and rescissions. (*See Budget Process, Deferral, Impoundment, Reconciliation, Rescission. See also Gramm-Rudman-Hollings Act of 1985.*)

Budget and Accounting Act of 1921—The law that, for the first time, authorized the president to submit to Congress an annual budget for the entire federal government. Prior to the act, most federal agencies sent their budget requests to the appropriate congressional committees without review by the president.

Budget Authority—Generally, the amount of money that may be spent or obligated by a government agency or for a government program or activity. Technically, it is statutory authority to enter into obligations that normally result in outlays. The main forms of budget authority are appropriations, borrowing authority, and contract authority. It also includes authority to obligate and expend the proceeds of offsetting receipts and collections. Congress may make budget authority available for only one year, several years, or an indefinite period, and it may specify definite or indefinite amounts.

Budget Process—(1) In Congress, the procedural system it uses (a) to approve an annual concurrent resolution on the budget that sets goals for aggregate and functional categories of federal expenditures, revenues, and the surplus or deficit for an upcoming fiscal year; and (b) to implement those goals in spending, revenue, and, if necessary, reconciliation and debt-limit legislation. (2) In the executive branch, the process of formulating the president's annual budget, submitting it to Congress, defending it before congressional committees, implementing subsequent budget-related legislation, impounding or sequestering expenditures as permitted by law, auditing and evaluating programs, and compiling final budget data. The Budget and Accounting Act of 1921 and the Congressional Budget and Impoundment Control Act of 1974 established the basic elements of the current budget process. Major revisions were enacted in the Gramm-Rudman-Hollings Act of 1985 and the Budget Enforcement Act of 1990.

Budget Resolution—A concurrent resolution in which Congress establishes or revises its version of the federal budget's broad financial features for the upcoming fiscal year and several additional fiscal years. Like other concurrent resolutions, it does not have the force of law, but it provides the framework within which Congress subsequently considers revenue, spending, and other budget-implementing legislation. The framework consists of two basic elements: (1) aggregate budget amounts (total revenues, new budget authority, outlays, loan obligations and loan guarantee commitments, deficit or surplus, and debt limit); and (2) subdivisions of the relevant aggregate amounts among the functional categories of the budget. Although it does not allocate funds to specific programs or accounts, the budget committees' reports accompanying the resolution often discuss the major program assumptions underlying its functional amounts. Unlike those amounts, however, the assumptions are not binding on Congress.

By Request—A designation indicating that a member has introduced a measure on behalf of the president, an executive agency, or a private individual or organization. Members often introduce such measures as a courtesy because neither the president nor any person other than a member of Congress can do so. The term, which appears next to the sponsor's name, implies that the member who introduced the measure does not necessarily endorse it. A House rule dealing with by-request introductions dates from 1888, but the practice goes back to the earliest history of Congress.

Calendar—A list of measures or other matters (most of them favorably reported by committees) that are eligible for floor consideration. The House has five calendars; the Senate has two. A place on a calendar does not guarantee consideration. Each house decides which measures and matters it will take up, when, and in what order, in accordance with its rules and practices.

Calendar Wednesday—A House procedure that on Wednesdays permits its committees to bring up for floor consideration nonprivileged measures they have reported. The procedure is so cumbersome and susceptible to dilatory tactics, however, that committees rarely use it.

Call of the Calendar—Senate bills that are not brought up for debate by a motion, unanimous consent, or a unanimous consent agreement are brought before the Senate for action when the calendar listing them is "called." Bills must be called in the order listed. Measures considered by this method usually are noncontroversial, and debate on the bill and any proposed amendments is limited to a total of five minutes for each senator.

Caucus—(1) A common term for the official organization of each party in each house. (2) The official title of the organization of House Democrats. House and Senate Republicans and Senate Democrats call their organizations "conferences." (3) A term for an informal group of members who share legislative interests, such as the Black Caucus, Hispanic Caucus, and Children's Caucus.

Censure—The strongest formal condemnation of a member for misconduct short of expulsion. A house usually adopts a resolution of censure to express its condemnation, after which the presiding officer reads its rebuke aloud to the member in the presence of his colleagues.

Chamber—The Capitol room in which a house of Congress normally holds its sessions. The chamber of the House of Representatives, officially called the Hall of the House, is consider-

ably larger than that of the Senate because it must accommodate 435 representatives, four delegates, and one resident commissioner. Unlike the Senate chamber, members have no desks or assigned seats. In both chambers, the floor slopes downward to the well in front of the presiding officer's raised desk. A chamber is often referred to as "the floor," as when members are said to be on or going to the floor. Those expressions usually imply that the member's house is in session.

Christmas Tree Bill—Jargon for a bill adorned with amendments, many of them unrelated to the bill's subject, that provide benefits for interest groups, specific states, congressional districts, companies, and individuals.

Classes of Senators—A class consists of the 33 or 34 senators elected to a six-year term in the same general election. Since the terms of approximately one-third of the senators expire every two years, there are three classes.

Clean Bill—After a House committee extensively amends a bill, it often assembles its amendments and what is left of the bill into a new measure that one or more of its members introduces as a "clean bill." The revised measure is assigned a new number.

Clerk of the House—An officer of the House of Representatives responsible principally for administrative support of the legislative process in the House. The clerk is invariably the candidate of the majority party.

Cloture—A Senate procedure that limits further consideration of a pending proposal to 30 hours in order to end a filibuster. Sixteen senators must first sign and submit a cloture motion to the presiding officer. One hour after the Senate meets on the second calendar day thereafter, the chair puts the motion to a yea-and-nay vote following a live quorum call. If three-fifths of all senators (60 if there are no vacancies) vote for the motion, the Senate must take final action on the cloture proposal by the end of the 30 hours of consideration and may consider no other business until it takes that action. Cloture on a proposal to amend the Senate's standing rules requires approval by two-thirds of the senators present and voting.

Code of Official Conduct—A House rule that bans certain actions by House members, officers, and employees; requires them to conduct themselves in ways that "reflect creditably" on the House; and orders them to adhere to the spirit and the letter of House rules and those of its committees. The code's provisions govern the receipt of outside compensation, gifts, and honoraria, and the use of campaign funds; prohibit members from using their clerk-hire allowance to pay anyone who does not perform duties commensurate with that pay; forbids discrimination in members' hiring or treatment of employees on the grounds of race, color, religion, sex, handicap, age, or national origin; orders members convicted of a crime who might be punished by imprisonment of two or more years not to participate in committee business or vote on the floor until exonerated or reelected; and restricts employees' contact with federal agencies on matters in which they have a significant financial interest. The Senate's rules contain some similar prohibitions.

College of Cardinals—A popular term for the subcommittee chairmen of the appropriations committees, reflecting their influence over appropriation measures. The chairmen of the full appropriations committees are sometimes referred to as popes.

Committee—A panel of members elected or appointed to perform some service or function for its parent body. Congress has four types of committees: standing, special or select, joint, and, in the House, a Committee of the Whole.

Committees conduct investigations, make studies, issue reports and recommendations, and, in the case of standing committees, review and prepare measures on their assigned subjects for action by their respective houses. Most committees divide their work among several subcommittees. With rare exceptions, the majority party in a house holds a majority of the seats on its committees, and their chairmen are also from that party.

Committee of the Whole—Common name of the Committee of the Whole House on the State of the Union, a committee consisting of all members of the House of Representatives. Measures from the union calendar must be considered in the Committee of the Whole before the House officially completes action on them; the committee often considers other major bills as well. A quorum of the committee is 100, and it meets in the House chamber under a chairman appointed by the Speaker. Procedures in the Committee of the Whole expedite consideration of legislation because of its smaller quorum requirement, its ban on certain motions, and its five-minute rule for debate on amendments. Those procedures usually permit more members to offer amendments and participate in the debate on a measure than is normally possible. The Senate no longer uses a Committee of the Whole.

Committee Veto—A procedure that requires an executive department or agency to submit certain proposed policies, programs, or action to designated committees for review before implementing them. Before 1983, when the Supreme Court declared that a legislative veto is unconstitutional, these provisions permitted committees to veto the proposals. They no longer do so, and the term is now something of a misnomer. Nevertheless, agencies usually take the pragmatic approach of trying to reach a consensus with the committees before carrying out their proposals, especially when an appropriations committee is involved.

Concurrent Resolution—A resolution that requires approval by both houses but is not sent to the president for his signature and therefore cannot have the force of law. Concurrent resolutions deal with the prerogatives or internal affairs of Congress as a whole. Designated H. Con. Res. in the House and S. Con. Res. in the Senate, they are numbered consecutively in each house in their order of introduction during a two-year Congress.

Conference—(1) A formal meeting or series of meetings between members representing each house to reconcile House and Senate differences on a measure (occasionally several measures). Since one house cannot require the other to agree to its proposals, the conference usually reaches agreement by compromise. When a conference completes action on a measure, or as much action as appears possible, it sends its recommendations to both houses in the form of a conference report, accompanied by an explanatory statement. (2) The official title of the organization of all Democrats or Republicans in the Senate and of all Republicans in the House of Representatives. (*See Party Caucus.*)

Confirmations—(*See Nomination.*)

Congress—(1) The national legislature of the United States, consisting of the House of Representatives and the Senate. (2) The national legislature in office during a two-year period. Congresses are numbered sequentially; thus, the 1st Congress of 1789–1791 and the 102d Congress of 1991–1993. Before 1935, the two-year period began on the first Monday in December of odd-numbered years. Since then it has extended from January of an odd-numbered year through noon on January 3 of the next odd-numbered year. A Congress usually holds two annual sessions, but some have had three sessions and the 67th Congress had four. When a Congress expires, measures die if they have not yet been enacted.

Congressional Record—The daily, printed, and substantially verbatim account of proceedings in both the House and Senate chambers. Extraneous materials submitted by members appear in a section titled "Extensions of Remarks." A "Daily Digest" appendix contains highlights of the day's floor and committee action plus a list of committee meetings and floor agendas for the next day's session.

Although the official reporters of each house take down every word spoken during the proceedings, members are permitted to edit and "revise and extend" their remarks before they are printed. In the Senate section, all speeches, articles, and other material submitted by senators but not actually spoken or read on the floor are set off by large black dots, called bullets. However, bullets do not appear when a senator reads part of a speech and inserts the rest. In the House section, undelivered speeches and materials are printed in a distinctive typeface. The term "permanent *Record*" refers to the bound volumes of the daily *Records* of an entire session of Congress.

Congressional Terms of Office—A term normally begins on January 3 of the year following a general election and runs two years for representatives and six years for senators. A representative chosen in a special election to fill a vacancy is sworn in for the remainder of his predecessor's term. An individual appointed to fill a Senate vacancy usually serves until the next general election or until the end of the predecessor's term, whichever comes first. Some states, however, require their governors to call a special election to fill a Senate vacancy shortly after an appointment has been made.

Continuing Resolution (CR)—A joint resolution that provides funds to continue the operation of federal agencies and programs at the beginning of a new fiscal year if their annual appropriation bills have not yet been enacted; also called continuing appropriations.

Contract Authority—Statutory authority permitting an agency to enter into contracts or incur other obligations even though it has not received an appropriation to pay for them. Congress must eventually fund them because the government is legally liable for such payments. The Congressional Budget Act of 1974 requires that new contract authority may not be used unless provided for in advance by an appropriation act, but it permits a few exceptions.

Controllable Expenditures—Federal spending that is permitted but not mandated by existing authorization law and therefore may be adjusted by congressional action in appropriation bills. (*See Appropriation.*)

Correcting Recorded Votes—The rules of both houses prohibit members from changing their votes after a vote result has been announced. Nevertheless, the Senate permits its members to withdraw or change their votes, by unanimous consent, immediately after the announcement. In rare instances, senators have been granted unanimous consent to change their votes several days or weeks after the announcement.

Votes tallied by the electronic voting system in the House may not be changed. But when a vote actually given is not recorded during an oral call of the roll, a member may demand a correction as a matter of right. On all other alleged errors in a recorded vote, the Speaker determines whether the circumstances justify a change. Occasionally, members merely announce that they were incorrectly recorded; announcements can occur hours, days, or even months after the vote and appear in the *Congressional Record*.

Corrections Calendar—Members of the House may place on this calendar bills reported favorably from committee that repeal rules and regulations considered excessive or unnecessary. Bills on the Corrections Calendar normally are called on the second and fourth Tuesday of each month at the discretion of the Speaker in consultation with the minority leader. A bill must be on the calendar for at least three legislative days before it can be brought up for floor consideration. Once on the floor, a bill is subject to one hour of debate equally divided between the chairman and ranking member of the committee of jurisdiction. A vote may be called on whether to recommit the bill to committee with or without instructions. To pass, a three-fifths majority, or 261 votes if all House members vote, is required.

Cosponsor—A member who has joined one or more other members to sponsor a measure. (*See Bills and Resolutions Introduced.*)

Current Services Estimates—Executive branch estimates of the anticipated costs of federal programs and operations for the next and future fiscal years at existing levels of service and assuming no new initiatives or changes in existing law. The president submits these estimates to Congress with his annual budget and includes an explanation of the underlying economic and policy assumptions on which they are based, such as anticipated rates of inflation, real economic growth, and unemployment, plus program caseloads and pay increases.

Custody of the Papers—Possession of an engrossed measure and certain related basic documents that the two houses produce as they try to resolve their differences over the measure.

Dance of the Swans and the Ducks—A whimsical description of the gestures some members use in connection with a request for a recorded vote, especially in the House. When a member wants his colleagues to stand in support of the request, he moves his hands and arms in a gentle upward motion resembling the beginning flight of a graceful swan. When he wants his colleagues to remain seated in order to avoid such a vote, he moves his hands and arms in a vigorous downward motion resembling a diving duck.

Dean—Within a state's delegation in the House of Representatives, the member with the longest continuous service.

Debt Limit—The maximum amount of outstanding federal public debt permitted by law. The limit (or ceiling) covers virtually all debt incurred by the government except agency debt. Each congressional budget resolution sets forth the new debt limit that may be required under its provisions.

Deferral—An impoundment of funds for a specific period of time that may not extend beyond the fiscal year in which it is proposed. Under the Impoundment Control Act of 1974, the president must notify Congress that he is deferring the spending or obligation of funds provided by law for a project or activity. Congress can disapprove the deferral by legislation.

Deficit—The amount by which the government's outlays exceed its budget receipts for a given fiscal year. Both the president's budget and the annual congressional budget resolution provide estimates of the deficit or surplus for the upcoming and several future fiscal years.

Degrees of Amendment—Designations that indicate the relationships of amendments to the text of a measure and to each other. In general, an amendment offered directly to the text of a measure is an amendment in the first degree, and an amendment to that amendment is an amendment in the second degree. Both houses normally prohibit amendments in the third degree—that is, an amendment to an amendment to an amendment.

Dilatory Tactics—Procedural actions intended to delay or prevent action by a house or a committee. They include, among others, offering numerous motions, demanding quorum calls and recorded votes at every opportunity, making numerous points of order and parliamentary inquiries, and speaking as long as the applicable rules permit. The Senate's rules permit a battery of dilatory tactics, especially lengthy speeches, except under cloture. In the House, possible dilatory tactics are more limited. Speeches are always subject to time limits and debate-ending motions. Moreover, a House rule instructs the Speaker not to entertain dilatory motions and lets the Speaker decide whether a motion is dilatory. However, the Speaker may not override the constitutional right of a member to demand the yeas and nays, and in practice usually waits for a point of order before exercising that authority. (*See Cloture.*)

Discharge a Committee—Remove a measure from a committee to which it has been referred in order to make it available for floor consideration. Noncontroversial measures are often discharged by unanimous consent. However, because congressional committees have no obligation to report measures referred to them, each house has procedures to extract controversial measures from recalcitrant committees. Six discharge procedures are available in the House of Representatives. The Senate uses a motion to discharge, which is usually converted into a discharge resolution.

Discharge Calendar—The House calendar to which motions to discharge committees are referred when they have the required number of signatures (218) and are awaiting floor action.

Discharge Petition—*(See Discharge a Committee.)*

Discharge Resolution—In the Senate, a special motion that any senator may introduce to relieve a committee from consideration of a bill before it. The resolution can be called up for Senate approval or disapproval in the same manner as any other Senate business. *(House procedure, see Discharge a Committee.)*

Division Vote—A vote in which the chair first counts those in favor of a proposition and then those opposed to it, with no record made of how each member votes. In the Senate, the chair may count raised hands or ask senators to stand, whereas the House requires members to stand; hence, often called a standing vote. Committees in both houses ordinarily use a show of hands. A division usually occurs after a voice vote and may be demanded by any member or ordered by the chair if there is any doubt about the outcome of the voice vote. The demand for a division can also come before a voice vote. In the Senate, the demand must come before the result of a voice vote is announced. It may be made after a voice vote announcement in the House, but only if no intervening business has transpired and only if the member was standing and seeking recognition at the time of the announcement. A demand for the yeas and nays or, in the House, for a recorded vote, takes precedence over a division vote.

Enacting Clause—The opening language of each bill, beginning "Be it enacted by the Senate and House of Representatives of the United States of America in Congress assembled..." This language gives legal force to measures approved by Congress and signed by the president or enacted over his veto. A successful motion to strike it from a bill kills the entire measure.

Engrossed Bill—The official copy of a bill or joint resolution as passed by one chamber, including the text as amended by floor action, and certified by the clerk of the House or the secretary of the Senate (as appropriate). Amendments by one house to a measure or amendments of the other also are engrossed. House engrossed documents are printed on blue paper; the Senate's are printed on white paper.

Enrolled Bill—The final official copy of a bill or joint resolution passed in identical form by both houses. An enrolled bill is printed on parchment. After it is certified by the chief officer of the house in which it originated and signed by the House Speaker and the Senate president pro tempore, the measure is sent to the president for his signature.

Entitlement Program—A federal program under which individuals, businesses, or units of government that meet the requirements or qualifications established by law are entitled to receive certain payments if they seek such payments. Major examples include Social Security, Medicare, Medicaid, unemployment insurance, and military and federal civilian pensions. Congress cannot control their expenditures by refusing to appropriate the sums necessary to fund them because the government is legally obligated to pay eligible recipients the amounts to which the law entitles them.

Executive Calendar—The Senate's calendar for committee reports on its executive business, namely treaties and nominations. The calendar numbers indicate the order in which items were referred to the calendar but have no bearing on when or if the Senate will consider them. The Senate, by motion or unanimous consent, resolves itself into executive session to consider them.

Executive Document—A document, usually a treaty, sent by the president to the Senate for approval. It is referred to a committee in the same manner as other measures. Resolutions to ratify treaties have their own "treaty document" numbers. For example, the first treaty submitted in the 106th Congress would be "Treaty Doc 106-1."

Executive Order—A unilateral proclamation by the president that has a policy-making or legislative impact. Members of Congress have challenged some executive orders on the grounds that they usurped the authority of the legislative branch. Although the Supreme Court has ruled that a particular order exceeded the president's authority, it has upheld others as falling within the president's general constitutional powers.

Executive Privilege—The assertion that presidents have the right to withhold certain information from Congress. Presidents have based their claim on: (1) the constitutional separation of powers; (2) the need for secrecy in military and diplomatic affairs; (3) the need to protect individuals from unfavorable publicity; (4) the need to safeguard the confidential exchange of ideas in the executive branch; and (5) the need to protect individuals who provide confidential advice to the president.

Executive Session—A meeting of a Senate or House committee (or occasionally of either chamber) that only its members may attend. Witnesses regularly appear at committee meetings in executive session — for example, Defense Department officials during presentations of classified defense information. Other members of Congress may be invited, but the public and press are not to attend.

Expenditures—The actual spending of money as distinguished from the appropriation of funds. Expenditures are made by the disbursing officers of the administration; appropriations are made only by Congress. The two are rarely identical in any fiscal year. In addition to some current budget authority, expenditures may represent budget authority made available one, two, or more years earlier.

Expulsion—A member's removal from office by a two-thirds vote of his house; the super majority is required by the Constitution. It is the most severe and most rarely used sanction a house can invoke against a member. Although the Constitution provides no explicit grounds for expulsion, the courts have ruled that it may be applied only for misconduct during a member's term of office, not for conduct before the member's election. Generally, neither house will consider expulsion of a member convicted of a crime until the judicial processes have been exhausted. At that stage, members sometimes resign rather than face expulsion. In 1977 the House adopted a rule urging members convicted of certain crimes to voluntarily abstain from voting or participating in other legislative business.

Federal Debt—The total amount of monies borrowed and not yet repaid by the federal government. Federal debt consists of public debt and agency debt. Public debt is the portion of the federal debt borrowed by the Treasury or the Federal Financing Bank directly from the public or from another federal fund or account. For example, the Treasury regularly borrows money from the Social Security trust fund. Public debt accounts for about 99 percent of the federal debt. Agency debt refers to the debt incurred by federal agencies like the Export-Import Bank, but excluding the Treasury and the Federal Financing Bank, which are authorized by law to borrow funds from the public or from another government fund or account.

Filibuster—The use of obstructive and time-consuming parliamentary tactics by one member or a minority of members to delay, modify, or defeat proposed legislation or rules changes. Filibusters are also sometimes used to delay urgently needed measures in order to force the body to accept other legislation. The Senate's rules permitting unlimited debate and the extraordinary majority it requires to impose cloture make filibustering particularly effective in that chamber. Under the stricter rules of the House, filibusters in that body are short-lived and therefore ineffective and rarely attempted

Fiscal Year—The federal government's annual accounting period. It begins October 1 and ends on the following September 30. A fiscal year is designated by the calendar year in which it ends and is often referred to as FY. Thus, fiscal year 1999 began October 1, 1998, ended September 30, 1999, and is called FY99. In theory, Congress is supposed to complete action on all budgetary measures applying to a fiscal year before that year begins. It rarely does so.

Five-Minute Rule—In its most common usage, a House rule that limits debate on an amendment offered in Committee of the Whole to five minutes for its sponsor and five minutes for an opponent. In practice, the committee routinely permits longer debate by two devices: the offering of pro forma amendments, each debatable for five minutes, and unanimous consent for a member to speak longer than five minutes. Also a House rule that limits a committee member to five minutes when questioning a witness at a hearing until each member has had an opportunity to question that witness.

Floor Manager—A majority party member responsible for guiding a measure through its floor consideration in a house and for devising the political and procedural strategies that might be required to get the measure passed. The presiding officer gives the floor manager priority recognition to debate, offer amendments, oppose amendments, and make crucial procedural motions.

Frank—Informally, a member's legal right to send official mail postage free under his or her signature; often called the franking privilege. Technically, it is the autographic or facsimile signature used on envelopes instead of stamps that permits members and certain congressional officers to send their official mail free of charge. The franking privilege has been authorized by law since the first Congress, except for a few months in 1873. Congress reimburses the U.S. Postal Service for the franked mail it handles.

Function or Functional Category—A broad category of national need and spending of budgetary significance. A category provides an accounting method for allocating and keeping track of budgetary resources and expenditures for that function because it includes all budget accounts related to the functions subject or purpose such as agriculture, administration of justice, commerce and housing and energy. Functions do not necessarily correspond with appropriations acts or with the budgets of individual agencies.

Germane—Basically, on the same subject as the matter under consideration. A House rule requires that all amendments be germane. In the Senate, only amendments proposed to general appropriation bills and budget resolutions or under cloture must be germane. Germaneness rules can be evaded by suspension of the rules in both houses, by unanimous consent agreements in the Senate, and by special rules from the Rules Committee in the House.

Gerrymandering—The manipulation of legislative district boundaries to benefit a particular party, politician, or minority group. The term originated in 1812 when the Massachusetts legislature redrew the lines of state legislative districts to favor the party of Gov. Elbridge Gerry, and some critics said one district looked like a salamander.

Gramm-Rudman-Hollings Act of 1985—Common name for the Balanced Budget and Emergency Deficit Control Act of 1985, which established new budget procedures intended to balance the federal budget by fiscal year 1991. The timetable subsequently was extended and then deleted. The act's chief sponsors were senators Phil Gramm (R-Texas), Warren Rudman (R-N.H.), and Ernest Hollings (D-S.C.).

Grandfather Clause—A provision in a measure, law, or rule that exempts an individual, entity, or a defined category of individuals or entities from complying with a new policy or restriction. For example, a bill that would raise taxes on persons who reach the age of 65 after a certain date inherently grandfathers out those who are 65 before that date. Similarly, a Senate rule limiting senators to two major committee assignments also grandfathers some senators who were sitting on a third major committee prior to a specified date.

Grants-in-Aid—Payments by the federal government to state and local governments to help provide for assistance programs or public services.

Hearing—Committee or subcommittee meetings to receive testimony from witnesses on proposed legislation during investigations or for oversight purposes. Relatively few bills are important enough to justify formal hearings. Witnesses often include experts, government officials, spokespersons for interested groups, officials of the General Accounting Office, and members of Congress. Also, the printed transcripts of hearings.

Hold—A senator's request that his or her party leaders delay floor consideration of certain legislation or presidential nominations. The majority leader usually honors a hold for a reasonable period of time, especially if its purpose is to assure the senator that the matter will not be called up during his or her absence or to give the senator time to gather necessary information.

Hold-Harmless Clause—In legislation providing a new formula for allocating federal funds, a clause to ensure that recipients of those funds do not receive less in a future year than they did in the current year if the new formula would result in a reduction for them. Similar to a grandfather clause, it has been used most frequently to soften the impact of sudden reductions in federal grants. (*See Grandfather Clause.*)

Hopper—A box on the clerk's desk in the House chamber into which members deposit bills and resolutions to introduce them. In House jargon, to drop a bill in the hopper is to introduce it.

Hour Rule—(1) A House rule that permits members, when recognized, to hold the floor in debate for no more than one hour each. The majority party member customarily yields one-half the time to a minority member. Although the hour rule applies to general debate in Committee of the Whole as well as in the House, special rules routinely vary the length of time for such debate and its control to fit the circumstances of particular measures.

House—The House of Representatives, as distinct from the Senate, although each body is a "house" of Congress.

House as in Committee of the Whole—A hybrid combination of procedures from the general rules of the House and from the rules of the Committee of the Whole, sometimes used to expedite consideration of a measure on the floor.

House Calendar—The calendar reserved for all public bills and resolutions that do not raise revenue or directly or indirectly appropriate money or property when they are favorably reported by House committees.

House Manual—A commonly used title for the handbook of the rules of the House of Representatives, published in each Congress. Its official title is *Constitution, Jefferson's Manual, and Rules of the House of Representatives*.

House of Representatives—The house of Congress in which states are represented roughly in proportion to their populations, but every state is guaranteed at least one representative. By law, the number of voting representatives is fixed at 435. Four delegates and one resident commissioner also serve in the House; they may vote in their committees but not on the House floor. Although the House and Senate have equal legislative power, the Constitution gives the House sole authority to originate revenue measures. The House also claims the right to originate appropriation measures, a claim the Senate disputes in theory but concedes in practice. The House has the sole power to impeach, and it elects the president when no candidate has received a majority of the electoral votes. It is sometimes referred to as the lower body.

Immunity—(1) Members' constitutional protection from lawsuits and arrest in connection with their legislative duties. They may not be tried for libel or slander for anything they say on the floor of a house or in committee. Nor may they be arrested while attending sessions of their houses or when traveling to or from sessions of Congress, except when charged with treason, a felony, or a breach of the peace. (2) In the case of a witness before a committee, a grant of protection from prosecution based on that person's testimony to the committee. It is used to compel witnesses to testify who would otherwise refuse to do so on the constitutional ground of possible self-incrimination. Under such a grant, none of a witness testimony may be used against him or her in a court proceeding except in a prosecution for perjury or for giving a false statement to Congress.

Impeachment—The first step to remove the president, vice president, or other federal civil officers from office and to disqualify them from any future federal office "of honor, Trust or Profit." An impeachment is a formal charge of treason, bribery, or "other high Crimes and Misdemeanors." The House has the sole power of impeachment and the Senate the sole power of trying the charges and convicting. The House impeaches by a simple majority vote; conviction requires a two-thirds vote of all senators present.

Impoundment—An executive branch action or inaction that delays or withholds the expenditure or obligation of budget authority provided by law. The Impoundment Control Act of 1974 classifies impoundments as either deferrals or rescissions, requires the president to notify Congress about all such actions, and gives Congress authority to approve or reject them. The Constitution is unclear on whether a president may refuse to spend appropriated money, but Congress usually expects the president to spend at least enough to achieve the purposes for which the money was provided whether or not he agrees with those purposes.

Joint Committee—A committee composed of members selected from each house. The functions of most joint committees involve investigation, research, or oversight of agencies closely related to Congress. Permanent joint committees, created by statute, are sometimes called standing joint committees. Once quite numerous, only four joint committees remained as of 1997: Joint Economic, Joint Taxation, Joint Library, and Joint Printing. No joint committee has authority to report legislation.

Joint Resolution—A legislative measure that Congress uses for purposes other than general legislation. Like a bill, it has the force of law when passed by both houses and either approved by the president or passed over the president's veto. Unlike a bill, a joint resolution enacted into law is not called an act; it retains its original title.

Most often, joint resolutions deal with such relatively limited matters as the correction of errors in existing law, continuing appropriations, a single appropriation, or the establishment of permanent joint committees. Unlike bills, however, joint resolutions also are used to propose constitutional amendments; these do not require the president's signature and become effective only when ratified by three-fourths of the states. The House designates joint resolutions as H.J. Res., the Senate as S.J. Res. Each house numbers its joint resolutions consecutively in the order of introduction during a two-year Congress.

Journal—The official record of House or Senate actions, including every motion offered, every vote cast, amendments agreed to, quorum calls, and so forth. Unlike the *Congressional Record*, it does not provide reports of speeches, debates, statements, and the like. The Constitution requires each house to maintain a *Journal* and to publish it periodically.

King of the Mountain (or Hill) Rule—(*See Queen of the Hill Rule.*)

Lame Duck—Jargon for a member who has not been reelected, or did not seek reelection, and is serving the balance of his or her term.

Lame Duck Session—A session of a Congress held after the election for the succeeding Congress, so-called after the lame duck members still serving.

Law—An act of Congress that has been signed by the president, passed over the president's veto, or allowed to become law without the president's signature.

Legislative Day—The day that begins when a house meets after an adjournment and ends when it next adjourns. Because the House of Representatives normally adjourns at the end of a daily session, its legislative and calendar days usually coincide. The Senate, however, frequently recesses at the end of a daily session, and its legislative day may extend over several calendar days, weeks, or months. Among other uses, this technicality permits the Senate to save time by circumventing its morning hour, a procedure required at the beginning of every legislative day

Legislative Veto—A procedure, declared unconstitutional in 1983, that allowed Congress or one of its houses to nullify certain actions of the president, executive branch agencies, or independent agencies. Sometimes called congressional vetoes or congressional disapprovals. Following the Supreme Court's 1983 decision, Congress amended several legislative veto statutes to require enactment of joint resolutions, which are subject to presidential veto, for nullifying executive branch actions.

Live Pair—A voluntary and informal agreement between two members on opposite sides of an issue under which the member who is present for a recorded vote withholds or withdraws his or her vote because the other member is absent.

Loan Guarantee—A statutory commitment by the federal government to pay part or all of a loans principal and interest to a lender or the holder of a security in case the borrower defaults.

Lobby—To try to persuade members of Congress to propose, pass, modify, or defeat proposed legislation or to change or repeal existing laws. A lobbyist attempts to promote his or her own preferences or those of a group, organization, or industry. Originally the term referred to persons frequenting the lobbies or corridors of legislative chambers in order to speak to lawmakers. In a general sense, lobbying includes not only direct contact with members but also indirect attempts to influence them, such as writing to them or persuading others to write or visit them, attempting to mold public opinion toward a desired legislative goal by various means, and contributing or arranging for contributions to members election campaigns. The right to lobby stems from the First Amendment to the Constitution, which bans laws that abridge the right of the people to petition the government for a redress of grievances.

Logrolling—Jargon for a legislative tactic or bargaining strategy in which members try to build support for their legislation by promising to support legislation desired by other members or by accepting amendments they hope will induce their colleagues to vote for their bill.

Mace—The symbol of the office of the House sergeant at arms. Under the direction of the Speaker, the sergeant at arms is responsible for preserving order on the House floor by holding up the mace in front of an unruly member, or by carrying the mace up and down the aisles to quell boisterous behavior. When the House is in session, the mace sits on a pedestal at the Speaker's right; when the House is in Committee of the Whole, it is moved to a lower pedestal. The mace is 46 inches high and consists of 13 ebony rods bound in silver and topped by a silver globe with a silver eagle, wings outstretched, perched on it.

Majority Leader—The majority party's chief floor spokesman, elected by that party's caucus—sometimes called floor leader. In the Senate, the majority leader also develops the party's political and procedural strategy, usually in collaboration with other party officials and committee chairmen. He negotiates the Senates agenda and committee ratios with the minority leader and usually calls up measures for floor action. The chamber traditionally concedes to the majority leader the right to determine the days on which it will meet and the hours at which it will convene and adjourn. In the House, the majority leader is the Speaker's deputy and heir apparent. He helps plan the floor agenda and the party's legislative strategy and often speaks for the party leadership in debate.

Majority Whip—In effect, the assistant majority leader, in either the House or Senate. His job is to help marshal majority forces in support of party strategy and legislation.

Manual—The official handbook in each house prescribing in detail its organization, procedures, and operations.

Marking Up a Bill—Going through the contents of a piece of legislation in committee or subcommittee to, for example, consider its provisions in large and small portions, act on amendments to provisions and proposed revisions to the language, and insert new sections and phraseology. If the bill is extensively amended, the committee's version may be introduced as a separate bill, with a new number, before being considered by the full House or Senate. (*See Clean Bill.*)

Method of Equal Proportions—The mathematical formula used since 1950 to determine how the 435 seats in the House of Representatives should be distributed among the 50 states in the apportionment following each decennial census. It minimizes as much as possible the proportional difference between the average district population in any two states. Because the Constitution guarantees each state at least one representative, 50 seats are automatically apportioned. The formula calculates priority numbers for each state, assigns the first of the 385 remaining seats to the state with the highest priority number, the second to the state with the next highest number, and so on until all seats are distributed. (*See Apportionment.*)

Midterm Election—The general election for members of Congress that occurs in November of the second year in a presidential term.

Minority Leader—The minority party's leader and chief floor spokesman, elected by the party caucus; sometimes called minority floor leader. With the assistance of other party officials and the ranking minority members of committees, the minority leader devises the party's political and procedural strategy.

Minority Whip—Performs duties of whip for the minority party. (*See also Majority Whip.*)

Minority Staff—Employees who assist the minority party members of a committee. Most committees hire separate majority and minority party staffs, but they also may hire nonpartisan staff.

Motion—A formal proposal for a procedural action, such as to consider, to amend, to lay on the table, to reconsider, to recess, or to adjourn. It has been estimated that at least 85 motions are possible under various circumstances in the House of Representatives, somewhat fewer in the Senate. Not all motions are created equal; some are privileged or preferential and enjoy priority over others. And some motions are debatable, amendable or divisible, while others are not.

Nomination—A proposed presidential appointment to a federal office submitted to the Senate for confirmation. Approval is by majority vote. The Constitution explicitly requires confirmation for ambassadors, consuls, public Ministers (department heads), and Supreme Court justices. By law, other federal judges, all military promotions of officers, and many high-level civilian officials must be confirmed.

Oath of Office—Upon taking office, members of Congress must swear or affirm that they will "support and defend the Constitution . . . against all enemies, foreign and domestic," that they will "bear true faith and allegiance" to the Constitution, that they take the obligation "freely, without any mental reservation or purpose of evasion," and that they will "well and faithfully discharge the duties" of their office. The oath is required by the Constitution; the wording is prescribed by a statute. All House members must take the oath at the beginning of each new Congress.

Obligations—Orders placed, contracts awarded, services received, and similar transactions during a given period that will require payments during the same or future period. Such amounts include outlays for which obligations had not been previously recorded and reflect adjustments for differences between obligations previously recorded and actual outlays to liquidate those obligations.

Omnibus Bill—A measure that combines the provisions of several disparate subjects into a single and often lengthy bill.

One-Minute Speeches—Addresses by House members at the beginning of a legislative day. The speeches may cover any subject but are limited to one minute's duration.

Order of Business (House)—The sequence of events during the meeting of the House on a new legislative day prescribed by a House rule; also called the general order of business. The sequence consists of (1) the chaplain's prayer; (2) approval of the *Journal;* (3) pledge of allegiance (4) correction of the reference of public bills; (5) disposal of business on the Speaker's table; (6) unfinished business; (7) the morning hour call of committees and consideration of their bills (largely obsolete); (8) motions to go into Committee of the Whole; and (9) orders of the day (also obsolete). In practice, on days specified in the rules, the items of business that follow approval of the *Journal* are supplanted in part by the special order of business (for example, the corrections, discharge, or private calendars or motions to suspend the rules) and on any day by other privileged business (for example, general appropriation bills and special rules)

or measures made in order by special rules. By this combination of an order of business with privileged interruptions, the House gives precedence to certain categories of important legislation, brings to the floor other major legislation from its calendars in any order it chooses, and provides expeditious processing for minor and noncontroversial measures.

Order of Business (Senate)—The sequence of events at the beginning of a new legislative day prescribed by Senate rules. The sequence consists of (1) the chaplain's prayer; (2) *Journal* reading and correction; (3) morning business in the morning hour; (4) call of the calendar during the morning hour; and (5) unfinished business.

Outlays—Amounts of government spending. They consist of payments, usually by check or in cash, to liquidate obligations incurred in prior fiscal years as well as in the current year, including the net lending of funds under budget authority. In federal budget accounting, net outlays are calculated by subtracting the amounts of refunds and various kinds of reimbursements to the government from actual spending.

Override a Veto—Congressional enactment of a measure over the president's veto. A veto override requires a recorded two-thirds vote of those voting in each house, a quorum being present. Because the president must return the vetoed measure to its house of origin, that house votes first, but neither house is required to attempt an override, whether immediately or at all. If an override attempt fails in the house of origin, the veto stands and the measure dies.

Oversight—Congressional review of the way in which federal agencies implement laws to ensure that they are carrying out the intent of Congress and to inquire into the efficiency of the implementation and the effectiveness of the law. The Legislative Reorganization Act of 1946 defined oversight as the function of exercising continuous watchfulness over the execution of the laws by the executive branch.

Pairing—A procedure that permits two or three members to enter into voluntary arrangements that offset their votes so that one or more of the members can be absent without changing the result. The names of paired members and their positions on the vote (except on general pairs) appear in the *Congressional Record.* Members can be paired on one vote or on a series of votes.

Parliamentarian—The official advisor to the presiding officer in each house on questions of procedure. The parliamentarian and his assistants also answer procedural questions from members and congressional staff, refer measures to committees on behalf of the presiding officer, and maintain compilations of the precedents. The House parliamentarian revises the House Manual at the beginning of every Congress and usually reviews special rules before the Rules Committee reports them to the House. Either a parliamentarian or an assistant is always present and near the podium during sessions of each house.

Party Caucus—Generic term for each party's official organization in each house. Only House Democrats officially call their organization a caucus. House and Senate Republicans and Senate Democrats call their organizations conferences. The party caucuses elect their leaders, approve committee assignments and chairmanships (or ranking minority members, if the party is in the minority), establish party committees and study groups, and discuss party and legislative policies. On rare occasions, they have stripped members of committee seniority or expelled them from the caucus for party disloyalty.

Petition—A request or plea sent to one or both chambers from an organization or private citizens' group asking support of particular legislation or favorable consideration of a matter not yet receiving congressional attention. Petitions are referred to appropriate committees.

Pocket Veto—The indirect veto of a bill as a result of the president withholding approval of it until after Congress has adjourned sine die. A bill the president does not sign, but does not formally veto while Congress is in session, automatically becomes a law 10 days (excluding Sundays) after it is received. But if Congress adjourns its annual session during that 10-day period, the measure dies even if the president does not formally veto it.

Point of Order—A parliamentary term used in committee and on the floor to object to an alleged violation of a rule and to demand that the chair enforce the rule. The point of order immediately halts the proceedings until the chair decides whether the contention is valid.

Pork or Pork Barrel Legislation—Pejorative terms for federal appropriations, bills, or policies that provide funds to benefit a legislator's district or state, with the implication that the legislator presses for enactment of such benefits to ingratiate himself or herself with constituents rather than on the basis of an impartial, objective assessment of need or merit.

The terms are often applied to such benefits as new parks, post offices, dams, canals, bridges, roads, water projects, sewage treatment plants, and public works of any kind, as well as demonstration projects, research grants, and relocation of government facilities. Funds released by the president for various kinds of benefits or government contracts approved by him allegedly for political purposes are also sometimes referred to as pork.

Postcloture Filibuster—A filibuster conducted after the Senate invokes cloture. It employs an array of procedural tactics rather than lengthy speeches to delay final action. The Senate curtailed the postcloture filibusters effectiveness by closing a variety of loopholes in the cloture rule in 1979 and 1986.

President of the Senate—The vice president of the United States in his constitutional role as presiding officer of the Senate. The Constitution permits the vice president to cast a vote in the Senate only to break a tie, but he is not required to do so.

President Pro Tempore—Under the Constitution, an officer elected by the Senate to preside over it during the absence of the vice president of the United States. Often referred to as the "pro tem," he is usually the majority party senator with the longest continuous service in the chamber and also, by virtue of his seniority, a committee chairman. When attending to committee and other duties, the president pro tempore appoints other senators to preside.

Previous Question—A nondebatable motion which, when agreed to by majority vote, usually cuts off further debate, prevents the offering of additional amendments, and brings the pending matter to an immediate vote. It is a major debate-limiting device in the House; it is not permitted in Committee of the Whole or in the Senate.

Printed Amendment—A House rule guarantees five minutes of floor debate in support and five minutes in opposition, and no other debate time, on amendments printed in the Congressional Record at least one day prior to the amendment's consideration in the Committee of the Whole. In the Senate, although amendments may be submitted for printing, they have no parliamentary standing or status. An amendment submitted for printing in the Senate, however, may be called up by any senator.

Private Bill—A bill that applies to one or more specified persons, corporations, institutions, or other entities, usually to grant relief when no other legal remedy is available to them. Many private bills deal with claims against the federal government, immigration and naturalization cases, and land titles.

Private Calendar—Commonly used title for a calendar in the House reserved for private bills and resolutions favorably reported by committees. The private calendar is officially called the Calendar of the Committee of the Whole House.

Privilege—An attribute of a motion, measure, report, question, or proposition that gives it priority status for consideration. Privileged motions and motions to bring up privileged questions are not debatable.

Privileged Questions—The order in which bills, motions, and other legislative measures are considered by Congress is governed by strict priorities. A motion to table, for instance, is more privileged than a motion to recommit. Thus, a motion to recommit can be superseded by a motion to table, and a vote would be forced on the latter motion only. A motion to adjourn, however, takes precedence over a tabling motion and thus is considered of the "highest privilege." (*See also Questions of Privilege.*)

Pro Forma Amendment—In the House, an amendment that ostensibly proposes to change a measure or another amendment by moving "to strike the last word" or "to strike the requisite number of words." A member offers it not to make any actual change in the measure or amendment but only to obtain time for debate.

Proxy Voting—The practice of permitting a member to cast the vote of an absent colleague in addition to his own vote. Proxy voting is prohibited on the floors of the House and Senate, but the Senate permits its committees to authorize proxy voting, and most do. In 1995, House rules were changed to prohibit proxy voting in committee.

Public Law—A public bill or joint resolution enacted into law. It is cited by the letters P.L. followed by a hyphenated number. The digits before the hyphen indicate the number of the Congress in which it was enacted; the digits after the hyphen indicate its position in the numerical sequence of public measures that became law during that Congress. For example, the

Budget Enforcement Act of 1990 became P.L. 101-508 because it was the 508th measure in that sequence for the 101st Congress. (*See also Private Bill.*)

Queen of the Hill Rule—A special rule from the House Rules Committee that permits votes on a series of amendments, especially complete substitutes for a measure, in a specified order, but directs that the amendment receiving the greatest number of votes shall be the winning one. This kind of rule permits the House to vote directly on a variety of alternatives to a measure. In doing so, it sets aside the precedent that once an amendment has been adopted, no further amendments may be offered to the text it has amended. Under an earlier practice, the Rules Committee reported "king of the hill" rules under which there also could be votes on a series of amendments, again in a specified order. If more than one of the amendments was adopted under this kind of rule, it was the last amendment to receive a majority vote that was considered as having been finally adopted, whether or not it had received the greatest number of votes.

Questions of Privilege—These are matters affecting members of Congress individually or collectively. Matters affecting the rights, safety, dignity, and integrity of proceedings of the House or Senate as a whole are questions of privilege in both chambers.

Questions involving individual members are called questions of "personal privilege." A member rising to ask a question of personal privilege is given precedence over almost all other proceedings. An annotation in the House rules points out that the privilege rests primarily on the Constitution, which gives a member a conditional immunity from arrest and an unconditional freedom to speak in the House. (*See also Privileged Questions.*)

Quorum—The minimum number of members required to be present for the transaction of business. Under the Constitution, a quorum in each house is a majority of its members: 218 in the House and 51 in the Senate when there are no vacancies. By House rule, a quorum in Committee of the Whole is 100. In practice, both houses usually assume a quorum is present even if it is not, unless a member makes a point of no quorum in the House or suggests the absence of a quorum in the Senate. Consequently, each house transacts much of its business, and even passes bills, when only a few members are present.

For House and Senate committees, chamber rules allow a minimum quorum of one-third of a committee's members to conduct most types of business.

Ramseyer Rule—A House rule that requires a committee's report on a bill or joint resolution to show the changes the measure, and any committee amendments to it, would make in existing law.

Readings of Bills—Traditional parliamentary procedure required bills to be read three times before they were passed. This custom is of little modern significance. Normally a bill is considered to have its first reading when it is introduced and printed, by title, in the *Congressional Record*. In the House, its second reading comes when floor consideration begins. (This is the most likely point at which there is an actual reading of the bill, if there is any.) The second reading in the Senate is supposed to occur on the legislative day after the measure is introduced, but

before it is referred to committee. The third reading (again, usually by title) takes place when floor action has been completed on amendments.

Reapportionment—(*See Apportionment.*)

Recess—(1) A temporary interruption or suspension of a meeting of a chamber or committee. Unlike an adjournment, a recess does not end a legislative day. Because the Senate often recesses from one calendar day to another, its legislative day may extend over several calendar days, weeks, or even months. (2) A period of adjournment for more than three days to a day certain, especially over a holiday or in August during odd-numbered years.

Recognition—The power of recognition of a member is lodged in the Speaker of the House and the presiding officer of the Senate. The presiding officer names the member who will speak first when two or more members simultaneously request recognition.

Recommit—To send a measure back to the committee that reported it; sometimes called a straight motion to recommit to distinguish it from a motion to recommit with instructions. A successful motion to recommit kills the measure unless it is accompanied by instructions.

Reconciliation—A procedure for changing existing revenue and spending laws to bring total federal revenues and spending within the limits established in a budget resolution. Congress has applied reconciliation chiefly to revenues and mandatory spending programs, especially entitlements. Discretionary spending is controlled through annual appropriation bills.

Reconsider a Vote—A motion to reconsider the vote by which an action was taken has, until it is disposed of, the effect of putting the action in abeyance. In the Senate, the motion can be made only by a member who voted on the prevailing side of the original question or by a member who did not vote at all. In the House, it can be made only by a member on the prevailing side.

A common practice in the Senate after close votes on an issue is a motion to reconsider, followed by a motion to table the motion to reconsider. On this motion to table, senators vote as they voted on the original question, which allows the motion to table to prevail, assuming there are no switches. The matter then is finally closed and further motions to reconsider are not entertained. In the House, as a routine precaution, a motion to reconsider usually is made every time a measure is passed. Such a motion almost always is tabled immediately, thus shutting off the possibility of future reconsideration, except by unanimous consent.

Motions to reconsider must be entered in the Senate within the next two days of actual session after the original vote has been taken. In the House they must be entered either on the same day or on the next succeeding day the House is in session.

Recorded Vote—(1) Generally, any vote in which members are recorded by name for or against a measure; also called a record vote or roll-call vote. The only recorded vote in the Senate is a vote by the yeas and nays and is commonly called a roll-call vote. (2) Technically, a recorded vote is one demanded in the House of Representatives and supported by at least one-fifth of a quorum (44 members) in the House sitting as the House or at least 25 members in Committee of the Whole.

Report—(1) As a verb, a committee is said to report when it submits a measure or other document to its parent chamber. (2) A clerk is said to report when he or she reads a measure's title, text, or the text of an amendment to the body at the direction of the chair. (3) As a noun, a committee document that accompanies a reported measure. It describes the measure, the committee's views on it, its costs, and the changes it proposes to make in existing law; it also includes certain impact statements. (4) A committee document submitted to its parent chamber that describes the results of an investigation or other study or provides information the committee is required to provide by rule or law.

Reprimand—A formal condemnation of a member for misbehavior, considered a milder reproof than censure. The House of Representatives first used it in 1976. The Senate first used it in 1991. (*See also Censure, Code of Official Conduct, Expulsion.*)

Rescission—A provision of law that repeals previously enacted budget authority in whole or in part. Under the Impoundment Control Act of 1974, the president can impound such funds by sending a message to Congress requesting one or more rescissions and the reasons for doing so. If Congress does not pass a rescission bill for the programs requested by the president within 45 days of continuous session after receiving the message, the president must make the funds available for obligation and expenditure. If the president does not, the comptroller general of the United States is authorized to bring suit to compel the release of those funds. A rescission bill may rescind all, part, or none of an amount proposed by the president, and may rescind funds the president has not impounded.

Resolution—(1) A simple resolution; that is, a nonlegislative measure effective only in the house in which it is proposed and not requiring concurrence by the other chamber or approval by the president. Simple resolutions are designated H. Res. in the House and S. Res. in the Senate. Simple resolutions express nonbinding opinions on policies or issues or deal with the internal affairs or prerogatives of a house. (2) Any type of resolution: simple, concurrent, or joint. (*See Concurrent Resolution, Joint Resolution.*)

Revise and Extend One's Remarks—A unanimous consent request to publish in the *Congressional Record* a statement a member did not deliver on the floor, a longer statement than the one made on the floor, or miscellaneous extraneous material.

Rider—Congressional slang for an amendment unrelated or extraneous to the subject matter of the measure to which it is attached. Riders often contain proposals that are less likely to become law on their own merits as separate bills, either because of opposition in the committee of jurisdiction, resistance in the other house, or the probability of a presidential veto. Riders are more common in the Senate.

Rule—(1) A permanent regulation that a house adopts to govern its conduct of business, its procedures, its internal organization, behavior of its members, regulation of its facilities, duties of an officer, or some other subject it chooses to govern in that form. (2) In the House, a privileged simple resolution reported by the Rules Committee that provides methods and conditions for floor consideration of a measure or, rarely, several measures.

Secretary of the Senate—The chief administrative and budgetary officer of the Senate. The secretary manages a wide range of functions that support the operation of the Senate as an organization as well as those functions necessary to its legislative process, including recordkeeping, document management, certifications, housekeeping services, administration of oaths, and lobbyist registrations.

Select or Special Committee—A committee established by a resolution in either house for a special purpose and, usually, for a limited time. Most select and special committees are assigned specific investigations or studies, but are not authorized to report measures to their chambers.

Senate—The house of Congress in which each state is represented by two senators; each senator has one vote. Article V of the Constitution declares that "No State, without its Consent, shall be deprived of its equal Suffrage in the Senate." The Constitution also gives the Senate equal legislative power with the House of Representatives. Although the Senate is prohibited from originating revenue measures, and as a matter of practice it does not originate appropriation measures, it can amend both. Only the Senate can give or withhold consent to treaties and nominations from the president. It also acts as a court to try impeachments by the House and elects the vice president when no candidate receives a majority of the electoral votes. It is often referred to as "the upper body," but not by members of the House.

Senate Manual—The handbook of the Senate's standing rules and orders and the laws and other regulations that apply to the Senate, usually published once each Congress.

Senatorial Courtesy—The Senate's practice of declining to confirm a presidential nominee for an office in the state of a senator of the president's party unless that senator approves.

Sequestration—A procedure for canceling budgetary resources that is, money available for obligation or spending to enforce budget limitations established in law. Sequestered funds are no longer available for obligation or expenditure.

Sine Die—(*See Adjournment Sine Die.*)

Slip Law—The first official publication of a measure that has become law. It is published separately in unbound, single-sheet form or pamphlet form. A slip law usually is available two or three days after the date of the law's enactment.

Speaker—The presiding officer of the House of Representatives and the leader of its majority party. The Speaker is selected by the majority party and formally elected by the House at the beginning of each Congress. Although the Constitution does not require the Speaker to be a member of the House, in fact, all Speakers have been members.

Special Session—A session of Congress convened by the president, under his constitutional authority, after Congress has adjourned sine die at the end of a regular session. (*See Adjournment Sine Die.*)

Spending Authority—The technical term for backdoor spending. The Congressional Budget Act of 1974 defines it as borrowing authority, contract authority, and entitlement authority for which appropriation acts do not provide budget authority in advance. Under the Budget Act, legislation that provides new spending authority may not be considered unless it provides that the authority shall be effective only to the extent or in such amounts as provided in an appropriation act.

Sponsor—The principal proponent and introducer of a measure or an amendment.

Standing Committee—A permanent committee established by a House or Senate standing rule or standing order. The rule also describes the subject areas on which the committee may report bills and resolutions and conduct oversight. Most introduced measures must be referred to one or more standing committees according to their jurisdictions.

Standing Vote—An alternative and informal term for a division vote, during which members in favor of a proposal and then members opposed stand and are counted by the chair. (*See Division Vote.*)

Star Print—A reprint of a bill, resolution, amendment, or committee report correcting technical or substantive errors in a previous printing; so called because of the small black star that appears on the front page or cover.

Statutes at Large—A chronological arrangement of the laws enacted in each session of Congress. Though indexed, the laws are not arranged by subject matter nor is there an indication of how they affect or change previously enacted laws. The volumes are numbered by Congress, and the laws are cited by their volume and page number. The Gramm-Rudman-Hollings Act, for example, appears as 99 Stat. 1037.

Strike from the *Record*—Expunge objectionable remarks from the *Congressional Record,* after a member's words have been taken down on a point of order.

Strike Out the Last Word—A motion whereby a House member is entitled to speak for five minutes on an amendment then being debated by the chamber. A member gains recognition from the chair by moving to "strike out the last word" of the amendment or section of the bill under consideration. The motion is proforma, requires no vote, and does not change the amendment being debated.

Substitute—A motion, amendment, or entire bill introduced in place of the pending legislative business. Passage of a substitute measure kills the original measure by supplanting it. The substitute also may be amended. (*See also Amendment in the Nature of a Substitute.*)

Sunshine Rules—Rules requiring open committee hearings and business meetings, including markup sessions, in both houses, and also open conference committee meetings. However, all may be closed under certain circumstances and using certain procedures required by the rules.

Super Majority—A term sometimes used for a vote on a matter that requires approval by more than a simple majority of those members present and voting; also referred to as extraordinary majority.

Supplemental Appropriation Bill—A measure providing appropriations for use in the current fiscal year, in addition to those already provided in annual general appropriation bills. Supplemental appropriations are often for unforeseen emergencies.

Suspension of the Rules (House)—An expeditious procedure for passing relatively noncontroversial or emergency measures by a two-thirds vote of those members voting, a quorum being present.

Suspension of the Rules (Senate)—A procedure to set aside one or more of the Senate's rules; it is used infrequently, and then most often to suspend the rule banning legislative amendments to appropriation bills.

Table a Bill—Motions to table, or to "lay on the table," are used to block or kill amendments or other parliamentary questions. When approved, a tabling motion is considered the final disposition of that issue. One of the most widely used parliamentary procedures, the motion to table is not debatable, and adoption requires a simple majority vote.

In the Senate, however, different language sometimes is used. The motion may be worded to let a bill "lie on the table," perhaps for subsequent "picking up." This motion is more flexible, keeping the bill pending for later action, if desired. Tabling motions on amendments are effective debate-ending devices in the Senate.

Teller Vote—A voting procedure, formerly used in the House, in which members cast their votes by passing through the center aisle to be counted, but not recorded by name, by a member from each party appointed by the chair. The House deleted the procedure from its rules in 1993, but during floor discussion of the deletion a leading member stated that a teller vote would still be available in the event of a breakdown of the electronic voting system.

Treaty—A formal document containing an agreement between two or more sovereign nations. The Constitution authorizes the president to make treaties, but he must submit them to the Senate for its approval by a two-thirds vote of the senators present. Under the Senate's rules, that vote actually occurs on a resolution of ratification. Although the Constitution does not give the House a direct role in approving treaties, that body has sometimes insisted that a revenue treaty is an invasion of its prerogatives. In any case, the House may significantly affect the application of a treaty by its equal role in enacting legislation to implement the treaty.

Trust Funds—Special accounts in the Treasury that receive earmarked taxes or other kinds of revenue collections, such as user fees, and from which payments are made for special purposes or to recipients who meet the requirements of the trust funds as established by law. Of the more than 150 federal government trust funds, several finance major entitlement programs, such as Social Security, Medicare, and retired federal employees' pensions. Others fund infrastructure construction and improvements, such as highways and airports.

Unanimous Consent—Without an objection by any member. A unanimous consent request asks permission, explicitly or implicitly, to set aside one or more rules. Both houses and their committees frequently use such requests to expedite their proceedings.

Unanimous Consent Agreement—A device used in the Senate to expedite legislation. Much of the Senate's legislative business, dealing with both minor and controversial issues, is conducted through unanimous consent or unanimous consent agreements. On major legislation, such agreements usually are printed and transmitted to all senators in advance of floor debate. Once agreed to, they are binding on all members unless the Senate, by unanimous consent, agrees to modify them. An agreement may list the order in which various bills are to be considered, specify the length of time bills and contested amendments are to be debated and when they are to be voted upon, and, frequently, require that all amendments introduced be germane to the bill under consideration. In this regard, unanimous consent agreements are similar to the "rules" issued by the House Rules Committee for bills pending in the House.

Unfunded Mandate—Generally, any provision in federal law or regulation that imposes a duty or obligation on a state or local government or private sector entity without providing the necessary funds to comply. The Unfunded Mandates Reform Act of 1995 amended the Congressional Budget Act of 1974 to provide a mechanism for the control of new unfunded mandates.

Union Calendar—A calendar of the House of Representatives for bills and resolutions favorably reported by committees that raise revenue or directly or indirectly appropriate money or property. In addition to appropriation bills, measures that authorize expenditures are also placed on this calendar. The calendar's full title is the Calendar of the Committee of the Whole House on the State of the Union.

U.S. Code—Popular title for the *United States Code: Containing the General and Permanent Laws of the United States in Force on. . . .* It is a consolidation and partial codification of the general and permanent laws of the United States arranged by subject under 50 titles. The first six titles deal with general or political subjects, the other 44 with subjects ranging from agriculture to war, alphabetically arranged. A supplement is published after each session of Congress, and the entire Code is revised every six years.

Veto—The president's disapproval of a legislative measure passed by Congress. He returns the measure to the house in which it originated without his signature but with a veto message stating his objections to it. When Congress is in session, the president must veto a bill within 10 days, excluding Sundays, after he has received it; otherwise it becomes law without his signature. The 10-day clock begins to run at midnight following his receipt of the bill. (*See also Committee Veto, Item Veto, Override a Veto, Pocket Veto.*)

Voice Vote—A method of voting in which members who favor a question answer aye in chorus, after which those opposed answer no in chorus, and the chair decides which position prevails.

War Powers Resolution of 1973—An act that requires the president "in every possible instance" to consult Congress before he commits U.S. forces to ongoing or imminent hostilities. If he commits them to a combat situation without congressional consultation, he must notify Congress within 48 hours. Unless Congress declares war or otherwise authorizes the operation to continue, the forces must be withdrawn within 60 or 90 days, depending on certain conditions. No president has ever acknowleged the constitutionality of the resolution.

Whip—The majority or minority party member in each house who acts as assistant leader, helps plan and marshal support for party strategies, encourages party discipline, and advises his leader on how his colleagues intend to vote on the floor. In the Senate, the Republican whip's official title is assistant leader.

Without Objection—Used in lieu of a vote on noncontroversial motions, amendments, or bills that may be passed in either the House or Senate if no member voices an objection.

Yeas and Nays—A vote in which members usually respond "aye" or "no" (despite the official title of the vote) on a question when their names are called in alphabetical order. The Constitution requires the yeas and nays when a demand for it is supported by one-fifth of the members present, and it also requires an automatic yea-and-nay vote on overriding a veto. Senate precedents require the support of at least one-fifth of a quorum, a minimum of 11 members with the present membership of 100.

Yielding—When a member has been recognized to speak, no other member may speak unless he or she obtains permission from the member recognized. This permission is called yielding and usually is requested in the form, "Will the gentleman yield to me?" While this activity occasionally is seen in the Senate, the Senate has no rule or practice to parcel out time.

Constitution of the United States

We the People of the United States, in Order to form a more perfect Union, establish Justice, insure domestic Tranquility, provide for the common defence, promote the general Welfare, and secure the Blessings of Liberty to ourselves and our Posterity, do ordain and establish this Constitution for the United States of America.

ARTICLE I

Section 1. All legislative Powers herein granted shall be vested in a Congress of the United States, which shall consist of a Senate and House of Representatives.

Section 2. The House of Representatives shall be composed of Members chosen every second Year by the People of the several States, and the Electors in each State shall have the Qualifications requisite for Electors of the most numerous Branch of the State Legislature.

No Person shall be a Representative who shall not have attained to the age of twenty five Years, and been seven Years a Citizen of the United States, and who shall not, when elected, be an Inhabitant of that State in which he shall be chosen.

[Representatives and direct Taxes shall be apportioned among the several States which may be included within this Union, according to their respective Numbers, which shall be determined by adding to the whole Number of free Persons, including those bound to Service for a Term of Years, and excluding Indians not taxed, three fifths of all other Persons.][1] The actual Enumeration shall be made within three Years after the first Meeting of the Congress of the United States, and within every subsequent Term of ten Years, in such Manner as they shall by Law direct. The Number of Representatives shall not exceed one for every thirty Thousand, but each State shall have at Least one Representative; and until such enumeration shall be made, the State of New Hampshire shall be entitled to chuse three, Massachusetts eight, Rhode-Island and Providence Plantations one, Connecticut five, New-York six, New Jersey four, Pennsylvania eight, Delaware one, Maryland six, Virginia ten, North Carolina five, South Carolina five, and Georgia three.

When vacancies happen in the Representation from any State, the Executive Authority thereof shall issue Writs of Election to fill such Vacancies.

The House of Representatives shall chuse their Speaker and other Officers; and shall have the sole Power of Impeachment.

Section 3. The Senate of the United States shall be composed of two Senators from each State, [chosen by the Legislature thereof,][2] for six Years; and each Senator shall have one Vote.

Immediately after they shall be assembled in Consequence of the first Election, they shall be divided as equally as may be into three Classes. The Seats of the Senators of the first Class shall be vacated at the Expiration of the second Year, of the second Class at the Expiration of the fourth Year, and of the third Class at the Expiration of the sixth Year, so that one third may be chosen every second Year; [and if Vacancies happen by Resignation, or otherwise, during the Recess of the Legislature of any State, the Executive thereof may make temporary Appointments until the next Meeting of the Legislature, which shall then fill such Vacancies.][3]

No Person shall be a Senator who shall not have attained to the Age of thirty Years, and been nine Years a Citizen of the United States, and who shall not, when elected, be an Inhabitant of that State for which he shall be chosen.

The Vice President of the United States shall be President of the Senate, but shall have no Vote, unless they be equally divided.

The Senate shall chuse their other Officers, and also a President pro tempore, in the Absence of the Vice President, or when he shall exercise the Office of President of the United States.

The Senate shall have the sole Power to try all Impeachments. When sitting for that Purpose, they shall be on Oath or Affirmation. When the President of the United States is tried, the Chief Justice shall preside: And no Person shall be convicted without the Concurrence of two thirds of the Members present.

Judgment in Cases of Impeachment shall not extend further than to removal from Office, and disqualification to hold and enjoy any Office of honor, Trust or Profit under the United States: but the Party convicted shall nevertheless be liable and subject to Indictment, Trial, Judgment and Punishment, according to Law.

Section 4. The Times, Places and Manner of holding Elections for Senators and Representatives, shall be prescribed in each State by the Legislature thereof; but the Congress may at any time by Law make or alter such Regulations, except as to the Places of chusing Senators.

The Congress shall assemble at least once in every Year, and such Meeting shall [be on the first Monday in December],[4] unless they shall by Law appoint a different Day.

Section 5. Each House shall be the Judge of the Elections, Returns and Qualifications of its own Members, and a Majority of each shall constitute a Quorum to do Business; but a smaller Number may adjourn from day to day, and may be authorized to compel the Attendance of absent Members, in such Manner, and under such Penalties as each House may provide.

Each House may determine the Rules of its Proceedings, punish its Members for disorderly Behaviour, and, with the Concurrence of two thirds, expel a Member.

Each House shall keep a Journal of its Proceedings, and from time to time publish the same, excepting such Parts as may in their Judgment require Secrecy; and the Yeas and Nays of the Members of either House on any question shall, at the Desire of one fifth of those Present, be entered on the Journal.

Neither House, during the Session of Congress, shall, without the Consent of the other, adjourn for more than three days, nor to any other Place than that in which the two Houses shall be sitting.

Section 6. The Senators and Representatives shall receive a Compensation for their Services, to be ascertained by Law, and paid out of the Treasury of the United States. They shall in all Cases, except Treason, Felony and Breach of the Peace, be privileged from Arrest during their Attendance at the Session of their respective Houses, and in going to and returning from the same; and for any Speech or Debate in either House, they shall not be questioned in any other Place.

No Senator or Representative shall, during the Time for which he was elected, be appointed to any civil Office under the Authority of the United States, which shall have been created, or the Emoluments whereof shall have been encreased during such time; and no Person holding any Office under the United States, shall be a Member of either House during his Continuance in Office.

Section 7. All Bills for raising Revenue shall originate in the House of Representatives; but the Senate may propose or concur with Amendments as on other Bills.

Every Bill which shall have passed the House of Representatives and the Senate, shall, before it become a Law, be presented to the President of the United States; If he approve he shall sign it, but if not he shall return it, with his Objections to that House in which it shall have originated, who shall enter the Objections at large on their Journal, and proceed to reconsider it. If after such Reconsideration two thirds of that House shall agree to pass the Bill, it shall be sent, together with the Objections, to the other House, by which it shall likewise be reconsidered, and if approved by two thirds of that House, it shall become a Law. But in all such Cases the Votes of both Houses shall be determined by yeas and Nays, and the Names of the Persons voting for and against the Bill shall be entered on the Journal of each House respectively. If any Bill shall not be returned by the President within ten Days (Sundays excepted) after it shall have been presented to him, the Same shall be a Law, in like Manner as if he had signed it, unless the Congress by their Adjournment prevent its Return, in which Case it shall not be a Law.

Every Order, Resolution, or Vote to which the Concurrence of the Senate and House of Representatives may be necessary (except on a question of Adjournment) shall be presented to the President of the United States; and before the Same shall take Effect, shall be approved by him, or being disapproved by him, shall be repassed by two thirds of the Senate and House of Representatives, according to the Rules and Limitations prescribed in the Case of a Bill.

Section 8. The Congress shall have Power To lay and collect Taxes, Duties, Imposts and Excises, to pay the Debts and provide for the common Defence and general Welfare of the United States; but all Duties, Imposts and Excises shall be uniform throughout the United States;

To borrow Money on the credit of the United States;

To regulate Commerce with foreign Nations, and among the several States, and with the Indian Tribes;

To establish an uniform Rule of Naturalization, and uniform Laws on the subject of Bankruptcies throughout the United States;

To coin Money, regulate the Value thereof, and of foreign Coin, and fix the Standard of Weights and Measures;

To provide for the Punishment of counterfeiting the Securities and current Coin of the United States;

To establish Post Offices and post Roads;

To promote the Progress of Science and useful Arts, by securing for limited Times to Authors and Inventors the exclusive Right to their respective Writings and Discoveries;

To constitute Tribunals inferior to the supreme Court;

To define and punish Piracies and Felonies committed on the high Seas, and Offences against the Law of Nations;

To declare War, grant Letters of Marque and Reprisal, and make Rules concerning Captures on Land and Water;

To raise and support Armies, but no Appropriation of Money to that Use shall be for a longer Term than two Years;

To provide and maintain a Navy;

To make Rules for the Government and Regulation of the land and naval Forces;

To provide for calling forth the Militia to execute the Laws of the Union, suppress Insurrections and repel Invasions;

To provide for organizing, arming, and disciplining, the Militia, and for governing such Part of them as may be employed in the Service of the United States, reserving to the States respectively, the Appointment of the Officers, and the Authority of training the Militia according to the discipline prescribed by Congress;

To exercise exclusive Legislation in all Cases whatsoever, over such District (not exceeding ten Miles square) as may, by Cession of particular States, and the Acceptance of Congress, become the Seat of the Government of the United States, and to exercise like Authority over all Places purchased by the Consent of the Legislature of the State in which the Same shall be, for the Erection of Forts, Magazines, Arsenals, dock-Yards, and other needful Buildings; — And

To make all Laws which shall be necessary and proper for carrying into Execution the foregoing Powers, and all other Powers vested by this Constitution in the Government of the United States, or in any Department or Officer thereof.

Section 9. The Migration or Importation of such Persons as any of the States now existing shall think proper to admit, shall not be prohibited by the Congress prior to the Year one thousand eight hundred and eight, but a Tax or duty may be imposed on such Importation, not exceeding ten dollars for each Person.

The Privilege of the Writ of Habeas Corpus shall not be suspended, unless when in Cases of Rebellion or Invasion the public Safety may require it.

No Bill of Attainder or ex post facto Law shall be passed.

No Capitation, or other direct, Tax shall be laid, unless in Proportion to the Census or Enumeration herein before directed to be taken.[5]

No Tax or Duty shall be laid on Articles exported from any State.

No Preference shall be given by any Regulation of Commerce or Revenue to the Ports of one State over those of another; nor shall Vessels bound to, or from, one State, be obliged to enter, clear, or pay Duties in another.

No Money shall be drawn from the Treasury, but in Consequence of Appropriations made by Law; and a regular Statement and Account of the Receipts and Expenditures of all public Money shall be published from time to time.

No Title of Nobility shall be granted by the United States: And no Person holding any Office of Profit or Trust under them, shall, without the Consent of the Congress, accept of any present, Emolument, Office, or Title, of any kind whatever, from any King, Prince, or foreign State.

Section 10. No State shall enter into any Treaty, Alliance, or Confederation; grant Letters of Marque and Reprisal; coin Money; emit Bills of Credit; make any Thing but gold and silver Coin a Tender in Payment of Debts; pass any Bill of Attainder, ex post facto Law, or Law impairing the Obligation of Contracts, or grant any Title of Nobility.

No State shall, without the Consent of the Congress, **lay** any Imposts or Duties on Imports or Exports, except what may be absolutely necessary for executing it's inspection Laws: and the net Produce of all Duties and Imposts, laid by any State on Imports or Exports, shall be for the Use of the Treasury of the United States; and all such Laws shall be subject to the Revision and Controul of the Congress.

No State shall, without the Consent of Congress, lay any Duty of Tonnage, keep Troops, or Ships of War in time of Peace, enter into any Agreement or Compact with another State, or with a foreign Power, or engage in War, unless actually invaded, or in such imminent Danger as will not admit of delay.

ARTICLE II

Section 1. The executive Power shall be vested in a President of the United States of America. He shall hold his Office during the Term of four Years, and, together with the Vice President, chosen for the same Term, be elected, as follows

Each State shall appoint, in such Manner as the Legislature thereof may direct, a Number of Electors, equal to the whole Number of Senators and Representatives to which the State may be entitled in the Congress: but no Senator or Representative, or Person holding an Office of Trust or Profit under the United States, shall be appointed an Elector.

[The Electors shall meet in their respective States, and vote by Ballot for two Persons, of whom one at least shall not be an Inhabitant of the same State with themselves. And they shall make a List of all the Persons voted for, and of the Number of Votes for each; which List they shall sign and certify, and transmit sealed to the Seat of the Government of the United States, directed to the President of the Senate. The President of the Senate shall, in the Presence of the Senate and House of Representatives, open all the Certificates, and the Votes shall then be counted. The Person having the greatest Number of Votes shall be the President, if such Number be a Majority of the whole Number of Electors appointed; and if there be more than one who have such Majority, and have an equal Number of Votes, then the House of Representatives shall immediately chuse by Ballot one of them for President; and if no Person have a Majority, then from the five highest on the list the said House shall in like Manner chuse the President. But in chusing the President, the Votes shall be taken by States, the Representation from each State having one Vote; A quorum for this Purpose shall consist of a Member or Members from two thirds of the States, and a Majority of all the States shall be necessary to a Choice. In every Case, after the Choice of the President, the Person having the greatest Number of Votes of the Electors shall be the Vice President. But if there should remain two or more who have equal Votes, the Senate shall chuse from them by Ballot the Vice President.][6]

The Congress may determine the Time of chusing the Electors, and the Day on which they shall give their Votes; which Day shall be the same throughout the United States.

No Person except a natural born Citizen, or a Citizen of the United States, at the time of the Adoption of this Constitution, shall be eligible to the Office of President; neither shall any Person be eligible to that Office who shall not have attained to the Age of thirty five Years, and been fourteen Years a Resident within the United States.

In Case of the Removal of the President from Office, or of his Death, Resignation, or Inability to discharge the Powers and Duties of the said Office,[7] the Same shall devolve on the Vice President, and the Congress may by Law provide for the Case of Removal, Death, Resignation or Inability, both of the President and Vice President, declaring what Officer shall then act as President, and such Officer shall act accordingly, until the Disability be removed, or a President shall be elected.

The President shall, at stated Times, receive for his Services, a Compensation, which shall neither be encreased nor diminished during the Period for which he shall have been elected, and he shall not receive within that Period any other Emolument from the United States, or any of them.

Before he enter on the Execution of his Office, he shall take the following Oath or Affirmation: — "I do solemnly swear (or affirm) that I will faithfully execute the Office of President of the United States, and will to the best of my Ability, preserve, protect and defend the Constitution of the United States."

Section 2. The President shall be Commander in Chief of the Army and Navy of the United States, and of the Militia of the several States, when called into the actual Service of the United States; he may require the Opinion, in writing, of the principal Officer in each of the executive Departments, upon any Subject relating to the Duties of their respective Offices, and he shall have Power to grant Reprieves and Pardons for Offences against the United States, except in Cases of Impeachment.

He shall have Power, by and with the Advice and Consent of the Senate, to make Treaties, provided two thirds of the Senators present concur; and he shall nominate, and by and with the Advice and Consent of the Senate, shall appoint Ambassadors, other public Ministers and Consuls, Judges of the supreme Court, and all other Officers of the United States, whose Appointments are not herein otherwise provided for, and which shall be established by Law: but the Congress may by Law vest the Appointment of such inferior Officers, as they think proper, in the President alone, in the Courts of Law, or in the Heads of Departments.

The President shall have Power to fill up all Vacancies that may happen during the Recess of the Senate, by granting Commissions which shall expire at the End of their next Session.

Section 3. He shall from time to time give to the Congress Information of the State of the Union, and recommend to their Consideration such Measures as he shall judge necessary and expedient; he may, on extraordinary Occasions, convene both Houses, or either of them, and in Case of Disagreement between them, with Respect to the Time of Adjournment, he may adjourn them to such Time as he shall think proper; he shall receive Ambassadors and other public Ministers; he shall take Care that the Laws be faithfully executed, and shall Commission all the Officers of the United States.

Section 4. The President, Vice President and all civil Officers of the United States, shall be removed from Office on Impeachment for, and Conviction of, Treason, Bribery, or other high Crimes and Misdemeanors.

ARTICLE III

Section 1. The judicial Power of the United States, shall be vested in one supreme Court, and in such inferior Courts as the Congress may from time to time ordain and establish. The Judges, both of the supreme and inferior Courts, shall hold their

Offices during good Behaviour, and shall, at stated Times, receive for their Services, a Compensation, which shall not be diminished during their Continuance in Office.

Section 2. The judicial Power shall extend to all Cases, in Law and Equity, arising under this Constitution, the Laws of the United States, and Treaties made, or which shall be made, under their Authority; — to all Cases affecting Ambassadors, other public Ministers and Consuls; — to all Cases of admiralty and maritime Jurisdiction; — to Controversies to which the United States shall be a Party; — to Controversies between two or more States; — between a State and Citizens of another State;[8] — between Citizens of different States; — between Citizens of the same State claiming Lands under Grants of different States, and between a State, or the Citizens thereof, and foreign States, Citizens or Subjects.

In all Cases affecting Ambassadors, other public Ministers and Consuls, and those in which a State shall be Party, the supreme Court shall have original Jurisdiction. In all the other Cases before mentioned, the supreme Court shall have appellate Jurisdiction, both as to Law and Fact, with such Exceptions, and under such Regulations as the Congress shall make.

The Trial of all Crimes, except in Cases of Impeachment, shall be by Jury; and such Trial shall be held in the State where the said Crimes shall have been committed; but when not committed within any State, the Trial shall be at such Place or Places as the Congress may by Law have directed.

Section 3. Treason against the United States, shall consist only in levying War against them, or in adhering to their Enemies, giving them Aid and Comfort. No Person shall be convicted of Treason unless on the Testimony of two Witnesses to the same overt Act, or on Confession in open Court.

The Congress shall have Power to declare the Punishment of Treason, but no Attainder of Treason shall work Corruption of Blood, or Forfeiture except during the Life of the Person attainted.

ARTICLE IV

Section 1. Full Faith and Credit shall be given in each State to the public Acts, Records, and judicial Proceedings of every other State. And the Congress may by general Laws prescribe the Manner in which such Acts, Records and Proceedings shall be proved, and the Effect thereof.

Section 2. The Citizens of each State shall be entitled to all Privileges and Immunities of Citizens in the several States.

A Person charged in any State with Treason, Felony, or other Crime, who shall flee from Justice, and be found in another State, shall on Demand of the executive Authority of the State from which he fled, be delivered up, to be removed to the State having Jurisdiction of the Crime.

[No Person held to Service or Labour in one State, under the Laws thereof, escaping into another, shall, in Consequence of any Law or Regulation therein, be discharged from such Service or Labour, but shall be delivered up on Claim of the Party to whom such Service or Labour may be due.][9]

Section 3. New States may be admitted by the Congress into this Union; but no new State shall be formed or erected within the Jurisdiction of any other State; nor any State be formed by the Junction of two or more States, or Parts of States, without the Consent of the Legislatures of the States concerned as well as of the Congress.

The Congress shall have Power to dispose of and make all needful Rules and Regulations respecting the Territory or other Property belonging to the United States; and nothing in this Constitution shall be so construed as to Prejudice any Claims of the United States, or of any particular State.

Section 4. The United States shall guarantee to every State in this Union a Republican Form of Government, and shall protect each of them against Invasion; and on Application of the Legislature, or of the Executive (when the Legislature cannot be convened) against domestic Violence.

ARTICLE V

The Congress, whenever two thirds of both Houses shall deem it necessary, shall propose Amendments to this Constitution, or, on the Application of the Legislatures of two thirds of the several States, shall call a Convention for proposing Amendments, which, in either Case, shall be valid to all Intents and Purposes, as Part of this Constitution, when ratified by the Legislatures of three fourths of the several States, or by Conventions in three fourths thereof, as the one or the other Mode of Ratification may be proposed by the Congress; Provided [that no Amendment which may be made prior to the Year One thousand eight hundred and eight shall in any Manner affect the first and fourth Clauses in the Ninth Section of the first Article; and][10] that no State, without its Consent, shall be deprived of its equal Suffrage in the Senate.

ARTICLE VI

All Debts contracted and Engagements entered into, before the Adoption of this Constitution, shall be as valid against the United States under this Constitution, as under the Confederation.

This Constitution, and the Laws of the United States which shall be made in Pursuance thereof; and all Treaties made, or which shall be made, under the Authority of the United States, shall be the supreme Law of the Land; and the Judges in every State shall be bound thereby, any Thing in the Constitution or Laws of any State to the Contrary notwithstanding.

The Senators and Representatives before mentioned, and the Members of the several State Legislatures, and all executive and judicial Officers, both of the United States and of the several States, shall be bound by Oath or Affirmation, to support this Constitution; but no religious Test shall ever be required as a Qualification to any Office or public Trust under the United States.

ARTICLE VII

The Ratification of the Conventions of nine States, shall be sufficient for the Establishment of this Constitution between the States so ratifying the Same.

Done in Convention by the Unanimous Consent of the States present the Seventeenth Day of September in the Year of our Lord one thousand seven hundred and Eighty seven and of the Independence of the United States of America the Twelfth. IN WITNESS whereof We have hereunto subscribed our Names,

George Washington,
President and
deputy from Virginia.

New Hampshire:	John Langdon
	Nicholas Gilman.
Massachusetts:	Nathaniel Gorham,
	Rufus King.
Connecticut:	William Samuel Johnson,
	Roger Sherman.

New York:	Alexander Hamilton.
New Jersey:	William Livingston,
	David Brearley,
	William Paterson,
	Jonathan Dayton.
Pennsylvania:	Benjamin Franklin,
	Thomas Mifflin,
	Robert Morris,
	George Clymer,
	Thomas FitzSimons,
	Jared Ingersoll,
	James Wilson,
	Gouverneur Morris.
Delaware:	George Read,
	Gunning Bedford Jr.,
	John Dickinson,
	Richard Bassett,
	Jacob Broom.
Maryland:	James McHenry,
	Daniel of St. Thomas Jenifer,
	Daniel Carroll.
Virginia:	John Blair,
	James Madison Jr.
North Carolina:	William Blount,
	Richard Dobbs Spaight,
	Hugh Williamson.
South Carolina:	John Rutledge,
	Charles Cotesworth Pinckney,
	Charles Pinckney,
	Pierce Butler.
Georgia:	William Few,
	Abraham Baldwin.

[The language of the original Constitution, not including the Amendments, was adopted by a convention of the states on September 17, 1787, and was subsequently ratified by the states on the following dates: Delaware, December 7, 1787; Pennsylvania, December 12, 1787; New Jersey, December 18, 1787; Georgia, January 2, 1788; Connecticut, January 9, 1788; Massachusetts, February 6, 1788; Maryland, April 28, 1788; South Carolina, May 23, 1788; New Hampshire, June 21, 1788.

Ratification was completed on June 21, 1788.

The Constitution subsequently was ratified by Virginia, June 25, 1788; New York, July 26, 1788; North Carolina, November 21, 1789; Rhode Island, May 29, 1790; and Vermont, January 10, 1791.]

Amendments

Amendment I

(First ten amendments ratified December 15, 1791.)

Congress shall make no law respecting an establishment of religion, or prohibiting the free exercise thereof; or abridging the freedom of speech, or of the press; or the right of the people peaceably to assemble, and to petition the Government for a redress of grievances.

Amendment II

A well regulated Militia, being necessary to the security of a free State, the right of the people to keep and bear Arms, shall not be infringed.

Amendment III

No Soldier shall, in time of peace be quartered in any house, without the consent of the Owner, nor in time of war, but in a manner to be prescribed by law.

Amendment IV

The right of the people to be secure in their persons, houses, papers, and effects, against unreasonable searches and seizures, shall not be violated, and no Warrants shall issue, but upon probable cause, supported by Oath or affirmation, and particularly describing the place to be searched, and the persons or things to be seized.

Amendment V

No person shall be held to answer for a capital, or otherwise infamous crime, unless on a presentment or indictment of a Grand Jury, except in cases arising in the land or naval forces, or in the Militia, when in actual service in time of War or public danger; nor shall any person be subject for the same offence to be twice put in jeopardy of life or limb; nor shall be compelled in any criminal case to be a witness against himself, nor be deprived of life, liberty, or property, without due process of law; nor shall private property be taken for public use, without just compensation.

Amendment VI

In all criminal prosecutions, the accused shall enjoy the right to a speedy and public trial, by an impartial jury of the State and district wherein the crime shall have been committed, which district shall have been previously ascertained by law, and to be informed of the nature and cause of the accusation; to be confronted with the witnesses against him; to have compulsory process for obtaining witnesses in his favor, and to have the Assistance of Counsel for his defence.

Amendment VII

In Suits at common law, where the value in controversy shall exceed twenty dollars, the right of trial by jury shall be preserved, and no fact tried by a jury, shall be otherwise re-examined in any Court of the United States, than according to the rules of the common law.

Amendment VIII

Excessive bail shall not be required, nor excessive fines imposed, nor cruel and unusual punishments inflicted.

Amendment IX

The enumeration in the Constitution, of certain rights, shall not be construed to deny or disparage others retained by the people.

Amendment X

The powers not delegated to the United States by the Constitution, nor prohibited by it to the States, are reserved to the States respectively, or to the people.

Amendment XI (Ratified February 7, 1795)

The Judicial power of the United States shall not be construed to extend to any suit in law or equity, commenced or prosecuted against one of the United States by Citizens of another State, or by Citizens or Subjects of any Foreign State.

Amendment XII (Ratified June 15, 1804)

The Electors shall meet in their respective states and vote by ballot for President and Vice-President, one of whom, at least, shall not be an inhabitant of the same state with themselves; they shall name in their ballots the person voted for as President, and in distinct ballots the person voted for as Vice-President, and they shall make distinct lists of all persons voted for as President, and of all persons voted for as Vice-President, and of the number of votes for each, which lists they shall sign and certify, and transmit sealed to the seat of the government of the United States, directed to the President of the Senate; — The President of the Senate shall, in the presence of the Senate and House of Representatives, open all the certificates and the votes shall then be counted; — The person having the greatest number of votes for President, shall be the President, if such number be a majority of the whole number of Electors appointed; and if no person have such majority, then from the persons having the highest numbers not exceeding three on the list of those voted for as President, the House of Representatives shall choose immediately, by ballot, the President. But in choosing the President, the votes shall be taken by states, the representation from each state having one vote; a quorum for this purpose shall consist of a member or members from two-thirds of the states, and a majority of all the states shall be necessary to a choice. [And if the House of Representatives shall not choose a President whenever the right of choice shall devolve upon them, before the fourth day of March next following, then the Vice-President shall act as President, as in the case of the death or other constitutional disability of the President. —][11] The person having the greatest number of votes as Vice-President, shall be the Vice-President, if such number be a majority of the whole number of Electors appointed, and if no person have a majority, then from the two highest numbers on the list, the Senate shall choose the Vice-President; a quorum for the purpose shall consist of two-thirds of the whole number of Senators, and a majority of the whole number shall be necessary to a choice. But no person constitutionally ineligible to the office of President shall be eligible to that of Vice-President of the United States.

Amendment XIII (Ratified December 6, 1865)

Section 1. Neither slavery nor involuntary servitude, except as a punishment for crime whereof the party shall have been duly convicted, shall exist within the United States, or any place subject to their jurisdiction.

Section 2. Congress shall have power to enforce this article by appropriate legislation.

Amendment XIV (Ratified July 9, 1868)

Section 1. All persons born or naturalized in the United States, and subject to the jurisdiction thereof, are citizens of the United States and of the State wherein they reside. No State shall make or enforce any law which shall abridge the privileges or immunities of citizens of the United States; nor shall any State deprive any person of life, liberty, or property, without due process of law; nor deny to any person within its jurisdiction the equal protection of the laws.

Section 2. Representatives shall be apportioned among the several States according to their respective numbers, counting the whole number of persons in each State, excluding Indians not taxed. But when the right to vote at any election for the choice of electors for President and Vice President of the United States, Representatives in Congress, the Executive and Judicial officers of a State, or the members of the Legislature thereof, is denied to any of the male inhabitants of such State, being

twenty-one years of age,[12] and citizens of the United States, or in any way abridged, except for participation in rebellion, or other crime, the basis of representation therein shall be reduced in the proportion which the number of such male citizens shall bear to the whole number of male citizens twenty-one years of age in such State.

Section 3. No person shall be a Senator or Representative in Congress, or elector of President and Vice President, or hold any office, civil or military, under the United States, or under any State, who, having previously taken an oath, as a member of Congress, or as an officer of the United States, or as a member of any State legislature, or as an executive or judicial officer of any State, to support the Constitution of the United States, shall have engaged in insurrection or rebellion against the same, or given aid or comfort to the enemies thereof. But Congress may by a vote of two-thirds of each House, remove such disability.

Section 4. The validity of the public debt of the United States, authorized by law, including debts incurred for payment of pensions and bounties for services in suppressing insurrection or rebellion, shall not be questioned. But neither the United States nor any State shall assume or pay any debt or obligation incurred in aid of insurrection or rebellion against the United States, or any claim for the loss or emancipation of any slave; but all such debts, obligations and claims shall be held illegal and void.

Section 5. The Congress shall have power to enforce, by appropriate legislation, the provisions of this article.

Amendment XV (Ratified February 3, 1870)

Section 1. The right of citizens of the United States to vote shall not be denied or abridged by the United States or by any State on account of race, color, or previous condition of servitude.

Section 2. The Congress shall have power to enforce this article by appropriate legislation.

Amendment XVI (Ratified February 3, 1913)

The Congress shall have power to lay and collect taxes on incomes, from whatever source derived, without apportionment among the several States, and without regard to any census or enumeration.

Amendment XVII (Ratified April 8, 1913)

The Senate of the United States shall be composed of two Senators from each State, elected by the people thereof, for six years; and each Senator shall have one vote. The electors in each State shall have the qualifications requisite for electors of the most numerous branch of the State legislatures.

When vacancies happen in the representation of any State in the Senate, the executive authority of such State shall issue writs of election to fill such vacancies: *Provided,* That the legislature of any State may empower the executive thereof to make temporary appointments until the people fill the vacancies by election as the legislature may direct.

This amendment shall not be so construed as to affect the election or term of any Senator chosen before it becomes valid as part of the Constitution.

Amendment XVIII (Ratified January 16, 1919)[13]

Section 1. After one year from the ratification of this article the manufacture, sale, or transportation of intoxicating liquors within, the importation thereof into, or the exportation thereof from the United States and all territory subject to the jurisdiction thereof for beverage purposes is hereby prohibited.

Section 2. The Congress and the several States shall have concurrent power to enforce this article by appropriate legislation.

Section 3. This article shall be inoperative unless it shall have been ratified as an amendment to the Constitution by the legislatures of the several States, as provided in the Constitution, within seven years from the date of the submission hereof to the States by the Congress.

Amendment XIX (Ratified August 18, 1920)

The right of citizens of the United States to vote shall not be denied or abridged by the United States or by any State on account of sex.

Congress shall have power to enforce this article by appropriate legislation.

Amendment XX (Ratified January 23, 1933)

Section 1. The terms of the President and Vice President shall end at noon on the 20th day of January, and the terms of Senators and Representatives at noon on the 3d day of January, of the years in which such terms would have ended if this article had not been ratified; and the terms of their successors shall then begin.

Section 2. The Congress shall assemble at least once in every year, and such meeting shall begin at noon on the 3d day of January, unless they shall by law appoint a different day.

Section 3.[14] If, at the time fixed for the beginning of the term of the President, the President elect shall have died, the Vice President elect shall become President. If a President shall not have been chosen before the time fixed for the beginning of his term, or if the President elect shall have failed to qualify, then the Vice President elect shall act as President until a President shall have qualified; and the Congress may by law provide for the case wherein neither a President elect nor a Vice President elect shall have qualified, declaring who shall then act as President, or the manner in which one who is to act shall be selected, and such person shall act accordingly until a President or Vice President shall have qualified.

Section 4. The Congress may by law provide for the case of the death of any of the persons from whom the House of Representatives may choose a President whenever the right of choice shall have devolved upon them, and for the case of the death of any of the persons from whom the Senate may choose a Vice President whenever the right of choice shall have devolved upon them.

Section 5. Sections 1 and 2 shall take effect on the 15th day of October following the ratification of this article.

Section 6. This article shall be inoperative unless it shall have been ratified as an amendment to the Constitution by the legislatures of three-fourths of the several States within seven years from the date of its submission.

Amendment XXI (Ratified December 5, 1933)

Section 1. The eighteenth article of amendment to the Constitution of the United States is hereby repealed.

Section 2. The transportation or importation into any State, Territory, or possession of the United States for delivery or use therein of intoxicating liquors, in violation of the laws thereof, is hereby prohibited.

Section 3. This article shall be inoperative unless it shall have been ratified as an amendment to the Constitution by conventions in the several States, as provided in the Constitution, within seven years from the date of the submission hereof to the States by the Congress.

Amendment XXII (Ratified February 27, 1951)

Section 1. No person shall be elected to the office of the President more than twice, and no person who has held the office of President, or acted as President, for more than two years of a term to which some other person was elected President shall be elected to the office of the President more than once. But this Article shall not apply to any person holding the office of President when this Article was proposed by the Congress, and shall not prevent any person who may be holding the office of President, or acting as President, during the term within which this Article become operative from holding the office of President or acting as President during the remainder of such term.

Section 2. This article shall be inoperative unless it shall have been ratified as an amendment to the Constitution by the legislatures of three-fourths of the several States within seven years from the date of its submission to the States by the Congress.

Amendment XXIII (Ratified March 29, 1961)

Section 1. The District constituting the seat of Government of the United States shall appoint in such manner as the Congress may direct:

A number of electors of President and Vice President equal to the whole number of Senators and Representatives in Congress to which the District would be entitled if it were a State, but in no event more than the least populous State; they shall be in addition to those appointed by the States, but they shall be considered, for the purposes of the election of President and Vice President, to be electors appointed by a State; and they shall meet in the District and perform such duties as provided by the twelfth article of amendment.

Section 2. The Congress shall have power to enforce this article by appropriate legislation.

Amendment XXIV (Ratified January 23, 1964)

Section 1. The right of citizens of the United States to vote in any primary or other election for President or Vice President, for electors for President or Vice President, or for Senator or Representative in Congress, shall not be denied or abridged by the United States or any State by reason of failure to pay any poll tax or other tax.

Section 2. The Congress shall have power to enforce this article by appropriate legislation.

Amendment XXV (Ratified February 10, 1967)

Section 1. In case of the removal of the President from office or of his death or resignation, the Vice President shall become President.

Section 2. Whenever there is a vacancy in the office of the Vice President, the President shall nominate a Vice President who shall take office upon confirmation by a majority vote of both Houses of Congress.

Section 3. Whenever the President transmits to the President pro tempore of the Senate and the Speaker of the House of Representatives his written declaration that he is unable to discharge the powers and duties of his office, and until he transmits to them a written declaration to the contrary, such powers and duties shall be discharged by the Vice President as Acting President.

Section 4. Whenever the Vice President and a majority of either the principal officers of the executive departments or of such other body as Congress may by law provide, transmit to the President pro tempore of the Senate and the Speaker of the House of Representatives their written declaration that the President is unable to discharge the powers and duties of his office, the Vice President shall immediately assume the powers and duties of the office as Acting President.

Thereafter, when the President transmits to the President pro tempore of the Senate and the Speaker of the House of Representatives his written declaration that no inability exists, he shall resume the powers and duties of his office unless the Vice President and a majority of either the principal officers of the executive department or of such other body as Congress may by law provide, transmit within four days to the President pro tempore of the Senate and the Speaker of the House of Representatives their written declaration that the President is unable to discharge the powers and duties of his office. Thereupon Congress shall decide the issue, assembling within forty-eight hours for that purpose if not in session. If the Congress, within twenty-one days after receipt of the latter written declaration, or, if Congress is not in session, within twenty-one days after Congress is required to assemble, determines by two-thirds vote of both Houses that the President is unable to discharge the powers and duties of his office, the Vice President shall continue to discharge the same as Acting President; otherwise, the President shall resume the powers and duties of his office.

Amendment XXVI (Ratified July 1, 1971)

Section 1. The right of citizens of the United States, who are eighteen years of age or older, to vote shall not be denied or abridged by the United States or by any State on account of age.

Section 2. The Congress shall have power to enforce this article by appropriate legislation.

Amendment XXVII (Ratified May 7, 1992)

No law varying the compensation for the services of the Senators and Representatives shall take effect, until an election of Representatives shall have intervened.

Notes

1. The part in brackets was changed by section 2 of the Fourteenth Amendment.
2. The part in brackets was changed by the first paragraph of the Seventeenth Amendment.
3. The part in brackets was changed by the second paragraph of the Seventeenth Amendment.
4. The part in brackets was changed by section 2 of the Twentieth Amendment.
5. The Sixteenth Amendment gave Congress the power to tax incomes.
6. The material in brackets has been superseded by the Twelfth Amendment.
7. This provision has been affected by the Twenty-fifth Amendment.
8. These clauses were affected by the Eleventh Amendment.
9. This paragraph has been superseded by the Thirteenth Amendment.
10. Obsolete.
11. The part in brackets has been superseded by section 3 of the Twentieth Amendment.
12. See the Nineteenth and Twenty-sixth Amendments.
13. This Amendment was repealed by section 1 of the Twenty-first Amendment.
14. See the Twenty-fifth Amendment.

SOURCE: U.S. Congress, House, Committee on the Judiciary, *The Constitution of the United States of America, as Amended*, 100th Cong., 1st sess., 1987, H Doc 100-94.

Congressional Information on the Internet

A huge array of congressional information is available for free at Internet sites operated by the federal government, colleges and universities, and commercial firms. The sites offer the full text of bills introduced in the House and Senate, voting records, campaign finance information, transcripts of selected congressional hearings, investigative reports, and much more.

THOMAS

The most important site for congressional information is THOMAS (*http://thomas.loc.gov*), which is named for Thomas Jefferson and operated by the Library of Congress. THOMAS's highlight is its databases containing the full text of all bills introduced in Congress since 1989, the full text of the *Congressional Record* since 1989, and the status and summary information for all bills introduced since 1973.

THOMAS also offers special links to bills that have received or are expected to receive floor action during the current week and newsworthy bills that are pending or that have recently been approved. Finally, THOMAS has selected committee reports, answers to frequently asked questions about accessing congressional information, publications titled *How Our Laws Are Made* and *Enactment of a Law,* and links to lots of other congressional Web sites.

House of Representatives

The U.S. House of Representatives site (*http://www.house. gov*) offers the schedule of bills, resolutions, and other legislative issues the House will consider in the current week. It also has updates about current proceedings on the House floor and a list of the next day's meeting of House committees. Other highlights include a database that helps users identify their representative, a directory of House members and committees, the House ethics manual, links to Web pages maintained by House members and committees, a calendar of congressional primary dates and candidate-filing deadlines for ballot access, the full text of all amendments to the Constitution that have been ratified and those that have been proposed but not ratified, and lots of information about Washington, D.C., for visitors.

Another key House site is The Office of the Clerk On-line Information Center (*http://clerkweb.house.gov*), which has records of all roll-call votes taken since 1990. The votes are recorded by bill, so it is a lengthy process to compile a particular representative's voting record. The site also has lists of committee assignments, a telephone directory for members and committees, mailing label templates for members and committees, rules of the current Congress, election statistics from 1920 to the present, biographies of Speakers of the House, biographies of women who have served since 1917, and a virtual tour of the House Chamber.

One of the more interesting House sites is operated by the Subcommittee on Rules and Organization of the House

Committee on Rules (*http://www.house.gov/rules/crs_reports. htm*). Its highlight is dozens of Congressional Research Service reports about the legislative process. Some of the available titles include *Legislative Research in Congressional Offices: A Primer, How to Follow Current Federal Legislation and Regulations, Investigative Oversight: An Introduction to the Law, Practice, and Procedure of Congressional Inquiry,* and *Presidential Vetoes 1789–1996: A Summary Overview.*

A final House site is the Internet Law Library (*http://law. house.gov*). This site has a searchable version of the U.S. Code, which contains the text of public laws enacted by Congress, and a tutorial for searching the Code. There also is a huge collection of links to other Internet sites that provide state and territorial laws, laws of other nations, and treaties and international laws.

Senate

At least in the Internet world, the Senate is not as active as the House. Its main Web site (*http://www.senate.gov*) has records of all roll-call votes taken since 1989 (arranged by bill), brief descriptions of all bills and joint resolutions introduced in the Senate during the past week, and a calendar of upcoming committee hearings. The site also provides the standing rules of the Senate, a directory of senators and their committee assignments, lists of nominations that the president has submitted to the Senate for approval, links to Web pages operated by senators and committees, and a virtual tour of the Senate.

Information about the membership, jurisdiction, and rules of each congressional committee is available at the U.S. Government Printing Office site (*http://www.access.gpo.gov/congress/ index.html*). It also has transcripts of selected congressional hearings, the full text of selected House and Senate reports, and the House and Senate rules manuals.

General Reference

The U.S. General Accounting Office, the investigative arm of Congress, operates a site (*http://www.gao.gov*) that provides the full text of its reports from 1996 to the present. The reports cover a wide range of topics: aviation safety, combating terrorism, counternarcotics efforts in Mexico, defense contracting, electronic warfare, food assistance programs, Gulf War illness, health insurance, illegal aliens, information technology, long-term care, mass transit, Medicare, military readiness, money laundering, national parks, nuclear waste, organ donation, student loan defaults, and the year 2000 computing crisis, among others.

The GAO Daybook is an excellent current awareness tool. This electronic mailing list distributes a daily list of reports and testimony released by the GAO. Subscriptions are available by sending an E-mail message to *majordomo@www.gao.gov,* and in the message area typing "subscribe daybook" (without the quotation marks).

Current budget and economic projections are provided at the Congressional Budget Office Web site (*http://www.cbo.gov*). The site also has reports about the economic and budget outlook for the next decade, the president's budget proposals, federal civilian employment, Social Security privatization, tax reform, water use conflicts in the West, marriage and the federal income tax, and the role of foreign aid in development, among other topics. Other highlights include monthly budget updates, historical budget data, cost estimates for bills reported by congressional committees, and transcripts of congressional testimony by CBO officials.

Campaign Finance

Several Internet sites provide detailed campaign finance data for congressional elections. The official site is operated by the Federal Election Commission (*http://www.fec.gov*), which regulates political spending. The site's highlight is its database of campaign reports filed from May 1996 to the present by House and presidential candidates, political action committees, and political party committees. Senate reports are not included because they are filed with the Secretary of the Senate. The reports in the FEC's database are scanned images of paper reports filed with the commission.

The FEC site also has summary financial data for House and Senate candidates in the current election cycle, abstracts of court decisions pertaining to federal election law from 1976 to 1997, a graph showing the number of political action committees in existence each year from 1974 to the present, and a directory of national and state agencies that are responsible for releasing information about campaign financing, candidates on the ballot, election results, lobbying, and other issues. Another useful feature is a collection of brochures about federal election law, public funding of presidential elections, the ban on contributions by foreign nationals, independent expenditures supporting or opposing a candidate for federal office, contribution limits, filing a complaint, researching public records at the FEC, and other topics. Finally, the site provides the FEC's legislative

recommendations, its annual report, a report about its first twenty years in existence, the FEC's monthly newsletter, several reports about voter registration, election results for the most recent presidential and congressional elections, and campaign guides for corporations and labor organizations, congressional candidates and committees, political party committees, and nonconnected committees.

The best online source for campaign finance data is FECInfo (*http://www.tray.com/fecinfo*), which is operated by former Federal Election Commission employee Tony Raymond. FECInfo's searchable databases provide extensive itemized information about receipts and expenditures by federal candidates and political action committees from 1980 to the present. The data, which are obtained from the FEC, are quite detailed. For example, for candidates contributions can be searched by Zip Code. The site also has data on soft money contributions, lists of the top political action committees in various categories, lists of the top contributors from each state, and much more.

Another interesting site is Campaign Finance Data on the Internet (*http://www.soc.american.edu/campfin*), which is operated by the American University School of Communication. It provides electronic files from the FEC that have been reformatted in .dbf format so they can be used in database programs such as Paradox, Access, and FoxPro. The files contain data on PAC, committee, and individual contributions to individual congressional candidates.

More campaign finance data is available from the Center for Responsive Politics (*http://www.opensecrets.org*), a public interest organization. The center provides a list of all "soft money" donations to political parties of $100,000 or more in the current election cycle and data about "leadership" political action committees associated with individual politicians. Other databases at the site provide information about travel expenses that House members received from private sources for attending meetings and other events, activities of registered federal lobbyists, and activities of foreign agents who are registered in the United States.

Index

Index